Murder / *by Accident*

Murder /*by Accident*

MEDIEVAL THEATER,
MODERN MEDIA,
CRITICAL INTENTIONS

Jody Enders

THE UNIVERSITY OF CHICAGO PRESS /
CHICAGO AND LONDON

Jody Enders is professor of French and
theater at the University of California, Santa
Barbara. She is the author of three books, most
recently of *Death by Drama and Other Medieval
Urban Legends* (2002), published by the University of Chicago Press.

The University of Chicago Press, Chicago 60637
The University of Chicago Press, Ltd., London
© 2009 by The University of Chicago
All rights reserved. Published 2009
Printed in the United States of America
18 17 16 15 14 13 12 11 10 09
1 2 3 4 5
ISBN-13: 978-0-226-20783-4 (cloth)
ISBN-10: 0-226-20783-8 (cloth)
Library of Congress Cataloging-in-Publication
   Data
Enders, Jody, 1955–
Murder by accident : medieval theater, modern
media, critical intentions / Jody Enders.
      p. cm.
Includes bibliographical references and index.
ISBN-13: 978-0-226-20783-4 (cloth : alk. paper)
ISBN-10: 0-226-20783-8 (cloth : alk. paper)
1. Drama, Medieval—History and criticism.
2. Theater—History—Medieval, 500–1500.
3. Violence in the theater. 4. Intention in litera-
ture. I. Title.
PN2152.E544 2009
809.2'9355—dc22
                                 2008048165

To the Memory of Bert O. States

What did I just do? I analyzed what I accidentally felt and what I accidentally did as a result of those feelings.

CONSTANTIN STANISLAVSKI, *Creating a Role*

Not much is common between going to the theater and taking up a book.

ERVING GOFFMAN, *Frame Analysis*

CONTENTS

ACKNOWLEDGMENTS

I have profited enormously over the past several years from the insights and expertise of many colleagues whom I wish to thank for their invaluable intellectual feedback during the preparation of this book. Any and all shortcomings are my own.

At a very early stage, my colleagues Paul Hernadi, David Marshall, and the late Bert States offered that rare combination of generosity and brilliance as they engaged me in numerous dialogues and debates; much earlier than that, David Lee Rubin was my first undergraduate teacher to introduce me to the very concept of literary theory. Three readers for the University of Chicago Press—David Bevington, Steven Mailloux, and Julie Stone Peters—challenged and encouraged me with their sage advice. At the University of Illinois, Chicago, Marya Schechtman has always had an uncanny ability to refer me to fascinating work in philosophy. For their willingness to brainstorm with me, I also acknowledge Philip Auslander, William Condee, Tracy Davis, Shannon Jackson, Elizabeth MacArthur, Clare Macdonald, Didier Maleuvre, Stephen Nichols, Rebecca Schneider, Darwin Smith, Jack Talbott, and William Warner. And it is a special pleasure to thank by name a number of graduate students whom it has been an honor to teach. In the course of their work in seminars, they grappled intelligently with the ethical dimensions of theater, for ten weeks at a time, in ways that I found inspirational: Clareann Despain, Carol Fischer, Andrew Gibb, Jason Narvy, Emily Weisberg, Hank Willenbrink, and Beth Wynstra. Very special thanks go as well to my friend Rita Copeland, who encouraged me to develop for Oxford's *New Medieval Literatures* an early version of my first thoughts on this topic.

I am thankful to the Interlibrary Loan Office at Davidson Library of my home institution, whose staff diligently assisted me in securing even the most obscure documents. Once again, Randy Petilos of the University of Chicago Press was the ideal editor, incarnating as he does that rare blend of intellectual engagement, sustenance, and generosity. Andrew Gibb and Clareann Despain were heaven-sent with their careful editorial assistance.

Finally, I wish to express once again my deep indebtedness to the John Simon Guggenheim Memorial Foundation. When the Foundation magnanimously funded a different project in 1999, I had the opportunity to develop the present one as well.

Above all, and as always, I am grateful for the love and support of my husband, Eric D'Hoker.

ABBREVIATIONS

Full citations for the frequently cited works listed here will be found in the list of Works Cited, at the back of the book.

AA	Shadi Bartsch, *Actors in the Audience: Theatricality and Doublespeak from Nero to Hadrian*
AIR	Robert Audi, *Action, Intention, and Reason*
AM	Joel Black, *The Aesthetics of Murder: A Study in Romantic Literature and Contemporary Culture*
AN	Paris, Archives Nationales
AP	Constantin Stanislavski, *An Actor Prepares*
APLC	Mike Sell, *Avant-garde Performance and the Limits of Criticism*
AS	Michael Bérubé, "Against Subjectivity"
ASCM	Anthony Giddens, "Action, Subjectivity, and the Constitution of Meaning"
AT	Steven Knapp and Walter Benn Michaels, "Against Theory"
AT2	Steven Knapp and Walter Benn Michaels, "Against Theory 2: Sentence Meaning, Hermeneutics"
BP	Elaine Scarry, *The Body in Pain: The Making and Unmaking of the World*
BTA	Richard Schechner, *Between Theater and Anthropology*
CA	Michael Witmore, *Culture of Accidents: Unexpected Knowledges in Early Modern England*
CMJH	*La Chronique de Metz de Jacomin Husson, 1200–1525*, ed. H. Michelant
CML	Steven Sverdlik, "Crime and Moral Luck"

CPV	*La Chronique de Philippe de Vigneulles,* ed. Charles Bruneau
CR	George A. Kennedy, *Classical Rhetoric and Its Christian and Secular Tradition from Ancient to Modern Times*
CVM	*Les Chroniques de la ville de Metz,* ed. Jean François Huguenin.
DAP	Alice Rayner, *To Do, to Act, to Perform: Drama and the Phenomenology of Action*
DBD	Jody Enders, *Death by Drama and Other Medieval Urban Legends*
DJ	*Digest of Justinian,* ed. Theodor Mommsen and Paul Krueger; trans. Alan Watson
DP	Michel Foucault, *Discipline and Punish: The Birth of the Prison*
EHTF	Gustave Cohen, *Études d'histoire du théâtre en France au Moyen-âge et à la Renaissance*
EVNA	Bradley Butterfield, "Ethical Value and Negative Aesthetics: Reconsidering the Baudrillard-Ballard Connection"
FA	Erving Goffman, *Frame Analysis: An Essay on the Organization of Experience*
FF	Susanne K. Langer, *Feeling and Form: A Theory of Art Developed from Philosophy in a New Key*
FIA	Natalie Zemon Davis, *Fiction in the Archives: Pardon Tales and Their Tellers in Sixteenth-Century France*
FLT	Roman Ingarden, "The Functions of Language in the Theater"
FRT	Victor Turner, *From Ritual to Theatre: The Human Seriousness of Play*
FT	Michael Kirby, *A Formalist Theatre*
GR	Bert States, *Great Reckonings in Little Rooms: On the Phenomenology of Theatre*
HDTW	J. L. Austin, *How to Do Things with Words*
HL	Johan Huizinga, *Homo Ludens: A Study of the Play Element in Culture*
ID	Umberto Eco, "Interpreting Drama"
IF	Monroe C. Beardsley and W. K. Wimsatt Jr., "The Intentional Fallacy"
IO	Quintilian, *Institutio oratoria*
IPE	Lawrence Buell, "In Pursuit of Ethics"
IS	Daniel C. Dennett, *The Intentional Stance*

IT	Paul Ricoeur, *Interpretation Theory: Discourse and the Surplus of Meaning*
LC	Suetonius, *The Lives of the Caesars*
LCR	*Livre de conduite,* ed. Gustave Cohen
LM	L. Petit de Julleville, *Les Mystères*
LMRSL	Wendell Harris, *Literary Meaning: Reclaiming the Study of Literature*
LS	*Law's Stories: Narrative and Rhetoric in the Law,* ed. Peter Brooks and Paul Gewirtz
LSFD	John Searle, "The Logical Status of Fictional Discourse"
LT	Terry Eagleton, *Literary Theory: An Introduction*
MC	Jacques Le Goff, *Medieval Civilization, 400–1500*
MES	*The Medieval European Stage, 500–1550,* ed. William Tydeman
MM	Kendall L. Walton, *Mimesis as Make-Believe*
MTOC	Jody Enders, *The Medieval Theater of Cruelty: Rhetoric, Memory, Violence*
MWM	Stanley Cavell, *Must We Mean What We Say? A Book of Essays*
NI	Ian D. Leader-Elliott, "Negotiating Intentions in Trials of Guilt and Punishment"
NS	Raymond Tallis: *Not Saussure: A Critique of Post-Saussurean Literary Theory*
OW	Umberto Eco, *The Open Work*
PE	Wendy Lesser, *Pictures at an Execution: An Inquiry into the Subject of Murder*
PEL	Michel de Certeau, *The Practice of Everyday Life*
POLF	Kenneth Burke, *Philosophy of Literary Form: Studies in Symbolic Action*
PP	J. L. Austin, *Philosophical Papers*
PSR	*The Performance Studies Reader,* ed. Henry Bial, 2d ed.
QA	Hans Robert Jauss, *Question and Answer: Forms of Dialogic Understanding*
RAH	*Rhetorica ad Herennium,* ed. Harry Caplan
ROMD	Jody Enders, *Rhetoric and the Origins of Medieval Drama*
RPI	Bruce Wilshire, *Role Playing and Identity: The Limits of Theatre as Metaphor*
SES	David Marshall, *The Surprising Effects of Sympathy: Marivaux, Diderot, Rousseau, and Mary Shelley*
SP	Wendy Steiner, *The Scandal of Pleasure: Art in an Age of Fundamentalism*

SRT   Geoff Pywell, *Staging Real Things: The Performance of Ordinary Events*

STP   Umberto Eco, "The Semiotics of Theatrical Performance"

SW   Jean Baudrillard, *Selected Writings*

TA   Jacob Larwood, *Theatrical Anecdotes or Fun and Curiosities of the Play, the Playhouse, and the Players*

TC   Reed Way Dasenbrock, *Truth and Consequences: Intentions, Conventions, and the New Thematics*

TD   Antonin Artaud, *The Theatre and Its Double*

TEL   Alan Read, *Theatre and Everyday Life: An Ethics of Performance*

TFR   *Le Théâtre français avant la Renaissance,* ed. Édouard Fournier

TI   Luke Wilson, *Theaters of Intention: Drama and the Law in Early Modern England*

TL   René Wellek and Austin Warren, *Theory of Literature,* 3d ed.

TMA   William Tydeman, *The Theatre in the Middle Ages: Western European Stage Conditions, c. 800–1576*

UP   Timothy Gould, "The Unhappy Performative"

VI   E. D. Hirsch, *Validity in Interpretation*

WH   Michel de Certeau, *The Writing of History*

WWW   *Why We Watch: The Attractions of Violent Entertainment,* ed. Jeffrey H. Goldstein

Mise en Scène

ACCIDENT, n. An inevitable occurrence due to the action of
immutable natural laws.
AMBROSE BIERCE, *The Devil's Dictionary*

My title, *Murder by Accident,* is a deliberate misnomer.
There is no such thing as murder by accident. Murder is not an accident
but an intentional act. And that is the whole point: sometimes, one would
never know that when reading literary theory. Sometimes, there are a lot
of questions to ask about what happened on a given night during a play or
a performance, a film or a filming, a television show or a taping. Many of
those questions are not about art at all.

This book is an interdisciplinary inquiry into several interrelated phenomena: the medieval theater, the modern media, the ethical problems
inherent in spectacles of real violence, theater phenomenology, "performativity," reception theory, the law and literature movement, and that old
critical chestnut known to generations of literary theorists as the "Intentional Fallacy"—a concept that, for better or for worse, made it unfashionable for students of literature to discuss what authors meant when they
penned their texts.[1] There will be a great deal to say in the chapters that
follow about the so-called fallaciousness of investigating authorial intention, about an initial critical emphasis on written literature, and about the
dogmatism with which the Intentional Fallacy (as described by W. K. Wimsatt Jr. and Monroe C. Beardsley in the 1940s) was applied and misapplied,
unsubtly dismissed, and subtly or not so subtly resurrected. But the point of
this prefatory mise en scène is to pose a deceptively simple question: What
is *supposed to happen* at the theater—and from whose perspective? Things
that are *supposed to happen* are not accidents; and *supposed to,* I will be arguing throughout, is tantamount to saying "what individuals involved in
making theater *intend them to be.*" That statement might seem obvious; but,
as we shall see through a series of comparative readings of *the theatrically
unexpected* in both medieval and modern times, it is not. And that prompts a

companion question that has long preoccupied performance theorists: *What counts as theater, anyway?*

Given Jacques Le Goff's remark that medieval society displayed a widespread tendency to theatricalize itself,[2] medieval theatricality was as ubiquitous, as "receptive to changes in the social structure," and as revelatory of the same as any "theater of everyday life" that Paul Zumthor, Victor Turner, Michel de Certeau, Marvin Carlson, or Alan Read might theorize.[3] Medieval theater is so tricky to define and identify that its very name is interspersed liberally in criticism with such terms as *spectacle, performance, sport, ritual, battle-play, pageant, parade, procession, dance, song,* and even *allegory* or *dialogue.*[4] Whence the persistence of "theater" as a metaphor for so many aspects of social life: theater of justice, military theater, even Erich Auerbach's "great drama of Christianity."[5] In many ways, theater is the place where our current debates about art begin.[6]

Even so, as present and influential as it once was in the Middle Ages (and in many oral cultures), that is how marginalized theater often finds itself in debates about the effects of mass media on culture. Whatever the reasons—soaring costs of tickets, the need to leave behind the television or the computer screen to see a play, the comparative size of the venue— theater has lost much of its collective rhetorical impact at the same time that print, cinematic, and electronic cultures have proved more accessible and influential.[7] The films, television programs, and, to a lesser extent, theater pieces of the present day reach audiences that early spectators could never have imagined as they gathered on public squares.[8] But medieval theater was probably the most popular and available literary form of its day and the site of immense controversy about how literature shapes character, life, and death. In medieval France, for example, theater history itself emerges from the shadows of crime and punishment: two mortal accidents at the theater and one conspiratorially intentional rape committed by a group of theatergoers in 1380, 1384, and 1395, respectively.[9]

Historians, of course, record the extraordinary, and they generally pass over, uncommented, the innumerable plays or performances that appeared uneventful (even though a theater piece is always an event of sorts). Consequently, as in the exceptional events that form the case studies of this book, we often come to know that a given play was performed at all only because something illegal, immoral, or at least exceptional happened in its wake. All of this forces us to concede two things from the outset. On one hand, even in these modern critical days of theatrical performativity in the service of social change, not every real thing that is created in association with theater is positive; on the other hand, despite the laudable openness of performance studies to noncanonical theatrical and ritual forms (most of which had already been identified by Isidore of Seville as early as the seventh century),[10] some events that occur during a theatrical performance are *not theater* and should not be called by that name.

At this point, some readers may be objecting already that theater is supposed to *represent* things, not to rape or kill people; or that not every theater piece or performance event houses criminal acts. My preliminary response is straightforward enough. If theater is *supposed to do* anything at all, then *we are talking about intentions.*[11]

Likewise, they might further object, with Alice Rayner, to the reductionism with which law courts must distill "action to its intentional features because legal and social consequences depend upon identifying the voluntary, motivational intent of an agent, as distinct from circumstances beyond the control of the agent."[12] Or they might counter that it is better to study all the accidents in theater in which the law *does not* intervene; or that it is no help to theater to look at the atypical. Here, we may respond with the ordinary language philosopher, J. L. Austin, that despite Terry Eagleton's impatience with the "unhealthily juridical" nature of speech act theory,[13] "the abnormal will throw light on the normal, will help us to penetrate the blinding veil of ease and obviousness that hides the mechanisms of the natural successful act" (*PP*, 128). Fortunately, most aesthetic media do not result in criminal acts or culminate in deaths requiring murder trials; and, habituated as medieval people were to what Patrick Geary calls "living with the dead," they did not expect to cohabit with them at the theater.[14]

In analyzing a series of largely violent theatrical occurrences, medieval and modern (which I seek nonetheless *not* to sensationalize), I am interested in the intersection of theatrical and legal institutions and the meaning of that intersection to drama, violence, ethics, and the consequences of action (or lack thereof). Theater poses special challenges to our notions of art and law by offering up a model *of and for action,* aesthetic, aestheticized, or other. Notwithstanding a remarkable critical reticence in the face of those challenges, theater cannot be illegal: it cannot be "against the law." That is by no means to say that theater cannot be subversive. Far from it. Theater artists have long protested the spirit of the law, sometimes subverting the letter of that law merely by taking to the stage in the first place.[15] I do say, however—albeit with numerous caveats, precisions, and refinements to come—that theater, like law, must always concern itself with life and with the equities of social interaction. It must do so because, even in the most traditional sense of performed drama, theater is always real, always legally actionable.

Of the art form that, for Anthony Kubiak, places on stage "real bodies living and dying in real time,"[16] it is fair to say that, in live media like theater, real things happen—*and do not happen*—all the time. One actor really *is* puncturing the hidden pouch that simulates bleeding, even when she is not actually bleeding; another really *is* taking a sip of that brown liquid that is not really scotch . . . or maybe it *is* scotch. Most observers do not much care when actors truly smoke cigarettes, truly drink, or when they exchange real kisses during love scenes. That is because, normally, such moments of realism do not result in legal or ethical dilemmas—unless, of course, the righteous nonsmoker were to object to the secondhand smoke, the moralist or police officer to underage drinking, or the spouses of the kissers—or their director[17]—to real tumescence. Despite the popular wisdom that asserts the jadedness of both medieval and modern audiences with respect to the ubiquitous violence of their respective cultures,[18] we all seem to care very much about events as varied as these: an ancient Greek performance of the *Eumenides* that allegedly caused terrified children to die and women to miscarry; the deaths of Romans in the gladiatorial amphitheater; or the actress who was beaten unconscious during an apparently consensual onstage assault at London's Real and True Theatre (RATT).[19] Evan Handler also cared about the nonconsensual attack that he endured in 1991 when an allegedly drunken Nicol Williamson pummeled him with a sword during *I Hate Hamlet*.[20] The fact is that we *do* care when such things happen because, just as there is a difference between drinking a Coke—or a scotch—and *pretending* to drink one, just as there is a difference between *faking* intercourse and *having* intercourse (art vs. pornography?), there is a vast difference between faking a punch or a gunshot or a strangulation and *not faking one*. Such events might well present the same ontological and phenomenological problems; but *assaulting* (as opposed to *pretending to assault*) is subject to both moral and legal intervention. And so it should be. The kiss might compromise the experience of art, but violence compromises the experience of life.[21] And the late medieval cultural imagination has much to teach us about what is *not* play—with a punch powerful enough to send any contemporary aficionado of the arts hurtling back to a kind of medieval future.[22]

Why intentionality at all? Why theater and theatricality? Why the Middle Ages? And why medieval France in particular?[23] Intentions do not *need* an audience to be intentions. And yet, when they *have* an audience, as they so often do, they are paramount to the everyday judgments that we make about everyday life, and which judgments lead to the social construction of equity, to say nothing of civilization.[24] Of even such a quotidian performance as modeling a dress, Umberto Eco posits that "with this simple gesture I am doing something that is theater at its best, since I not only tell you something, but I also am offering you a model, giving you an order or a suggestion, outlining a utopia or a feasible project. I am not only picturing a given behavior, I am also in fact eliciting a behavior, emphasizing a duty, *mirroring your future.*"[25]

It is a future in which intention matters as much as it has in the past. So, despite the "alterity" or "otherness" that have, in recent years, made for such good medievalism and such good medievalist politics, if one focuses exclusively on cultural difference, one runs the risk of failing to perceive cultural similarity.[26] Theater is a powerful medium that discloses much about both.

To that end, I will be comparing medieval events to modern ones and theater to other media that push their apparent boundaries, most notably cinema, television, and even telejournalism. Notwithstanding certain substantial differences in agency, scripting, and viewership to which we return throughout, those comparisons are not as audacious as they might initially appear, and they warrant a few precisions.[27] On what grounds, for instance, do I begin my Introduction by comparing a medieval Passion play to a contemporary televised broadcast of a traffic report? Or, to rephrase the question in the vernacular: Where does she get off?

Here.

Medieval theater audiences exhibited their spiritual dependency on the *mystère de la Passion* for guidance in navigating themselves through the space of the world on their way "home," more or less pragmatically, to the rewards of heaven. Modern Americans tune into their local traffic reports for assistance in navigating their bodies through space, bowing to ends that are highly pragmatic and attending to the wisdom of narrators who signal various impediments to their progress during that long road home. Medieval Christian entrepreneurs and theatergoers would have held that, for all its pleasurable didacticism, a Passion play sponsored by their local media outlet, the Church, was a true story of local heroes staged for "the edification, honor, utility, and profit of the city."[28] Likewise, modern television executives would doubtless profess their sincere journalistic goal to be the enlightenment of the public through the transmission of useful and profitable information of direct relevance to daily life; just as the ostensibly more secular American television viewer (reared on at least the *appearance* of a separation of church and state)[29] would be likely to profess that the content of a plethora of news shows and news magazines is true. In a latter-day Horatian *dulce/utile,* contemporary programmers like Neal Shapiro of *Dateline NBC* increasingly aestheticize their wares, ever attentive to finding "dramatic ways" to relate "important information" about the truths of real life, such that Joan Konner of the Columbia School of Broadcast Journalism averred that there is little distinction between "entertaining news and newsy entertainment."[30] Indeed, telejournalists might also feel justified in "helping out" reality as much as their medieval forebears did theatrically, the better to share those truths, as in the notorious enhancement of automotive explosions by *Dateline NBC* in support of an otherwise true report on motor vehicles that were dangerous to drive.[31] Even so, the aesthetic pursuit, display, and dissemination of knowledge could be dangerous, even deadly.

None of that is shocking in the slightest to aficionados of medieval performance genres or, for that matter, to the historians who have long recognized—if by nothing else than a proliferation of scare quotes—that there is no such thing as a simple dividing line between "fiction" and "nonfiction."[32] That amorphous site, moreover, is precisely where Michael Witmore situates the (early modern) accident itself: we "ought to think of accidents as existing halfway between the realms of fact and fiction" (*CA*, 6). As the case studies that follow will disclose all too compellingly, dangers lurk even in the amorphous—and in ways that call into question Bruce Wilshire's judgment that "in the experience of violence in the world one realizes that his own and others' lives are in jeopardy . . . [w]hile in the theatre, one is at least marginally aware, on the critical level of consciousness, that *the violence is not really happening*" (*RPI*, 249–50; my emphasis). Following Austin (who was himself following Wittgenstein), Erving Goffman rightly reminds us that the question of "what we mean by 'really happening' is complicated, and that although an individual may dream unrealities, it is still proper to say of him on that occasion that he is really dreaming" (*FA*, 7). Sometimes, dreams come true as the nightmares of the chapters of Part I.

As always, the challenge of any book is to find an orderly way of adapting to the linear chronology of reading what often seems an irresolutely tangled nexus. Thinkers as disparate as Cicero and Goffman have described that challenge so well that I always find myself repeating their wisdom. The former resorted to poetry when he observed that "a division into parts is more indefinite, like drawing streams of water from a fountain,"[33] while the latter acknowledged the writer's complaint that "linear presentation constrains what is actually a circular affair, ideally requiring simultaneous introduction of terms." "Nothing coming earlier," Goffman insisted, "depends on something coming later, and, hopefully, terms developed at any one point are actually used in what comes thereafter" (*FA*, 11). But that ideal is virtually impossible to achieve in practice, such that readers frequently find themselves complaining that "concepts elaborately defined are not much used beyond the point at which the fuss is made about their meaning" (*FA*, 11). For want of a better way of expressing phenomena that occur simultaneously, I have tried to preserve as much of the chronological and inductive nature of the events as possible without too much frontloading of theory. Despite my best efforts, however, it seems that one cannot approach intention without some prior, lengthy disquisition about what it is, even as the disquisition itself makes sense only when preceded by an entire framework of examples and histories that illustrate its stakes, scope, and ontology.

There are other issues of presentation as well. This book, ten years in the making, cannot be considered in any way definitive. It is the kind of book that is never finished, never exhaustive but usually exhausting (more for me, I hope, than for readers). For one thing, I invariably found myself retorting to each one of my own assertions, "Yes, but . . . what about *this* example?" I expect readers to do the same because, for almost every case that I will adduce, one could pursue ad infinitum a series of counterexamples that raise more and more questions. The impossibility of completing the sequence does not mean that we should not *begin* the sequence; so I can ask only that readers be patient enough to allow me some time to answer all their objections as those arise. I have done my best to think of each objection (if not in the body of the text, then in the occasional endnote that pops up to say "Yes, but . . . . "). But I doubt very much that I will have answered them all. If, by the end of this book, readers still disagree or still think that I have failed to consider some or other crucial aspect of intention at the theater, it is then that truly stimulating critical debate can continue. Among other things, I know that many will consider this to be a profoundly conservative book; but to those who abhor taxonomies and categories, I say, with no ill will: Please refute me; and, in so doing , you will find what you think really matters at the theater.

Caveats about matters of style are easier to express, if occasionally difficult to execute. A singular hurdle arose, for instance, regarding the passive voice, which is counterproductive in a book about agency: I have done my best to avoid it.

Also, since this is, in large part, a book that reconceptualizes the usual terminologies, I often introduce contested terms in scare quotes and, thereafter, I cease and desist. That does not mean that I have ceased to consider them controversial.

Regarding the critical apparatus, in trying to call attention to a number of unusual medieval documents, I have endeavored to keep notes to a minimum so that they do not disrupt the narrative; and, with the exception of the isolated turn of phrase, only English translations appear in the body of the text. All translations from French sources are my own unless otherwise indicated; and, in the case of my translations of French legalese, I have broken up some of its interminable sentences into more manageable semantic units. When a good published translation of a work exists (such as Greek or Latin sources in the bilingual editions of the Loeb Classical Library), I do not reproduce the original. If an original citation is relatively short (under five lines), I have included it in the relevant endnote. Otherwise, all original-language documents appear in the Appendix, where, as a rule, I reprint them exactly as they appeared. Whenever it is practical to do so, I refer to frequently cited works by abbreviations, a list of which appears in the front matter.

Finally, I am not a philosopher and even less so a philosopher of psychology.[34] Thus, while certain strands of philosophy and psychology appear and reappear, this is not a book about meaning, semantics, consequentialism, moral luck, the individual or collective unconscious, the work of Freud or Lacan, or, for that matter, about philosophical intentionalism vs. intentionality, including the relative merits of both terms.[35] Instead, for a medievalist writing from two departments (French and Theater), a project like this has a special meaning. Amongst medievalists, theater is barely part of the literary canon, while in a seemingly unrelated development, enrollments in college-level French courses have been declining nationwide.[36] Nevertheless, if French as a discipline exists in a relationship of simultaneous attraction to and revulsion from its canon, it is also true that, just on the fringe, an intensely forward-looking literary medium demonstrates with cannon-fire both what is right and what is wrong with any canon: the medieval theater. The violent theatrical past has much to tell us about the role of drama, French, and the Middle Ages in the future, including just who is more "medieval": citizens of the fourteenth or the twenty-first century.

Intention is a tough interdisciplinary nut to crack; and I am probably cracked even to try. Naturally, it will not tell "the whole story" any more than reception or anything else does. And many would be inclined to heed Stanley Cavell's warning that "intention is no more an efficient cause of an object of art than it is of a human action; in both cases it is a way of understanding the thing done, of describing what happens" (*MWM,* 230). But, as Susanne K. Langer commented long ago, "limitation is not itself a reason for rejecting a theory."[37] If representation is a deliberate act—and there will be ample evidence to suggest that it is—then it will have little meaning without due regard for the intentions of the individuals who elect to represent.[38]

Raymond Tallis writes that "there is a darkness at the heart of intention and there is an inescapable indeterminacy in their relation even to the actions that seem most precisely to realise them."[39] It is my contention that we will not fully grasp the darkness of today's real-life spectacles until we grasp a history that reckons with the proverbial "Dark Ages": a history that has consistently taught, for better or for worse, the necessity of understanding how intention affects the commission or omission of acts. Medieval and modern theatricality shines a spotlight on that darkness which lies at the heart of intention and at the heart of this book.

Introduction / *Doing Theater Justice*

> Pretend is an intentional verb: that is, it is one of those verbs
> which contain the concept of intention built into it.
> **JOHN SEARLE,** "The Logical Status of Fictional Discourse"

This is the story of two very public deaths that occurred
before the eyes of two very different audiences, one medieval and one modern. On 27 March 1380, a Parisian audience went to the theater to watch the
simulated life of Christ in a Passion play. Instead, they saw a man, Jehan
Hemont, accidentally wounded—mortally, it turned out—by a special effect
gone wrong. On the afternoon of 6 May 1998, Los Angeles adults tuned their
televisions to various programs (and children to their cartoons) only to see
regular programming interrupted by cameras scrutinizing a distraught
man wielding both a banner denouncing HMOs and a rifle. After threatening suicide, he proceeded to blow his brains out before viewers.[1]

When Jehan Hemont died at a Passion play in 1380, when an anonymous
man died on the freeway in 1998, both audiences felt a kindred shock. Two
"media outlets" of their respective eras had violated the audiences' expectations or, at a minimum, what they believed those expectations to be.
Both venues had been interrupted by a powerful dose of the violent pain
of reality, the medieval theater piece presumably by accident, the modern
one—cartoons, talk shows, game shows, the traffic report—by design. But
whose?

In 1380 and 1998, both a medieval play and a modern piece of breaking
news stepped over some kind of imaginary line in the sand. The Passion
play was *supposed to be* a representation, yet it supplied a real death. The
breaking news was *supposed to be* just that: news that conveyed to motorists which freeways they might avoid that afternoon. It, too, supplied much
more. During both events, each audience member who was banking on instruction, entertainment, or both was transformed legally, morally, and
aesthetically into a witness (or a potential witness) to a spectacular death
that might or not might not have been criminal (or, in the case of suicide,

1

considered sinful by certain religious standards).[2] Did spectators see a play? A sport? An accident? Did they see an instance of what we now call manslaughter? A murder? An execution? A suicide? An initial threat of suicide that changed once the predicted and predictable cameras were rolling?

In the name of civilization, both events cried out for evaluation and judgment; both were indecipherable without recourse to intentionality and its special relevance to theatrical spectacle. In 1380 and 1998, verdicts were forthcoming in the realms of law, morality, and aesthetics that rendered the participants guilty or not guilty, liable or not liable for events that would come to be defined post hoc as "crimes" or "not crimes"—which is a definition of another order than that of "art" vs. "not art."[3]

In 1380, a criminal investigation was launched for the purpose of determining whether the death of Jehan Hemont had occurred accidentally or intentionally. In 1998, an incensed American public demanded an answer to the question of whether or not the *airing* of a real death had occurred accidentally or intentionally. Jehan Hemont was killed by accident; an unnamed man's suicide was aired by accident.

In 1380, there was no live theater without someone's intent to put on a play; and in 1998, there was no airing of breaking news without someone's intent to broadcast it.

In the fourteenth century, it was a question of life and death. At the end of the twentieth century, it was a question of the spectacular phenomenology of life and death.

In 1380, audience sentiments about a theatrical explosion were clearly less important than the cause (accidental or intentional) of the victim's deadly wound. In 1998, the incendiary death of another man at his own hands was clearly more important than the fact that some people saw it and others filmed it (regardless of whether the filming served as a catalyst of sorts for the man's actions).

In both eras, the brutality of the events was somehow tempered by a judgment about accidents: a medieval cannon had misfired; a modern news anchor assured viewers that "we never meant that to happen."[4] Simply put, the proper moral, cultural, and aesthetic response to two sudden, violent, sensational deaths involved alleging (sincerely, disingenuously, or confusingly) that those deaths had occurred accidentally. It mattered a great deal whether or not Jehan Hemont and the man on the freeway had intended to die or intended for their deaths to be public. It also mattered whether or not anyone else had intended for them to die, or intended to display their deaths, or intended for others to see them, and under what circumstances. Independent of whether the audiences in question enjoyed the sight of real death, were shocked or repelled by it, or felt something else altogether, it was vital to assess who was responsible for their enjoyment, their indignation, or even their indifference.

But for intention, the outrage provoked by both events in their respective eras (in the form of juridical, parajuridical, and popular intervention) would have been meaningless. It was not meaningless.

The aftermath of both events interrogated a moment that existed before performance or reception ever took place. So, before there could be any ruling about the intention to watch, there had to be a ruling about the intention to *do* and the intention to *show*. Regardless of whether the events of 1380 and 1998 were *witnessed* deliberately or accidentally, observers needed to determine whether the events themselves had *come to pass* deliberately or accidentally. Both communities needed to ask who had intended to perform what. As if populated by Friedrich Schlegel's curious "prophets looking backwards," they addressed their questions in a post hoc analysis of ad hoc intent.[5]

In 1380 as in 1998, intention was the first thing to be investigated because, at some level, our two audiences seem to have known what the sociologist Anthony Giddens knows today: that not everything that happens—artistically or inartistically, criminally or noncriminally—is done on purpose. Social life, says Giddens, "escape[s] the intentional input of its creators. In other words, one of the most distinctive qualities of social activity concerns the significance of the unintended consequences of action."[6] And even if social life did *not* escape that intentional input, Raymond Tallis asserts that "an intention can never absolutely specify a unique action corresponding to it and the intention itself can never be fully elucidated" (*NS*, 234). In that sense, both events—extreme specimens in which death is the consequence of acts associated with spectatorship—offer special access to the crucial role of intentionality in the much debated intersections of art, action, representation, agency, and legal accountability.[7] Both events accost individuals and communities with a commanding moment when *specific spectacular acts may be legally actionable*—but only when the intentions are clear.

Furthermore, in raising the specter of legal accountability, both defy Stanley Cavell's statement that *"games are places where intention does not count* [my emphasis], human activities in which intention need not generally be taken into account; because in games *what happens* [his emphasis] is described solely in terms set by the game itself, because the consequences one is responsible for are limited a priori by the rules of the game" (*MWM*, 236). The boundaries of a theater piece of 1380 and a piece of telejournalism were set by the rules of the game of life. Thus, they also render moot the argument by Stephen Knapp and Walter Benn Michaels that "the mistake on which all critical theory rests has been to imagine that these problems [of intention, literary language, and interpretive assumptions] are real" (AT, 12). For Jehan Hemont and the man on the freeway, the problems were all too real: so real that it can hardly be suitable to resolve, with Terry Eagleton, that "[to] think of literary discourse in terms of human subjects is not in the first place to think of it in terms of *actual human subjects*. . . . [A] literary work is not actually a 'living' dialogue or monologue. It is a piece of language which has been *detached from any specific 'living' relationship*" (*LT*, 119; my emphasis).[8] Such statements constitute the antithesis of the living theatrical situation.

In this book, I take these two exemplary and cautionary tales as a point of departure for broader speculation about the absolute value of intentionality in theater and other live media. While it might seem odd at first blush to invoke intention precisely where it is said to lapse (involuntary manslaughter, acts of God, accidents, and the like), it is in that context—one that has long made room for the compatibility of chance and agency[9]—that it is actually the most important. In the accident, an "event" with vast semantic and, increasingly, narrative resonances of its own,[10] intention was incontrovertibly important, as in the medieval legal codes known as the *Digest of Justinian,* which stipulated that "he who kills a man, if he committed this act without the intention of causing death, could be acquitted; and he who did not kill a man but wounded him with the intention [in his soul] of killing ought to be found guilty of homicide."[11] It was important in early English law, which grappled with the paradox of murder by accident by making "specific provisions for pardoning unintentional or accidental criminal acts, particularly homicide" (*CA,* 26).[12] It was even more important in sixteenth-century France, where, as Natalie Zemon Davis demonstrates, jurists did not distinguish conceptually between *homicide involontaire* and *homicide volontaire,* both of which were punishable by death.[13] And it is important nowadays because, although the *American Heritage Dictionary* (among many others) peacefully warrants that an "accident" is an event in which intent *does not* come into play—that is, anything that "occurs unexpectedly or unintentionally"—Wendell Harris cannily affirms that "one cannot *not* intend; to not intend is to have intended something else. Not to have intended to knock over and break one of my hostess's crystal wine glasses is to have intended to pick up the salt or pass the roast beef."[14]

As we shall have occasion to see throughout, though with the requisite caveats, *there is no such thing as accidental intention; one cannot intend accidentally.* Nor can one intend "unconsciously" in that such an intention would fail to meet the conditions of its own ontology.[15] Like "murder by accident," "accidental intention" is a contradiction in terms, a misnomer, an oxymoron. Thus, in 1380 and 1998, the only way to make sense of the deaths of two presumably innocent men and the only available escape hatch to morality was the recognition of the *absence* of murderous intentions and, consequently, of the *de facto presence* of other intentions ascribed to everyone involved, to communicators and receivers alike.[16] Regardless of whether the findings were correct, incorrect, indeterminate, or unknowable, it was essential that spectators find a way of saying that they had not bargained on beholding the infliction of mortal wounds (*unless* they *had*, or *even if* they had). While E. D. Hirsch was among the first to predict the intellectual relativism that would attend the banishment of an author's intentions, at issue in our discussion about intention, action, agency, and aesthetics is the moral relativism that attends the "authors," as it were, of *action*.[17]

Hence, we come face to face with one of the greatest ironies of our times. In the real world, we never hesitate to ask: "Who did it?" or "Whodunit? And Why?" So it may be a manifestation of what Gerald Graff dubs the "cluelessness" of academia that it once became so unfashionable to ask: "Who wrote it? And why?"—to say nothing of a variant that is as crucial to theater as it is to law and life: "*Who acted? And why?*"[18] Certainly, Cavell was not clueless when he noted of the aesthetic critique of Federico Fellini that "'It is what he has *done* that matters.' But it is exactly to find out what someone has done, what he is responsible for, that one investigates his intentions" (*MWM*, 231; his emphasis).[19] Nor is there anything clueless about Reed Way Dasenbrock's contention that a host of daily events—"What did that person mean by honking his horn at me?"—are not unintelligible. What makes a given act intelligible, he asserts, "is above all our assumption that it is intelligible, that the actor intends an intelligible action that can be understood once we grasp the actor's intention in so acting. Thus, our belief that there is an intentional meaning to the object of interpretation is what drives our process of interpretation: we interpret until we think we have understood what initially we did not understand."[20] In that respect, perhaps the strangest thing of all is that, in a kind of academic version of what contemporary lawyers call "work product," it is as if critics were no longer authorized to investigate and judge the causes that bring works of art—and, especially, *works of action*—into existence.[21] In a peculiar carry-over from the 1940s and 1950s, modern and postmodern literary critics have tended to view accidents with all the panache of a Jean Baudrillard, but they have largely eschewed accident's natural counterpart: intention.[22]

And yet, if ascertaining noble intentions seems to make the difference between human and inhuman, "civilized" or "uncivilized" in the face of death, then how did they come to be perceived as so unimportant by so many theorists? Especially to any trustee of the New Criticism, to its poststructuralist descendants, and even to breakaway postmodernists? If intentionality is vital to both the court of law and the court of public opinion, then how did it come to be barred from literary opinion? If the interrelations between law and literature have never been more in vogue—thanks to something like the Court Television network (now truTV) and to an entire critical movement consecrated to the role of "law in everyday life"—why has the certainty about the legal and moral value of intentionality been matched by such uncertainty about its literary value?[23] Is it really as seemingly straightforward as acknowledging that, in a postmodern world characterized by such epitaphs as Roland Barthes's "Death of the Author," authors' intentions just died along with that author—or as most anti-intentionalists framed it, with *him*?[24] Might we instead focus less on the death and resurrection of the author and more on the death and resurrection of intention? Might we engage in a cultural history and a literary theory that heed the nature of performance (textual or otherwise) before, during, and after it occurs?

In framing those questions, I do not mean to discount the important, revisionist work in textual scholarship of such scholars as Fredson Bowers, Stanley Fish, Stephen Mailloux, Jerome McGann, Daniel Melia, Hershel Parker, Peter Rabinowitz, and G. Thomas Tanselle (to name but a few). In their different yet compatible ways, they have all reasserted the importance of intentionality to the authorial writing, the editorial establishment, and the readerly reception of literary texts; they have all shown that there can be no interpretation (and subsequent effects) without a *reader* first positing an authorial intention for a speech act.[25] Nor do I mean to deride in any way much valuable scholarship on the interplay between intention and the linguistic, historical, and sociocultural ways in which individuals and cultures make meaning.[26] I mean very much, however, to stress throughout this book that, with the exception of the enduring performativity of legal "acts" (and not the enduring textuality of French conference proceedings called *actes*), a written document is not—or at most, is *no longer*—an act. I mean to pursue that line of inquiry, moreover, without quibbling semantically about whether a performance is itself a text.[27] Relative to this last point, let us simply say for now that while a dramatic script is subject to textual analysis (as is, for that matter, a prompt book or an extant account of a performance past), the intention to act—which an agent may or may not memorialize in writing—is a virtual performance of sorts: a series of future actions envisaged not only by someone writing a text but by someone committing an act.

But a text is not the same thing as a performance, nor is a literary text performative in the same way as contracts, writs, guilty verdicts, or the formal, legal acts of forgiveness that appear in the medieval letters of remission that we study in the first part of this book.[28] Human interaction is hardly limited to acts of speech; and theater, following Austin, is a place where people "do things with words" and do things *period*. In extending the focus of literary intentionality beyond acts of writing, this book is a meditation on a question that is related to Cavell's: *must we mean what we do?* It is a question that Austin himself seems to elide by favoring speakers over doers when urging that, "since our acts are actions, we must always remember the distinction between producing effects or consequences which are intended or unintended; and (i) when the speaker intends to produce an effect it may nevertheless not occur, and (ii) when he does not intend to produce it or intends not to produce it it may nevertheless occur" (*HDTW*, 106).

It proves useful, then, to employ Alice Rayner's term *actant*, by which she separates "'really' doing something from just thinking about it" (*DAP*, 2).[29] Here, it will denote the person who is actively, presently, and, for the most part, deliberately engaged in an activity in such a way as to be able to provide a legitimate answer to the question, "What are you doing?" But where Rayner's ethical emphasis on the "rhetorical strategies by which intention is attributed and meaning conferred" lead her to conclude that acts "cannot escape the perspective of the onlookers" (*DAP*, 13), I submit that acts cannot escape the perspective of the actant. If an act has meaning, it is not because people say it does or try to say it does, but because it does, first and foremost, to the person or persons performing it.

Once upon a time, in one of the favorite critical meditations about the Intentional Fallacy, various interlocutors imagined that William Wordsworth's lyric poem, "A Slumber Did my Spirit Seal," materialized mystically as random marks on the sand, washed up by the tide but still legible and discernible as the Wordsworth text. On that beach, we find Knapp and Michaels drawing their own critical line in the sand about literary intention: "marks produced by chance are not words at all but only resemble them" (AT, 20). Even if one were to accept the binary that "either the marks are a poem and hence a speech act, or they are not a poem and *just happen to resemble* a speech act" (AT, 24; my emphasis), consider now how absurd it would be to substitute *action* for *words* in that first sentence—or in many others like it.

Keeping in mind that other line in the sand which representation itself is never supposed to cross,[30] we could not say that "acts produced by chance are not acts at all but only resemble them." Notwithstanding Hamilton's assertion that, over the centuries, we have lost touch with their intention-driven nature, we nonetheless employ a special word for acts produced by chance—*accidents.*[31] Usually, these are acts of nature, "acts of God," acts in which the actant intended to do something else, or acts in which the actant makes a "mistake" (a term defined in *Webster's Dictionary* as "an unintentional departure from truth or accuracy"). Likewise, while Hamilton elegantly refutes how "we have been conditioned to think that accidents involve physical change" (*Accident,* 1), such physical change is the essence of theater. No matter how pithy Witmore's recapitulation of Aristotelian wisdom that accidents "were events instead of actions" (*CA,* 28), such events have not ceased to be acts because they are unintended or because someone has intended to do something in a different way. An unintentional act—an accident—is still an act with consequences, some more noteworthy than others.

On the beach, there is a Wordsworth poem in the sand just as surely as there was, off stage in 1380, a dying man at the theater and, on the air in 1998, a dying man on the freeway. For as much ink as has been spilled, then, over the wave poem, and regardless of Hirsch's declaration that "whenever meaning is attached to a sequence of words, it is impossible to escape an author" (*VI,* 5), one conclusion is inalterable: *Whenever meaning is attached to a sequence of human actions, it is impossible to escape an agent,* whether human, divine, or mythic.[32] If actions are meaningful, then, that is at least in part because people *mean them to mean something.*[33] And no matter how appealing the Keatsian negative capability, no matter how enduring the existential fascination with a "Stranger's" absence of intent, a murderer's "gratuitous act," the surrealist experiments with unintentional or "automatic" writing, or the phenomenon of "intentionless meaning," most discussions of accidents presuppose discussions of intention, if only to verify, as jurists do, its absence.[34] "If a person kills for no reason at all," writes Ian Leader-Elliot, "that is a reason for doubting whether they really understand what killing is about."[35] The choice, note Knapp and Michaels of de Man's position, "is not between one intentional meaning and many intentionless meanings but between intentional meaning and no meaning at all" (AT, 23). Outside the most implausible coincidences, a text does not construct itself anymore than does a poem in the sand. Books on the shelves, paintings on the walls do not

do anything, however huge their emotional effects. A novel never killed anyone . . . unless, in some *fait divers,* a volume of the *Patrologia latina* were to
fall out of a tenth-story window and hit someone on the head, crushing the
victim to death.[36] The *appearance* of design, as Aristotle put it, might indeed
appear as marvelous as it once did when "the statue of Mitys at Argos killed
the author of Mitys' death by falling down on him when he was looking
at it; for incidents like that we think to be not without a meaning."[37] But
works of art—*objets d'art* and *objets,* period—do not have intentions: their
authors and creators do. Nor do actions have intentions: their agents do. To
fail to see that is to prefer pseudoagency to agency, pseudoperformativity to
performativity.

Performativity itself, as understood by Austin, arrived late and often
problematically to theater studies;[38] and Austin is rightly revered for having
emphasized that language is not limited to reflecting or describing reality
but can actually *create* reality under such fixed, ritualized circumstances
as marriages, promises, threats, and bets: "the issuing of the utterance is
the performing of an action—it is not normally thought of as just saying
something" (*HDTW,* 6–7). Thus, when the poker player says "I bet   "
while anteing up, he is betting and has bet; when the bride and groom say
"I do," they are not speaking about marriage but are genuinely committing
the performative act of getting married (assuming all the other requisite
conditions have been properly fulfilled).[39] But Austin's intuition that theater *cannot* be performative is substantially troubled by the events of 1380
and 1998, and by the other case studies of this book: "we can issue an utterance of any kind whatsoever, in the course, for example, of *acting a play*
or making a joke or writing a poem—in which case of course *it would not be
seriously meant* and we shall not be able to say that we seriously performed
the act concerned. If the poet says 'Go and catch a falling star' or whatever
it may be, he doesn't seriously issue an order" (*PP,* 228; my emphasis).[40] In a
conspicuous shift to the passive voice—"it would not be seriously meant"—
and an equally conspicuous slipperiness between writing poems and performing actions—Austin handily disposes of theatrical intent. And yet, if an
utterance and, more important, an *action* during a play is *meant* as anything
at all, that is because it is both meant and *performed by someone* and understood by someone else.[41] It is an example of neither "intentionless meaning"[42] nor intentionless action.

Normally, Austin is right, of course, about the classic representation
scenarios of theater, film, and television, which are "performed" and not
"performative"—a point that has become increasingly obscure in the secondary literatures in which *performative* has come to denote, misleadingly,

anything that is performed.[43] Not every theatrical consequence is "performative" precisely because not every on-stage action or event is brought about by someone who intends that specific action or event. When a character issues a threat like "I'm going to beat you up," the actor usually harms no one, having committed only to an imitation that is more or less representative of the real thing. When *Friends* is taped before that live studio audience, and Monica and Chandler say "I do," it should be obvious to everybody that there is no legal marriage between Courtney Cox Arquette and Matthew Perry (for one thing, because one of them is already married). Common sense further tells us that Goffman was right to posit that plays are bracketed from reality by a "theatrical frame" that ensures that they are not "real life" but "art."[44] But the uncommon sense of 1380, 1998, and countless other events hints that Austin was wrong and that real theatrical performativity is possible. We shall see that, from lethal pratfalls to playing with weapons to militaristic sieges, theater history is positively exploding with instances of comic and tragic performativity.[45]

Two men were mortally wounded in 1380 and 1998, one at the theater, the other on the freeway and on television. In the face of those deaths, it is woefully inadequate to pose the usual questions about the phenomenology of audience response, the ontology of art, or even their interdependency as articulated by Isidore of Seville. Long before Goffman ever contended that "onlooking belongs from the start to the theatrical frame" (*FA*, 130), Isidore had pointed out that theater owes its very name to "the act of watching" by people who "stood high up and watched the plays from there."[46] Furthermore, given that audience response has been a cornerstone of dramatic theory from Aristotle to Isidore to Herbert Blau to Susan Bennett,[47] it is just as inadequate to marry audience response to the ontology of spectacle by asking, were spectators entertained? If so, it was art; if not, it was not art.[48] As Timothy Gould admonishes wisely, it is a grave error to "reduce our ability to identify the action performed in a performative utterance to a matter of calculating the effects on some audience, real or imagined" (*UP*, 21).

Equally inadequate is Goffman's normally helpful ontological distinction between the physical "theatergoer" (who buys tickets, checks coats, or thinks that the theater is too cold) and the psychic "onlooker" (who participates vicariously in the representation on stage) (*FA*, 129–30). The family of Jehan Hemont would not have been much comforted to learn that it was Jehan-the-theatergoer who died and not Jehan-the-onlooker: Aside from that, Mrs. Lincoln, how did you enjoy the play?[49] Instead, a shift in our critical focus encourages us to ask not just "Do spectators like or understand what they see?" but "What do the performers intend to do *and do*?" Such a focus moves us beyond the limitations of questions like these: At the actual theatrical instant when Jehan Hemont received his fatal wound in 1380, was the *Mystère de la Passion* still a play? Did it cease to be one because, following Walter Benjamin on artistic "reproducibility" or Richard Schechner on theater as "twice-behaved" behavior, death can never be "behaved" twice—at least, not by the same protagonist?[50] Likewise, in 1998, was the twentieth-century video spectacle of "breaking news" journalism, spectacle, or both? Did it cease to be one or the other (or both) at the moment when the victim's head exploded? Despite Bradley Butterfield's having drawn on Baudrillard to remark that "whether real or imaginary death initiates the [symbolic] exchange is beside the point," it was scarcely "beside the point" for Jehan Hemont or for the unnamed man on the freeway (EVNA, 70).[51] One can hardly advance the cinematographic, aesthetic, and economic agendas over the legal and moral ones. Nor can one divorce acts—or the appearance of acts—from their consequences: a coherency that has been obfuscated by the intensely political tenor of contemporary critical engagements.

When two men die before spectators, they are not merely signs of themselves, despite Baudrillard's celebrated scenario in which a *personage pretending to be a thief* goes through all the motions of stealing something from a department store. The ersatz thief might well place an expensive scarf in his pocket, glance at the video monitors, and head casually toward the store's exit; but the difference between his own status as theft-simulator and that of a real thief is only—thus far—the intent to steal. Baudrillard famously observes that "the same gestures and the same signs exist as for a real theft; in fact the signs incline neither to one side nor the other."[52] But he ends his theft scenario *before* they *do*—incline, that is, either to theft or pretense.[53] In order to be an ersatz criminal simulating theft, and not a real thief stealing, the "true simulator" must *at some point* enact his noncriminal (or less criminal) intent only to simulate a robbery; he must do so by returning the merchandise.[54] Eventually, the signs (perceived, misperceived, or ignored) do indeed incline to one side or the other, confirming (or not) the intent that makes for a thief. It may or may not matter that an audience, if present, constructs its own meaning of a theft or a simulation: security personnel might intervene based on their reading of the signs; other shoppers might fail to notice the signs. But ultimately, with or without the sound of one hand clapping, a crime does not need to be witnessed to be a crime; and, as we all know, the most successful crimes are those that are never witnessed at all.

While the purpose of the pages that follow is to document and justify what I am about to say, I prefer to lay my critical cards on the table right now. If there is a single thread of argumentation that runs through this book, it is this:

To a greater or lesser degree, and not as tautologically as it might sound, the integrity of theater derives from an axiom that it seems impossible to rebut: Just as there is *no murder by accident* because there is *no accidental intention,* there is *no theater by accident* because there is *no accidental impersonation* and *no accidental representation* (inasmuch as impersonation, representation, or, for that matter, theatrical nonrepresentation are themselves intentional acts). Without a cognizance of intent, there is no murder in the first place. And no theater. "There is no intentionality in nature," asserts Kirby (*FT,* xi). And Searle also states squarely that "one cannot truly be said to have pretended to do something unless one *intended to pretend to do it,*"[55] from which Luke Wilson concludes, "*To pretend is to pretend to intend,* to intend to spread out a covering intent; intent and pretense are layered one on another" (*TI,* 11; my emphasis).[56] We may also say that, if "language has intention already built into it" (AT, 24), so, too, does theatrical action.[57] Any interpretation of the conception, performance, or reception of theater must recognize that individuals or collectives who make theater *intend to make theater.* In theater, there is no such thing as the Intentional Fallacy and there never has been.[58]

To put the matter even more plainly, theater is prone to accidents in ways that "texts" are not; and those accidents are meaningful in light of intention. We understand the meaningless in the context of the meaningful. So, once we refocus our attention on where intentionality actually lies—with agents or actants—we open new vistas on other aspects of literary critique, which need in no way be discarded: the ontological, phenomenological, ethical, and moral dimensions of action, on or off stage. As we shall see, what has been lost in the shuffle of literary theory (if less so in philosophy and rhetoric) is the aesthetic phenomenon that derives so much of its strength from its quintessential ability to make the move *from thought* (or from meaning or text when the latter exists or is extant) *to action:* theater. To this day, there is no single satisfactory study of intentionality on the stage; and only a handful of critics have addressed the subject head-on.[59]

Among those few, Witmore has produced an astute philosophy of the interplay between accident and the Aristotelian probabilities of tragic plot. Drawing on Susan Suavé Meyer's work on Aristotle's *Poetics,* he defines the accident as "any noteworthy or astonishing event which had not been predicted in advance" (*CA,* 19), and argues that "the theater was a ready model for an accident-prone world, supplying a controlled space in which to plot sudden events and reflect on their causes" (*CA,* 7).[60] As stunning, however, as is his insight from *Poetics* 1452a that the accident "transforms an individual . . . into a protagonist in a dramatic scene, qualifying him for any number of stories which could be used to make sense of what happened from a particular interested perspective" (*CA*, 12), there is something profoundly nontheatrical about even the interpretations of those who study drama without really analyzing *performance*.[61] In short, it is time to put theater back into drama.

—————————

Intentions need not necessarily lead to actions, and a person may intend— and do—a great many things that are not actions: "Why is your sister crying? What did you do?" "I hurt her feelings" as opposed to "I hit her."[62] In everyday conversation, we regularly invoke intention when speaking of actions or, at a minimum, the emotionally actionable. But for purposes of the exposition and delimitation of our subject, we are not concerned with all the rhetorical intangibles of sentiment that attend both intention and its achievement(s): "By reading a romance novel, I intended to feel better, to zone out"; "By insulting you, I intend to hurt your feelings"; "In telling you this joke, I intended to cheer you up" . . . and I do. "By lancing this boil, I intend to inflict a painful cure and heal."[63] That is not to say that affective situations are unimportant. Quite to the contrary, theater's modus operandi is to provoke changes in emotion, character, and even consciousness in distinct ways. It is only to say that we focus here, with special relevance to theater, on the question of *"What did you mean to do?"* We focus on acts that an actant can intend, commit, and complete, regardless of whether their affective consequences last a second or a lifetime.

In approaching the theory and practice of intentionality, I further suggest, building upon the work of the new-wave intentionalists, that rhetorics of action matter in different ways—and often simply *matter more*—than rhetorics of writing. Writing can alter thoughts and feelings, just as it can impel rhetorically to action, but words on a page do not *act* (whatever their potential to impel again, as they endure in a variety of textual, plastic, video, and audio monuments).[64] Writing something, reading something (silently or aloud), watching something (like a videotape or DVD), or saying something are not the same things as doing something.[65] People do—or do not—do things. But people are not texts and they are not things.[66] And that is true despite Goffman's pragmatist equation of acts to objects: "the meaning of an object (or act) is a product of social definition" (*FA*, 39n). We no longer inhabit a primordial legal world that assigns divine agency to falling objects, a world in which ancient and medieval lawyers prosecuted statues, pigs, and other beasts for crimes like murder.[67] If Alan Dershowitz believes that life is *not* a dramatic narrative, then the vagaries of existence can no longer be explained as they once were by the medieval and early modern "theater of God's judgment": "like accidents on stage, those in the world were subject to a curious form of premeditation: while they might appear to come about spontaneously, accidents were actually arranged by some kind of superordinant agency that staged them for a dramatic or didactic end" (*CA, 7*).[68]

People who do things may or may not know the full extent of their intentions before (or after) they act. As Cavell points out, "it is obvious enough that not everything you know you are doing is something you are intending to be doing (though it will also not be, except in odd circumstances, something you are doing unintentionally either)" (*MWM,* 231). Individuals may not know their intentions at all. Or try to know them. They may know their intentions and lie about them, in lies that bespeak many of the same perils of modern-day legal allocutions. Even so, one thing is clear. Absent the lifeline extended by the existence of intentions, our two audiences of 1380 and 1998 (and all others like them) would have been forever dehumanized, relegated to the dark corners of history with the likes of the infamous Nero or Gaius Caligula, the latter of whom enjoyed watching prisoners being decapitated while he was dining.[69] Absent the idea of the accident, absent the saving grace of an *absence* of criminal intention, all cultural arenas in which spectators view real death or real violence would be no more salvageable than their real or imagined counterparts in snuff films or "snuff dramas."[70] All such "spectacles" would necessarily be considered immoral for having rendered their audiences voyeuristically complicit in the commission of an entire range of crimes from assault to homicide—unless, of course, spectators were able to say "No, I never intended to see that" or "No, I intended to divert myself only with the sight of simulated death, not real death."

Recuperating intentionality is thus entirely about morality or, to use the more fashionable term that somehow sounds more objective, about the "ethics" of agency. As Lawrence Buell states persuasively, "it has become increasingly difficult in the poststructuralist world to finesse the question of ethics (and, one might assert logically) the questions of intentionality that undergird any sort of ethical reflection."[71] But what is ethics, anyway, if not the moral compass of any movement from thought to action? What is theater if not a morally imbued aesthetic version of the same thing? Nevertheless, Buell stresses a situational ethics of the "virtual interpersonality" of the experience of *reading*—not the *actual experience* of behaving (IPE, 13). Even Eve Sedgwick's ground-breaking inquiry into the politics of interpersonality in "The Spectacle of the Closet" takes place within the textual space of the novel (a prelude, perhaps, to her own reexploration of the subject with Andrew Parker in *Performativity and Performance*).[72] Theater is the elephant in the critical room. It is the artistic medium that has eternally demonstrated that interpersonality is more than virtual, more than seen through the glass of a computer screen darkly: it brings people face to face.

In the end, those developments are not so surprising. The early debates about the Intentional Fallacy had virtually nothing to do with action and even less to do with theater, except for the occasional metaphorical allusion of Wimsatt and Beardsley: "we ought to impute the thoughts and attitudes of the poem immediately to *the dramatic speaker,* and if to the author at all, only by an act of biographical inference" (IF, 5; my emphasis). Those debates were almost exclusively text-bound, even though theater, like live television, is about actions, their consequences, and the intentions imbricated in those consequences. In other words, the literary genre that has so much in common with the spoken, enacted literatures of early cultures was finessed right out of the picture as critics chose to theorize intention in sonnets, novels, and other written documents, in the beaux-arts, and, more recently, in film. In light of Dasenbrock's contention, however, that "there is no fundamental difference between the way we try to figure out a speaker's intentions and the way we figure out the intentions of anyone performing an action" (*TC,* 172), the question is how and why an obsession with the former—especially when that speaker is really a *writer*—could have foreclosed the latter. Theater proved distinctly unsuited to theoretical reflections about the Intentional Fallacy. But the reasons why it was unsuited stand to topple an entire set of assumptions that gave rise to the critical dismissal of intention.

There was a certain logic to excluding theater from the (in)famous discussions about the Intentional Fallacy. To use a term beloved by medievalists, intention demands the *lectio difficilior* or the "more difficult," and thus more likely, "reading" of events; and theater draws on the intentions of multiple parties. At each performance event, a play represents ephemerally but repeatedly the varied and variable intentions of any number of players (and virtual players) who might be multiplied exponentially: authors, playwrights, adapters, producers, sponsors (medieval guilds or modern advertisers), directors, crews, actors, audiences, viewers, playbill and libretto readers, and so on, all of whom understand—or attempt to understand—both their own intentions and the intentions of others. Furthermore, those intentions vary from place to place, person to person, period to period, in time and over time. They also vary in the same place, in the same person, in the same time period, and from moment to moment. Even if an authorial or authoritative text survives, even if that text appears to reflect its creator's (or creators') intention(s), even if one prefers the reader's intentions to the author's, it is still true that, each and every time a play is staged, each and every time it brings those variegated intentions into an active, dialectical relationship with audiences and their own intentions, performance has the potential—because of people acting accidentally or on purpose—to revivify, undercut, or alter any or all of those intentions.[73]

Add to that the need, in matters of medieval textuality,[74] to multiply just as exponentially the meanings of each textual variant, and early theater throws down the gauntlet of a *lectio difficilissima*, its only real stability being that of a virtually infinite capacity for instability. In accordance with his commitment to "validity in interpretation," Hirsch objected that "to banish the original author as the determiner of meaning was to reject the only compelling normative principle that could lend validity to an interpretation" (*VI, 5*). But, given theater's multiple agents (who work with or without the aid of texts), dramatic literature could never have participated in such validity; those studying it faced an uphill battle from the start against a large-scale invalidation of theater.[75] The comfort of a "compelling normative principle" as incarnated anachronistically by a single "original author" has never been available; that personage is a fantasy, especially for classicists, medievalists, and all those working on periods before the advent of print culture. In the ancient and medieval worlds, the reading experience itself was largely public and interactive, a cultural praxis that is surprisingly compatible with Hirsch's observation that "textual meaning is a public affair" (*VI, 11*) and that is not so surprisingly resistant to the textual constraints of structuralism, formalism, and even canonical traditions of "establishing a text" (without which most of us would have nothing to study at all outside of dusty manuscript libraries).[76] Faced with manuscript evidence that has been ravaged by time, hungry animals feasting on vellum, and, above all, tired or incompetent scribes who have made mistakes or lost their places, the scholars who establish texts are in the business of recovering the lost intentionalities of the authors whose work they seek so carefully to preserve and redisseminate by providing informed answers (sometimes, a learned best guess) to this question: What did the author—or the scribe or both—mean and intend to write?[77] Daniel Melia even went so far as to question whether medieval literature in general had "*any* meaning" to him whatsoever if he could not make "basic decision[s] about the (implied) author's intention."[78]

Given the instability of medieval texts, characterized by *mouvance* and *variance,* most medievalists would be hard-pressed to agree with Knapp and Michaels that "a text only has a single meaning—the meaning its author intends it to have. If it is understood 'in a different way,' it is either misunderstood or it is a different text" (AT2, 9).[79] Even if there *were* such a thing as a single medieval or a single theatrical text,[80] to accept their statement at face value would be to relegate any theatrical performance to a collective (or not so collective) misunderstanding. One would hope that even the most ardent reader of texts (literary, plastic, or cinematic) would have no trouble admitting that theater need not be about the written word. One would also hope that such a reader would admit that, while the metaphors and practices of writing or textuality are just as apt to reflect the move from invisible to visible meaning, they cannot account adequately for the multidimensional nature of action or for the play of perceptions that is theater, a medium that makes the invisible become visible and makes silence speak.

Whether the *lectio* of medieval theater be *difficilior, difficilissima,* or even impossible, that is no reason not to undertake it. Investigations into the intentions of others will never be satisfactory to a degree of certainty (despite so many medieval inquisitorial pronouncements to the contrary).[81] Even Hirsch avowed that "I can never know another person's intended meaning with certainty because I cannot get inside his head to compare the meaning he intends with the meaning I understand." But it is unreasonable to spurn the question of intention for fear of never getting it right: "It is a logical mistake to confuse the impossibility of certainty in understanding with the impossibility of understanding" (*VI,* 17). Certainly, there can be no hope of getting it right in law, morality, or aesthetics if we do not inquire.

Whence the present inquiry and my proposal that, in spite of the hard times on which any version of the Intentional Fallacy has fallen, it is urgent that we reintegrate intentionality into the contemporary critical dialogue in general and into theater studies in particular. I argue that the misunderstanding and marginalization of intention has had a great deal to do with the misunderstanding and marginalization of theater, not only as a literary genre but as a medium of action—action that requires the evaluations and judgments that can be wrought only by the reintegration of theater into the critical canon . . . sometimes, to the sound of medieval cannons. Inasmuch as theater primarily stages real (imitative and, thus, intentional) acts committed in real time by real individuals, I further submit that intention is not a fallacy at all. If one of Aristotle's signal contributions to the very nature of dramatic plot was to tease out the providential and *nonaccidental* nature of what only *appeared to be,*[82] then let us say this: To paraphrase Luce Irigaray, just as murder is an accident that is not one—a notion that obsessed some of the earliest detractors of the Intentional Fallacy—intention is that fallacy which is not one.[83] If gender studies have taught us that actionable bias can inhere uncommented in gendered language, then liable agents can inhere unaccountable in passive language for acts they commit.

I have no wish to oversimplify complex acts that must always be studied in context, but I believe it will be helpful to outline the two interrelated taxonomies that form the argumentative crux of this book. They are starting points only, and their complexities will become positively kaleidoscopic as we proceed. The first taxonomy treats, with special relevance to theater, four fundamental ways in which intention comes into play in the performance of action (linked, for the time being, to the violence of our case studies); the second taxonomy treats the types of intentions we shall be exploring throughout: ACTUAL, ACHIEVED, DECLARED, and PERCEIVED INTENTIONS.[84] I describe both taxonomies with all due caution because I also aim to analyze the insufficiency of the categories when addressing (for each actor in each social drama) such attendant circumstances, in any combination, as free will, coercion, changes of mind, risk management, malfeasance, negligence, and above all, good faith.[85]

As we shall see, to intend is, by nature, to have good faith, even when it is a good-faith effort to have bad faith, even if the intent is to do evil, and even if one embarks on a problematic course toward a worthy goal or a problem-free course toward an unworthy one. Consider, for instance, the modern criminal who instigates a car wreck at some risk to himself and to others, all for the purpose of collecting settlement money, either off the books or as insurance fraud. The other driver, who crashes into him as a result of the setup, has had an accident. The criminal, however, has not legitimately had an accident because, whatever else might have gone wrong, he intended to crash, arranged for the necessary conditions to fulfill that crash, and did crash.[86] The nonaccidental medium of theater also emerges from a good-faith effort to engage in it in a social context that includes a minimal respect for the letter and spirit of the law.[87] For our first taxonomy, then:

1. There are acts (including violent theatrical acts) *committed accidentally* and *viewed—or experienced—deliberately*.[88] (Jehan Hemont's mortal accident of 1380 already illustrates the limitations of this category in that theatergoers had doubtless committed—deliberately—to watching a play, which normally hosts neither death nor "acting" by those behind the scenes.)

2. There are acts *committed accidentally* and *viewed or experienced accidentally*. In theater studies, this second scenario corresponds to someone

stumbling quite by chance upon an accident, on stage or off, never having intended to witness any such thing or even to attend or observe the theatrical venue. (Worthy of note at this stage is that there is, in fact, such a thing as an accidental act of reading. Normally, people do not read by accident, with such notable exceptions as Augustine's famous accident-that-was-not-one in the *Tolle et lege* moment.[89] But the following are indeed possible: before you know it, you're reading the billboard as you drive; you're browsing at Borders and find yourself reading a book you had not meant to select; the staff-member at the Bibliothèque Nationale brings you the wrong volume, an error you don't notice until you've read for a while).[90]

3. There are acts *committed deliberately* and *viewed or experienced accidentally*. In this scenario, another somebody might happen upon a violent spectacle or a crime-in-progress. On the face of things, that sounds like what happened in 1998 when, with little or no warning, viewers of traffic reports and cartoons found themselves watching breaking news about a deliberate suicide watch.[91]

4. And there are acts, including representation, that are *committed deliberately* and *viewed or experienced deliberately*. As far as we know, this fourth scenario may also correspond at best to (artistic) complicity or voyeurism and, at worst, to snuff films. When considered in connection with an ontology-making (or ontology-breaking) violence, it also corresponds to theater.

Our second taxonomy concerns the type of intentionalities at work—and at play—in the world of action, theatrical or other: ACTUAL, ACHIEVED, PERCEIVED, and DECLARED INTENTIONS. While each is elaborated in the case studies that follow, it is helpful to begin with a few relatively simple examples of ACTUAL and ACHIEVED INTENTIONS inasmuch as those are the intentions about which actants state their DECLARED INTENTIONS, and which intentions, achievements, and declarations are perceived by others (PERCEIVED INTENTIONS).

Long before the term *multitasking* came into vogue, individuals have negotiated multiple intentions while performing multiple activities that do not provide the kind of one-to-one correlation so frequently admired by politicians or literary theorists. As Tallis elucidates the matter so effectively, chance and agency, accident and intention go together. "I am walking on the beach," he muses—Is the Wordsworth poem there, too?—"and I pick up a stone. There can be no doubt that I intend to pick up *a* stone; but the *choice* of this particular stone out of the many thousands that lie to hand is left [by whom?] to chance" (*NS*, 233; his emphasis).[92] So let us imagine that a woman, whom we will call Sarah, intends to compose a poem, drink a cup of coffee, and smoke a cigarette (ACTUAL INTENTIONS) . . . and she does all three of those things successfully (ACHIEVED INTENTIONS).[93] It is perfectly logical or "happy" (for Austin) that an agent might execute successfully one intended behavior and fail, "unhappily," at the other:[94] if, say, Sarah were to compose the poem, but put out her cigarette in the coffee, rendering it undrinkable.

Or consider Jack, who intends, while playing Hamlet, to enter stage left while zipping up his fly; and he succeeds at playing Hamlet, moving, and zipping. Peter intends to drive to the market, talk to his realtor on his cell phone, and read the sports section (ACTUAL INTENTIONS), but he achieves only two of those things successfully after crashing, accidentally, into a tree (partially ACHIEVED INTENTIONS). And Oliver intends to model his tuxedo while walking down the stairs on the way to get his iced tea in the living room (ACTUAL INTENTIONS). For one thing, Oliver can change his intentions mid-course: seeing an old friend downstairs, he runs, doesn't walk, down the stairs. Or he notices a big stain on the tux and decides not to model it. For another thing, Oliver might have any number of accidents that impede the achievement of any or all of his ACTUAL INTENTIONS and/or which prompt him to reevaluate: he trips and falls because the cat runs in front of him; he splits the seam of his Armani; he is so preoccupied with the pain in his ankle or the cost of the torn formal wear that he no longer cares about the iced tea, the modeling, or seeing his friends downstairs until he has had time to change. Furthermore, changes of course include Oliver's being knocked completely off course (*NS*, 233) in ways that may or may not be anodyne but are always illuminating, especially in light of Witmore's observation that "the example starts to become a story at the instant when an intention (embodied in the man's 'course') becomes subject to alteration" (*CA*, 10).[95] They can be accidental or intentional, due to the omissions or commissions of Oliver or others, to acts of God, etc.[96] Finally, the Armani-clad Oliver might make, ad hoc, in medias res, or post hoc, any number of true or false, implicit or explicit declarations (DECLARED INTENTIONS) about his ACTUAL INTENTIONS, and even his misACHIEVEMENTS, in heading to the iced tea and group of friends downstairs, while his friends might wonder: What on earth is he doing? What's he trying to do? (PERCEIVED INTENTIONS). The same caveats apply as for the first taxonomy; and, although it will prove practically impossible to disentangle ACTUAL, ACHIEVED, PERCEIVED, and DECLARED INTENTIONS, for the moment, I classify them roughly as follows (as a prelude of sorts to the more specific theatrical considerations of chapter 5):

> ACTUAL INTENTIONS refer here to what an agent (and virtual actant) intends to do. They are invisible, and their invisibility informs a cultural history that embraces everything from the emergence of confession as the "queen of proofs" to literary debates about authorial sincerity.[97]
>
> ACHIEVED INTENTIONS refer to what an agent actually *does*, successfully or unsuccessfully, in carrying out his or her ACTUAL INTENTIONS— if, as is often logical, that agent in fact makes the effort to do so.[98] (Police forces, of course, would certainly have an easier time of it if criminals *did not* make that effort; and one may also intend *inaction*.) ACHIEVED INTENTIONS thus concern moments when the invisible becomes visible not just in words but in action. The relation between ACTUAL and ACHIEVED INTENTIONS is crucial to our analysis of the accidents that follow, in which we shall see that an accident in theater is something that occurs *on the way* from ACTUAL to ACHIEVED INTENTION.
>
> The situation becomes even more complex once intentions are DE-CLARED by an actant and PERCEIVED by someone else (though they need not be). I use the term DECLARED INTENTIONS to denote the true or false,[99] informed or misinformed declarations (linguistic, gestural, and so on) that agents make—before, during, or after the commission of their acts—about their ACTUAL and ACHIEVED INTENTIONS. Thus, ad hoc or in medias res, our friend Oliver might say, "Check out my new tux!" or "Just let me get my drink" or "I'll be right there but I can't run in this thing." Post hoc, to compensate for clumsiness, embarrassment, and the like, he might just as readily tell his friends that he was practicing a pratfall for tomorrow's play. Again, strictly speaking, it is not necessary to communicate an intention at all, and, sometimes, it is commendable not to: "I don't love you, I'm just using you"; "When I tell you I'm a tragedy-relief worker, I intend to scam you." But when DECLARED INTENTIONS enter the realm of communication, as they invariably do in our medieval legal cases, they proffer significant clarification—sometimes confusion—about why people do what they do. They are, moreover, the *raison d'être* of medieval letters of remission, which exist precisely to pronounce, clarify, and memorialize intention (even as they preserve meaningful gaps between intention and action).
>
> Last, PERCEIVED INTENTIONS denote what an audience makes of any of it, all of it, or none of it: these refer to the intention(s) that audi-

ence members, spectators, even readers attribute to any given author or authors, actor or actors, director or directors, and so on.[100] This category will later include self-perception (for both actants and audiences), as well as how spectators, watchers, and witnesses perceive the intentions of others, this latter feature sounding much more complicated than it is. We raise concerns about it every day when, in response to something unpleasant on stage or screen, we wonder not just: "What did that producer, director, actor, theater troupe, television station, newscaster mean to do?" but also, "Did the director really think I'd want to see that?"[101]

However imperfectly, when DECLARED and/or PERCEIVED INTENTIONS are available, they reexcavate what the alleged Intentional Fallacy has long buried. If an accident is decipherable only in terms of an actant's passage from ACTUAL TO ACHIEVED INTENTION, then what decades of phenomenology, reader response criticism, postmodernism, and even frame analysis have failed to resurrect is this: *the real fallacy is to think that the only relevant disconnect in human action is that between an agent's ACHIEVED INTENTIONS and an audience's PERCEIVED INTENTIONS.*[102]

Challenging though it is to unravel the strands of both taxonomies, our eight short chapters represent my best effort to do so. In Part I, "Back to the Medieval Future," four medieval case studies show that, for each contested topic of modernity, there is a medieval antecedent (and, for that matter, probably a classical one too) that underscores the unparalleled importance of intention in artistic action in general and theatrical action in particular. Those case studies—"arbitrary slice[s] . . . cut from the stream of ongoing activity" (*FA,* 10)—set the critical stage upon which we retheorize theatrical intentions, literally, by doing theater justice. Here, we make the acquaintance of four of the most unfortunate individuals ever to have encountered medieval theatrical life (three of whom are survived by letters of remission): a stagehand, a bystander at a rehearsal, a rape victim, and a dancer. They are all victims of violent acts related to a theater in which, for Peter Brook, "there is a deadly element everywhere."[103] Each one shines a spotlight on what theater is not, and in so doing, they illuminate what it is supposed to be, meant to be, intended to be by those performing it.

In chapter 1, "Behind the Seen: All Hell Breaks Loose," we are concerned with the intentions of the stagehand, Guillaume Langlois, who, in 1380, was obliged to account for his role in the accidental death by cannon-fire of his colleague, Jehan Hemont. In an incident that assists us in amplifying the theatrical resonances of ACTUAL, ACHIEVED, DECLARED, and PERCEIVED

INTENTIONS, the two props men take us behind the scenes as well as "behind the seen" to just what it is that people mean to do, what they achieve successfully or unsuccessfully, and what they *say* they mean to do.

Next, in chapter 2, "The Final Run-Through," we attend another theatrical performance, this one in 1384, only to meet another casualty of medieval technical wizardry gone awry. This time, one Perrin Le Roux died at the hands of Fremin Severin from injuries sustained during a rehearsal of the *Miracle of Théophile*.[104] In addition to shedding new theatrical light on the nature of both "work performance" (*FA*, 126–27) and legal work product, the case of Perrin Le Roux justifies the assertion that *there is no such thing as accidental impersonation.*

Continuing to exploit that great untapped theatrical resource which is the medieval letter of remission,[105] we analyze in chapter 3 the numerous difficulties of agents' declarations of their intentions. In "Fear of Imminence and Virtual Ethics: Staging Rape in the Middle Ages," we consider two assaults with ties to the theater: the gang-rape of a woman in 1395 by a group of men who spent the night on the scaffolding erected for the following day's theatrical production;[106] and a medieval equivalent of today's marital rape when, almost a century later, in 1485, an actor returned home from his performance as a devil and, still in costume, allegedly forced himself sexually upon his wife.[107] Both texts take up what I term the fear of imminence, one of the greatest scare tactics of all time: if you yourself pretend—or witness pretending—for too long, then pretense will become reality.

Our final medieval case study appears in chapter 4, "Killing Himself by Accident: Of Broken Frames, Mimetic Blindness, and a Dance of Death," which completes the jigsaw puzzle of an agent's ACTUAL, ACHIEVED, and DECLARED INTENTIONS with that jagged piece known as an audience's PERCEIVED INTENTIONS—that is, their understanding(s) or misunderstanding(s) of a given act. Its subject is the spectacular death in 1507 of the jovial butcher, Henry D'Anoux, who fell on his knife while dancing, only to have his cries for help met with disbelief from his fellow dancers.[108] By investigating both what happens and what does not happen as he lies dying, we come to a new understanding of theatrical performativity, which, in turn, facilitates a critical reassessment of the dreaded Intentional Fallacy per se, and for which purpose I have created a liminal space.

In a theoretical Entr'Acte, I reappraise, in light of the applied critical history of the Intentional Fallacy, what the scenarios of Part I will have proved: intention is "this fallacy which is not one." Here, I complete my proposal that there can be no Intentional Fallacy when it comes to the theater by looking to the critical (mis)fortunes of the Intentional Fallacy itself.

The text-bound dismissal of intentionality, I argue—with its antitheatrical emphasis on text over actant—reveals an almost "agentless" quality that is characterized by three fallacies of logic and morality alike: the critical substitution of "accident" for "causation," of "reception" for "intention," and of "politics" for "agency." I further suggest that the pedagogy and the politicization (whether rightist or leftist) of literary theory have propagated, to the great detriment of our understanding of theater, *the mistaken and misleading view that art is performative—even politically performative—in a uniform way.*[109]

Having shed the necessary light on theatrical practice and critical theory, our opening taxonomies then yield a revised working definition of the theatrical contract itself, which informs Part II. Chapters 5 through 8 are all devoted to what one might dub (following Antonin Artaud, who strikingly invoked metatheatrically the medieval Black Death) "the theater and its trouble"[110] or, following Judith Butler in *Gender Trouble*, "theater trouble." Throughout Part II, I consider separately and sequentially (as far as that is possible), first, the intentions of the parties who are making theater; next, the intentions of those attending it; and, finally, what our understanding of both types of intentionality brings to the many and various ways in which the theatrical contract is broken by members of the theatrical collective (chapter 6) and by spectators (chapter 7), respectively.

Chapter 5, "The Theatrical Contract," explores its subject in full recognition of the legalistic dimensions of the term. Drawing on Goffman's signature definition of social involvement—and, by extension, *theatrical involvement*—as an "interlocking obligation" (*FA*, 346), I contend that there is nothing "unhealthily juridical" (*LT*, 119) about the mutual consideration—indeed, the *legal consideration*—that defines the theater: what individuals performing and spectating intend, both for themselves and for others. Once we look to the interrelations of what those making theater *intend to do,* what they achieve or misachieve, what they say (if anything) about all that, and what an audience perceives or misperceives about those intentions and their enactments, we are able not only to make moral, ethical, legal, and artistic sense of dramatic performance but also, at long last, *to determine what theater is not.*

Next, I offer in chapter 6, "In Flagrante Theatro," a series of real and hypothetical scenarios that illustrate the virtually infinite roles of intention on the stage, the better to reframe Goffman's own frame analysis. Initially from the standpoint of actors and other members of the theater collective (who presumably share both a common intention and a legal "standing" to act, to represent, to perform),[111] I focus on Goffman's theory—and the theatrical practices—of "breaking frame" (*FA*, chap. 10). In short, by pondering what the impossible murder by accident might look like on stage, I argue that a veritable critical obsession with breaking frame constitutes, in reality, an obsession with breaking the theatrical contract.

If, up to that point, we will have concentrated on the acts and accidents of both actors and those behind the scenes, we turn in chapter 7, "Theater Nullification," to various instances in which audience members themselves (appear to) break the theatrical contract.[112] Here, it is spectators who reject, as it were, the rules of the theatrical game, much as contemporary juries reject the rule of law when offering creative verdicts more consonant with their own sensibilities about what they think the law *should be*.[113] The responses (or nonresponses) of theater audiences (and also of nonspectators), their action(s) or inaction, depend not only upon their own intentions but on their perceptions of what others intend *for them*—all of it in ways that enhance our comprehension of violent contemporary experiments with those very responses.

Finally, we come full circle to my opening statement that the eminently sociable theater cannot—and should not—be illegal. With an emphasis on the dire consequences of ignoring intention in live media as well as in literary theory, past, present, and future, we return, in "Black Box and Idiot Box," to that pitiable man on the freeway, as contextualized by a host of other snuff-like incidents, including the notorious airing by *60 Minutes* of the Kevorkian-assisted suicide of Thomas Youk in May 1998.[114] I call this final chapter not a traditional "conclusion" but a theatrical Talk-Back, in part to encourage continued debate about the subject of intention.

It is not my own intention here to proffer some kind of apology for the good old days of the medieval world when intention ruled, a mindset that nurtured such repressive and imperialistic events as the Crusades or the persecution of Jews. But, from those proverbially Dark Ages there emerge a haunting series of accidents that had real consequences to real "bodies that mattered," and whose import is enhanced by intentions that mattered just as much.[115] They matter not just in theory but in practice: the practice of theater and the practice of life.

Part I / *Back to the Medieval Future*

1 / Behind the Seen:
All Hell Breaks Loose

> The artist is responsible for everything that happens in his
> work—and not just in the sense that it is done, but in the sense
> that it is *meant*. It is a terrible responsibility; very few men have
> the gift and the patience and the singleness to shoulder it. But it
> is all the more terrible, when it *is* shouldered, not to appreciate
> it, to refuse to understand something meant so well.
> **STANLEY CAVELL,** *Must We Mean What We Say?*

One fine Parisian day, Jehan Hemont, apprentice at the
bathhouse, went along to the theater to help out a friend of long standing, one Guillaume Langlois. Their lives were never to be the same. When
all was said and done, Guillaume found himself the subject of a criminal
investigation into his handling of the theatrical props in his charge; and Jehan Hemont had no life at all. On 27 March 1380, he was mortally wounded
during the Crucifixion scene of a Passion play during which, one might say,
all hell broke loose. Something had gone wrong with one of the ten cannon
that had simulated, according to "customary practice," the fire and brimstone of divine wrath.[1] It was something that raised serious legal questions
about liability, responsibility, and morality at the theater, just as it clarifies
now for us the types of intentionality that we shall be exploring: ACTUAL,
ACHIEVED, DECLARED, and PERCEIVED INTENTIONS.

Guillaume Langlois was the special effects man; Jehan Hemont was the
victim. But whose victim? How does something meant so well happen so
wrong? What are the ramifications of doing what one does not intend? Medieval Parisians also posed a question that few contemporary scholars dare
to ask in the current political climate: Was theater responsible for his death?
This chapter is devoted to the surprising answer to that question as we
focus, along the way, on the common-sense connections between theater
and law.

In 1380, Jehan Hemont did not die for political reasons, and his accidental
death had little to with any politics save those which had allowed representation to be so dangerous in the first place.[2] That is why we know about
these two men at all. Their story survives in a letter of remission that was
issued to Guillaume Langlois during the following month of April on an
unspecified day that seems to coincide with Jehan's passing. In that letter,

King Charles V absolved Guillaume of all criminal (if not civil) wrongdoing in the fatal accident that had caused the death of his friend Jehan. A remarkable document that was first edited and published in *Romania* in 1900 by Antoine Thomas, the letter tells a tale of that terrible moment when risky representation becomes reality.[3] Although Charles V might readily have pronounced theater guilty for the fatality, he arranged instead for all plays "staged and established in honor and remembrance of the death and passion of our Lord Jesus Christ" to get off scot-free (fol. 152v; Appendix, Document 1.1). Moreover, he forgave Guillaume Langlois, who had lacked the requisite intent to be branded a criminal, in large part because of the good life that Guillaume had led—and which goodness was demonstrable (tautologically) by his very participation in the useful, instructive, and godly commemoration of the life of Christ that had hosted the accident: "Disposed to grant his plea . . . and acknowledging that the plays in which he was engaged were in signification and example of goodness and that the aforesaid complainant is of good name, repute, and honest conversation, we have forgiven, acquitted, and pardoned the supplicant in the aforementioned case of the actions which thus occurred" (fol. 153r).

In this legal document about medieval theater gone awry, there is no such thing as an Intentional (or Biographical) Fallacy. Guillaume Langlois received a royal pardon because, before 27 March 1380, he had authenticated, with a history of good conduct, his noble intentions and his equally noble life story. It would therefore be a grave error today to discount as immaterial the very story that proved so material to both his terrestrial legal case and his eternal salvation.[4]

Other questions were to arise regarding Guillaume's civil liability; but, for now, we are obliged to admit that the one proposition that was not open to question was the absolute virtue of religious drama, regardless of its potential for mortal danger. No matter how vituperatively we might condemn medieval censorship and regulation of the stage, there is no escaping the fact that, in a culture in which men were what they did, Charles V defended the artistic medium in which art is action: theater. To paraphrase the Spanish humanist Juan Luis Vives, theater in 1380 was no "sword in the hand of a madman":[5] it was no sword at all so long as it was brandished by good men for good works.

Modern scholars thus find themselves in the curious position of acknowledging that a medieval king endorsed a relatively simple answer to the very question that haunts us today as lawsuits proliferate against various art forms.[6] Did the MTV cartoon figures, Beavis and Butthead, cause a Chicago child to set fire to his house? Did Oliver Stone's *Natural Born Killers* inspire copycat criminals? Did depressing rock music cause an unstable teenager to commit suicide? Did the spectacle of "fun-boxing" cause a young mother's death on 18 June 2003? Does rap music instigate real violence against women? Or, in perhaps the closest American equivalent to a medieval Passion play, does the latter-day pageant wagon known as Hell House, which depicts rape, abortion, and "sinners" dying of AIDS, foster hatred and homophobia?[7] All such inquiries hark back to Plato's complaints that theater precipitates transgression, anarchy, and unorthodox opinions, compromising the legal bedrock of the *polis*. Innumerable, likeminded medieval accusations charged that theater was guilty, by association, of all manner of sins of commission and omission: crime, violence, fornication, and all-around unchristian behavior.[8] Notwithstanding today's tendency to attribute such questions to the enemies of art who seek to contain, curtail, or censor it, the failure to ask such questions actually does a disservice to history, historiography, and to theater itself, which is largely absent from modern indictments of the arts. Not everything associated with art is artistic; and, if there is no guilt by association *alone,* there is no art by association.

No doubt about it: the usual clichés about the Middle Ages will not do as we try to understand the complexities of what is, at the very least, a story of religious art for art's sake. Passion plays and their participants were not criminally liable for the deadly acts that occurred within the so-called "boundaries" of those plays (however blurred and imprecise those boundaries might have been).[9] Jehan Hemont died in 1380, and it would have been very easy to say that, but for theater, he would have lived. However, it was also easy to respond that if an incontrovertibly legal, moral, and necessary theater were outlawed, then only outlaws would have theater.

Whence a startling insight. What sounds like the artistic version of the conservative slogan of the National Rifle Association—"if guns were outlawed, only outlaws would have guns"—actually corresponds to a contemporary, liberal, protheatrical position: a position voiced, no less, by what passes these days for the incarnation of repression, a medieval king. Charles V and/or his lieutenants recognized that while individual actors, special effects men, and the like might be held responsible for the equivalent of today's civil torts, their individual parts did not culminate in the condemnation of the whole of theater. That art form might well have constituted both the instrument and the scene of the crime, conjuring the wisdom of the *Digest of Justinian* that "it makes no difference whether someone kills, or provides the occasion of death."[10] Likewise, the death of Jehan Hemont was the outcome (*eventus*) of "what is done" (*facta*), which was "to be considered, even if [the act] was done by a most inoffensive man, although the law punishes the man who is in possession of a weapon for the purpose of homicide no less than him who kills."[11] But that same book of the *Digest* also proffered a clear distinction between murder and accident on the basis of intention: "[I]f someone draws his sword or strikes with a weapon, he undoubtedly did so *with the intention of causing death;* but if he struck some-one with a key or a saucepan in the course of a brawl, although he strikes [the blow] with iron, *yet it was not with the intention of killing.* From this it is deduced that he who has killed a man in a brawl *by accident rather than design* should suffer a lighter penalty."[12] The Passion play of 1380 definitely provided the "occasion of death," but by accident; and there was no doubt about the purity of the representational intentions behind both the production and its violence.

Jehan Hemont met the Grim Reaper when a theatrical imitation of fire and brimstone was trumped by the real explosion employed to produce that effect. He suffered for several weeks afterward and ultimately "passed from life to death on the 27th day of the present month [of April] or thereabouts" (fol. 153r). There is no evidence that Guillaume Langlois intended to harm him in any way, so this was no "snuff drama." Even in a culture that the-atricalized executions, interrogations, death, warfare, and other rituals, Jehan Hemont did not die on stage (as related to our earlier taxonomy) from the deliberate commission of real violence viewed deliberately.[13] He was no modern performance artist choosing notoriously to inflict pain upon his own body before spectators, *à la* Bob Flanagan or Karen Finley.[14] Nor did he resemble a London actress who had supposedly chosen to be as-saulted on the stage of the Real and True Theatre in the 1980s (*SRT,* 21). As far as we know, Jehan Hemont did not intend to commit "suicide by drama" (by analogy to the claims made by contemporary American law enforce-ment officers that the goal of certain individuals brandishing lethal weap-ons is to commit "suicide by police").[15] He did not choose to die at all; nor was he forced to participate in the spectacle of his own death. No actor he but, rather, a normally unseen stagehand,[16] he was not there to do any pre-tending in his own person. Instead, he was participating in the theatrical *esprit de corps* that creates overall scenic verisimilitude and which, despite a long history of on-stage accidents, was meant to represent death, not to render it.[17]

And yet, death was rendered, coinciding performatively with Hell's fire and brimstone. Was it an accident? A coincidence? An act of divine provi-dence?[18] Or was there, somewhere behind the seen, *someone's* underlying murderous intent? As investigators endeavored to determine whether Guillaume Langlois had been responsible for Jehan Hemont's death, they had a pressing question to resolve, which was not about the theater but about law and order: Did a crime occur or not?[19] If Guillaume had never intended to kill Jehan, then his community could speak not of murder but of accidents that could be forgiven and of agents who might pay lesser penalties. Instead of extensive discussion of the affect that attends reception—how are we all feeling about this?—they inquired about the liability and consequences of intentional and unintentional acts. What did Guillaume intend to do—and believe he was doing—at a time when belief was everything?[20]

The case of Jehan Hemont demanded a ruling as to whether death was creationally intentional and theater destructively performative. If, for J. Hillis Miller, a "true performative brings something into existence that has no basis except in the words,"[21] then, in 1380, another true performative appears to have brought not some*thing* but some*one* into nonexistence. The medieval case thus focused on the very aspect of speech act theory about which Eagleton was so apprehensive: its potential for "smuggling in the old 'intending subject' of phenomenology in order to anchor itself" (*LT,* 119). One cannot "smuggle in" something that is always already there; and the voice of Jehan Hemont speaks from beyond the grave to the importance of intentions, just as he had once spoken, before dying, to the issue of his own intentions. One week after the incident, on 3 April 1380, from his sickbed he memorialized in writing—so says Guillaume's letter of remission—his forgiveness of his friend in a notarized document that has not survived:[22]

> After these things had thus transpired, the aforesaid Hemont, who was a good and true friend to the aforementioned complainant and who, on account of the wound he had thus sustained from the plug of the said cannon, did not wish [Guillaume] to be damaged in any way or to be prosecuted, either by him or on his behalf, either now or at some future time, the aforesaid Jehan Hemont, being of sound mind and body, of his own free will, without any undue influence, declared and proclaimed—for Guillaume and for his heirs, or for anyone having legal business with him—that the aforementioned complainant was entirely, truly, and absolutely innocent of the deed which had thus transpired and of any [other] accusation which might reasonably ensue on account of the event at some future date, saying and confessing that the two of them had been good friends. (fol. 153r)

Both Jehan Hemont and Guillaume Langlois proclaimed their good intentions to their king in order to explain and to resolve legally an accidental death at the theater. In theater as in life, meaning something is not the same thing as doing something.

On the medieval stage, reality made for good representation, and a sophisticated theatrical culture rose to the challenge of the proviso that better effects made for the better acting that made for the better message.[23] Guillaume Langlois had been "asked, requested, and charged by the actors playing the roles of the enemies and the devils to be present at the aforementioned plays in order to fire the cannon at the right moment [during the Crucifixion] in order *to ensure that [the actors] would play their roles better*" (fol. 152v; my emphasis). We will never know which one of the ten pieces of artillery malfunctioned or why. What we do know is that a death in connection with the fourteenth-century Parisian stage could not have been ruled accidental without an elucidation of the intentions of Guillaume Langlois and Jehan Hemont. We also know that, in a cruel irony, the man who worked all day with water at the bathhouse as a *varlet d'estuves* found himself ill prepared for theater's deadly fireworks. Equally ironic is the portentous switch to the passive voice in Guillaume Langlois's letter of remission, which elides the question of agency at its very moment of truth: "a red-hot rammer *had been placed and stuffed* into one of the cannon."[24] Too tightly? Incorrectly? And by whom? We can only induce that Guillaume must have had some contact with the cannon, otherwise, he would never have needed a letter of remission when one of those cannon misfired—and in ways that even Austin could never have suspected when describing, as we shall see momentarily, the "unhappy performative" as a "misfire." Jehan and Guillaume had

> arranged and prepared the aforesaid group of cannon so that these would detonate and make noise at the specific time and place of the Crucifixion. And because, upon the place where the aforesaid complainant and Jehan Hemont were standing, there *had been placed* a hot rammer, which was stuffed into one of the cannon standing at that site, the plug [*cheville*] of the aforesaid cannon popped out and fired earlier and otherwise than the aforesaid supplicant and Hemont had anticipated or expected. [The explosion occurred] in such a way that the aforesaid Hemont was struck and, by chance [*d'aventure*],[25] wounded by this said plug in one of his legs; and from the strength of the explosion and of the flames that broke out, the aforesaid Guillaume was also burned and charred all over his face; and he was in great peril of being killed or mortally wounded. (152v; my emphasis)

In an unintentional and "infelicitous" act, the collateral deadliness of a deliberate theatrical explosion would not have met Austin's conditions for performativity; but it does anticipate in quite remarkable ways his definition of a misfire: "[When] the act that we purport to perform . . . [does] not come off—it will be, one might say, a misfire. This will be the case if, for example, we do not carry through the procedure—whatever it may be—correctly and completely, without a flaw and without a hitch. If any of these rules are not observed, we say that the act which we purported to perform is void, without effect" (*PP*, 225). Misfires notwithstanding, however, the performance of 1380 was not "without effect."

Independent of Austin's own rejection of true performativity on the stage, we cannot comprehend a theatrical misfire—whether metaphorical or as literal as it was in 1380—by focusing exclusively on the success, achievement, reception, or "happiness" of a given act.[26] For one thing, we know very little about who, aside from Guillaume, even saw Jehan Hemont's distress because, for all its detail, the letter of remission does not tell us whether the show went on; whether cast, crew, and audience members were even aware of the accident; or whether anyone rushed to the scene (or behind the scenes, if "behind" there was) to provide medical assistance. For another thing, the success, achievement, or happiness of the act in question was wholly different for at least two groups who faced the divine threat of Hell's fire and brimstone: the impersonated sinners "within" the play and the spectators "without" it.[27] As far as the first group was concerned, the dramatic storyline must surely have appeared to be the epitome of success in its threat to the *characters* of the Passion play. But for the second group, the misfire caused theater itself to backfire in what became, for Jehan Hemont, a living hell on earth, the ultimate "unhappy performative."

Baudrillardian symbolic exchange aside, there remains something profoundly unsettling about an "entry into the symbolic" that, for Butterfield, "severs the subject from the real" (EVNA, 68). If anything, Jehan Hemont's entry into the symbolic world of theater bound him all too closely to the real as it came close to severing his leg. Given that he was fatally "wounded . . . in one of his legs" (152v), it is impossible to accept the Baudrillardian notion that "every referent is fatally mediated, and *even a wounded leg* cannot be called on to issue the truth about its condition beyond representation" (EVNA, 69; my emphasis). Even Austin did not think so when he imagined a parlor game in which a man pretending to be a hyena carries his game too far and takes a bite out of yet another leg, Austin's own calf: "Try to plead that you were only pretending, and I shall advert forcibly to the state of my calf—not much pretence about that, is there? There are limits, old sport"

(*PP,* 204). Jehan Hemont's wounded leg issued a number of truths about its condition—as well as his and ours—when he died. One of those truths is that, if we see his pain solely as a referent, then the only thing "fatally mediated" will be reality and its own players.

Inasmuch as medieval artists sought, in Jauss's words, to "do justice to the transcendence of the Christian faith," their art forms "had to give the invisible or future and, consequently, unreal truth a degree of certainty in contrast to which all the probabilities of the visible, everyday world would pale into 'as ifs,' if not into delusions" (*QA,* 5). There was nothing delusional about Jehan Hemont's wound when, by mischance, by accident, but apparently not by design, theater played a role in his real death. At that very instant, theater, which functions as what we might call the great *as if,* became an *as is,*[28] exposing the limitations of Wilshire's violent spin on Austin's falling star (*PP,* 228): "Pestilence that 'kills' does not kill the beings performing or auditing; 'stabs to the heart' do not kill" (*RPI,* 262). In 1380, fire and brimstone *did* kill; and, to paraphrase Elaine Scarry, pain was pain and not a metaphor of pain.[29] Rather, as Barbara J. Eckstein frames her objection to a purely phenomenological approach to pain, "the daily assault on human flesh and all physical facts of life are not simply battles of words."[30]

Ever since the publication of Scarry's paradigm-shifting *Body in Pain,* no one would seriously maintain that we should not study what pain means to its sufferers simply because that pain "is usually private and incommunicable, contained within the boundaries of the sufferer's body" (*BP,* 27). The same thing ought to hold true for the investigation of the responsibilities of those who inflict pain, starting with whether they are doing it deliberately or not—and even when they are doing it during theater, an art form that displays both the truth of illusion and the illusion of truth.[31] "The experience of pain," writes Eckstein, "is factual truth for the person in pain. It is witnessed not with the *eyes* . . . but with other nerves of the body." But, in continuing her thought, she claims that "because pain does not relate to other people and cannot depend upon their testimony, its factual nature can be perceived as illusion or opinion by those who witness it and those who hear tell of it. In other words, they can doubt it" (72; her emphasis). The very mission of theater, which it has always shared with classical and medieval legal discourse, is to shape, create, or remake truths by bringing verisimilar illusions before the eyes of witnesses, whom we call "the audience."[32]

When Jehan Hemont eventually died of his wound, it was not because there had been an audience that day at the *Mystère de la Passion.* His death had nothing to do with their presence, their absence, or their interpretation of the events unfolding before them—unless, of course, as we shall see in chapter 4, that interpretation somehow included their recognition that a real wound required real life-saving intervention. Nor is anyone suggesting that his death was irrelevant to theater because it occurred behind the scenes. Nor would it be correct to assert that, had spectators truly felt entertained, then Jehan Hemont had not truly been wounded. Nor, conversely, would it be enough to say that, had audiences ceased to find the Passion play diverting at the interruptive moment of the fatal wound, then it had ceased to be theater.[33] Nor did the audience cause his death because of their reception needs—although that is the bottom line of many of the arguments that one hears today regarding the popularity of simulated violence in the media: that is, because audiences demand violence and advertisers invest huge revenues consistent with that perceived demand, both phenomena heighten the odds that real violence will occur.[34] Nor did the subsequent legal inquiry have anything to do with the bloodthirstiness of crowds or with the variety of solutions historically evinced to mollify that alleged bloodthirstiness.

The cause of Jehan Hemont's death was a cannon wound, not a social construction. And we call that death "an accident" because, while Guil laume was intending to do one thing, he achieved something else, which underscores our earlier point that an accident is something that occurs on the way from ACTUAL to ACHIEVED INTENTION. As Tallis states the case succinctly, "our intentions cannot be utterly specific, with absolute values assigned to all possible variables. The actual moves constituting the action do not uniquely realise the intention; or, to look at it the other way round, the intention cannot legislate over all the features of the action, even if one is knocked off course in the passage from intention to realization" (*NS*, 233). Sometimes, as for Wendell Harris, it is a simple matter of a clumsy protagonist knocking over the crystal glass on the way to reaching for the roast beef (*LMRSL*, 91). Sometimes, we face a vision of collateral damage that sounds positively Platonic: "When a man performs an act as a means to an end, he wills not his act, but the object of his act" (*Gorgias*, 466). Sometimes, as in 1380, it is a matter of life and death.

In the anodyne cases with which I introduced our taxonomy of ACTUAL, ACHIEVED, DECLARED, and PERCEIVED INTENTIONS, the reasons for the course correction were comparatively unimportant: cats, iced tea, and tuxedos. Not so for Jehan Hemont and Guillaume Langlois, knocked off course in and because of violence. As Cavell articulates the problem with language eerily appropriate to the events of 1380 (as well as to the type of logic that undergirds Good Samaritan laws in a country like France), "you know that firing a gun [or a cannon, for that matter] is making a lot of noise, but only in special circumstances will making the noise be (count as) what it is you are intending to do." However, once something happens, accidentally or on purpose, to knock the agent off course, there is no avoiding this imperative: "even in so simple a case as the firing gun: he may not have thought of it before, but he had better think of it now" (*MWM*, 231–32). So, too, should we.

For all the postmodern pleasure that it has been possible to take in various crises of representation, language, or theory, what faced Jehan Hemont in 1380 was a crisis of reality. Theory is not the same thing as practice; practice is not the same thing as rescue; and aesthetics is not the same thing as ethics. As Alan Read puts it forcefully, "though theatre might be said to be beyond good and evil, theoretical relativism is an inadequate response to its practices" (*TEL*, 1). Real violence calls for real justice, even when it occurs at the theater; and, barring acts of God or natural catastrophes, real violence has agents whom we judge, in part, on their intentions, which are real, no matter how intangible.

Jehan Hemont, his surviving relatives, and his king all sought to discern the intentions of Guillaume Langlois, who might well have felt partially or entirely responsible for the catastrophe; the pardon that resulted from those good intentions ensured a sort of happy ending for everyone involved. Jehan Hemont had presumably gone straight to heaven on the same grounds that his unwitting assailant was forgiven: both were good men who had led good lives. Guillaume Langlois and his heirs were spared the shame and stigma of having a convicted killer in the family, although they remained at risk in another arena; the benevolent monarch did not terminate Guillaume's civil liability, "should there be any party who wishes to pursue him in this matter in the civil courts alone" (fol. 153r). That was not surprising in a world where early Frankish laws had consistently sanctioned financial restitution as the expiation for a wide range of violent crimes, including murder.[35] What is surprising is that theater was also spared, despite a sweeping history of countless polemics against it. It is interesting to see how.

We do not normally think of Goffman's bracketed theatrical frame as legal insulation, but perhaps we should, as he himself seemed to do when opening *Frame Analysis:* "All the world is not a stage—certainly the theater isn't entirely. (Whether you organize a theater or an aircraft factory, you need to find places for cars to park and coats to be checked, and these had better be real places, which, incidentally, had better carry real insurance against theft)" (*FA*, 1).[36] Notwithstanding States's celebrated philosophizing about such cheerful theatrical occasions as real dogs or working clocks on stage, when it comes to "the upsurge of the real into the magic circle where the conventions of theatricality have assured us that the real has been subdued and transcended,"[37] that upsurge is not always so pleasantly surprising. The real world cannot be completely "subdued and transcended" any more than death itself. That is true despite the optimistic aphorism that has eternally indicated the contrary: that immortal arts can transcend even death. The upsurge of the real, be it verbal or physical, can be both permanent and illegal. And medieval communities knew it.

This was no medieval *théâtre vitrine,* or "theater as window," played out as if behind glass, closed in, separated by some kind of fourth wall, to be watched at arm's length, even though the origins of drama itself allegedly rested upon such a distinction.[38] Indeed, not all the medieval edicts and postmodern phenomenology in the world can erect a fourth wall, whether in a past era in which there was no such wall, or in a present one, the better to knock it down again. That did not stop medieval actors from breaking[39]— and medieval civic officials attempting painstakingly to demarcate—the privileged physical as well as psychic frames for the words and actions of a theater that had long surged from its official performance sites onto streets, church steps, and marketplaces (and vice versa).[40] Legislation of theatrical action may have arisen from a perceived need to protect communities from the unpremeditated—and premeditated—eruptions of violence which, according to Gosselin, were characteristic of the fifteenth- and sixteenth-century stage: "one could scarcely leave a mystery play without having been a witness to or an actor in 'a wounding and bloody battle.'"[41] Similarly, such legislation appears to have been connected to the effects of verbal violence from the stage, as communicated centuries prior to Ingarden's inquiry into the nature of theatrical language. In 1456, for example, a group of actors in Angers protested, from *inside* a *Mystère de la Passion,* against the legislation of theatrical language, concerned that their on-stage words might trigger accusations of heresy from *outside* the play: "I protest publicly on behalf of all players in this mystery play, jointly and severally, that, in the event that anything against the faith should be said or done by anyone, it shall be deemed null and void. For we do not intend [*entendre*] to say or do anything against the faith."[42]

True, the spoken and written word had eternally been reckoned mightier than any sword, stick, or dagger.[43] But, if we look back in Angers, the play's expositor petitioned on behalf of his fellow thespians that, within the proverbial magic circle of dramatic representation, theirs were legally protected utterances. His juridical language clarified the troupe's intentions and further situated any and all actors in Passion plays within a legal and theological tradition that had ever likened lawyers to actors by virtue of their special ability to speak in someone else's voice, to "interpret," translate, or impersonate.[44] Thus, one particularly intriguing case was prosecuted in fifteenth-century Paris by the royal prosecutor LeMaistre against Maître Chambellan of Parliament, whom the former had accused of defaming two other members of Parliament. In his own defense, Chambellan cited the precedent of none other than Saint Jerome, who had been accused of heresy "for having translated Greek into Latin." Chambellan contended that, like actors, lawyers were but "translators": they could not be held liable for verbal offenses that they had not uttered in their own voices.[45] Was there a comparable release from liability for actors regarding the bodily acts of theater, which they were not performing, as it were, *in their own bodies*?

The question makes no sense. Short of science fiction or cinematic comedies about corporeal and identity exchange (*Big, Freaky Friday, Prelude to a Kiss, Thirteen Going on Thirty,* and so on), *one cannot act in someone else's body;* actor and character inhabit the same body. No matter how many "presences" an actor's body establishes—at least seven for Graver[46]—and no matter how complex and kaleidoscopic an actor's communication networks, *actors act in their own bodies only.* Their characters on stage have only the appearance of agency, a point that various medieval French legal communities had no trouble at all resolving, despite the phenomenological difficulties that Cavell would evoke so famously in his meditation about the yokel who rushes the stage to stop "Othello" from murdering "Desdemona" because he cannot tell her apart from Mrs. Siddons (*MWM,* 328).[47] *The appearance of agency* is not the same thing as *the appearance of action;* and the appearance of one action might well be the commission of another. That is why action must continue to occupy such a crucial place in what is legally actionable on stage, screen, and television. It is also why questions about legally actionable artistic action return us unceasingly to intention. When things go criminally wrong with actions—or, depending on intention, when they go criminally "right"—acts are not bracketable by the theatrical frame and never have been. Nor should they be.

Obviously, my goal here is not to study the legal case against Jehan Hemont in the same way that a modern attorney would do when recalling the prevailing wisdom about intention, causation, and culpability that there is "no liability without fault."[48] Even so, several commonsensical objections—variations on those foregrounded in our Mise en Scène—must be addressed:

POINT: "You don't stage plays to kill people." **COUNTERPOINT:** Aside from the gladiatorial arena or the remote possibility that, in the stuff of Agatha Christie novels or episodes of *Columbo,* a given play might serve as the medium for murder—or might host spectators who hope that it will—any understanding of the death of Jehan Hemont depends nonetheless on ruling out Guillaume's murderous intentions *at the theater.* Risks during staging are subject to accusations (and verdicts) of recklessness; or, as Jackson recalls in the realm of legal philosophy, "we hold people morally—and legally—responsible for the bad that results from reckless behaviour despite the fact that the bad need not be intended."[49] But theatrical performances normally host neither murder nor accusations of murder.

POINT: "Of course the death of Jehan Hemont is not a problem for theater. It was an accident, for heaven's sake!" **COUNTERPOINT:** Plays do not stage themselves; people with intentions stage them. And it is on that basis that we employ the term *accident*—not *murder by accident*—in the first place.

POINT: "Don't be ridiculous! *Theater* wasn't responsible for the death of Jehan Hemont!" The more juridically inclined might also interject that the Passion play of 1380 was no more responsible for Jehan's death than, say, an antiques dealer would be responsible for having sold an attractive bejeweled dagger to a man who then trips and drops the dagger, only to see it plummet from a third-floor window straight into the neck of a pedestrian whom it stabs and kills. Or that theater was no more liable for Jehan's death than a car dealership would be for selling a vehicle to someone who drove it recklessly a single time in twenty years, only to run someone over. Common sense also tells us that the production company of the short-lived television series *Cover-Up* was not responsible for the fluky death of the actor Jon-Erik Hexum, who on 12 October 1984 jokingly took a props revolver loaded with blanks, fired it against his temple in such a way as to dislodge a piece of his skull, and precipitated the serious edema that resulted in his being taken off life support one week later (after a medical verdict of irreversible brain damage).[50]

COUNTERPOINT: There might be a certain logic to insisting that antiques dealers, car franchises, and production companies are no more liable for those "accidents" than theater was liable for the death of Jehan Hemont. But understanding such acts and actions is possible only in light of the intentions of the parties "in charge" of the objects in question: cannons, antiques, cars, or, more controversially, guns.[51]

POINT: "You can't look at theater that way! You're transforming it into a loaded gun, which is precisely the sort of argument that leads to censorship." **COUNTERPOINT:** "Funny you should mention it." As we shall now

see, that is exactly what happened to everything *but theater* in the proliferation of firearms that characterize debates about intention and its
fallacies.[52] Following Goffman's remark that "all things used for ham-
mering in nails are not hammers" (*FA,* 39n), if theater is a hammer, a
whip, a cannon, a loaded gun, then not every gun misfires . . . or fires at
all. Besides, even Charles V did not see it that way: It's not the gun, it's
the intent. To reinvoke the NRA analogy that opened this chapter, *Guns
don't kill people, people do.* But can that possibly mean *Theater doesn't kill
people, people do?* Not entirely.

In his 1940s critique of Wimsatt and Beardsley, Coomaraswamy offered
an extreme example of the dangers of neglecting intention by introducing
into the ongoing discussion the subject of murder. The difference between
a skillful murder and a skillful poem, he wrote, was "simply a 'moral' one,
not an 'artistic' one, since each if carried out according to plan is 'artistically' successful."[53] Some forty years later, Knapp and Michaels took up the
analogy toward a different end, suggesting nonetheless that thinking about
murder was a valuable way of thinking about meaning. Indeed, Sverdlik
submits that understanding intention in philosophy is "easier" when we
"simplify discussion" by confining our inquiry to a single example like "firing a gun with the intention of killing the person aimed at."[54] Extrapolating
from Gadamer's interest in moments when an agent's intentions fail to go
"according to plan," Knapp and Michaels theorized that "you try to shoot
someone and the gun isn't loaded; alternatively, you point what you think is
an unloaded gun at someone and the gun goes off. What happens is not what
you intended. But . . . the analogy between shooting someone and saying
something doesn't hold. In the case of shooting, you can fail to do what you
intended to do and you can succeed in doing something you didn't intend"
(AT2, 6).[55]

Knapp and Michaels are the first to recognize that meaning "is not like
acting," acknowledging that "the fact that people can do something other
than what they intend to does not show that people can mean something
other than what they intend to mean" ("AT2," 7). Still, the victim of this
imaginary scenario is not their concern. Rather, they devote their conclusion to the interrelations of language and meaning: "in language you can
never fail to mean what you intend and you can never succeed in meaning
something other than what you intend. You can, of course, fail to communicate what you mean, and failing to communicate is indeed analogous to
failure in the case of shooting: in both cases the consequences differ from

what you intended" (AT2, 6). Such seemingly sensible words fail to reassure, especially given the pair's earlier claim that "[t]here is a crucial difference between shooting someone and meaning something. No matter how many times you try to shoot someone with an unloaded gun, you can't succeed. But the case of language is obviously different" (AT2, 4).

The case of language is indeed different. It is different not only at the level of convention, which is very much their point. It is different because, as they readily admit in their refinement of Hirsch and Searle, "[t]he point . . . is not that there *need* be no gulf between intention and the meaning of its expression but that there *can* be no gulf" (AT, 17; their emphasis). It is different at the level of the consequences of actions in which there *can be* such a gulf: "attempted murder is not the same thing as real murder; to try to do something is not necessarily to do it. Perhaps conventions are essential to meaning something in the same way that a loaded gun is essential to shooting someone. You can't mean anything if you don't use the conventions; you can't shoot anyone if the gun isn't loaded" (AT2, 3). That statement passes for legal truth each time judges hand down lighter criminal sentences to defendants convicted of attempted murder than they do to those convicted of first-degree murder. But a plan is not the same thing as a plan that fails. And, even from the standpoint of reception, a meaning misunderstood is not a noncommunication; it is a miscommunication.

Knapp and Michaels do well, in their critique of de Man, to point out that "[w]hat reduces the signifier to noise and the speech act to an accident is the absence of intention" (AT, 23).[56] But, unless it is the general who, when saying "Hi," is misunderstood by the firing squad to mean "Fire!" (upon which they do so), the consequences of a misunderstanding do not usually result in instantaneous death.[57] Some might find it traumatic to be misunderstood; misunderstandings that build over the years may even spawn individual violence as well as the collective violence of war. But, upon its issuance, an act of speech (however emotionally damaging) is not the same thing as an act of physical assault or murder.[58] Furthermore, while an attempted murder that fails may be a nonmurder (like the well-aimed gunshot that misses the mark), it is not a nonact. And it is inconsistent with our understanding of the arts to bring communication into the picture for meaning and to fail to bring "result" or "consequence" into the picture for acts: simulated acts, too, which, even for Baudrillard, have consequences.

Consider Baudrillard's trademark argument about a "fake hold up" in which you "check that your weapons are harmless, and take the most trustworthy hostage, so that no life is in danger (*otherwise you risk committing an offence*)." Regardless of the simulator's intentions, "a police officer will really shoot on sight; a bank customer will faint and die of a heart attack; they will really turn the phoney [*sic*] ransom over to you," such that "you will *unwittingly* find yourself immediately in the real" (*SW*, 178; my emphasis). There is nothing "unwitting" about the simulator's acts that have provoked the crisis: even the most gifted simulator knows full well—or should know—that his demand for ransom will prompt precisely the real activities Baudrillard mentions. Moreover, following Goffman's pragmatism (*FA*, 39n), the ransom is *not* phony for those legitimately providing it (although it *could be* if the real victims of the alleged simulation had engaged in simulations of their own by filling up a briefcase with newspaper). It is, quite simply, as real as gravity, in the words of the controversial Alan Sokal: "Anyone who does not believe that gravity exists is invited to jump out the window of my apartment. I live on the tenth floor."[59] And it is as real as the felony murder rules that might hold the simulator responsible for the allegedly unintended murder by heart attack that he committed.

Finally, as compared to Baudrillard's own simulated theft scenario, cited earlier (*SW*, 178), inaction before a stolen item is of a very different order of magnitude than inaction before a dying man, and a theft that endangers property is no match for an act of violence that endangers human beings, even in a simulated holdup. While Baudrillard is intrigued by the impossibility of punishing simulation (whether of vice or virtue), the possibility of punishing theatrical feigning is what is at stake in the events of 1380. The accidental failure to (succeed at) murder might constitute an instance of Austinian performative "unhappiness" (if preceded by such a threat as "I'm going to kill you"); the failure to die is, in all likelihood, a happy event for the nonvictim. Independent of whether it is ever appropriate to call the unintended consequences of actions "successful" or "unsuccessful"—even Hirsch affirms that the "author's desire to communicate a particular meaning is not necessarily the same as his success in doing so" (*VI*, 11)—we cannot help but notice that all the philosophy in the world will not bring a dead man back to life or, if we now return to Austin, a dead animal.

While anyone familiar with the concept of performativity can probably cite chapter and verse of *How to Do Things with Words*, Austin's "Plea for Excuses" is one of the most provocative texts on the relationship between intention and action. Here, he invites us to imagine that he has "conceiv[ed] a dislike" for his own donkey as it grazes peacefully alongside his neighbor's donkey in the same field. Austin wonders what terminology he ought to use after an unsuccessful effort to kill the wretched beast: "I go to shoot it, draw a bead on it, fire: the brute falls in its tracks. I inspect the victim, and find to my horror that it is *your* donkey. I appear on your doorstep with the remains and say—what? 'I say, old sport, I'm awfully sorry, &c., I've shot your donkey *by accident*'? Or '*by mistake*'? Then again, I go to shoot my donkey as before, draw a bead on it, fire—but as I do so, the beasts move, and to my horror yours falls. Again the scene on the doorstep—what do I say? 'By mistake'? Or 'by accident'?" (*PP,* 133n; his emphasis).[60]

That scenario has inspired others such as Sverdlik to ruminate about moral luck, offering a human equivalent of those Austinian donkeys, in which the carefully scheming, would-be assassin "*A*" finds that, when he "fires a rifle at *B* . . . the bullet is deflected by a cigarette case in *B*'s pocket, or a bird suddenly darts in the way" (CML, 181; his emphasis). Be that as it may, human, divine, even avian intervention does not cancel out the murderous intentions of the individual who has unsuccessfully or erroneously fired a shot. In such cases, even a "nonmurder" is not a "nonaccident." Or, as Searle puts it eloquently, "in these cases it is, so to speak, *the fault of the world* if it fails to match the intention or the desire, and I cannot fix things up by saying it was a mistaken intention or desire in a way that I can fix things up by saying it was a mistaken belief" (*Intentionality,* 8; my emphasis). The world is not an intending subject, and the Intentional Fallacy itself is a mistaken belief that needs fixing.

From the numerous weapons strewn on the ground of philosophy—Cavell's noisy gun, Austin's donkey-killing rifles, Baudrillard's SWAT team—we see that, in theater as in life, if meaning something is not the same thing as doing something, then meaning to mean is not the same thing as meaning to do, an insight that moves us off the page and onto the stage. Thus, for Searle, "acts are things one *does,* but there is no answer to the question, 'What are you now doing?' which goes, 'I am now believing it will rain', or 'hoping that taxes will be lowered', or 'fearing a fall in the interest rate', or 'desiring to go to the movies'" (*Intentionality,* 3; his emphasis).[61] We can easily envisage asking Guillaume Langlois that question ad hoc, to which he could have responded, "I am preparing the cannon" or "Since this cannon is ready, I'm moving on to the next one," or something of the sort. Post hoc, the question is: "What did you do?" And his answer would not have been: "I was believing that the cannon was ready." Rather, it became: "I prepared the cannon (properly) for the representation of the Crucifixion and then left it alone;" or, depending on his level of guilt, "I accidentally killed a man."

To intend to kill does not always mean to succeed in committing murder; and death can result from actions that no one intended. In 1380, Charles V (or his lieutenants sensitive to any number of factors including economic inducement) officially had no trouble separating the two when he forgave the unintentional death of Jehan Hemont. Guillaume Langlois might well have been liable for moving on to that next cannon, misguided in his belief that it was safe to leave the first lethal weapon behind. But, since he never meant to kill anybody, he was not guilty of murder—a finding far more meaningful than being not guilty of meaning.

2 / The Final Run-Through

> As literature creates a virtual past, drama creates a virtual future.
> The literary mode is the mode of Memory; the dramatic is the
> mode of Destiny.
> **SUSANNE LANGER,** *Feeling and Form*

Jehan Hemont was not the only person to be mortally wounded at the theater. Just over four years later, on 19 June 1384, in the Parisian suburb of Aunay-lès-Bondy, one Perrin Le Roux was killed as a result of a remarkably similar accident that occurred during a rehearsal of the *Miracle of Théophile*. Another victim of special effects gone awry, he prompted another intervention by a new monarch, Charles VI, after another investigation of intentions.[1]

What occurred on that deadly day now has a familiar ring. "Charged with operating the said cannon" was a certain Fremin Severin, who "apparently filled the mouth [*bouete*] of this said cannon with paper alone, without placing any iron or wood there." He found himself nonetheless with a lethal weapon in his charge, just as Perrin found himself in the line of fire: "The late Perrin Le Roux *happened to place* himself [*se mist d'aventure*] in front of the aforementioned cannon as it was going off, in such a way that, while the aforesaid cannon was firing, the paper, which was in the barrel of this said cannon, hit him in the eye. . . . From this blast, the late Perrin Le Roux passed from life to death the following Friday; and, on account of this thing, the aforesaid blood relations [*amis charnelz*] of Fremin Severin have made the[ir] request to us" (fol. 7r–v; Appendix, Document 2.1; my emphasis).

Something was different this time. The participants were at church "in order to rehearse their roles [*pour recorder leurs personages*]" (fol. 7r). Perrin was killed not before the proverbial full house but in that special in-between or liminal space which is the rehearsal, not yet intended for an audience—at least not at that very moment.[2] He met the Grim Reaper during a representational event that was, at the time, a work-in-progress, even an artistic brand of Goffman's "work-performance" (*FA,* 126). To borrow

47

Antonin Artaud's famous phrase, Fremin Severin came to blows with the "theater and its double" almost as a *doubly liminal* personage: his work behind the scenes on the special effects was normally at most unseen and at least unobserved by the audience; and the rehearsal itself, before the anticipated official performance,[3] was not yet "the real thing." Unfortunately for Fremin, rehearsals host many real things, described compellingly by Goffman as follows: "Practicing provides us with a meaning for 'real thing,' namely, that which is no longer mere practicing. But, of course, this is only one meaning of real. A battle is to a war game as a piano recital is to a finger exercise; but this tells us nothing about the sense in which warfare and music are different orders of being" (*FA,* 62). In 1384, by the time the rehearsal was over, Perrin would be experiencing an "order of being" that was very different indeed in his passage "from life to death."

Highlighting the limitations of various critical approaches to liminality, I argue in this chapter that the very concept—and practice—of the rehearsal make sense only in light of intentionality: an intentionality that, in the case of 1384, may be accessed through the textual traces of what was once the fascinating, protodramatic performance known as the letter of remission.[4] Letters of remission, such as Guillaume Langlois's of chapter 1 and now Fremin Severin's, memorialize allocutions of the intentions and regrets associated with everyday lives and deaths long past. Crucial here is not only intention but *time,* the stock in trade of theater, about which popular wisdom has long held that "comedy is tragedy plus time." In 1384, a rehearsal was what a rehearsal always is: an intention to present something formally later, all the while really presenting it, previewing and *pre*-viewing it by doing it, acting and enacting the *faits, gestes,* and words that create art both in the present and in times to come. Whence Goffman's invocation of the phrase "no longer," my own use of "not yet," and Kirby's formalist and intentionalist insistence on presentation before spectators *at some time:* "By our definition, it would be theatre *as long as there was the intent to make theatre,* to show the performance *at some time* to an audience" (*FT,* xi; my emphasis).[5] Timing may be everything, but in 1384, so was intention.

Kirby proposes a single answer to the ontological problem of the rehearsal by asserting that "intent is a necessary and crucial element [of theater]. People make something that develops and changes in time—a performance—with the intent of having it affect an audience." In that way, he purports to "escape," minimally, at the level of affect, "from a theatre version of a very old philosophical question: Is there any sound if a tree falls in the middle of a huge forest and nobody is there to hear it? Is it theatre if a person performs something when alone or if a full rehearsal of a play is conducted without an audience?" (*FT,* x–xi). While an intention-oriented approach to theater cannot answer all of our questions about what is (or was) happening in 1384, we shall see nevertheless that it offers a remedy of sorts to the moral relativism that has dogged theater studies from Plato to Stanislavski to Wilshire, just as it ultimately assists us in comprehending that important but elusive subject of our chapter 5, the theatrical contract.

In spite of the many and varied teachings of formalism, phenomenology, performativity, reception theory, and postmodernism, it would be preposterous (to say nothing of cold-hearted) to assess the events of 19 June 1384 from a purely phenomenological perspective, reckoning, for instance, that Perrin's death "did not count" as theater because rehearsals always keep one foot in reality—though with Perrin's other foot in the grave. It would be equally preposterous to suggest, as if Perrin's blinding wound had extended to others, that if no one *saw* him struck down—or was meant yet to see him—then there was no dramatic spectacle.[6] One cannot simply ask: "If a man dies at the theater and nobody sees it, is he still dead?" The answer is unquestionably yes. Nor could any contemporary critic (whether liberal or conservative, New or Old Historicist, postmodernist or structuralist) reasonably state that mortal events that occur during rehearsals are nonevents. The same holds true for such a mortal filming as that of *The Twilight Zone Movie* when, in 1982, Vic Morrow and two children perished. One cannot deny that three human beings were dead because the film-in-progress was not yet a film. Or that the deaths of the children did not matter because their roles were peripheral to the action. Or that there was no film because they died. Eventually, there *was* a film; but, between the film and the dead actors, we must focus our attention upon the latter.

Like Jehan Hemont before him, Perrin Le Roux died from real injuries to his real body from real effects. He did not die from any theory of the rehearsal of real effects, but from the real effects themselves, which were being rehearsed at the time as representation. Theory pales by comparison to the fact that, if practice makes perfect, it can also make death: a death in 1384 that was not a "murder by accident" because of intention alone. And, unless we were to include, unspeakably and inhumanely, the progressive act of dying itself—even when elevated to the status of a medieval *ars moriendi*—death is not liminal, regardless of the medieval theological propensity to consider terrestrial living as but a prelude to, a pilgrimage toward, and even *a rehearsal for* eternal celestial life.[7] As Lady Mercy puts it when arguing in the heavenly court of Arnoul Gréban's *Mystère de la Passion,* humankind deserved redemption because "[man] committed the outrage on earth / which was but a pilgrimage / and a path by which to reach the kingdom without end."[8]

Once again, this is not to repudiate the substantial, significant, and fascinating phenomenological problems of liminal events like rehearsals or of liminality itself. The rehearsal is the site of some of the most suggestive inquiries into theater; and the concept of liminality has proved invaluable for deepening our understanding of where to look for medieval theater in the first place.[9] But when, as in 1384, rehearsals broach—and breach—intentions, the question to ask is not: Is it (or was it) art? art-in-progress? not art? Rather, we need to ask: What killed Perrin Le Roux? It is a question to which theater scholars are not immune, with Goffman himself musing that "when a coroner asks the *cause* of death, he wants an answer phrased in the natural schema of physiology; when he asks the *manner* of death, he wants a dramatically social answer, one that describes what is quite possibly part of an intent" (*FA*, 24–25; his emphasis). Perrin Le Roux probably died from infection, a physiology that belongs to the inquest;[10] but the social drama that now unfolds before us is a matter of intent, which sheds light on the ontology of art, if only by instructing us that, sometimes, art is not the issue at all. Still, what *is not art* tells us a great deal about what *is art* in the apparent cognitive dissonance with which, in this very chapter, those concerns move us toward a revised ontology of theater in terms of our initial taxonomies, now specifically related to theatrical acts of representation.

Just as there is no murder by accident, there is no accidental impersonation, whether during a rehearsal or during a so-called official performance. As we shall see, of the four cases enumerated earlier—namely, acts (1) committed accidentally and viewed deliberately; (2) committed accidentally and viewed accidentally; (3) committed deliberately and viewed accidentally; and (4) *committed deliberately and viewed deliberately*—only the fourth case is capacious enough to cover the communal experience of theater.

As the scribes J. Clerici and T. D'Estouteville lay a linguistic foundation in this new letter of remission for an exculpatory accident (invoking the chance, happenstance, and misfortune of what Perrin *happened to do*), they also place at center stage the question of Fremin Severin's intentions, even if "once removed" by their own narrative voices. It so happened that, in addition to his work behind the scenes, Fremin was also "playing a character" in the play of *Théophile* and was "supposed to fire a cannon [*ou quel jeu avoit un personnage de un qui devoit getter d'un canon*]" (fol. 7r).[11] What happened, then? And who did what at the scene of what else, which was eventually ruled a forgivable crime?

The scribes' locution, presumably based on Fremin Severin's own attestations before them, implies a legal strategy akin to that privileged "translator's" position once invoked by Saint Jerome, whereby even the most unsafe theater constituted a kind of legal safe house. It was a position that, at least theoretically, tendered two protections for actors: they were not to be held responsible for utterances spoken in the voices of others, nor for the theatrical acts committed by their characters whom they performed nonetheless in their own bodies.[12] In Fremin's case, that strategy turned on the distinction between his own allegedly noble intentions to represent (or to collaborate, as a stagehand, in representation) and the putative intentions of the character(s) he was playing . . . or, at times, *not playing,* since Fremin was also "supposed to fire a cannon." Predicaments of phenomenology, however, are not necessarily predicaments of law, despite what Cavell tells us about the difficulty of pointing simultaneously to both Desdemona and Sarah Siddons playing Desdemona (*MWM,* 328). In or out of character, Fremin Severin was operating a lethal weapon, and he perceived a clear and present danger to a group of bystanders, Perrin Le Roux among them, at which point he made an effort to intervene: "at the moment when he was supposed to fire this said cannon, the aforementioned Fremin apparently said to the people who were standing around there: 'Get back! You've got no business being so close! It's too dangerous!'" (fol. 7r).[13] Fremin had no trouble differentiating between his roles as actor, stagehand, and citizen anticipating his legal duties. Nor did his community who, in the end, pointed to *him* as the personage in the theater of life who required forgiveness. They did so, moreover, despite the legal precautions that Fremin had taken on his own behalf.

While Fremin's admonition seems to have laid the groundwork for legal insulation from a serious felony and for clemency to come, it did not go far enough to save the life of Perrin. Fremin Severin failed in what we would call today a "good-faith effort" to save Perrin's life; and in the Middle Ages "good faith" was a more expansive notion. So, too, was the kind of "act of God" that would prompt latter-day insurance companies to reject the wrongful death claim that would surely be filed under analogous circumstances.[14] Perrin's life depended on someone's—anyone's—ability to perceive changes in the dialectic between intended (or unintended) realism and intended (or unintended) reality on stage, regardless of whether realism or reality was being rehearsed at the time.[15] So, like Guillaume Langlois before him, Fremin *needed* a letter of remission because of the discrepancy between his ACTUAL INTENTIONS (to simulate divine wrath?) and his MISACHIEVED INTENTIONS (killing someone by accident).

Fremin Severin thus faced grave danger in 1384 from any number of medieval legal principles, the most perilous of which was expressed in the wisdom of the Lex Cornelia, according to which "guilty intention [*dolus*] is presumed from the deed."[16] Not only did Fremin shout out a warning, he did everything he could to avoid the presumption of guilty intention from his deed. He did so both at the scene and later when seeking a pardon by proclaiming that, in executing his duty to fire the cannon, he intended to harm no one. Rather, he served all within earshot with legal notice—*à tous ceux qui ces presents avertissements orront*?[17]—that if, at some point, they had put themselves at risk *unintentionally,* they were now doing so *intentionally.* His cry of "Get back!" was tantamount to saying: "I renounce my responsibility for this action and transfer that responsibility to you." This is a model reminiscent of time-honored forensic rhetorical strategies, or of those frequently theatricalized scriptural teachings about Pilate "washing his hands" of the Crucifixion of Christ,[18] and also anticipatory of Cavell's point that he "may not have thought of it before, but he had better think of it now": "[W]hen further relevances of what you are doing, or have done, are pointed out, then you cannot disclaim them by saying that it is not your intention to do those things but only the thing you're concentrating on. 'Unintentionally,' 'inadvertently,' 'thoughtlessly,' etc., would not serve as excuses unless, having needed the excuse, you stop doing the thing that keeps having the unintentional, inadvertent, thoughtless features" (*MWM,* 231–32). How unforeseeable would the death of Perrin Le Roux have been, for instance, to anyone familiar with the death of Jehan Hemont four years earlier? How unforeseeable would it have been a century later, given all the fighting that typically erupted during mystery plays and that culminated, says Gosselin, in the need to "explain oneself before the judge and tell him all about these incidents, which were *unpredictable but always assured*"?[19]

In an artistic medium whose dangerous acts might precipitate legal inquiries into the intentions of its actants, foresight was necessary; various medieval communities endeavored to rise to the challenge, as when, on 26 June 1501, the town council of Mons barred from entry to a Passion play "children under the age of ten," "senile old people," and "pregnant women."[20] Likewise, contemporary theater troupes to this day serve legal notice regarding their use of such effects as strobe lights, which pose a danger to epileptic theatergoers (but which, in all likelihood, are dangerous to no one else and, on many nights, to no one at all). My point is that when such legally self-interested notices announce the possibility of harm to an audience, their authors frequently follow up by shifting the blame to the victim who does not exercise due care: Why did the epileptic patron attend the performance in spite of the warning? More interesting still, when that individual later initiates a lawsuit because the warning was not made visible enough (or, for the blind epileptic patron, not audible enough), he or she unveils one of the most enduring legal entities of all time, which is nevertheless a construction as fictive as that of any literary enterprise: that proverbial "reasonable person," who represents reassuringly the only individual capable of "legitimate surprise" in the face of "legitimate accidents."[21] Classical rhetorical treatises had long codified such legitimacy.

As far as we know, Fremin was no lawyer and no rhetorician. But when acting in his own defense, he did not need to be; if anything, his thespian training would have helped. Even without specific knowledge of such a forensic manual as the widely circulated pseudo-Ciceronian *Rhetorica ad Herennium*, Fremin Severin deployed its wisdom quite skillfully while enacting the canonical techniques of stasis theory (Latin *constitutio*), especially the legal strategy called the Juridical Issue (*constitutio iuridicalis*). Of the two subtypes of the Juridical Issue, only one is relevant, the Assumptive Issue.[22] Fremin manages to touch all its legal bases—too many, in fact—by invoking each one of the four subtypes of the Assumptive Issue: "Acknowledgment of the Charge, Rejection of the Responsibility, Shifting of the Question of Guilt, Comparison with the Alternative Course" (*RAH,* 1.24). It is useful to address them here in reverse order.

First, while Comparison with the Alternative Course involves justifying that, when faced with a choice, the actant elected the better action, Fremin himself had urged, quite literally, an alternative course of action for the bystanders, among them, poor Perrin Le Roux. Second, with regard to Shifting the Guilt, Fremin acknowledges the act but defends himself "by diverting the issue of guilt from himself" to Perrin. For this subtype the Pseudo-Cicero cites the theatrical example of Orestes, driven to his crime "by the crimes of others" (*RAH,* 1.25). Granted, Fremin is not suggesting—at least not explicitly—that Perrin Le Roux's failure to exercise ordinary care of his person was criminal. Nevertheless, the idea of emphasizing the potentially criminal acts of others sets the stage for the subtype of Rejection of the Responsibility, "when we repudiate, not the act charged, but the responsibility, and either transfer it to another person or attribute it to some circumstance."[23] In that respect, Fremin's defense—"I was just following theatrical orders"?—was buttressed by none other than Perrin himself. Like Jehan Hemont before him, Perrin took responsibility for his actions and forgave his unwitting assailant on his deathbed: "the aforesaid deceased Perrin said that he [himself] was to blame for the aforesaid blow and not the aforesaid Fremin" (fol. 7v).

Furthermore, Rejection of the Responsibility was a legal principle staged time and time again in highly juridical moments of many a play's Garden of Eden, as when Adam faults Eve for the Fall, or in the celestial tribunals of the *procès de paradis,* which adjudicated theatrically the guilt of human-kind.[24] Similar accidents, negligence, and warnings (along lines spookily reminiscent of Fremin's) had long been treated in no less a venue than the *Digest of Justinian,* which indicated that "gross negligence is not interpreted as guilty intention. Accordingly, if . . . a pruner when throwing down a branch from a tree fails to shout a warning and kills a passer-by, punish-ment under this statute is not applicable."[25] That regulation does not pre-clude the possibility of punishment under another statute. But, as we shall see, it does mean that the Middle Ages elevated the relationship between acts, guilt, and interpretation to the art form known as the letter of remis-sion. As a written record of a legal performance about a past performance of (noncriminal) intention, the letter of remission acknowledges responsi-bility for acts that (accidentally) perpetrate evil, all the while formalizing a plea for mercy.

Thus, regarding the extant record of Fremin Severin's juridical (and, perhaps, prototheatrical) performance before two scribes, which detailed his intentions during a theatrical performance of 1384, the first subtype of the Assumptive Issue is of special importance: the Acknowledgment of the Charge (*concessio*), through which "we plead for pardon [*Concessio est per quam nobis ignosci postulamus*]" (*RAH,* 2.23). That defense includes the Ex-culpation and the Plea for Mercy, the former of which is identified as fol-lows: "The Exculpation is the defendant's denial that he acted with intent [*cum consulto*]" (*RAH,* 1.24) because "it is the intention which should al-ways be considered, and that unintentional acts ought not to be regarded as crimes" (*RAH,* 2.24).[26] Within the Exculpation, the Pseudo-Cicero contin-ues, there are "three subheads: Ignorance, Accident [*fortuna*], and Neces-sity" (*RAH,* 1.24).[27] Fremin offers such exculpatory evidence by invoking (mis)adventure (*aventure*) and insisting that his intent had been to provide special effects, not to kill.

More dispositive still is our recognition that the Plea for Mercy is every bit as theatrical and every bit as cathartic as the legal process itself, which purges communities of malefactors while offering solace to wronged citi-zens, all evidenced by the official Latin name for both catharsis and the Ex-culpation: *purgatio.*[28] As various medieval descendants of feudalism invoked the usual *topoi* of "humanity and pity" (*de humanitate, misericordia*), they also indicate today that among the most aesthetically undervalued aspects of the medieval letter of remission are its theatricalization and recontextualization (presumably in light of Christian forgiveness) of the classical forensic convention known as the Plea for Mercy—though with a twist that normally concedes the very premeditation that the Exculpation denies. "It is a Plea for Mercy when the defendant *confesses the crime and premeditation* [*consulto*], yet begs for compassion" (*RAH*, 1.24; my emphasis).[29] Fremin begged for mercy by insisting on the opposite of the technique elucidated in the *Ad Herennium:* his *lack of premeditation.* Thus, although the Pseudo-Cicero believed that throwing oneself upon the mercy of the court was "rarely practicable, except when we speak in defence of one whose good deeds are numerous and notable" (*RAH*, 1.24), it is precisely that which was once "rarely practicable" that medieval jurists transformed into the official letter of remission for men of good deeds—men like Fremin who were of "good reputation and character" (fol. 7v).

As we have already seen, to confess premeditation without calling upon "ignorance, chance, or necessity" was exceptionally hazardous territory in the Middle Ages; while such confessions were not unheard of (as in our next chapter), they were by no means the typical strategy of letters of remission. Letters such as those issued to Guillaume Langlois and Fremin Severin proclaimed the good intentions of men who, by dint of their good intentions, were *not* criminals . . . but also, who *would not* and *could not* have been criminals even if they *had* had evil intentions (the logic goes) on the one occasion memorialized by their letters. Even the indices of apparent malice would have paled by comparison to the weight of a man's usual virtue, especially if "in committing his mistakes he was moved not by hatred or cruelty, but by a sense of duty and right endeavour" (*RAH*, 2.25). Certainly Fremin had tried to do right; and he was forgiven by Charles VI, who offered him mercy and purported to resolve the affair to the satisfaction of all the parties.

Theater was safe again, and more than safe. The mere thought, the mere project of theater was also safe—even during rehearsal, a type of acting that, if anything, serves as both a declaration and a tangible, physical enactment of the intention to act again. To use, perhaps oddly, a term from the business world: a rehearsal is both an event in the present and an *option on future action,* a statement about, a promise of, even an experiment with the intentions to engage in performances to come.[30]

As paper ignites in the mouth of a cannon, intellectual sparks begin to fly from the friction with which the rehearsal meets that overdetermined genre of the letter of remission. If a theater rehearsal (as a tangible reality

in the present) constitutes an option on the future, then a medieval letter of remission takes out an option both on the past intentions of those
who are acting no longer and on the legal future. It memorializes post hoc
a phenomenon that exists only ad hoc: intention. Although the conservative Coomaraswamy was about as far removed from performance theory
as one might imagine, he was right about this: "We can, and have a right
to, criticise intentions; but we cannot criticise an actual performance *ante
factum*" ("Intention," 47; his emphasis). A rehearsal, however, lying somewhere between official and unofficial, incarnates one such way in which to
engage in that critique.

Fremin Severin's plea for mercy was a performance about a rehearsal, a
post hoc account of a phenomenon whose ontology is based on the ad hoc.
It is a retrospective evocative here of the allegedly "simpler" world of theatrical agency as described by Langer. "On the stage," she philosophized,
"we see acts in their entirety, as we do not see them in the real world *except
in retrospect*, that is, by constructive reflection. In the theatre they occur in
simplified and complete form, with visible motives, directions, and ends"
(*FF*, 310; my emphasis).[31] On one hand, she sounds like Aristotle, who wrote
in *Poetics* 1451a that a "representation of a piece of action [the plot] must
represent a single piece of action and the whole of it." On the other hand,
she also sounds like a Dershowitz *avant la lettre*, the latter arguing that,
since the events of daily life are "often simply meaningless, irrelevant to
what comes next . . . out of sequence, random, purely accidental, without
purpose," then the "business" of lawyers is to gain some control over that
chaos by offering a "plausible retrospective account, a story or a narrative
of what happened." In a view of temporality that, once again, sends us back
to that medieval future, Dershowitz endorses Sartre's position that, "when
you tell about life . . . you seem to start at the beginning. . . . But in reality
you have started at the end."[32]

Theater solicits retrospection the moment the proverbial curtain falls,
inviting numerous judgments about the acts of numerous intending selves.
But of equal and enduring relevance is its capacity for virtuality: theater is
pro-spective. In ways that are both aesthetically different and legally similar to the felony murder rule invoked earlier in the context of Knapp and
Michaels's loaded gun, theater is in the business of not just *after*sight but of
literal *fore*sight (of the kind, moreover, that leads to the fearful and fearsome imminence of our next chapter).[33] If the legal argument of the felony
murder rules basically runs that the allegedly unintended consequences of
a variety of crimes should have been *foreseen*, then what is a rehearsal if
not a literal act of foresight? Like Schlegel's "prophets looking backward,"

those who seek to understand actions and events also start at the end.[34] They await, as if reading one of those interminably long German sentences, the arrival of that peskily suspended verb that issues forth only at the end, bestowing significance upon all that precedes it. One need not be the gloomy Cassandra to notice that such is the essence of intention, which bestows meaning upon the actions that it inspires at the same time that any eventual assessments of its ad hoc existence take place post hoc.

While Langer is surely right to contend that theater is "form in suspense" (*FF*, 310), that art form is just as clearly *judgment in suspense*. Judgment that sometimes comes too late. Judgment about the nature and quality of acts, accidents, and art that cannot evade the intentions of those acting.[35] Judgment that points not just to "history in the making" but to lives themselves in the making—which lives are, not so curiously, decipherable only in retrospect and, as proponents of the law and literature movement have illustrated so cogently, decipherable by literary standards.[36] Differently from the murderer who intends to kill, observers decide only in retrospect whether something was *not* theater or *not* murder, even though it seemed so at the time . . . and even when everything that had prompted such questions in the first place occurred during rehearsal, an event that, among many other things, tests what is achievable and what is perceivable, whether in 1384 or 2008.

"Weird things happen in theatre," writes Wilshire, and "they are particularly arresting as they are discovered in rehearsal." The prevention of such "weirdness"—and, more often than not, the assurance of its opposite—is one of the primary reasons for *having* a rehearsal. But the fatal accident of 1384 was more than just "weird." With its mortal violence, it broached issues considerably larger than those of artistic control, the ultimate arbiter in Wilshire's definition of violent or pornographic art: "artists cannot achieve the level of control of the subject matter necessary for such art" (*RPI*, 251). Since the actor can never retain complete mastery over a moment of death, he continues in a more morbid vein, "he cannot artistically perform his own death" (*RPI*, 268).[37] Not only do a host of theatrical anecdotes proffer evidence to the contrary in the form of the ultimate on-stage performative that is the actor (like Edmund Kean or Montfleury) who dies on stage while invoking death.[38] If we read Wilshire's theory in connection with Goldstein's audience-centered approach to why we watch violence, the results are even more disturbing. Pondering the psychological definition of violence as "action *intended to harm*," he introduces *Why We Watch* by stating that "a boxing match would be regarded as a violent event while a simulated boxing match or a cartoon boxing match would not" (*WWW*, 2; my emphasis). To accept such a definition at face value would mean, absurdly, that an unintentionally committed violent act would not conform to the definition of violence. We would be obliged to conclude that, since no one had *intended to harm* Perrin Le Roux or Jehan Hemont, then the acts of bodily harm that resulted in their accidental deaths were not violent.

Moreover, by Wilshire's logic, when Kean and Montfleury allegedly expired on stage, their drama would have ceased to be art—or even art-in-progress. He leaves the door open, however, for the possibility that a play is still a play if someone *other than an actor* takes control of it: if, let us say, a stagehand, an actor off stage, or a bystander were to kill (accidentally or on purpose?) one of the actors on stage.[39] Untenably, then, if a Kean or a Montfleury dies while impersonating his character, losing artistic control, then the plays were not art; but if a Fremin Severin or a Guillaume Langlois kills them by accident with a special effect, then the plays *were* art. Furthermore, for Kirby, even Perrin Le Roux would have died during a bona fide theater piece because he (and his artistic collaborators) had the "intent to make theatre," which is "a performance intended to have an effect on an audience" (*FT*, xi, xiii). Still, even while retaining intentional (and primarily affective) effect upon an audience as a criterion of theater, Kirby acknowledges nonetheless that "the mere presence of an audience does not convert something done without intentionality into theatre" (*FT*, xi). In that respect, he seems to agree with Goffman (whom he never cites) that "it is not the mere act of performance that makes something theatre; all theatre is performance; but all performance is not theatre. . . . [T]hings may be theatrical—like theatre—without being theatre" (*FT*, xi).[40]

Whence a further modulation in Kirby's attempt to distinguish an audience-destined theater from other spectacular events during which audiences are *merely tolerated* (although *by whom* he does not say: apparently by the performer) (*FT*, xi–xi). "Eavesdropping and voyeurism are not theatre," he asserts, "because the perceived activity is not intended for an audience" (*FT*, x)—and we hear the popular version of that argument in the snide question asked by individuals who appreciate neither being watched (as unintentional performers) nor watching (as unintentional spectators): "What do you want to do? Sell tickets?" If, for Kirby, the mere existence of a spectatorial gaze cannot, in and of itself, transform such activities into theater unless they are intended as theater, then one might pose these questions to him:

Why is his intention-based definition of theater agentless at its most crucial moment? Just who is it that intends to make theater—and makes it? The director? The producer? The actors? Any and all of those who are working behind the scenes? May we use the term *theater* when referring to other activities orchestrated by agents who intend to affect their audiences with a performance, but not necessarily an aesthetic one? Or does he mean that any performance is by its nature theatrical? Would he concur with Joel Black, for instance, that there is an "aesthetics of murder"?[41] Would the staging of a high-stakes game of insurance fraud through rigged car wrecks be theater because those involved intended to have a financial effect (or affect) on Allstate and/or a life-threatening one on agent and victim alike?[42] What about unstaged roadway accidents that prompt rubbernecking? What about the type of car wreck imagined by J. G. Ballard and translated to the cinema by David Cronenberg in *Crash*? Happily, we now have a better understanding of such activities since they have found an intellectual home in the ever expanding discipline of performance studies, which welcomes Isidore of Seville's treatment of war and play (*Etymologiarum,* 2: book 18) alongside medieval tournaments, modern circuses, processions, sporting events, bridge matches, work sites, cocktail parties, parlor games, political rallies, funerals, classroom instruction, and even Reality TV.[43] But the multiplication of our objects of inquiry neither addresses nor resolves the moral and ethical issues of theater in general and of its rehearsals in particular.

Such issues arise even in Goffman's signature study of "work performance" and "rehearsal frames." When speaking of contests, for example, he maintains that sporting events *encourage* spectators but do not *require* them (although any baseball club owner desirous of making a profit would doubtless disagree).[44] People who attend weddings and funerals as "witnesses and as guests . . . usually come by invitation, not fee" (*FA,* 126). Likewise, a rocket launch would have a scientific mission, but during the spectacular launch itself, spectators would be "tolerated," not essential, to the event—although, again, part of NASA's funding has long depended on public interest. Perhaps most striking in Goffman's analysis, and most germane to rehearsals from 1384 to the present, is his summoning to service of two concepts that are positively medieval: *purity* and *impurity.* In an audience-based ontology that hosts again that element of chance or happenstance that we have been exploring, Goffman notes that

> Performances can be distinguished according to their *purity,* that is, according to the exclusiveness of the claim of the watchers on the activity they watch.
> Dramatic scriptings, nightclub acts, personal appearances of various sorts, the ballet, and much of orchestral music are *pure. No audience, no*

performance. The limiting cases here are *ad hoc performances,*[45] those that occur within a domestic circle when a party guest does a turn at the piano or guitar for the optional beguilement of other guests who *happen to be* close by. (*FA,* 125; my emphasis)

It is one of the projects of this book to show that one cannot speak of theater until such an "exclusive claim" made by an audience is the very claim invited by—*intended by*—those performing. Indeed, only from that vantage point do many of the semantic delimitations in current use for speaking of performance start to make sense, including Goffman's own finding that sporting events, bridge matches, construction sites, and cocktail parties are theatrical but not theater because "no *prior agenda* need be present to obligate the individual to perform" (*FA,* 125; my emphasis). What is a "prior agenda" if not an intention? Whose agenda is it, exactly? With whom does the obligation originate? And is it appropriate to speak of art at all if that agenda or obligation is imposed by someone else, as when Nero notoriously coerced performers into death-defying entertainments for a public doubtless just as "obligated" to attend the spectacle?[46]

Seen from Goffman's curious perspective of aesthetic purity, the rehearsal is a type of work product that unfolds before audiences who are more or less tolerated (by a theater collective) during an event that is both a real performance and the promise—the intent—of a future one. Thus, his "rehearsal frame," an entity that Perrin Le Roux's death would presumably have broken, circumscribes a variety of everyday opportunities to watch "process" or "work": "Most *impure* of all, I suppose, are work performances, those that occur, for example, at construction sites or rehearsals, where viewers openly watch persons at work who *openly show no regard or concern* for the dramatic elements of their labor." Notwithstanding the challenge of deciphering what an "open display" of the *absence* or *lack* of theatrical affect might look like, at stake here for Goffman is a patently legalistic assessment of intention: "distinctions among performances refer to the *official face of activity, not to its underlying character and intent*" (*FA,* 126; my emphasis). As for the "impurity" of the work performance, its "unofficial" quality lies in the "lack of regard or concern" of agents who, to put it squarely, have no intent to make theater. Even if they did, Goffman appears to be suggesting that they would see their own desires trumped by the overarching official face—that is, the official intent (as legislated by whom? their bosses?)—of the activity in question.

One might be tempted to say with Goffman that a rehearsal is not quite an official performance, but not quite an unofficial one, either. At Goffman's construction site, there is a productive interplay—not necessarily a theatrical one—between what the "performers" intend to do, what the "audience" intends to watch (whence, for Isidore, theater purportedly got its name), and what the now intentionless peephole at the construction site meant at the time of its construction—and continues to mean—for the intending subject who had once arranged for that construction.[47] That individual might well be drilling other peepholes, licit or illicit, so that more spectators can watch performances that were never intended as such by any of the agents engaged in their work. Their work performances are not theater because workers do not intend them as such; but, more interestingly, the popularity of such activities as spectacles of sorts might ultimately foster the belief, in voyeuristic individuals, that those individuals are indeed a legitimate audience of such spectacles. Consider the case of Reality TV, which regularly depicts the work product of real arrests in *Cops;* the real verdicts issued by Judge Judy; the allegedly true confessions made to Oprah, Ricki Lake, or Dr. Phil; or the real weight loss, dating, makeovers, surviving, and risktaking of countless other offerings. That apparent legitimation might even lead to people's later sense of entitlement to just what *should* fall under their gaze: "On-the-spot TV news coverage now offers up the world, including its battles, as work performances, this, incidentally, inclining the citizenry to accept the role of audience in connection with any and all events" (*FA,* 126). But just because, in a tradition once articulated by Lucretius, Marivaux, and the like,[48] we see ourselves as audiences, that does not mean that what we have witnessed is theater.

By the same token, just because a given individual has the intent to act, to represent, to perform, that does not necessarily mean that there will be a corresponding attempt to receive the performance. It all raises fascinating questions not only about theater audiences (to whom we turn in chapter 7) but about who has the "standing" to participate, at any given moment, in the making of theater: questions that shed new light on the theatrical contract that will occupy us throughout Part II.[49] For the time being, let it suffice to say this: Goffman never goes so far as to state what Kirby did years later when hanging his entire definition of theater on intentionality (an approach I am championing here in spirit if not in letter): "Theatre does not occur in nature. It is not accidental. It does not just happen" (*FT,* x). Nevertheless, the "impure" nature of Goffman's rehearsal is irremediably linked to the intention of the "workers" constructing not buildings over time but theater over time.[50]

Sensibly, Goffman questions his own observations almost immediately in a footnote in which he imagines this scenario: "Commercial recordings of orchestral rehearsals are now available, presumably to allow audiences an intimate glimpse of the conductor at work. One wonders how these strips differ from the real thing" (*FA*, 126n). Little of an "impure" nature comes to mind when one thinks of the common commercial practice of selling tickets to orchestra rehearsals, as is done every summer at the Aspen Music Festival, for instance, when music lovers who prefer to spend $20 instead of $66 (and rising) may substitute a dress rehearsal for a formal concert. Presumably, the impurity would lie in the possibility that if something were to go significantly wrong, the conductor would stop the whole rehearsal and have the orchestra do the botched section again (or *would* she?); while for $66 the show will certainly go on. But one may presume just as readily that the audience members, having paid a lesser fee to attend a rehearsal, realize that attention to error during work performances is possible. They might even like the idea, looking forward to the occasional phrase of bad music. At the same time, the expectations that producers, directors, crew, and actors have of themselves during these something-less-than-official performances might differ or change, given the expectations that they attribute rightly or wrongly to attendees (and which attendees attribute rightly or wrongly to themselves). Once the overarching project is to sell tickets "as if" to an "official performance," we are left with the anomaly that is the rehearsal: an officially unofficial performance. Or is it an unofficially official one?

What compels our attention in 1384, just as it will in our concluding Talk-Back (live television being a work performance of sorts), is the realization that not all theatrical work is quite so benign as the orchestra rehearsal, no matter how blustery the behavior of the maestro. Goffman understood that point in ways that now seem prescient, given the voyeurism associated with on-the-spot telejournalism as well as with hybrid television genres like *Cops*, and even with performances such as that of the suicidal man on the freeway in 1998. Moreover, the "terminological help" that he offers in the context of contests, the better to "relieve the burden carried by the word 'performance,'" is most welcome to anyone seeking to understand the nature and import of rehearsals such as the deadly one of 1384, especially within the ludic culture of the Middle Ages.[51] In lexical precisions that prove illuminating for the rehearsal, Goffman emphasizes the inextricable connection between intention and acting as he introduces a series of terms—*presented, dramatized, rigged,* and *re-presented:* "In order to be particularly clear about frame, one might say that a bridge game that is televised or otherwise placed before an audience is a *presented* match; as part of a scripted movie, a *dramatized* match; as something a cheater arranges, a *rigged* match. And presumably a play about cheating at bridge would provide viewers with a *dramatized rigged* match; and a news clip of a roller derby, a *re-presented rigged* match" (*FA*, 127; my emphasis). Since games do not televise themselves, scripts do not write themselves, films do not direct themselves, plays do not stage themselves, and news reports do not air themselves, it is productive to render explicitly what Goffman does not—except for the intentional orchestrations of the "cheater," which raise anew the specter of law and ethics, where intention always matters. Substituting "rehearsal" for Goffman's "match," we might say this:

A rehearsal that is deliberately disseminated to an audience is a *presented rehearsal;* as part of a theatrical script, a *dramatized rehearsal* (like the famous play within a play in *Hamlet*); as something a murderous props master[52] arranges, a *rigged rehearsal.* And presumably a play about a murderous props master would provide viewers with a *dramatized rigged* rehearsal; and a news clip of a rehearsal (or a medieval report of one declaimed during a letter of remission?), a *re-presented rigged rehearsal.* As far as we know, no "cheaters" were present to arrange for the murder of Perrin Le Roux in a spectacle that merely *looked like* an accident but was actually something else. But none of that alters the bottom line: all the presentations, disseminations, and redisseminations, all the cheating and honesty in the world involve the numerous intentionalities that lend meaning to acts, as committed by agents and understood or misunderstood by their viewers. For many, that is the very essence of theater, a medium devoted to acts that have meaning and whose rehearsals have meanings of their own. Although we shall see that any given individual can be *misperceived* as representing, pretending, or engaging in theater, that individual cannot represent, pretend, impersonate, simulate,[53] or *rehearse* by accident.

Returning, then, to the promised refinement of our initial taxonomy, we are now in a better position to affirm that our first two cases do not really apply to theater at all: that is, Case 1 (acts *committed accidentally* and *viewed deliberately*) and Case 2 (acts *committed accidentally* and *viewed accidentally*) are not acts of representation. Regarding the latter in particular, while it is perfectly plausible that one or more spectators might stumble accidentally upon a play-in-progress or a rehearsal[54]—not as unluckily, we hope, as poor Perrin Le Roux, who seemed barely aware that there *was* a play—that play exists perfectly well (or unwell) without them. It may be *viewed* accidentally, but it is not *performed* accidentally. That does not mean, however, that theater ceases to be theater when accidents occur. More often than not, the medieval and modern show goes on[55] since the collective's primary intent is still to make theater, to represent, to put on an "official" spectacle or an "unofficial" rehearsal. Indeed, our recognition of that overarching intent[56] enables us to account for deliberate acts committed during theater that are *not* representational, *no longer* representational, or *never intended* (by a member of the collective with the standing to so intend) *to be* representational. Furthermore, that holds true for Case 3 as well, which we may now understand, theatrically speaking, as acts of representation *committed deliberately* and *viewed accidentally*. In the troupe rehearsing the *Miracle of Théophile,* the players in question did not intend to kill onlookers or bystanders (unless someone among them had actually crafted, with extreme malice aforethought, a complex murder plot to rub out Perrin Le Roux using theater as cover).[57] Instead, this was a case of the players' theatrical intentions gone awry, allegedly—whence the investigation—through no fault of their own.

The present point, oddly obscured by the openness of performance studies, is relatively simple even if rarely made: just because something occurs *during* a representation does not mean that it *is* a representation; just because something is *performative* does not mean that it is a *theatrical performance;* and just because something *is* a *theatrical performance* does not mean that it is *an Austinian performative.* None of the inflammatory events above were performatives in the Austinian sense in that they were not intended as such. As conservative as it may sound, what I am suggesting is this:

Without wishing to imply that countless thrilling avant-garde performances are *not* theater, I contend nonetheless that the investigation of rehearsals demonstrates with unusual clarity that we are in the presence of theater when someone with the "standing" to represent follows through on his or her intention to make theater. With additional precisions of the juridical nature of that standing to come later, I further contend that there is indeed such a thing as *theatrical standing,* regardless of how frequently it is transferred, willingly or unwillingly, from performers to spectators—and regardless of the latter's sense of entitlement to that standing. It all returns us to Case 4, acts of representation *committed deliberately* and *viewed deliberately:* the case that most faithfully and appropriately describes the implicit contract that is the experience of theater.

Isidore's etymology notwithstanding, theater is not just any kind of action or any kind of witnessing: it is the witnessing of representation. Before we can attain any real understanding of the cognitive, rhetorical, affective, or physical results of such witnessing (including whether audiences are invited or uninvited, aware or unaware, right or wrong about what others are doing—as well as about what those audiences themselves are doing and should do), we need to address first what it means to intend to represent. Theatrical representation is decipherable on the basis of the intention(s) of

a variety of agents to do, to act, to perform, and sometimes—not always—
to be seen by others who have intentions of their own.[58] Therefore, when
dealing with acts of representation that are disseminated deliberately and
viewed deliberately, let us consider, at least provisionally, that theater is this
(or, to sound less conservative, *classic theater* is this):

> The deliberate creation—by one or more parties and of their own free
> will—of effects and behaviors that simulate reality (whether violent
> or nonviolent), but which effects are *not* the realities that their cre-
> ators strive to make them appear to be to others (or to virtual others),
> regardless of the postmodernist propensity toward the Baudrillard-
> ian hyperreal or the Borgesian blurring of maps and territories (*SW*,
> 166–67), and regardless of the panoply of techniques of realism that
> go into "building a character," such as taking a sip of that colored
> water, smoking a real cigarette, going off choreography accidentally
> or on purpose to inflict real injury, and so on.[59] Walking is still walk-
> ing, just as breathing is still breathing. But even those acts, shared by
> actor and character, breathe new life into the fictional universe that a
> collective intends to create.

While I reserve for chapter 5 the discussion of the bona fide theatrical
contract, this provisional definition has several immediate advantages: It
offers an artistic way of responding to the numerous issues of liability that
arise when theater becomes the site of accidents that hurt actors, spectators,
or, as was the case for Perrin Le Roux, nonspectators. It demands that we
take into account modes of coercion, especially in the huge financial un-
dertaking that was a Passion play, which include such economic coercion as
the obligatory participation in 1513 of the clergyman of Metz in the processional spectacles of pardon parades "under penalty of forfeiting one silver
mark."[60] By the same token, from the standpoint of the audience, spectators also attend the theater voluntarily. Under ordinary circumstances, they
have not been forced to do so—although one might think here of children
constrained to submit to their parents' desire to inculcate a love of the arts.[61]
Rather, of their own free will, they expect to see—and, more often than not,
do see—what Aristotle termed, in his foundational definition of tragedy,
"imitations of actions":[62] those are the province of the actor who performs
them, not the spectator (who must nonetheless recognize their objects).

Finally, the provisional definition embraces ethics as a formal feature
of the theater and excludes, at least from purely artistic consideration, instances in which human beings are placed on stage to "represent" (para-

doxically) against their will—or even to do so consensually, as when the RATT actress allegedly ceded her ability to consent (which was no longer extant once she was beaten unconscious [*SRT,* 21]). Likewise, it excludes the coercive spectacles of both the Roman amphitheater and the contemporary terroristic attack,[63] both medieval "snuff drama" and modern snuff films, along with what I can only think to call the "snuff journalism" that has culminated in the airing of executions as different in substance as those of Daniel Pearl and Saddam Hussein. All such events trouble the standard representation scenarios of theater insofar as the actants (who are making a spectacle of themselves and of others) intend to—and do—provide real violence of so extreme a nature that it preempts the primary representational goal of a communicative medium that they may even consider to *be* theater, raising exceptionally vexed questions as to whether one can speak of theater at all in such contexts. I say that one cannot.

Whatever our take on those things, there are two very unfashionable consequences of any analysis of legally actionable acts that occur on and off the stage: *we must judge them,* which means evaluating the intentions of those who committed them. Two medieval kings did as much in 1380 and 1384, but their forgiveness did not extend to civil liability. So unless we are game to issue a blanket statement that nothing that happens on stage is illegal because it is protected by the intent to represent, then we are forced to include that "unhealthily juridical" consideration (*LT,* 119) in our definition of theater. Once we refocus our attention on where intentionality actually belongs—with agents—new perspectives are possible on the ontological, phenomenological, ethical, and moral dimensions of theatrical action.

3 Fear of Imminence and Virtual Ethics:
Staging Rape in the Middle Ages

> A murderer is regarded by the conventional world as something
> almost monstrous, but a murderer to himself is only an ordinary
> man. It is only if the murderer is a good man that he can be
> regarded as monstrous.
> GRAHAM GREENE

The Devil made him do it. Or was it theater? If we believe
several chroniclers of Metz, there survived in 1485 a living testimonial to
the dangers of theater so monstrous that it was the stuff of legend. Although
the great Petit de Julleville elected to shroud the events in silence, what survived was the living, dying offspring of what we could call today a marital
rape (and what I shall call a rape in this chapter).[1]

As is the case with so much of the extant evidence of the medieval stage,
we know that a play—probably a Passion play—was performed that year
in the French city of Bar-le-Duc, and we know that for one reason only:
something terrible happened. One fine day, an unnamed actor returned
home after his performance and, still clad in his devil suit, he proceeded
to force himself sexually upon his unnamed wife, who tried repeatedly
to resist him. While medieval law had no category for "marital rape" as
we currently understand that felony, the point is that, by committing an
act that was, at a medieval minimum, unchristian and unchaste, this actor made a transition so seamless that it has haunted theater history for
centuries.[2] Moving effortlessly from make-believe to making, he stopped
impersonating a devil (*contrefaire le dyable*) and *became* a devil in real life
(*faire le dyable*). In other words, he stopped representing altogether; he simply was.[3] And what he was, according to the voracious chronicler, Philippe
de Vigneulles, was an intending subject vowing to break an earlier vow in
a kind of "preperformative" declaration.[4] He was as good—and as bad—as
his word: "It next came to pass that, at this same time, there was performed
in Bar-le-Duc a play in which there were several men playing the parts of
devils. Among them, there was one who, in that get-up, wished to enjoy
consortium with his wife. And she was putting him off and asking him what
he was trying to do; and he responded: 'I wish,' said he, 'to make the beast

with two backs [*faire le dyable*].' And, hard as she tried to resist, she was forced to obey him."[5] The fear is familiar, as is the troubling violence from medieval domestic life: a theatrical self *cannot* be slipped on and off like a costume; the general aesthetic rendering of evil on stage propagates specific misconduct off stage. Before we turn to what is unfamiliar, however, about the fascinating conclusion of this story, we should recall that it dramatizes some very old questions.

Do such theatrical portrayals implant evil there where there is no evil to begin with? Or, as popular wisdom about hypnosis would have it, do they only reveal, enable, hasten, or execute something that is always already there? Should we side with Massumi, who contends that the "problem with acting isn't that it carries the actor out of himself, out of his character into another, out of his real self into a false double; it is that it doesn't take the actor *far enough* outside of himself"?[6] And if any of those things are true, then what did theater bring out—or risk bringing out—in the good souls who sallied forth to make Passion plays and who announced repeatedly their desire to edify their Christian communities?[7] What do character, intent, and the character of intent tell us about what it means both to make theater and to be made by it? At what point does an actor cease both *intending to represent* and *representing*?[8] The allegedly terrifying ebb and flow of intent between official and unofficial sites of performance (including the performance of the reciprocal obligations of daily life) is the subject of the apocryphal events of Bar-le-Duc and of this chapter.

Regardless of whether the diabolical traits of the actor from Bar-le-Duc were manifest, dormant, or latent, he does not stop his performance once at home because it is no longer a performance—that is, if playing evil had ever been a performance for him at all. Bar-le-Duc posits a direct causal connection between a medieval play and a rape; so, whatever contemporary vocabulary we choose to invoke—triggers, catalysts, prompters,[9] and so on—the assault of a medieval wife demonstrates the relevance of medieval theatricality to modern and even postmodern conceptions of ethics as a body of knowledge. By reading together the make-believe tale from Bar-le-Duc with both the *Miracle of the Child Given to the Devil* and the all-too-real gang-rape of another unnamed medieval woman on the eve of a Passion play in 1395, I make here the following argument:

From the standpoint of literature, law, education, folklore, and "folk law,"[10] these examples dramatize intentionality by bringing together what should never have been separated: *ethics as a body of knowledge* and *theater's knowledge of bodies.* In that sense, they illuminate even today the shared subject of ethics and theater, one that theater enacts better than any other literary medium as it sheds new artistic light on the well-known legal triad of motive, means, and opportunity: the interplay between thought and action. Although theater offers up a world of virtual ethics, its human subjects-in-action are engaged in representational behaviors that are nonetheless real behaviors that necessarily broach questions of real ethics, *theatrical ethics.* Drawing on philosophical approaches to moral luck as well as on a new misnomer—the "accidental contract"—I further submit that theatrical performance is inseparable from ethics.[11]

Most of the time, theater survives and thrives very well under those circumstances, so long as no severe legal, ethical, or moral violations occur, at which point we shall finally be able to say when theater ceases to be theater. In that respect, the posttheatrical story of Bar-le-Duc illustrates a massive cultural anxiety about the cooptation of intent. One might best call it the *fear of imminence,* and it shall denote here the fear that theater can do to a community precisely what it allegedly did in 1485 to individuals. In a theatrical twist on the religious notion that life is but a dress-rehearsal for heaven, the fear of imminence bedevils us with the possibility—nay, the *probability*—that when actors represent on stage the passage from criminal intention to criminal action, they are but rehearsing the real thing in the ongoing performance that is social life. It is the fear once described by Plato that theatrical mimesis cultivates, especially through "the emotions of sex and anger . . . all the appetites and pains and pleasures of the soul . . . when what we ought to do is to dry them up."[12] It is the fear expressed by a host of fifteenth-century thinkers that theater might lead to a "cessation of the divine office, a cooling off in charity and alms, infinite adultery and fornication, scandals, derisions, and mockery."[13] And it is the fear that taunts us—and haunts us—with the hunch that theorists like Wilshire are wrong to say that theater's broken hearts "cease to be when the curtain falls and the mind turns from their contemplation" (*RPI,* 262). The tale from Bar-le-Duc warns that, sometimes, realities endure long after the curtain has fallen and that ethics prevents us from turning away from the contemplation of the real traces of the real bodies left behind.[14]

So it is that the fear of imminence conjoins historically—but also disjoins—these two parties: the medieval Devil in theater's flesh and Sartre's actor. The actor, observes Sartre, "is the reverse of the player, who becomes a person like anyone else when he has finished work, whereas the actor 'plays himself' every second of his life. It is both a marvelous gift and a curse; *he is his own victim,* never knowing who he really is or whether he is acting or not."[15] In Bar-le-Duc, someone else was the victim: someone to whom it likely did not matter whether *he* was acting because *she was not.* In

1485, there was no player; there was only an actor "cursed" with the instability not just of theater but of his own intentions.

Instructive in that respect is Langer's comment about the not-necessarily-fearful imminence of theater: "Dramatic action is a semblance of action so constructed that a whole, indivisible piece of virtual history is implicit in it, as a yet unrealized form, long before the presentation is completed. This *constant illusion of an imminent future,* this vivid appearance of a growing situation before anything startling has occurred, is *'form in suspense.'* It is a human destiny that unfolds before us" (*FF,* 310; my emphasis). Although today's performance theorists and theater historians would likely substitute "virtuality" for Langer's "imminence," they would surely agree that theater speaks eternally to the potentiality of actions. Nor is there any reason to limit "form in suspense" to the stage, although Langer gives some very good reasons why we could: "Since stage action is not, like genuine action, embedded in a welter of irrelevant doings and divided interests . . . it is possible there to see a person's feelings grow into passions, and those passions issue in words and deeds" (*FF,* 310; my emphasis).[16] The translation of a passion into a deed is as good a definition as one might formulate of the imminence of artistic intention, both on stage and off; when actors take up roles, they translate artistic intention into bodily art and bodily action.

In the world of theater, where virtual becomes actual in every performance, where form is always in suspense (*FF,* 310), what else is in suspense? And what else (besides spectators' disbelief) is suspended? Ethics can only be suspended so far, and never, I submit, so far as to erase the fearsome link between theatrical imminence and the legal concept (when appropriate) of "imminent threat." Furthermore, once imminence is politicized, as it is so often these days, it engages and enrages liberals and conservatives alike, as when the fear of what *might* happen gives birth not just to imaginary medieval devils in a *pro-spective* theater but to real legislative interventions that are preventive, designed by their creators to stop the feared result *before it occurs.*[17] Consider the myriad ways in which those who fear imminent danger (real and imaginary) act on their fears: the censorship of pornography to forestall violence against women, the eavesdropping authorized by the Patriot Act, the torture of suspicious individuals to thwart future terrorism, the use of agentless but morality-friendly devices like the V-Chip and the nanny-cam?[18] What, then, are we to make of the imminence of theater itself?

Ultimately, the legend of Bar-le-Duc hints that even the existentially inclined Sartre did not go quite far enough when he philosophized that, in theater, "participation is the experience of an almost carnal relationship with an image, not merely a knowledge of it."[19] In 1485, theater was a carnal relationship not with an image but with a body—even with one of Scarry's bodies in pain. As it packs a moralistic punch that modern monitory tales can barely rival, Bar-le-Duc bequeaths so-called documentary evidence about the hideous imminence of theater, as exemplified by an actor who not only impersonates (*contrefaire*) the Devil and becomes one (*faire le dyable*): he sires one in his own image (*faire un diable*). Extending theatrically, as legal Exhibit A, a body of evidence that is a monstrous body, the devil of Bar-le-Duc threatens—in the most literal sense possible—that *intentions can be embodied;* and that theater provides both a venue and a model for how that takes place. "It then came to pass that she was pregnant and brought the child to term. But it came to pass that she gave birth and *was delivered of a body* which was, from the mid-torso down, the form of a [hu]man, and, from the mid-torso up, the form of a devil. People were much astonished by this thing. And no one dared baptize the child until a trip had been made to Rome in order to determine what was to be done with it" (*CPV*, 3:114-15; Appendix, Document 3.1; my emphasis).[20] With the exception of birth itself, nothing embodies, nothing incarnates like theater.[21]

Oddly enough, the Devil has not marked the infant at the carnal domain that was his purview (the *lower torso* at the genitalia). Quite to the contrary, Philippe states squarely that "from the mid-torso down," the child had a human form (*forme d'homme*).[22] The freakish creature is a chip off the old block in that what is monstrous about the baby is the *upper torso,* including brain, heart, and intellect: the child has no "better half," it is incapable of conscience, incapable of forming good intentions.[23] So, although this particular monster probably never existed—(if papal intervention there was, no record survives)—it had antecedents from medical literature and lore.[24] Unlike much medical lore, however, which located the blame for deformed children within the wombs of women, Philippe's narrative keeps diabolical parentage where it belongs: not with the hapless expectant mother who had perhaps looked at a picture of a devil during her pregnancy, but with the seed of man and, in this case, of man on stage.[25]

A medieval man is what he does, and to make sense of what he does, we must have recourse to intention, as decisive to theater as to law, but in a seemingly perpetual state of flux, subject to criminal, even diabolical, catalysts on and off the stage. Theater demonstrates the instability of intention at the heart of agency (*NS,* 234) as Bar-le-Duc admonishes that, whatever the intentions that precede theater, that art form may give rise to new evil intentions, which in turn give rise to bad acts and give birth to monstrosity. One need not have waited for the legal analysis of Berns that "intention in the common law is a wondrous beast, at once illusory and monstrous."[26] If there really is some sort of monstrous devil in the flesh, that monster is intention.

In 1485, an actor allegedly made the move from ersatz or virtual devil to actual sexual aggressor because, while he was acting, something happened at the most impenetrable levels of character and consciousness, the very entities that theater exists to externalize. It was something that preempted civilized, lawful, or moral behavior. Something that facilitated a trans-formation, *in* theater but, as we shall see, not necessarily *by* theater, and which moved a man from noncriminal represented action to real unethical (if not necessarily or not yet criminal) action. Something that tells us that what Stanislavski calls "building a character" on stage also builds criminal character off stage. Bar-le-Duc thus urges us to investigate what is always unseen: intention, even as what *is* seen in an extant text already proves challenging enough to access.[27]

With no specific information about which play was performed in 1485, we have no way of evaluating the alleged causal connection between the-ater and today's rape because we do not know whether the play in question even represented a rape. Given that "there were several men playing the parts of devils," it sounds as though it was a Passion play; so it probably did not portray rape.[28] But part of the problem is that even if the unnamed play *had* staged a rape, there is an extreme paucity of *didascalia* or audience testimonies to indicate precisely how acts of sexual violence were brought to life on the medieval stage, if at all. Indeed, dramatized rapes tend to un-fold over the brief time span of some dozen verses and sometimes, as in the fifteenth-century *Rape of Dinah,* within a single octosyllabic verse. To Dinah's pleas for mercy, for instance, her assailant, Sichem, responds that "It's all for naught!" and by the end of the verse, the deed is done: "Now sated is / my sensual affection."[29] More legally relevant to Bar-le-Duc is this question: How did anybody even know that the actor came home in costume and assaulted his wife? Were there witnesses? Did the husband boast about his exploit in town the next day?[30] Did his wife file a complaint against her husband? Did the husband receive some sort of pardon based on his alleg-edly good intentions, detailed in some lost letter of remission? Did the baby die en route to see the pope?

Most germane to our inquiry into the fear of imminence and virtual eth-ics is this: Philippe's language leaves open the prospect that theatrically in-spired crime happened—or could have happened—any number of times. It sounds as though it happened only once after a single performance of a single play. But Passion plays normally took several days to perform and they mobilized communities for weeks on end. What happened on Day Two? Or Day Three? Was theater's potentially reckless endangerment of character apparent at every rehearsal, too? What kind of time needs to elapse between theatrical performance and bad act to make the criminal connection to a liable theater? What if the rape had been perpetrated one day later? Two days later? What are we to make of the fact that, if theater truly *were* the incubator for danger, there had been *several men* playing devils? Even in a folkloric culture of Passion-play devils appearing in hordes during *diableries* (both on and off stage with varying degrees of criminality),[31] it seems that, in 1485, none of *those* men raped *their* wives, or anyone at all. Nor, as far as we know, did theatrical events perversely inspire any audience members to violate ethics (at least, in non-Sadian universes that *have* ethics) to the point of committing copycat crimes.[32] If theatrical imminence is perilous to and for some, is it not perilous to and for all?

Furthermore, if Bar-le-Duc sounds the alarm, lest theater bring out the devil in a man, then what about staged events that *fail to coincide* with real ones? What if playing at evil were to spawn good, and vice versa?[33] Since, again, we tend to hear about a medieval performance only when something goes wrong, it seems just as plausible that *another* devil left the stage in 1485 more moved by the Crucifixion than by his own diabolical role. Perhaps he decided to give alms to the poor, an outcome consistent with what municipalities hoped that the religious theater would do. Perhaps yet another devil resolved to stop beating his wife—and did. We simply know nothing about it. Nor is there any evidence (yet) that any Cains ever went home in costume and killed their brothers, biological or Christian. Nor that the medieval *jongleurs* and authors who wrote, spoke, or sang of rape went on to commit rape themselves (although that very possibility has been the subject of much speculation in Chaucer studies).[34] Nor, from the standpoint of the audience, has anyone to my knowledge suggested that a story like the thirteenth-century *Romance of Silence* taught women how to stage, to the detriment of honorable men, the false appearances of rapes that never occurred.[35] Indeed, as tempting as it has been to consider, *à la* Derrida and Foucault, a general violence of epistemology, no scholar has yet substantiated Marjorie Curry Woods's speculation that young medieval scholars would have been prone to violence against women from having cut their teeth on such great Senecan display pieces as "The Man Who Raped Two Girls" on a single night.[36]

All that by way of saying that we know surprisingly little, from reliable sources, about the exact behaviors, good or bad, that theater inspired, instigated, facilitated, coerced, and so on within individual actors and audience members, or in what time frame. True, one finds other apocryphal stories, such as the unnamed actor playing Despair in a Passion play, whose speeches exhorting Judas to suicide were apparently so persuasive that he eventually committed suicide himself.[37] And, in 1503, the seamster and actor Jehan Mangin "had violently and forcefully raped and deflowered" a young girl; but his thespian skills enabled him to disguise himself as a washerwoman and "in that get-up, pretending to go off to the river to do the washing, he crossed over the city gate at the bridge" and escaped the jurisdiction of Metz.[38] But there is no reason to rule out the possibility of "good ostension" related to the medieval theater.[39] If costume does not make the man but, rather, the man makes the costume, then the imminence of theater must also lie in a not-so-fearful potential to spawn the commission of acts of virtue.

Maybe it is not theater, then, that is dangerous but something else: something that theater hosts but which it is not. Something about character, embodiment, and the intentions that precede action. In the *Morality Play of the Uncle Who Killed his Nephew,* a rapist announces, "Thus, I have enacted my will [*Or ay-je acomply ma pence*]."[40] That is the business, both metaphorical and practical, of theater: to accomplish thought. It is also the fearful business of Bar-le-Duc, a tale that concretizes, corporealizes, and enacts the passage from intention to action. As proof that theater can alter the character of bodies at play at the level of intention, Bar-le-Duc cautions that, as there are no accidents in theater, there are also no accidents in life, a message that handily dispenses with the paradox of acting as stunningly captured by Stanislavski: "What did I just do? I analyzed what I accidentally felt and what I accidentally did as result of those feelings."[41]

Most of the time, what is created by human agents in theater is no accident. On one hand, though, the fear-mongering associated with theater casts *as one* theater's panoply of intending subjects; on the other hand, more "sympathetic" assessments foster the misleading notion that if we ignore causality altogether, we can toss aside evidence of individual evil in otherwise noble art forms simply by calling them accidents. I submit instead that, if there is truly an imminence to be feared in theater and its history, it is any morally and ethically bankrupt foreclosure of intent. Although the tale from Bar-le-Duc paints a troubling picture of actorly openness to theatrical possession (which sounds more like witchcraft or succubi), unless we plan to treat theater as a type of mental illness during which actors who lose themselves on stage are no longer responsible for their own actions,[42] unless we mean to exempt actors from the capacity to form any other intent except representation, then we will have nothing but paradoxes to consider. Those would be theater by accident, murder by accident, and a final terrifying entity that we have yet to consider but which the Middle Ages did: the *accidental* or *unintentional contract,* which would be impossible in speech-act theory because it would imply the equally oxymoronic promise by accident.

The notion that it is not theater which is prone to evil but individual character(s) is confirmed by the outcome of one of the most beloved theatrical offerings of medieval France. In the fourteenth-century *Miracle of the Child Given to the Devil,* the Virgin Mary rescues from Hell a young man whose mother had wished him there after suffering another marital rape.[43] The chronicler Jacomin Husson even pauses in the midst of his history of the city of Metz to tell the whole story, as he saw it staged on 10 October 1512. Minus the theatrical prologue to the husband's violent action, the subject of this particular miracle play is remarkably similar to that of Bar-le-Duc, its epilogue captured by an actual theater piece. In another tale of domestic sexual abuse, another unnamed husband forces his unnamed wife to submit to him sexually, even though they have previously sworn to a life of chastity. With a marked juridical vocabulary, Husson relates that the wife blames the Devil for the rupture of their mutual promise to one another and pledges any fruit of the coerced union to him: "After they had been married for a while, they entered together into an agreement [*aiccord*] to live chastely for the duration of their marriage. And so it came to pass that the husband wished to have consortium with his wife, who resisted with all her strength on account of the vow that they had taken [*pour le voeu qu'ils avoient faict*]. Nevertheless, it had to be. The angry wife said that the devil had played his part in this [*le diable y heust part*], and that if she were to conceive a child, that it would be the Devil's and that she was giving it to him. And this was ill-advised, for at that very hour, she conceived a son: whence she cursed the evil hour more than one hundred thousand times" (*CMJH,* 268–69; Appendix, Document 3.2). Having thus invoked the Devil's name, she also invokes one of the primary subjects of both the play and its afterlife. Careless contracts result in careless living and, one might say, in accidents that are not accidents because they illustrate a lack of resolve on the part of those who have sworn to a certain kind of moral rectitude in life.

To make a long story short, when her son turns fifteen, both he and his mother are poised to pay a penalty that is all the more steep in that this child is no monster: he is a beautiful, pious lad who is steadfastly devoted to the Virgin Mary. Enter, *dea ex machina,* the Virgin Mary, who retrieves the boy from Satan's clutches and nullifies what the wife had probably never meant to be a contract as she was fighting off her husband and attempting to honor the contract that she herself had made in good faith—but which her husband (thoughtlessly? lustfully?) sought to, meant to, vowed to, intended to, and did break. In the *Miracle of the Child Given to the Devil,* it does not seem to matter that, but for the fruition of her husband's sinister intentions, she would never even have entered, in the heat of her justifiable rage, into such a diabolical contract in the first place. Her careless speech is punished more severely than his evil actions as the tale, buttressed by popular folkloric motifs, warns that any hasty summons issued to the Devil might bind the speaker to that "unintentional contract."

Legally speaking, the *Miracle of the Child Given to the Devil* raises the same issues of Bar-le-Duc as to how, in a world where all were contractually bound to God, intending medieval subjects entered into their own contracts. After all, this was no *Miracle of Théophile,* in which an all too worldly priest had conjured the Devil through magic words and contracted officially with the Prince of Darkness for a larger prebend in exchange for a life of service to the horned creature—all memorialized in an official written document with the proper seals.[44] Nor was this the equally popular cardplayer at the gambling table who swears hastily "to God and his saints" that he will renounce card-playing forever or "the Devil should twist his neck." Philippe de Vigneulles claims that, in 1512, the Devil obliged post haste, producing an entity not unlike the monstrous baby of Bar-le-Duc, another diabolically fashioned half-a-body: "And upon saying those words, he lost half of himself" at the same time that he lost forever his power of speech and, thus, the ability to make any more careless invocations or to carry through to completion—to perform—any further acts, legal, theatrical, or other.[45] In a fascinating literal use of the adverb *perfectly—parfaictement* denotes both perfection and legal completion (*parfaire*)—the protagonist (who is called Blanctrain) also loses his power of legal speech: "And he could never again speak perfectly again."[46] Furthermore, in an unusual pun on his name, we find one more intriguing legal message about just what it means to put both halves back together again.

"Blanctrain" the cardplayer is a wretched soul who had "no other job except carting straw for sale throughout the city, whence people used to call him Blan Trains."[47] The verb *trainer* means "to carry a burden"; while *train* could refer to a beast of burden, a lifestyle, a prosecution, or a mistreatment. But, legally, *blancs* also referred to the "blank spaces" of today's "boilerplate" contract, which he unwittingly ratified (oxymoronically, of course) with the Devil. Blanctrain's lesson is that, in a terrestrial existence that is but a virtual rehearsal for heaven, our lives are boilerplates, and we must fill in the *blancs* as virtuously as we can. But there are no half-sizes when it comes to intention.

So it was that folklore warned repeatedly of a supremely fearsome imminence. Contracts, like lust, were virtually "incitable" at any time but especially in theater, one of the Devil's favorite playgrounds. Intending subjects needed ever to have a care, lest they fill in the blanks of the contracts of their lives unintentionally. As we also learn from one of the most bizarre extant cases from medieval legal history, even evil intention was not in and of itself sufficient to fill in those blanks. But that does not mean that historians should not try to fill in the notoriously blank spaces of rape.

Bar-le-Duc was not the first time that rape and theater had come together in the Middle Ages, nor would it be the last. On 13 August 1395, a corrupt local law officer (*prevost fermier*) by the name of Jehan Martin received a letter of remission from King Charles VI for his participation in a gang-rape of 1 May of that year. That document later attracted the attention of the archivist Antoine Thomas, who noticed that the malefactors had spent the night on the scaffolding that had been erected for the next day's Passion play, all of which inspired Gustave Cohen to publish the document as if its subject were theater only (*EHTF*, 170).[48] Jehan Martin acknowledged having played a major role in plotting (with his friend Jehanin le Cave) the gang-rape of the former concubine Mrs. Coton, which was committed in Chelles (near Paris) by a conspiracy of at least three men. In a document that brings together rape, criminal intent, voyeurism, and theatrical space, Martin further acknowledged multiple times his criminal intentions in that conspiracy, which had begun over drinks at an inn when Jehanin le Cave had leaned over to "whisper in the ear of the aforesaid supplicant [Jehan Martin] that, if he wanted, he could set it up so that this said woman would go outside of this said inn, so that the two of them could know her carnally."[49]

Conspiracy (*coniuratio*) was a serious crime in the Middle Ages, as evidenced by the wisdom of the *Digest of Justinian* which cites both "things counseled" and "guilty knowledge" as a basis upon which "the scale of the crime is the same for those who aid others by advice."[50] Reminiscent of today's felony murder rule, the outcome-oriented directive of the statute was to punish the murder-minded possessor of weapons "no less than him who kills" (*DJ*, 48.16.8).[51] But this medieval version of *mens rea* in the presence of a vicious will takes a troubling turn in 1395.[52] Martin put forward successfully a most unusual defense that enabled him to obtain a lighter sentence—namely, the reclassification of a criminal matter into a civil one.[53] His letter of remission reveals a malevolent but instructive counterpoint to the events of Bar-le-Duc in that Jehan Martin swore that, on the eve of a Passion play, he had not actually raped the woman in question but had *only intended to.* Unlike Baudrillard's simulator who fulfilled all the conditions for theft *except intention,*[54] Martin testified that he had possessed *criminal intention alone:* "And the aforesaid supplicant [Jehan Martin], *with the intention of having relations with the aforesaid woman* . . . followed [the others] out to the fields outside this said city . . . in order to see if he could find this said woman so that he might do his business with her as the others. . . . They spent that night fully clothed on the scaffolding that had been made for this aforesaid holiday, *without having relations with this woman*" (fols. 74v–75r; my emphasis). In a story with as many holes as the tale of Blanctrain and Bar-le-Duc had blank spaces, at least that is how the scribes recorded what he said.[55]

Martin rationalized (or someone else did on his behalf) that in spite of his patently criminal intentions, he deserved a lesser punishment because he had not carried out those intentions to their plotted consequence. Counterintuitively, he asked forgiveness because he had "only intended to rape" but did not rape; he had committed "only" a virtual rape, not an actual one. In a devious inversion of the usual medieval reasoning that "I am what I have done," Martin proffers the converse rationale: "I am not what I have not done." In so doing, he finesses the entire question of evil by separating it from his allegedly unenacted intentions.

Whether the setting be inside or outside the law, there is something "off" about severing intention from action, all the more so in that both ethics and law rely on their interdependence. Modern philosophers might well carve out a theory that Martin and his prince were consequentialists of sorts for having found that, given the choice between an additional sexual assault upon Mrs. Coton on one hand and the end of her gang-rape on the other, Jehan Martin's "failure" to rape her was a better outcome. Consequentialism, explains Scheffler, "in its purest and simplest form is a moral doctrine which says that the right act in any given situation is the one that will produce the best overall outcome, as judged from an impersonal standpoint which gives equal weight to the interests of everyone."[56] But in elevating outcome over evil intention, Jehan Martin and his prince also responded legally to the fear of imminence with the suggestion that, even in the midst of criminal conspiracy, evil can still be thwarted, if only by happenstance, permitting a fascinating glimpse into what a medieval philosophical theory of moral luck might look like.

As expounded by Austin in his ingenious distinction between killing a donkey by "accident" vs. "by mistake" (bad aim? wrong animal?), moral luck is that branch of philosophy that invites us to ponder the intervention, into the acts of intending subjects, of various twists of fate.[57] Austin, Williams, and Sverdlik all ruminate about such conundrums as this one: a drunk driver runs a stop sign and, luckily, kills no one simply because no one happened to be crossing the street or driving through the intersection at that very moment. Likewise, in 1395, Martin claimed a certain moral luck (immoral luck?) in that something intervened—in his case, someone—to prevent him from completing his criminally conspiratorial act of rape. He and three coconspirators, says Martin, were barred from the crime scene by a fourth coconspirator who "knocked them off course" (*NS*, 233) by wielding a rod and threatening that "if he [Martin] didn't leave, he would be beaten." After that threat, the group allegedly headed back to the theatrical site that had ostensibly attracted them to Chelles in the first place (fol. 75r), prompting Martin to contend that the law should not consider his initial intent. Through no fault of his own, he alleges, he was unable to carry it out, even though, as Sverdlik puts it, this is a clear-cut case in criminal law in which the agent "believes that he or she has done everything necessary to assure that the harm occurs. It is well known that the law will accept behavior that falls somewhat short of this point as being an attempt" (CML, 183).

Given the nature of a letter of remission as a medieval form of the legal allocution of intention, the legal strategy of Jehan Martin sheds new and sinister light on the eternally vexed question of sincerity. It is a strategy based on an oxymoron as potent as that of murder by accident: Jehan Martin's was a *good-faith display of bad faith,* an entity that anticipates Searle's observations about the philosophical curiosities of intentionality in speech acts. Granted, a rape is not a "speech act." It is not *speech* at all (although it might include speech and although one might argue that a threat to rape that is followed by an assault is indeed a speech act). But letters of remission *are* speech acts, memorializing in writing a monarch's official pardon to an officially spoken request for royal forgiveness. On one hand, Jehan Martin seems to know what Searle asserted centuries later: "if I fail to carry out my intentions or if my desires are unfulfilled I cannot in that way correct the situation by simply changing the intention or desire." Searle also noticed that "it is logically odd, though not self-contradictory, to perform the speech act and deny the presence of the corresponding Intentional state." You cannot say, he elaborates, "'I apologize for insulting you, but I am not sorry that I insulted you', 'Congratulations on winning the prize, but I am not glad that you won the prize', and so on. All of these sound odd for the same reason," which Searle identifies as an improper "direction of fit." A speech act *"will be satisfied if and only if the expressed psychological state is satisfied, and the conditions of satisfaction of speech act and expressed psychological state are identical"* (*Intentionality,* 8–11; his emphasis).

Jehan Martin's letter of remission is odd for similar reasons. It departs, moreover, from one of Austin's claims that rivals any stasis theory that Hermagoras or Hermogenes ever invented: in one sort of defense, "we accept responsibility but deny that it was bad: in the other, we admit that it was bad but don't accept full, or even any, responsibility" (*PP,* 124). Even if we were to take Jehan Martin's word for it, at the very minimum, he plotted a rape, committed to a conspiracy, and enabled a rape by others. He also acknowledged both the corresponding intentional state and the partial execution of the criminal action, disavowing only that it was committed by him. But nowhere in the lengthy document of some 1,600 words does he apologize: he is not sorry for his corresponding intentional state. Nor is he sorry, it seems, for the rape. Thus, his nonapology takes place within the very document that formalizes the forgiveness extended to remorseful subjects. As Searle adds, "if I apologize for stepping on your cat, I express remorse for stepping on your cat" (*Intentionality,* 10). In a piece of pseudo-logic, the ramifications of which extend far beyond household pets into a plethora of (pseudo)apologies from contemporary figures,[58] Jehan Martin seeks—and receives—forgiveness for a criminal act that he says he did not commit and for which he is not sorry.

And yet, at the same time that Jehan Martin is not sorry, he also acknowledges the truth of the proposition that a woman was raped because of a series of actions that he facilitated and precipitated. The apology, recalls Searle, "presupposes the truth of the proposition that I stepped on your cat, and the remorse contains a belief that I stepped on your cat" (*Intentionality,* 10). Martin had made quite sure that Mrs. Coton and her husband would be denied lodging everywhere in town, he had refused to intervene on their behalf when the beleaguered couple begged him for help, and he had ensured that the former concubine would be left prey for the marauding gang (fol. 74v). In a sophistic approach to his having been derelict in his duty to enforce the law (fol. 75r), Martin articulates what Sverdlik calls a legal and ethical absurdity: "With respect to acts that involve an intention to inflict harm, the problem of moral luck amounts to the question of whether a complete *attempt* to commit a crime or to do wrong is morally equivalent to *success* in committing the crime or doing the wrong. (Obviously talk of 'successful negligence' is absurd)" (CML, 181; his emphasis).[59] Jehan Martin's defense is equally absurd. For instance, in defense of his dereliction of his duty (a crime characterized not by action but *inaction*), he appears to apologize for his intended inaction—"I did not intervene"—but not for his thwarted intended action (to rape).[60] In other words, he was "successfully negligent" in a case of "not-rape by accident."

In our ongoing endeavors to trace any elusive passage from thought to action, it remains critical to recognize that there is a difference between a plan, a plan that fails, a plan that is never enacted, and a plan that succeeds. Like the mystery play set for the next day, the rape of Mrs. Coton followed a path from intention to enactment, from virtuality to actuality. But Mrs. Coton endured an actual rape, not a virtual one, after Jehan Martin and his cronies had imagined it, scripted it, and made it material in accordance with their criminal intentions: all in such a way as to lend new meaning to the term *dramatic plot* as well as to the spectatorship associated with the dastardly, voyeuristic violation that is gang-rape. It all prompts additional questions which, *pace* Eagleton, remind us that, from antiquity to the present day, the vocabulary of theater has always been as juridical as that of the law has been theatrical.[61] Plays have plots, characters have motives, trials host "courtroom drama," police rush to "the scene of the crime," and so on. Given that modern theorists of performance would likely agree that a play is a play, regardless of whether or not a specific plan for performance is consummated, is a man who scripts a rape a rapist? an attempted rapist? a virtual rapist? Where does that leave the accountability and even the culpability of theater, whose participants regularly intend to—and do—engage artistically in the representation of countless crimes? What are the moral ramifications of theater's own scripting and virtuality (criminal, representational, or otherwise)? As Wilson frames the question, "What then is the relation between the agency with which you murder someone and that with which you enter into a contract by promising a certain future performance?" (*TI*, 6). Is entertaining the idea of rape tantamount to a crime? A thought-crime of intention in a medieval world (and beyond) where, supposedly, "no one is punished for thinking" (*DJ*, 2:48.19.18)?

The questions are almost as frightening as the answers. Anyone who recognizes freedom of thought would have a difficult time saying that a man is, by definition, a killer or a rapist because he would like to kill or rape. Even so, in Chelles in 1395, a play-to-be appears to have provided the opportunity for a rapist-to-be; and the opportunity of theater helped to provide imminent rapists with an imminent victim. To invoke the final feature of the present argument—the well-known modern legal triad of motive, means, and opportunity—the problem here is that the fear of imminence rests on the incorrect association of *opportunity* with criminal *means* and *motive*.[62]

First of all, even the *Digest of Justinian* distinguished between a variety of *motives* for the intentional infliction of violence, as when flogging "goes unpunished if administered by a magistrate or parent, because it is inflicted for the purpose of correction not for the sake of insult; but it is punished when someone has been beaten up in anger by an outsider."[63] Anscombe frames the problem especially clearly when emphasizing the distinction between the spirit *in which,* as opposed to the end *to which,* one man kills another: "We should say: popularly, 'motive for an action' has a rather wider and more diverse application than 'intention with which the action was done.' . . . Motives may explain actions to us; but that is not to say that they 'determine,' in the sense of causing, actions" (*Intentionality*, 19). Moreover, one can have all sorts of motives for doing something or for wanting to do something: but having reasons for doing something does not mean that a subject will do it or even that he or she intends to do it. (Thus, the jury in the criminal trial of O. J. Simpson rejected Marcia Clark's Disneyesque theory that "a dream is a wish your heart makes.") Theater was not a *motive* in the deaths of Jean Hemont and Perrin Le Roux, the rape of Mrs. Coton, or the fictional violations of Bar-le-Duc and the *Miracle of the Child*. Although it is the artistic product of one or more intending subjects, theater is not itself an intending subject; it cannot be guilty of the numerous crimes associated with it because theater does not "intend." Only those engaging in it can intend. It is possible, of course, to envisage the transformation of theater *into a motive* that fuels doing something else: "I did X because of theater"; "I killed someone for the sake of theater"; "I am blowing up this theater because my friend was trampled to death at the theater"; "I am closing down this theater because theater is evil and damages my community." But even if theater *were* an intending subject, a motive is not the same thing as an intention (although intentions can motivate), and an intention is not the same thing as a cause: especially a "cause of death" or a "cause of rape." "As for the importance of considering the motives of an action," writes Anscombe, "as opposed to considering the intention, I am very glad not to be writing either ethics or literary criticism, to which this question belongs" (*Intentionality*, 19). She can say that again.

Second, despite a long history of real and apocryphal on-stage violence and death, theater does not provide a *means* for rape, murder, or assault.[64] Even in the sadomasochistic bodily mutilations by Belle de Jour at her New York club (*BTA*, 298–301), even in isolated cases when Murder Mystery

Theater hosts a real murder, even if one were to imagine that "Lady Macbeth" were to take her dagger and stab a fellow actor or that one of the players from Stephen Sondheim's *Assassins* were to open fire, one does not kill *by means of theater*, no matter how many wrongful-death suits crowd American court dockets, the complainants alleging that a piece of art, tape, music, or drama has incited a murder or a suicide.[65] Despite our earlier "loaded gun" analogy, theater is not itself a weapon but, rather, one of any number of potential sites for weaponry. One does not say that "theater killed someone," however convincing Montfleury might have been when attributing his untimely demise not to "the fever, the dropsy, or the gout, but . . . [to Racine's] the *Andromache!*"[66]

Regarding *opportunity*, however, the third member of our current legal trinity, the legend of Bar-le-Duc and the facts of Chelles truly do drive home the point that theater *can* be a trigger, an opportunity of sorts for criminal conduct. If Le Goff associated medieval ludic culture with "opportunities for ostentation and advertisement" (*MC*, 360–61), in 1395, they were also opportunities for rape. Likewise, Jehan Martin's letter of remission makes it painfully clear that a venal law officer and his unsavory cronies would probably never have come to Chelles at all on that fateful night had it not been for the impending theatrical festivities. But Martin certainly did not *need* theater to fulfill his corrupt nature; and there is little credible evidence that theater was any more "opportunistic," any more likely to nurture such fulfillment than any other event that raises issues of crowd control: parades, tournaments, public trials, hangings, or, should we now head back to that medieval future, contemporary rugby matches. Theater is not an agent or a silent coconspirator, so it cannot be "theater's fault" that Mrs. Coton was raped or that Jehan Hemont and Perrin Le Roux were killed. Indeed, the letters issued to Guillaume Langlois and Fremin Severin memorialized the thinking that theater remained a great good, even if it was the site of mortal wounds. Thus, medieval kings extended forgiveness not to things and certainly not to guilty art forms but to accountable human agents.

Even so—and notwithstanding what sometimes looks like medieval hysteria or hostility toward the arts—we would be wrong to discount completely the medieval fears of theatrical imminence. In at least that one well-documented case of 1395, theater really *did* attract that proverbial bad element to town; and Mrs. Coton would doubtless have appreciated a little protection. By no means am I advancing here the extreme position that, since theater is dangerous, it must be carefully supervised and censored (although Mrs. Coton might well have supported that position). One may elect not to participate in art, and one may turn off the television or walk out of the play or the film. Nor am I arguing, *à la* MacKinnon, that Mrs. Coton was raped *because of theater.* But we do no service to the victim if we imply that theater raises no issues of crowd control, or that Mrs. Coton was perfectly safe. Nor can we arrive at the verdict that theater is "not guilty" if we refuse to admit that it was probably the catalyst that brought Jehan Martin to town. If we fail to see that, we miss the very grounds on which theater *is* not guilty.

At this stage, equally relevant to the fear of imminence are the following questions: What does it mean, exactly, to act on one's fears? Or to fail to act on them? Based on which fears do individuals act preemptively or preventively, seeking to discipline and punish crime even before it occurs?[67] Truth be told, we know a great deal about such medieval prevention. In acts of "preregulation," numerous citizenries reinforced their police forces when theater came to town, or forbade the carrying of weapons, or advised surveillance of guests at inns.[68] But such medieval efforts to maintain the proverbial safe distance between theater and audience through the ad hoc prevention of crimes of opportunity do not (yet) translate into a post hoc legislative ban on all theater.[69] The problem is that there can be no safe distance from intentions.

In investigating such matters, we do well to avoid some of the perils of philosophical pragmatism, on one hand—judging theater by its use (*FA,* 39n)—and of consequentialism, on the other, as in judging theater by its outcome. Even if we go so far as to call theater an inducement or an entrapment, it is neither means nor motive. It is only opportunity: an opportunity that, under normal circumstances, represents the opposite of criminal intent. While a certain blurring occurs at the level of freedom of speech and artistic freedom, when, for example, actors illegally put on plays in open defiance of political and legal repressions of the arts, that does not alter the bottom line: people making theater intend (primarily) to put on plays, not to commit crimes.[70] Most of the time, they intend to and do perform Aristotle's "representation (mimesis) of an action" (*Poetics,* 1449b) and Langer's "semblance" of one (*FF,* 310). At the same time, their play constitutes a promise of sorts, a commitment to performing (through real actions and activities) the verisimilar appearance of fictional action. Jehan Martin had no such intention (he was not engaged in theater, even though it was theater studies that helped us to see him); the legendary man from Bar-le-Duc seemingly had the intention to do both. So despite Black's palinode to the artistic potential of murdering someone beautifully (*AM,* 1–5), the intention to make theater is wholly unlike the intention to commit murder. Just because one can plan, promise, and plot a crime does not mean that any commitment to future action is of similar quality to a plan, promise, and plot to make theater.

What, then, are we to make of the medieval take on virtual ethics and the fear of imminence? What does it teach us today? Notwithstanding how easy it would be to politicize the present discussion in the context of war and regime change, our focus on the legal politics of theater is problematic enough, thank you. Legally speaking, we might wonder what would happen if the events of Bar-le-Duc were to take place in the twenty-first century. The bad husband (or bad Christian) would be a felonious marital rapist, at least since the 1978 case against John Rideout; and, depending on the verdict, his wife would be (or would not be) the official victim of a crime. But what if she had found a way to prevent the rape by defending herself against her husband? Even by killing him in self-defense? What if, as in such well-received films as *The Burning Bed* (1984), which was allegedly based on a true story, she had killed her husband while he slept in order to prevent more abuse the next day? Zealous prosecutors would likely reject a plea of self-defense on the grounds that the abuser posed no "imminent threat" to her as he slept; while a good defense attorney would surely look to such contemporary legal *topoi* as this one: "to establish duress which will excuse a criminal act, the degree of coercion must be present, imminent, and of such a nature as to induce a well-grounded apprehension of death or serious bodily harm if the act is not done." Imminent danger was and remains a matter of perception for that proverbial "reasonable person," whose reasonableness would likely be disputed by the opposing counsel's retort that "coercion is no defense if there is any reasonable way, other than committing the crime, to escape the threat of harm; the fear of injury must be reasonable."[71]

Lest such contemporary legal questions strike the reader as a leap, consider the case of Marguerite Vallée in the skillful hands of Natalie Zemon Davis. When Francis I pardoned Marguerite in February 1537 for having killed her long abusive husband, the letter of remission read that, after a particularly violent day, he had begun to attack her with an ax: "She turned away his blow as best she could and started to flee. He hurled the ax after her, and it just missed her head. And seeing her husband's rage and that he was running to get the ax and hit her, Marguerite, sick at heart and a desperate woman, turned around and suddenly picked up the ax and, repelling his violence, turned around and defending herself, gave Valenton two or three blows. She doesn't know rightly where for she was so upset by his beating that she didn't know what she was doing" (*FIA,* 78; her translation).[72] At the heart of the "battered wife syndrome" defense or, for that matter, the self-defense of Marguerite Vallée, lies a legal argument about the fear of imminence that is based on a pathology of perception in those for whom pathology has become the norm: "At first blush, it would seem impossible to claim that a sleeping person posed an *imminent threat of death or great bodily harm.* To counter this initial impression, it is crucial to explain to the jury how the battered woman's perception of imminent danger and the necessity to use deadly force was influenced by her status as a battered woman."[73] One might be tempted here to refute simultaneously, with Knapp and Michaels, Plato's doxa and Fish's philosophy of knowledge by proclaiming that "having beliefs just *is* being committed to the truth of what one believes and the falsehood of what one doesn't believe" (AT, 26; their emphasis). But even that insight is insufficient when we attempt to assess everything that happened—or did not happen—in 1395 and 1485.

Regardless of the dispute between prosecution and defense as to the reasonableness of what a battered wife believes to be true about her imminent danger, there is no way to test (with the usual inadequacies) her belief because that imminence has been thwarted by the death of the violent man who may or may not have had the intent to harm her at that particular moment. When a costumed devil announces his intention to "make the beast with two backs" before raping his wife, when another spousal rape victim enters unwittingly into a contract with the Devil, and when Jehan Martin makes a series of self-serving statements about the rape of Mrs. Coton, all of them declare their intentions: the first, ad hoc as a promise that is a threat; the second, ad hoc as a promise by accident; and the third, post hoc as a legal strategy. In rendering audible and/or visible that which is always invisible—a subject's ACTUAL INTENTIONS—such declarations illuminate with uncommon clarity the uncompromised importance of intention in matters of law, theater, and life. In the law, premeditation is the script for criminal behavior (or the lack thereof); in Bar-le-Duc, a scripted stage devil became a real one in the performance of life; and in Chelles, the scripting of a conspiracy to commit rape should have been legally actionable even if never performed (or, as Martin maintained, even if it was "only" virtual for some and actual for others).

Unlike the chronicles of Philippe de Vigneulles or the miracles of the Virgin, which happily recount the intentions of others, the medieval letters of remission that we have been studying formalize a series of statements (and misstatements), a series of DECLARED INTENTIONS that agents themselves have issued about their own *legally* actionable activities (mediated though those statements might be by extant scribal voices). As noted in the Introduction, DECLARED INTENTIONS need not be present for ACTUAL or ACHIEVED INTENTIONS to exist; that is, people have intentions, independent of whether they declare them or otherwise communicate them. Indeed, Giddens cautions that it is only sometimes—and "fluctuating according to historically given social circumstances"—that agents can even "give a discursive account of the circumstances of their action," communicating the "intentions and reasons which agents have for what they do" (ASCM, 165). But, like the modern legal allocution, the letter of remission exists to elucidate the (criminal or noncriminal) ACTUAL INTENTIONS of individual actants. It is a venue in which they explain their actions (and inactions) by DECLARING post hoc their ACHIEVED, misACHIEVED, or unACHIEVED INTENTIONS. And they make those declarations, honestly or dishonestly, for the enlightenment or confusion of those listening or reading. A focus on ACHIEVED INTENTIONS (which are sometimes legally manifest as facts that are not in dispute) brings us no closer to the saving grace of the alleged purity of ACTUAL INTENTIONS, the latter constituting a frequent and anything-but-pure rationale for torture but also the very entity that Jehan Martin transmutes so malevolently into the forgivable impurity of his own intentions. In so doing, he issues a haunting conclusion that is relevant today: when it comes to the fear of imminence, unless we are prepared to say that we are all virtual criminals on the stage of the world, all virtual witnesses to virtual crimes (which are all virtually subject to actual prosecution), we have no choice but to account for intention—in the theater and everywhere else.

4 / Killing Himself by Accident:
Of Broken Frames, Mimetic Blindness,
and a Dance of Death

> Fascinated, he was enjoying himself hugely. The wounded
> falling, and the dead lying stretched out, did not look as if
> they were really wounded or dead. He felt as though he were
> watching a play.
>
> **GUSTAVE FLAUBERT,** *The Sentimental Education*

The year is 1504, the setting a joyous one as man and
woman are joined in holy wedlock in the northern French city of Metz. On
Wednesday, 9 October, a wedding dinner is being held for Jehan Blanchair,
followed by dancing in the reception hall, a celebration that tugs irresist-
ibly at Henry D'Anoux, the strapping young butcher and *bon compaignon*
who has been serving the meat at the feast. Since Henry has completed his
duties, he goes into the great hall to dance. There will soon be a dramatic
twist. Literally.

According to Philippe de Vigneulles, who reports the events in his memoirs, the time came for a dance in which Henry excelled: the acrobatic display of face and figure known as *Le Grant Turdion,* which might be translated
loosely as "The Big Twist."[1] With two separate lines of ladies and gentlemen
sending couples two by two to meet up in the middle, this particular dance
got its name (*turdion* from *tordion* from *tordre*) because of its characteristic con*tort*ions: its grimacing, squeezing, pressing, twirling, and twisting.
"The first one to lead the dance," explains Philippe, "leaves his spot and his
place in line, and, in the middle of the floor, he does several turns and goes
round and round. And then, *he and the girl make a series of faces together,* and
then he escorts her back to her place. And everybody does this in turn to the
very best of his or her ability—with great strides [*gambairdes*] or somersaults or some other way—and they all do it *one after the other until the end*"
(*CPV,* 4:35; Appendix, Document 4.1; my emphasis).[2] It turns out that Henry
D'Anoux "did it all the way until the end" of his life. An eerie throwback to
the contorted countenances of the *danse macabre,* Henry's *tordion* was true
to its purported origins in the Dance of Death.[3]

In a stunningly detailed account that is of interest to any dance historian
(and which, not coincidentally, follows Philippe's unusually lengthy de-

scription of the death-defying feats of a visiting circus [*CPV*, 4: 30–34]), we
learn that one of Henry's knives was still dangling dangerously "above his
ass" (*dessus son cul*) as he mixed acrobatics, somersaults, tumbling, mime,
and even something that sounds like a kind of break-dancing *avant la lettre*.
It all came together in the butcher's trademark spin on the sensational move
called the *cul tumerel*, which we might render as "The Dervish Derrière,"
"The Contorted Caboose," or, in a more vulgar vein that retains the con-
notations of *cul*, "The Tumble-Butt" (*tumerel* = acrobat / tumbler): "When
it came time for Henry's turn, he made a hundred thousand grimaces and
faces. Among those, it was his habit to do one called the *cul tumerel*, which
is very challenging to do in the way that he used to do it: because he would
hop up and down on one foot, while holding the other foot up in the air
with one hand, and, at the same time, keeping the other hand at the back
of his head holding his neck. Then, all of a sudden, without losing his grip,
he would thrust his head down into the *cul tumerel*, doing a complete som-
ersault, and then get up again—all without losing his grip" (*CPV*, 4:35).[4] At
this point, we know where this sporty story of dance theater is going, and
it is a pity for Henry that he does not: he is apparently unaware of Marcus
Aurelius's dictum that "the art of living is more like wrestling than dancing, in so far as it stands ready against the accidental and the unforeseen,
and is not apt to fall."[5]

Dangling knives. Jumping around. Virtuoso performance worthy of any
saltator. Knife essentially drilled by the dance deep into Henry's body. Dance
of Death. Cry for help. Cry initially unheard. Cry unheard because it issues within the spectacular frame of the *tordion*, a dance in which mimicry,
exaggeration, and pained countenances are the order of the day. As Henry
was turning round and round and up and down, "the point of this knife
went right through his leggings and doublet just above his right hip and
penetrated completely into his body," digging "into the bone in such a way
that it was all stuck and buckled [*reboullés*]."[6] Upon realizing that he was
dying, Henry communicated the urgency of his situation by asking for a
priest. At first, no one believed him: "Then, as he was getting up, he felt
the point of the knife and asked for confession; but everybody thought he
was only kidding or just playing around [*qu'il se juait ou truffait*]—that is,
until they saw him altered" (*CPV*, 4:35). To borrow a maxim from an Italian
legal document of 1304, that is, at least, what his fellow revelers thought
until "the spectacle changed from jest to the truth."[7] As Philippe himself
turns the phrase in his *Gedenkbuch*, Henry was a man who was "*killing himself by accident [qui par fortune se tuait]*"; and, believe you me, no one has
ever seen a man die such a death or die the way that he died; and that is

why I want to tell it here" (147; Appendix, Document 4.2; my emphasis). So do I.

Dance or not dance? Dying or not dying? Theater or not theater? Art or not art? Even crime or not crime? As far as we know, there was no legal intervention this time in the form of a letter of remission. Instead, at issue in 1504, and also in this chapter, are the legal, moral, and ethical dimensions of making a spectacle of oneself in everyday life, as well as the nature and timing of the reactions to such spectacles, not just in narrative, as for Ricoeur, but in the actions of agents and spectators.[8] Sometimes, as Henry's case illustrates so forcefully, a proper understanding of framed activities is a matter of life and death. Nevertheless, as in the preceding chapters, there is something ethically amiss with the critical interpretation that favors the broken frame over the broken man. That is not to say that the frame is unimportant. It *is* important—but, in 1504, only insofar as it reveals the potentially enormous gap between an agent's intentions and what a frame can prevent onlookers from seeing, even when it is right before their very eyes. As a medium that relies on pretense and disguise for the representation of tangible demonstrations that we both see and do not see, theater (as mimed dance or *saltatio*)[9] suggests that frame analysis is not fatally flawed but, rather, that it can be flawed by fate . . . or by intention.

Goffman's foundational insight retains its relevance—namely, that in framed activities, observers "actively project their frames of reference into the world immediately around them, and one *fails to see* their so doing only because events ordinarily confirm these projections, causing the assumptions to *disappear* into the smooth flow of activity" (*FA*, 39; my emphasis). But it is valuable to make those assumptions so that those frames of reference *appear* again. Like the people we have already met—Jehan Hemont, Perrin Le Roux, the unnamed wife of Bar-le-Duc, and Mrs. Coton—Henry D'Anoux escaped neither Philippe's notice nor ours because his dance played out contrary to expectations: not just his audience's but his own. Goffman's "failure to see" is more than the canonical "suspension of disbelief" and more than Langer's "disengagement from belief," which she deems "the very opposite" of make-believe (*FF*, 49). After all, what *is* suspension of disbelief if not *voluntary suspension*? An agreement to disengage? A temporary commitment to see fiction as reality and reality as fiction? There is also more at stake than what Cavell sensibly asserts of the hypervisible behaviors that direct us toward invisible intention in the first place: in "ordinary conduct, nothing is more *visible* than actions which are not meant, visible *in* the slip, the mistake, the accident, the inadvertence . . . and by what follows (the embarrassment, confusion, remorse, apology, attempts to correct . . .)"

(*MWM*, 226–27; his emphasis and ellipsis). In 1504, we have before us the converse: a kind of *mimetic blindness* that afflicts both observers and agents.

If the world of painting makes occasional use of the *trompe l'oeil*,[10] then theater's regular state is one of *trompe le corps*. Bodies on stage enact both the semblance of action and real actions; and they do so as both signs of themselves and themselves,[11] ever signifying something else in an art form that issues not just tricks of the eye but *tricks of the body*. If, following Goffman, the perception of norms changes with the transgression of norms,[12] then it is crucial to recall that a transgression is committed *by someone:* by an agent who acts accidentally or on purpose based on what he or she intends to do and regardless of whether those activities are witnessed accidentally, on purpose, or at all.

Drawing here on the work of Goffman, Eco, and others, I argue that Goffman's "interlocking obligation" (*FA,* 346) lays an excellent foundation for speaking (throughout Part II) about the fortunes and misfortunes of theater as contract. It is an implicit contract, a "common consent" in which all parties understand and accept voluntarily the roles consistent with theatrical framing—roles they recognize as such based, in large part, on the legibility and appropriateness of the available signs.[13] As we shall see, both contracts and frames can be broken deliberately or by accident; and both types of breakage have consequences. I contend, however, that, when scholars focus, as they so often do, on the broken theatrical frame, they are actually interested in the broken contract between the various intending subjects known as actors and audiences.

The theatrical contract, like any other, will require consideration (in the legal sense)of the interplay between ACTUAL, ACHIEVED, and DECLARED INTENTIONS, as defined earlier. In the meantime, though, the case of Henry D'Anoux spotlights here a final type of intentionality that has thus far remained backstage: PERCEIVED INTENTIONS, that is, what others (observers, spectators, audiences, onlookers, and so forth) make of an agent's ACTUAL, ACHIEVED, and DECLARED intentions. For Henry D'Anoux, PERCEIVED INTENTIONS are critical inasmuch as his fellow dancers decide to intervene (or not) based on what they perceive his ACTUAL (and his interconnected ACHIEVED) INTENTIONS to be. They also do so based on whether they deem his DECLARED INTENTIONS an accurate or inaccurate, honest or dishonest, sincere or insincere rendering of his ACTUAL INTENTIONS. All of it opens the door to what spectators themselves do (and even what fellow actors do) as a result of those perceptions and misperceptions, themselves becoming intervening agents who enact (also successfully or unsuccessfully) their own ACTUAL INTENTIONS, which they then ACHIEVE or misACHIEVE, and which are PERCEIVED or misPERCEIVED by others, and so on ad infinitum.[14] But to view the events of 1504 from the standpoint of reception alone would be to substitute implied viewer for actual agent.[15] Until and unless intention becomes part of the picture, reception theories inevitably fall flat due to a failure to recognize that audience perceptions and misperceptions of acts depend, at least in part, on what spectators make of an actant's ACTUAL INTENTIONS, on one hand, and of that actant's ACHIEVED INTENTIONS, on the other (regardless of whether either or both are DECLARED or UNDECLARED).

Again, difficult though it is to disentangle those intentionalities, the story of Henry D'Anoux demands just that. For one thing, any DECLARA-TION, implicit or explicit, is bound to at least a minimal rhetorical con-struction of audience: the declaration must be made in a language that the addressee understands; it must be audible; addressees must be awake, and so on. Indeed, I further argue that the dialectical relationship between DE-CLARED and PERCEIVED INTENTIONS is paramount to a veritable rhetoric of theatricality. For another thing, since those making theater invariably have multiple intentions at any given moment, then the essence of theater's mimetic blindness appears to lie in the temporary blackout of all intention-alities except one, which itself ultimately disappears in favor of characters' intentionalities: the actants' intentions to impersonate (to represent, to cre-ate, to behave as if they were) personae other than who they are.[16] True, so-called good acting often renders that primary intent invisible enough to give way to the intentions of a character. Suspended disbelief becomes an audience's belief in the ongoing fictions; or it prompts (only apparently conversely) an alienation effect in spectators who register (involuntarily?) the artifice of the performance. In the case of murder, theater, or suicide by accident, it all permits the identification of an elusive but no less critical entity that we might call IMPLIED DECLARED INTENTION—and, by *implied*, I mean "*implied by* the actor or the theatrical collective *to* the audience."

The term doubtless seems unwieldy to some. Why not just say "implied meaning," "implied promise," "implied intention," or (following Eco, Pa-vis, and de Marinis) "implied receiver" or "model spectator"?[17] Why not just say "semiotics" or "frame analysis"? My response is threefold:

First, notwithstanding the tenacious anthropomorphism of Goffman's assertion that the frame "organizes more than meaning; it also organizes involvement" (*FA*, 345), a frame has no intent, no consciousness, no agency. It has never "organized" human action in its nonexistent life: not, that is, *until human beings organize their own behaviors* in accordance with what their surroundings (appear to) suggest to them—which suggestions, outside the natural world, are often arranged by other human beings. We thus do well to avoid the passive voice whenever we can, because it seriously clouds the issues: crimes do not commit themselves, and even the haunting idea of the thought-crime, as once conjured in the *Digest of Justinian* (2:48.19.18), is still something that someone thinks up. It is not an agentless entity.

Second, as retrograde as this might sound (and I hope that this chapter will show that it is not), theater (or, if postmodernists prefer, nonrepresentational metatheater) is always an informed IMPLIED DECLARATION about the primacy of representation, as related to Goffman's "prior agenda to perform" (*FA,* 125) in all its various stages of being and becoming.[18] If it is not, then it should be.

And third, I will be proposing that, ideally, IMPLIED DECLARED INTENTION blinds spectators to all other intentions; and, that, without it, little in the theater makes sense. That includes both audience response (as when spectators honor theatrical action with silence and applause at the right moments) and all those avant-garde attempts to subvert those very conventions, in part because they *are* conventions—but those attempts at some point may *themselves* become the new conventions of radicalism.[19]

The question of IMPLIED DECLARED INTENTION is exactly what Henry's fellow dancers were obliged to ponder in 1504; similar questions arise each time audiences ask themselves of theater, dance, mime, radio, or opera (despite the differences in dissemination) whether the actors who are representing characters also intend to do, are doing, or have done something else as well. For our present purposes, IMPLIED DECLARED INTENTION is the primary unspoken premise of an unspoken contract—a phenomenon, moreover, for which rhetorical theory has long had a name: the *enthymeme,* or rhetorical syllogism, in which one premise of a deductive line of reasoning is so clear, so culturally and contextually contingent that it need not be spoken.[20] Sometimes, of course, that premise actually *is* spoken, as when the expositor of a medieval Passion play comes forward to expound on the goodness of God that lies at the root of all things.[21] Sometimes, theater or cinema explores the notion of self-impersonation, as when John Malkovich plays John Malkovich in a vestige of sorts of the author vs. narrator debate. But as an antidote to theater's mimetic blindness, it is eye-opening to think about the stage as a semiotic space[22] in which the communication of mimetic intentions (by intending subjects) is enthymematic.

In theater, representation is the enthymematic premise of an unspoken rhetorical syllogism that ostensibly need never be declared: "I am an actor and I intend to represent something for you here today." Essential to the aesthetic, legal, moral, and ethical distinctions between what is and what is not theater, that premise might well be altered accidentally, as it was in 1504 by Henry D'Anoux during his mimed dance. But whatever the alteration, if the enthymeme helps us to uncover a compelling case of mimetic blindness, then it is our duty to turn blindness into insight.[23] Might we then say that there are none so blind as those who do not see that we cannot substitute frames and responses for intentions?

On the day of the wedding feast, Henry D'Anoux was not acting. He was no Mercutio to Shakespeare's Tybalt, claiming, when mortally wounded in *Romeo and Juliet,* that "it's nothing."[24] His distress did not constitute, as in Baudrillard's ersatz holdup (*SW,* 178), some kind of postmodern test of just what it takes for an audience to break that proverbial fourth wall. He was committing neither "suicide by theater" nor "suicide by sport" (by analogy to the contemporary "suicide by police"). He did not inflict intentionally the mortal wound that killed him "at the end of three days"; and he did not engineer a way for others to kill him. Instead, his demise joins the ranks of such other presumably accidental deaths as those of the wrestlers Owen Hart and Stacy Young: that of Hart, a professional, due to an equipment malfunction at Kemper Arena; that of Young, an amateur, due to a knockout punch in the course of "fun-boxing" on 14 June 2003 (she then lay dying in full view of her husband and two daughters).[25] In Philippe's turn of phrase, which unambiguously situates the butcher's death in the context of ethics and luck, Henry *"killed himself by accident"*: the knives had "slipped out of their sheaths; and, in one of those one-in-a-million pieces of *bad luck* that just doesn't happen, when the knives were coming loose, one of them *wound up* pointing upward with its handle against the floor" (*CPV,* 4:35; my emphasis). The problem for Henry is that his cry for help was not accidental but very much intentional.

Henry D'Anoux's death by dance was a matter of bad luck in both action and perception. As far as we know, when he took to the dance floor that evening, he had not been thinking, "My knife isn't properly fastened, but I like to live dangerously." Nor does any question appear to have been asked or answered as to whether his sheath was defective (although one can only begin to imagine the product liability issues that would be raised today). Rather, Henry had intended a fabulous performance of the *cul tumerel,* which he executed completely (ACHIEVED INTENTION) in accordance with that ACTUAL INTENTION—and about which intentions (both ACTUAL and ACHIEVED) there was no confusion. At the same time, however, that he was in the midst of achieving that intention to dance and to mime, he also did something else by accident: something that Henry himself failed to grasp, at least initially; something that, as previously noted, we are hard-pressed to call an achievement or a success since it was unintentional.[26] Given that one cannot intend accidentally, given that an accident is something that occurs *on the way from* ACTUAL to ACHIEVED INTENTION, there was, in point of fact, great confusion—for both dancer and audience—about Henry's other "achievement": "killing himself by accident."

Part of the now familiar problem is the presence of constantly negotiated multiple intentions, the achievement of any one of which can be compromised by a variety of accidents, as Henry D'Anoux learned to his consternation. (In the Introduction, we considered the more anodyne example of "Oliver," who trips while drinking coffee and walking down the stairs to model his tux, a "misachievement" of sorts attributable to any number of factors that may or may not be under his control—a moment of inattention, a cat knocking over the water glass, an earthquake, and so on—and about which factors he might issue, at any time, any number of true or false declarations about his ACTUAL INTENTIONS.) Now, we find Henry D'Anoux at center stage as the actor/dancer in a mortal stunt that neither he nor his audience expected and which he barely believed himself, in part because of the absence of visual clues like bloodshed. Even the surgeon found later that the knife "was so deep inside that they could hardly see it."

Still, at some point, Henry "felt that he had injured himself"; so, like any other observer, he resorted to interpreting the signs. "Not thinking that it was what it was," explains Philippe, "he was still escorting the aforesaid girl back to her place; and then he went back to the spot [and bent down] to pick up his knives. But when he found only one of the knives, he was much astonished."[27] With the same logic that dominates law, storytelling, and legal storytelling, Henry put two and two together much as the Pseudo-Cicero had once advised, "gather[ing] all these indications into one, and arriv[ing] at definite knowledge" that he was wounded.[28] In a riveting turn of phrase, we read that it was only upon making that realization while getting up that Henry even "felt his wound for the first time," all followed by an almost unbearable irony in which Philippe's bizarre orthography makes for this morbid double-entendre: *"Dieu ait son airme"* might mean either "May God take his soul!" or "May God take his weapon!" (*Gedenkbuch*, 148). The real trick in a dance of tricks was to cue a parallel realization for those watching.

Henry's case exemplifies a palpable gap between intention and action, between ACTUAL and ACHIEVED INTENTIONS (dancing vs. wounding) as well as between what Henry declared implicitly ("I will dance," "I am dancing," "I have danced") and what he later declared explicitly, when calling for a priest, as a result of a new intention (or a revised set of intentions). His call for help bespeaks a similar gap between what audiences saw, heard, perceived, or misperceived and what any of them did or did not do as a result of any of those perceptions or misperceptions, the latter nurtured in no small part by Henry's own initial misperception of what he himself had done by accident. Very much on point, then, in ways that seem much too literal here, is Tallis's observation that "chance penetrates to the core of agency not merely because intentions are externally prompted, formed on the spur of the moment, in response to something that is external to oneself, but also because there can be no 'uniquely referring' intentions" (*NS*, 234).[29] *During* the *cul tumerel,* Henry had not changed his primary intention one iota: unaware of his wound, he thought only that he was dancing the *tordion* in accordance with those intentions and, doubtless, that he was achieving them, too (which also gives us some idea of the physical pain associated with such recreational activities). Just as the dance prevented everyone, including him, from *seeing* the accident that he did not even *feel*—and which would normally have knocked him off course in the achievement of his ACTUAL INTENTIONS—so now, in a curious synaesthesia, did that dance also blind Henry's comrades post hoc from seeing *and hearing* the truth of Henry's condition when he spoke.

In 1504, something happened during a dance that was not a dance and for which help was needed. Such things happen; we just don't know it because no one has told us to know it; and if we've peacefully suspended our disbelief, we're not even *supposed* to know it, even when told. Which is what makes Henry's task so difficult: difficult for him, not for philosophy. Difficult because he must communicate these three pieces of news: what *looks like* an achievement is *not one;* what *was once* a representation is *not one*—or is no longer one; and, somehow, a dance that has not played out in complete accordance with *anyone's* expectations *both is and is not, was and was not one.* Without that new information, "Help!" does not mean "Help!" even though Henry is speaking the same language as his auditors and doing so, we presume, correctly. That is to say that, during the *Grant Turdion* (as during a play), "Help!" usually means "the character I am playing in this dance is grimacing as if he were dying" and not "the man who is dancing is dying."

Furthermore, in the veritable antithesis of crying "Fire!" in a crowded theater, mimed dance empties language as well as gesture of their usual meanings, afflicting its audiences with a kind of theatrical double-blind that ensures that even a "clear and present danger" is, for a time, unclear, seemingly absent, not dangerous at all.[30] Although Lucian of Samosata had once lauded mime as a "manual philosophy" that makes "intelligible what is obscure,"[31] in 1504, mimed dance rendered all too obscure the change in Henry's intentions. Afflicted not only by his wound but by its unfortunate coincidence with the grimace-conventions of the *Grant Turdion,* Henry D'Anoux needed urgently to pierce through the usual fictional meaning of those gestures in order to communicate to his fellow revelers unusual new information about his unusual new intentions regarding a dangerously obscure reality.

At stake here, then, is more than the doctrine of infelicities, in which Austin casts poetry, theater, and joking as linguistic parasites exempt from performative status: "a performative utterance will, for example, be *in a peculiar way* hollow or void if said by an actor on the stage, or if introduced in a poem, or spoken in soliloquy" (*HDTW,* 22; his emphasis).[32] That doctrine is not capacious enough to account for the peculiarities and dangers of Henry's condition. When he asks to be confessed—the last performative act of any dying Catholic[33]—the real infelicity for Henry is that it *is* "seriously meant" (*PP,* 228). And while Philippe de Vigneulles does not record the exact words of the SOS, those words could mean only one thing: "I think I'm dying."

Dying he is, even though, from the audience's perspective, Henry seems only to have broken frame or, more accurately, broken *a frame within a frame.* Having escorted his partner back to her place within the *Grant Tordion,* Henry has already done something "out of turn" for the dance by revisiting center stage to inspect the site of his *cul tumerel:* since his turn is over, he should not be there. The challenge for Henry is to establish that he has not only left his spot but left the dance entirely. He must signal his exit from the *tordion* or languish in the circles of dance Hell. Additionally, since he has no one to announce *for him,* as would Owen Hart over four hundred years later in 1999, that his distress was "not a part of the entertainment here tonight,"[34] Henry must himself take a stab at "outing" his unseen pain and its unseen frame. He must convey to his listeners that any remaining grimaces are not feigned but real indices of a real pain with signals of its own: signals that, unluckily, resemble those of that particular dance. In the twinkling of a tearful eye, he must ensure that his onlookers will step outside the magic circle(s) with him and that, as Boece had once put it of another deadly wedding feast of 1285 at Jedburgh Abbey, those onlookers will "quit the masquerade" and provide not aesthetic reflection and not applause, but physical, medical, and religious intervention (or what Goffman calls "interception").[35] Until Henry is able to convey that message, his fellow revelers will remain blinded by the frame of the dance: a frame that fosters what Eco would call the "de-realization" (ID, 103) of Henry's own body at the very moment when it is on the verge of being de-realized by death.

Henry D'Anoux has a problem. His audience initially disbelieves his plea for aid because they see not the specific behavior before them but the generic, framed behavior of the *tordion*. Pretense, recalls, Austin, "must be not merely like but *distinctively* like the genuine article simulated" (*PP*, 214; his emphasis). So, in the sort of scenario that has intrigued the likes of Borges and Baudrillard (*SW*, 166–67), Henry's pretense has become so distinct that it *is* the thing imitated, pretense no longer. Even so, it is only after spectators determine whether Henry is acting or not acting that they themselves will be prepared to respond by acting or not acting and, as we shall see in chapter 7, in ways that are welcome or unwelcome—in this case, of course, most welcome. Would they be as quick as Henry in putting two and two together?

Naturally, Henry's fellow revelers are thinking that he is miming a grimace, which they believe to be consistent with successful, intentional, representational dancing; but unbeknownst to them all, Henry is both representing a Dance of Death and representing death nevermore. Or is it evermore? Only if they believe his unseen pain will they "unsuspend" their earlier disbelief. Therefore, what Henry needs to convey is a little studied entity dubbed by Goffman "intention display," an "exaggerated externalization" common to both real life and bad acting, which "seems to involve two elements, somewhat phased. The first is 'registering,' namely, the exhibition, often furtive, of the consequences for oneself of what one has just heard or witnessed. The second is 'intention display,' the portraying of what one is inclined now to do because of what has just happened" (*FA*, 235). The question is: When—and how—did Henry's compatriots register *his* intention display? When did they make a judgment, however transitory or instinctive, that Henry's intentional "playing around" had stopped and that the crisis of an unintentional Dance of Death was at hand?

Despite such folkloric evidence as the silly spectators of Riga fleeing the armed characters of a *Ludus prophetarum* of 1204,[36] there is every indication that medieval audiences were not too ignorant to notice that the theatrical "frames" to which they brought ethical responsibilities could be broken. Just as fellow actors and/or bystanders had rushed to the assistance of Jehan Hemont and Perrin Le Roux during a play of 1380 and the rehearsal of one in 1384, so too, later, would a similar urgency attend the rescue of two priests playing Christ and Judas during a Passion play of 1437, when those men almost lost their lives during their respective Crucifixion and hanging scenes.[37] The individuals who helped them were not Cavellian yokels, doing the right thing for the wrong reasons; they "broke frame"—however fluid its boundaries—not because they *did not* understand the ontology of the theater but *because they did.* Even within a culture characterized by highly aestheticized legalistic spectacles of the scaffold, they recognized the distinction between endangered characters and endangered actors, between watching miming and watching dying.[38] And they were not "morally lucky": they were simply acting morally and ethically, all too happy to do the right thing . . . as soon as they could figure out what that was.

In terms of when the revelers of 1504 responded to Henry D'Anoux, Philippe tells us that they did so "immediately" upon seeing his altered state, presumably when Henry fainted or collapsed: "Immediately, they took him by the arms and he was led off to a butcher of Quairtaul; and he was confessed before they pulled out the aforesaid knife" (*CPV,* 4:35–36). Philippe also tells us, however, that "at first" the others did not believe Henry, suggesting a chronological chasm (at least, for the dying man) between *at first* and *immediately.*[39] How long was it before mimetic blindness dissipated and reality came into focus? Until a group escorts Henry to the surgeon, Philippe de Vigneulles describes only an absence of response: "they did not believe him."

Nevertheless, an absence of recorded response does not mean no response. Perhaps one spectator thought, "There he goes again!" or another "Well done!" or yet another "How tasteless!" Or perhaps yet another spectator found Henry D'Anoux a kind of medieval version of Austin's hyena (whom we met in chapter 1), an imitator who, "with a touch of realism possibly exceeding your hopes," pushes his divertissement so far that he takes a bite out of Austin's leg (*PP,* 204). Perhaps Henry, too, had gone too far, prompting spectators to conclude that he deserved to be ignored. After all, "overreaching" a performance had long aroused the curiosity of audiences and the wrath of partisans of *bienséance,* as when Lucian complained about mimes who exceeded "the due limit of mimicry and put forth greater effort than they should" ("Saltatio," 82). Thus, Stanislavski himself would complain much later that "the moment you lose yourself on the stage marks the departure from *truly living your part* and the beginning of *exaggerated false acting*" (*AP,* 177; my emphasis). For Henry D'Anoux, losing himself on the dance stage was not false acting but a hyperreal event that marked a departure from truly living to truly dying. Given that all three medieval accounts mention jest, play, joking, and mockery, it is probable that most of those in attendance simply laughed (like or unlike hyenas), offering up one of many types of affective response when what Henry needed was action.[40] So the question is: Under what circumstances does theater call not only rhetorically for audience reflection and response (be it verbal or non-verbal) but performatively (or, at a minimum, in an illocutionary manner) for immediate action?

In one of the most fascinating sections of *Frame Analysis,* Goffman argues from Langer's work (*FF,* 342) that spectators laugh as onlookers "in sympathetic response to an effective bit of buffoonery by a staged character" but as theatergoers when their laughter "greet[s] an actor who flubs, trips, or breaks up in some *unscripted* way" (*FA,* 130; my emphasis).[41] In that sense, the case of laughter effectively marries audience response to thespian intention, inasmuch as *unscripted* here can only mean *"unintentional on the part of the actor."* Moreover, as Goffman begs numerous questions of reception, ethics, and agency, he further elides the multiple intending subjects of theater in that the person who "scripts" might be a writer, director, producer, actor, and so on. Also, he places, under the same umbrella of *the unscripted,* events that are the result of human agency as well as those that are not: the accidental stumble, the "freak accident" of the lightning strike, the technical negligence of a spotlight falling, and a host of other possibilities to come. But our approach to theater need not replicate consequentialism.

On one hand, if the onlooker laughs sympathetically at an actor's—or a character's—buffoonery, then that spectator must be minimally aware that the actor is playing buffoonery by design, *intentionally,* for an audience. Not only is such recognition the essence of sympathy, but also a comic actor's success is often measured (by audiences) by his or her ability to elicit such laughter. On the other hand, if that same spectator laughs as theatergoer at an unscripted event that is *unintentional* (and which appears thus to the audience), we are faced anew with the moral dilemmas that have long dogged theater. Enlightenment theorists problematized those dilemmas especially pointedly, raising questions about the degree of sympathy or cruelty with which audiences respond not to characters but to other living beings, on stage or off. Imagine, for instance, that when the eighteenth-century actor Whitfield exposed the bald pate of Samuel Reddish during some botched stage choreography in *Hamlet* "to the laughter of the audience," he had actually *meant to* embarrass his fellow actor (*TA,* 214). Despite Artaud's pretensions to the contrary, theater should not be cruel.

All such incidents imply the troubling flip side of the elegant theory articulated by Marshall for a later period: that "the frame of theater signals the pleasure of the audience in beholding a spectacle of suffering, yet it does not signal the secret awareness that the spectacle is false" (*SES,* 25). In Metz in 1504, dance does not seem to have signaled any distress, save Henry's, that some spectacles of suffering are true. When spectators laugh at something

embarrassing or painful, we assume—and we hope—that they do so in the
knowledge that the painful behavior was caused unintentionally. It does not
matter that Chevy Chase is playing "Chevy Chase" in the opening pratfalls
of *Saturday Night Live*. Independent of the producers' desires for ratings
and the audience's desire to laugh, it does not even seem to matter whether
that audience laughs at the man or at his character (if it *is* a character and if
they *should not* laugh because he is in pain). What matters is that he intends
to fall, he intends for the fall to elicit laughter, and he apparently succeeds
at both.[42] But it would be unkind to laugh at the fact that such repeated
tumbles injured him; just as it would have been unkind to have laughed in
1504 when Henry D'Anoux killed himself. The audience didn't know, nor
did the falling man himself; nor had anyone told them to know it.

Regardless of whether an actant ACHIEVES his or her ACTUAL INTEN-
TIONS successfully or unsuccessfully, effectively or ineffectively, happily or
unhappily (as Austin would say), and regardless of whether an audience
perceives any of it correctly, incorrectly, or at all, the issue is this: No matter
how many splintered psyches contribute to the theater (whether it be Goffman's schizoid audience with its two roles of theatergoer and onlooker, or
Graver's multiple-personality-laden actor with his seven bodies to match),
none of it is decipherable without an understanding—preferably a correct
one—of intention.

In 1380, a special effects man was mortally injured by stray cannon fire; but
Jehan Hemont declared his worthy intentions to help with the performance
of a Passion play. In 1384, a curious spectator wandered by an outdoor rehearsal and ignored, at the eventual cost of his life, a warning from another special effects man to stand back; but Fremin Severin memorialized
his intent to serve and protect. In 1395, a law officer allegedly did nothing
to serve and protect as a woman was gang-raped; instead, that same Jehan
Martin made a series of self-serving statements about having failed to enact
his evil intentions to rape Mrs. Coton. In 1485, a costumed devil allegedly
announced his intention to "make the beast with two backs" before raping
his wife; and he made no later mitigating declaration, either because there
was no excuse or because the man never existed. In 1504, Henry D'Anoux
lay bleeding internally while his fellow dancers laughed; but eventually,
he successfully contradicted his earlier IMPLIED DECLARED INTENTION to
engage in mimed dance.

Closer to our own era, a theater audience watched, initially motion-
less, as an actress was beaten unconscious and, for all the audience knew,

dead, on a London stage (*SRT,* 21). In 1998, police officers and telejournalists watched an impending suicide, the former responding with caution, the latter with live feeds, proffering help of sorts (we shall see) by publicizing the man's message about HMOs but not necessarily the help that he really needed. In 1380, 1384, 1395, and now 1504, a proper understanding of an agent's accident (or alleged accident) facilitates a proper understanding of a spectator's misperception.

In 1380 and 1384, there was no time to save Jehan Hemont and Perrin Le Roux. In 1395, there was plenty of time to save Mrs. Coton. In 1504, even if audiences *had* recognized that Henry's distress was real, it is unlikely that they could have saved him from a deep puncture wound. And in 1998, there was plenty of time at least *to attempt to stop* the man on the freeway from killing himself, had the negotiations begun (and the filming stopped?). In all those cases, any given spectator (or group of spectators) acts or fails to act, breaks or fails to break the proverbial frame, having made a judgment about the primary intention(s) of the people before them who are engaged in various acts, including acts of representation.

Ultimately, then, it is not enough to ask if, when, or how a spectator's conception of art is related to (or compromised by) the collapse of the proverbial "safe distance" of theater. With the exception of the patently criminal, extratheatrical rape of Mrs. Coton, each medieval event of l'art 1 demanded that a theatrical frame be broken, not with Goffman's applause, boos, or laughter but with interception (*FA,* 127): interception that derives from a moral, legal, or ethical imperative and not—at the very least, not *exclusively*—from an aesthetic one. It is intention that advances our understanding of not just a *prise de conscience* but a *prise d'action.*

Once upon a time, Erving Goffman paused to ponder the case of the woman who encounters a mirror alternatively in a dressing room and at an auction house. In his celebrated illustration of the theatrical frame, he argued that frames enable agents and observers to identify all those invisible lines in the sand beyond which they "normally" do not go (or intend to go) and beyond which no one expects to see them go: "[A] properly dressed woman who closely examines the frame of a mirror on sale at an auction house and then stands back to check on the trueness of the mirror's reflection can well be seen by others present as someone who *hasn't really been seen.* But if she uses the mirror to adjust her hat, *then* [his emphasis] others present can become aware that only a certain sort of looking had all along been *what was expected* and that the object on the wall [on display] was not so much a mirror as a mirror-for-sale; and this experience can be reversed should she appraisingly examine a mirror in a dressing room instead of ex amining herself in the mirror" (*FA,* 39; my emphasis). Just because the lady is "unseen," however, does not mean that she is not there. So, as a perplexed Henry D'Anoux once wondered, what does that individual need to do to be seen?

Inspired by Goffman's suggestive scenario of the mirror and the lady, Eco reprised it as the point of departure for "Interpreting Drama" by placing the mirror in both an antique store *and* a beauty parlor, and by characterizing the lady's behavior not as "unexpected" but as "irregular": "First situation: The mirror is in a beauty parlor, and the lady, instead of using it to adjust her hairdo, inspects the quality of its frame. That seems irregular. Second situation: The mirror is exhibited in an antiques shop, and the lady, instead of considering the quality of the frame, mirrors herself and adjusts her hair. That seems irregular" (ID, 105).

It is productive to point out that readers and observers, medieval or modern, would likely agree that the lady's responses do indeed seem irregular—unless, of course, they are convinced of the relentless narcissism, vanity, or acquisitiveness of women. Certainly the Middle Ages contributed no dearth of misogynistic literature that regularly expounded on such vices—and long before ladies could pick up hand-mirrors at any drug store.[43] "The difference in the mode of framing," continues Eco, "has *changed the meaning of the actions* of the characters in play. The contextual frame has changed the meaning of the mirror's carved frame—that is, the frame as situation has given a different semiotic purport to the frame as object. In both cases, however, there is a framing, an ideal platforming or staging, that *imposes and prescribes the semiotic pertinence both of the objects and of the actions,* even though they are not intentional behavior or nonartificial items" (ID, 105; my emphasis).[44] Barring a claim that, in a sociological version of the Tower of Babel, frames and norms (like language) once emerged ex nihilo from a divine hand (or a diabolical or naturalistic one), we are obliged to admit this: Culturally loaded (or overloaded) though objects might be, *they do not display themselves* nor do they just *happen to be* on display. A mirror on display has no agency;[45] nor does an auction house, a beauty parlor, or a theater. Not so for the people who display mirrors, other objects, or themselves at the theater.

How a culturally and historically contingent entity like a frame comes to "impose" or "prescribe" anything whatsoever is not a neutral act. That is, if "semiotic purport" is directed, guided, ascribed, or imposed, then the directing, guiding, ascribing, or imposing is done *by someone*—in the present case, by whoever placed the mirror in the human-made salon or art-house in the first place. We see this easily in such extreme examples as the amphitheaters and arenas of Nero's Rome or of Kim Il-Sung's North Korea.[46] It is also visible, however, on a smaller scale: the unruly preschooler standing in the corner, or Eco's moralistic spectacle of the drunk in front of the Salvation Army who has "lost his original nature of 'real' body among real bodies." For Eco, he has been *"picked up* among the existing physical bodies,"[47] such that he is "no more a world object among world objects—he has become a semiotic device" (ID, 102–3; his emphasis). Does the drunk *intend to perform*? Perhaps he has merely entered into a different contract: in exchange for accepting his new role as device, he will receive food or shelter. Such critical traces of agency elided are only the beginning of the interpretational difficulties of the mirror, the lady, and the theater.

On one hand, Goffman's mirror is "on display" because someone has decided to display it, banal though the intention to do so might be. It is on display for reasons that, whether recognized or unrecognized, known or known, knowable or unknowable to observers, are *not unknown* to the person or persons who actually placed that mirror at the auction house with a certain agenda or agendas in mind. On the other hand, there is a significant difference between the individual who displays him- or herself and the individual who is placed on display by someone else, possibly against his or her will. Does a given actant intend or desire to be the recipient of an observer's gaze?

I submit that, in a rush to judgment of the "irregular" or "unexpected" behaviors of Goffman's curious lady, theater scholars have largely concentrated on audience response: if the lady's actions are irregular, they are irregular *to* someone. Not that there's anything wrong with that. But a focus on how observers perceive and respond to frames presents a skewed picture of human activity. Norms and expectations of framed activities may or may not be understood for a variety of reasons, ranging from cultural difference to historical variation to a yokel-like ignorance of conventions (*MWM*, 326–27) to, as Lucy once said to Charlie Brown, stupidity. Therefore, we must also ask, with respect to Goffman's lady (who is gazing as much as she is gazed upon): What exactly is she doing? Is she doing it accidentally or on purpose?

How easy it is to generate a list of all the things she might do in front of that mirror at the auction house, assuming that she pays attention to it at all: check her waistline, redo her makeup, look for a pimple, notice that one of her buttons is undone, call her husband on her cell phone, study the glass or the frame, recognize the object as stolen, call the police, or even take a gun to her head and fire. What if her "irregular" responses are appropriate and the seemingly abnormal is normal? What if the woman adjusting her hat at the auction house was told by her dermatologist to check her face every hour for the return of a rash? What if even an irregular response is somehow appropriate? What if, in a twist of moral luck, Goffman's lady calls the police after identifying the mirror as a stolen object—and the police, once on the scene, subsequently arrest the culprit who turns out to be not just a mirror-stealer but a murderer? What if two negatives make a positive? What if, in addition to an agent's multitasking, there are one or more frames at once[48] that inform not just an artistic *mise-en-abîme* but a theatrical *mise-en-action*? That is to say that, if a frame is both an idea and a space, if a frame both creates and is created by a meaningful universe, then we must set our theoretical stage with people—not things—the better to determine whether certain seemingly irregular behaviors are, in reality, regular to the real persons creating such scenes and performing in them.[49]

In 1504, Henry D'Anoux's behavior was irregular for a dancer, but not for a person who is dying. Regardless of audience perceptions and judgments about appropriateness to the setting, any actant who is performing an action in accordance with his or her intent is doing something "regular," not "irregular," for him- or herself (even if that activity *seems* or *is* culturally irregular to others). Whatever the verdict on questions of regular vs. irregular, whatever the myriad ways in which intent informs reception and vice versa, whatever the perceptions and misperceptions, responses and lack of response by observers, in the case of the mirror and the lady, none of it obviates the fact that the lady is doing something voluntarily or involuntarily, accidentally or on purpose which we must assess on its own terms. Seen, unseen, or almost unseen, wherever the lady does her preening or inspecting—auction house, beauty parlor, office, living room, theater—she is still preening or inspecting before an object that is still a mirror—and which is located in an auction house that is still an auction house or a salon that is still a salon. Broken or unbroken, a frame is still a frame. Mahogany is still mahogany. Glass is still glass. A room is still a room. A dance is still a dance. Action is still action. Stasis is still stasis. A play is still a play. Theater is still theater, even when unusual, unintended, or unexpected things transpire . . . unless, as we shall see, a collective (or certain others) elect to compromise the entire process, abandoning their primary intent to make theater.

Perrin Le Roux, Fremin Severin, and Henry D'Anoux were still dying, within or without frames that circumscribed, within their so-called bounds, imitations, realities, or any combination thereof. And unless death itself were physiologically dependent on the timeliness of the intervention, the presence of observers *does not* alter that reality, its outcome, or even the reality of those imitations (though it is a commonplace of behavioral science to notice that people behave differently when observed, photographed, or filmed). We are not dealing exclusively here with some kind of quantum theater according to which it would be impossible even to observe frames and framed activities without changing their makeup, despite Sartre's worries about just that: "If you 'participate'—and this is what troubled Brecht—you change what you participate in."[50] Long before modern theorists ever spoke of horizons of expectation, reception theory, or feedback, audience participation in early theater had collapsed the now familiar binary of "inside" vs. "outside," inasmuch as observation, feedback, and even the changes they precipitate were organic to that art. So it was that, ever since the apocryphal origins of theater in ancient Greece, theater—barely bounded by convenient ropes or walls—has always constituted a frame capacious enough to include change, disruption, "breakage," process, and the transformative—though not ontologically transformative—power of an audience's gaze.[51] No one ever suggests that the preening or inspecting by Goffman's lady has transformed an antique store or a beauty parlor into something else. And yet, although sometimes theater can be—and should be—stopped in its tracks, we shall see that critical approaches to the theater often remain caught stubbornly at that very juncture, bound up as they have been to questions of response. The question remains as to how that came to pass.

In the final analysis, frames renew and revisit the very moral, legal, and ethical relationships with the real which the living arts never truly leave behind. It all makes for a peculiar brand of "theory trouble" that is related to a companion brand of legal trouble, which is just as peculiar for theater as it is to its double—life.

Entr'Acte / *This Fallacy Which Is Not One*

> In morality, tracing an intention limits a man's responsibility; in
> art it dilates it completely.
> **STANLEY CAVELL,** *Must We Mean What We Say?*

There is a fallacy that underlies the Intentional Fallacy.
There always has been. It is more clear-cut than the general revisionist stance of being "against theory," as formulated in 1982 by Knapp and
Michaels. It is more universal than the characterization by Wimsatt and
Beardsley that "the design or intention of the author is neither available
nor desirable as a standard for judging the success of a work of literary art"
(IF, 3). It is more commonsensical than Cavell's query about what one "lis-
tens for" in music: "Is there any reason other than philosophical possession
which should prevent us from saying, what seems most natural to say, that
such questions discover the artist's intention in a work?" (*MWM*, 225). And
it is more expansive than Hirsch's pronouncement that "no logical necessity
compels a critic to banish an author in order to analyze his text" (*VI*, 2).[1]

After a brief discussion of the applied critical history of the Intentional
Fallacy, I make a tripartite argument in this theoretical Entr'Acte that has
been somewhat obscured by the teachings of phenomenology, reception
theory, and performativity: The Intentional Fallacy consists of three ques-
tionable and interrelated substitutions that appear logical but tend to be
more political than logical (assuming as I do, in disagreement with many,
that there is such a thing as an apolitical logic).[2] Numerous critics have
engaged in the following critical exchanges (with interesting pedagogical
effects to boot):

1. They have replaced *intention* with *accident*.

2. They have replaced *action* and, more specifically, *agent* with *words,
text,* and even *image*.[3]

3. Aided and abetted by the almost unrecognizable contortion if not
cooptation of agency wrought by the two understudies above, they have

replaced *author* with *audience*—often *audience of literary critics and theorists*. At a minimum, they have replaced the perceived singularity of authorial meaning with the plurality of audience meanings (whatever the latter's potential for change and evolution) and, more and more these days, with audience agency.[4]

As we shall see, all three critical preferences for accidents, texts, and audiences have compromised the agency of the real people performing their art(s), despite Buell's optimism that "the new ethical inquiry tends to favor recuperation of authorial agency in the production of texts, without ceasing to acknowledge that texts are also in some sense socially constructed" (IPE, 12). Indeed, our medieval case studies have now shown that the problem for intentionality in theater studies is this: When critics shift the emphasis from "deliberate" to "accidental," from animate agent to inanimate (though occasionally anthropomorphized) *texts,* and from intention to reception, the concomitant shift from pragmatism to politics fosters a heady but impractical conception of the myriad physical ways of making meaning and an impaired understanding of speech acts. There are exceptions, of course, such as the many theorists who have nurtured the resurrection of Barthes's allegedly dead author and the "ethical turn" in contemporary literary theory.[5] Lipking claims, for instance, that the critical proponents of Barthes's dead author "who disclaim any interest in intentions and careers . . . have replaced subjects with spaces and writers with traces."[6] But it is high time to acknowledge that if an author constructs meaning and agency, if he or she *does* anything at all, it is as an actant grappling with intention. One cannot, by sheer whim or individual intention, handily dispense with the intentions of the authors, producers, and disseminators of art simply by electing to talk about something else.

Initially, that "something else" was a formalist, linguistic, or ontological analysis of a poetic text through the proverbial close reading. Later, the closeness of such readings inspired the deconstruction of the very meanings that had seemed to emerge with such stability—a stability, however, that no one familiar with performance or, for that matter, codicology and the establishment of texts would ever have acknowledged.[7] And, elsewhere, that "something else" was thought to inhabit a readership, another entity that, with the exception of theater companies working from a script, is at least nonessential and at most tangential to live theater (if not to live teaching). It all happened because, ever since the teams of Wimsatt with Beardsley plus Wellek with Warren (unintentionally) demonized intention in the 1940s and 1950s, generations of literary critics have approached authorial intention with disbelief, disdain, distrust, and even disgust, pronouncing mantra-like with Wimsatt and Beardsley the phrase cited at the outset of this chapter about the unavailability and undesirability of the author's intention for critical judgments about literature (IF, 3).[8] But, somehow, the criterion of "the success of a work" dropped out of the original equation in what Hirsch termed "the false and facile dogma that what an author intended is irrelevant to the meaning of his text" (*VI*, 12).

Whether expressed or unexpressed, conscious or unconscious, recuperable or lost, intentions were perforce linked to the real lives of men and, eventually, women writing. Thus, an author's "original intent" was doubly subjected to scorn in that "his" irrelevant motives went hand in hand with his equally irrelevant biography, all of which raised the specter of the equally dreaded Biographical Fallacy. "Whatever the importance of biography," declared Wellek and Warren, "it seems dangerous to ascribe to it any specifically *critical* importance. No biographical evidence can change or influence critical evaluation" (*TL*, 80; their emphasis).[9] Intention's fallacy, then, amounted to its being too "extrinsic" to be appropriate for illuminating the "intrinsic" structures of poetry. It was also too extraneous, too extratextual, too impressionistic, and later, too phallocentric to survive the portentous shift in critical attention from biography-driven literary histories to sociohistorical circumstance.

Naturally, it was vital to release imaginative literature from the historiographical practices that had long found critics attempting to evaluate poetry as if it were a transcript of lived experience. By that logic, the key to understanding what the nineteenth-century French Romantic poet Lamartine had "really meant" when he penned "The Lake" would have resided in the discovery of the exact pastoral site of his romantic assignations. The so-called truth of the work of Céline or, more recently, of de Man would likewise have lain in the discovery of a fascist past that was relevant, to be sure, but as the key to entire *oeuvres,* much less sure. By that logic, Coomaraswamy issued proclamations about intention and literary worth, the likes of which are familiar to most of us only in those jettisoned textbooks from *Dead Poets' Society:* "We can, however, go behind the work of art itself, *as if it were not yet extant,* to enquire whether or not it *'ought' ever to have been undertaken at all,* and so also decide whether or not it is 'worth' preserving."[10] Nevertheless, when formalists dismissed an antiquated view of the author in favor of a decontextualized, ahistorical, intrinsically poetic text, and when their successors dismissed an antiquated view of the text in favor of a hypercontextualized, extrinsic, and sociohistorical theory, the former deemphasized the connection between the literary imagination and the real

world, while the latter often overemphasized it.[11] Both practices have obfuscated the stakes of theatrical action, medieval and modern.

Accident as Surrogate Intention

In the early history of the Intentional Fallacy, intentionality occasionally
appeared as its own opposite, denoting precisely what it does not: the happy
(or unhappy) *accident* or coincidence, as if happenstance were a sufficient
explanation for the human motivations (or the lack thereof) that inaugu-
rate human action.[12] For example, when Stallman reviewed Wimsatt and
Beardsley in his 1965 definition of intention for readers of the *Princeton Encyclopedia of Poetry and Poetics,* he differentiated, as we have done for action,
between these types of meaning: what an author *says* he—(yes, always *he*)—
means (which Stallman calls *declared intentions*); what he *really means* (*actual
intentions*); what he manages to "achieve" as "meaning within the work"
(*achieved intentions*); and what his audiences *think* he means (*perceived
intentions*). Stallman then made room, however, for one special scenario in
which an author's declared and achieved intentions are identical. It is a scenario of accident, coincidence, and literal *coincide*-ence: "The problem of
i[ntentions] arises from the fact that the author's declared i[ntentions] as
to his design or meaning are one thing, and his achieved i[ntentions]—the
actual intention or meaning framed within the work itself—quite another
thing, even when the one and other *happen to* agree or coincide."[13] As if authorial intent had nothing to do with extant writing, Stallman places the
author outside the frame of his literary creation in such a way that that
creator, the proximate cause of the work of art, no longer has any relevance
to its production. At the same time, he relegates even readerly response to a
matter of chance, despite centuries of codification in the history of rhetoric
about how to achieve such response, not coincidentally but intentionally.

Although Ricoeur affirms that, in written discourse, "the author's intention and the meaning of the text cease to coincide" (*IT,* 29),[14] any success
in writing what one means—and what one means to say[15]—can scarcely be
coincidental. Action involves meaning to do; and "accident" cannot stand
in for the coincide-ence of intentions, authorial or otherwise, because, accidents make sense only when judged in the context of intentions. And, in
living arts like theater, the actor is not only the deliverer of language but the
performer of acts.[16]

By Stallman's logic, none of the case studies of Part I would make any
sense at all. In 1380, the good intentions that had meant that Jehan Hemont's
accidental assailant, Guillaume Langlois, was not a murderer would have

been pure coincide-ence. In 1384, Fremin Severin's insulating admonition to Perrin Le Roux would merely have coincided with his *desire* to warn. In 1395, the forgiveness extended to Jehan Martin would have been right on the money, given a "mere coincidence" of his criminal intentions with a brutal gang-rape. And, in 1504, a group of dancers who intended to dance would have achieved the *Grant Turdion* just as coincidentally as the nonsuicidal butcher "killed himself by accident." None of that *is* logical; none of it is so. When someone deliberately enacts his or her intentions successfully, with or without having honestly declared those intentions, the successful commission of the intentional act is not an accident.

In that respect, perhaps the most interesting twist of all is that Hirsch invoked accidents even in the context of readerly performance, although with that entity psychologically confined to a kind of middle ground between critical overidentification *à la* Poulet and oxymoronic nihilism *à la* Nicholas of Cusa.[17] Replicating the tenet that "the author's meaning is inaccessible" (*VI*, 14–19), Hirsch explains that "since we are all different from the author, we cannot *reproduce his intended meaning in ourselves, and even if by some accident we could,* we still would not be certain that we had done so" (*VI*, 14; my emphasis). Enacting, recommunicating, or experiencing a never verifiable authorial intent is not the same thing as understanding it (however imperfectly), trying to understand it, or understanding it based on our limited ability to summon all the probabilities to our side—probabilities on which our legal system is based. Literary criticism does not proceed "accidentally on purpose." So if being a positive theorist bespeaks both an unwillingness to face nihilistically the events of Part I and an insistence on ethics in societies with laws, then maybe intentionality is not so bad.

"Word" or "Text" as Surrogate for Agent or Actant

More conveniently for anti-intentionalists, the proffer of *accident* as the dubious replacement for *intention* has facilitated the equally dubious replacement of *action* with *text,* a large-scale intellectual finesse of the problem of agency with grave ramifications as much for theater as for the theater of everyday life. In another coincidence that is not one, ever since the much touted Barthesian death of a flesh-and-blood author, that long-gone human agent has tended to appear on the critical stage as a *thing:* the intentionless text, an entity critiqued by Ricoeur as "the fallacy of hypostasizing [*sic*] the text as an authorless entity" (*IT,* 30). In the same way that students pepper their writing with passive voices, eliding agency for fear that they will have to name the human actant responsible for what they're talking about, we are witnessing a revival of sorts of that old standby, intentionless mean-ing,[18] according to which acts are indeed committed (and even motivated and willed): just not by anyone in particular. That situation is impossible in theater studies. Consider also those ubiquitous compound subjects of contemporary critical writing and everyday conversation which make for seemingly agent-free agency: "hate crimes" and "hate speech" exist because we recognize that actual *speakers*—not *speeches*—are the ones doing the hat-ing (even though words regularly carry vestiges of such hatred).

Thus, Harris notices the birth of *the text as person,* even in Eco's own redeployment of the work of Wimsatt, Beardsley, and Hirsch with the In-tentional Fallacy: "Only the phrasing is different as Eco seeks to define the limits of reasonable interpretation; regarding 'the intention of [the] author' as referring to the unknown intentions with which the author sat down to write, Eco *chooses to speak of 'the intention of the text'* " (*LMRSL,* 96; my em-phasis).[19] Who cuts the cord? Eco does not say. But in recasting the great topos of the poet-creator, he responds to the death of the author by anthro-pomorphizing that author's offspring: the text. It was a move not unknown to Wimsatt and Beardsley themselves, who postulated, in another ellipsis of authorial agency, that a poem "*is detached* from the author *at birth* and goes about the world beyond his power to intend about it or control it" (IF, 5; my emphasis).[20] Newly endowed with consciousness, agency, subjectivity, and intentions, that Pygmalion-like text now possesses the ability to *intend to do things* that, frankly, only authors can intend to do.[21] It has become human in ways that even Ricoeur does not seem to have anticipated and against which Giddens counsels explicitly: "the theme of the decentering of the subject, therefore, should not lead to the disappearance of the self as agent" (ASCM, 165). The only way, it seems, to stop talking about a human (male) author is to kill him off and convert his text into a human being that is capable of the feats of agency we normally associate with animate beings only.

There is nothing wrong, of course, with inquiring about the effects of art, which is a variation on the theme of asking what art does. But we can-not substitute intentional *textual* agency (if such a thing existed) for in-tentional *human* agency, whether in 1380 or in 2008. As we noted earlier, a work of art does not have an intention. Its author or authors do. In the-ater, so too do its producer or producers, director or directors, performer or performers, and so on, along with the spectator or spectators who come into contact with the myriad artistic intentions of all those parties. A text is not a friend,[22] a person, or an agent, even though, at extreme moments in history—or extreme metaphors, such as the pen as mightier than the sword—political regimes have been known to burn (to kill?) books because of what texts supposedly *do*. Indeed, it is of no small consequence that medieval literate culture once concretized *on stage* the notion that textual agency is but a dramatic fiction.

For one thing, medieval dramatists frequently referred to their finished plays as books (*livres*), in a culture in which the performative properties of the book have been well documented.[23] In the little-known fifteenth-century *Farce de Digeste Viel et Digeste Neuve* (loosely translated as *The Farce of the Old Legal Code vs. the New Legal Code*), books materially took to the stage as the incarnation of de Certeau's contention that "books are only metaphors of the body" (*PEL*, 140).[24] In this brief romp (487 verses) through the university community of late medieval Paris, the two main characters are living, breathing textbooks who debate their respective merits with their users. To Old Digest's claim that "[s]ince [the beginning], I've been fruitful and multiplied / And my text has been published," New Digest retorts: "All of my chapters are well-written, / And my text is beautifully illuminated . . . / Down with [you], that old parchment!"[25] As the two fight for their very lives (against one another and against the students who prefer no books at all), their literal battle of the books demonstrates that orality and literacy, speaking and writing, theatricality and textuality were not binaries. Rather, they were—and are—points on a performance continuum in which books—including scripts—are both records of past performances and virtual spaces for future ones.[26] As books in performance, the two Digests lend a whole new meaning to the term *legal representation*, both on stage and off: they are legal representations of the criminal or noncriminal intentions embodied only by living beings.

Audience Meaning as Surrogate for Authorial Meaning (At the Expense of Actant's Meaning)

What happened to the possessor of intent? Convenient though it has been to tout the death of the author, reports of which have been greatly exaggerated, the kindest interpretation is to view that death as a murder by accident. Nowadays, many critics have replaced the author with a new intending subject: the critical self. When Wimsatt and Beardsley wrote that "there is hardly a problem of literary criticism in which the critic's approach will not be qualified by his view of 'intention'" (IF, 3), it is doubtful that even they could have predicted the transmutation of "his view of intention" into "his or her view of his or her own intention(s)," which undergird audience agency and critical action. Though they did caution that "there is danger of confusing personal and poetic studies" (IF, 10), intentionality has passed from author to text to audience, such that one of the great ironies to emerge from generations of rejection of the Intentional Fallacy is this: Even as a dead author is no longer an intending agent, "his" wrested personhood seems to apply to everybody but "him." We thus do well to address the political climate that has propagated a veritable obsession with the receivers, as opposed to the producers of art, and in which theorists from all walks of life focus on personal consequences without due regard for the intentions of the agents demanding their perception in the first place.

We now find readers clamoring vociferously for their own intentionalities, righteously seeking to rectify any and all authorial (mis)perceptions of who they are, and agitating about what they should do about it. Instead of "What happened and why?" or even "How did this happen?" innumerable literary critics prefer to ask: "How is this about me?" or "How do I stage myself as a critical player in my interaction with this work?" If long gone are such questions as "What did the author mean, feel, and intend for his text?", not so for "What do I, the critic, mean, feel, and intend for it?" Witness the metamorphoses, fueled by the *Rezeptionsasthetik* of the 1970s and 1980s, of audience into readership into critical readership, as evidenced even today by the rise of homages to the "place of the personal" in literary criticism.[27] Witness also the large-scale, if varied, replacement of the disgraced "author's intentions" with literary theorists' own intentions, their own subjectivities, and even their own life stories as they self-identify by race, class, gender, age, or geography as a prelude to speaking and writing.[28] For example, in a 1996 forum in *PMLA,* Molloy presents a self-conscious assessment of her own self-consciousness as a queer Latina in "Mock Heroics;" while Davidson emphasizes the fictionalizing aspects of personal diary entries: "Whether we put ourselves in or think we are leaving ourselves out, we are always in what we write. That is our place; like it or not, there is no other."[29]

So it is that, today, at a moment when authorial agency has never seemed so passé, critical agency has never been so "in" as *enfin le critique—et aussi la critique—vint.*[30] But there is something quite strange about the way in which modern literary theorists ruled authors irrelevant to their own life stories while simultaneously ruling both audiences and themselves in as key players in those very stories.[31] If an author's intentions were no longer relevant, each and every reader's response supposedly *was,* as theories of reception oftentimes morphed into studies of intention in disguise.[32] Whether consciously, subconsciously, or unconsciously, many theorists now consign to the oblivion of an oversimplified reception theory any vestiges of authorial intentionality and agency that get in the way of their ability to talk about their own intentionalities. That is presumably because—and here they would be surprised to learn that they agree with both Hirsch and early legal theories of confession—no one's intentions but their own can be verified.[33] In an equally curious twist on the otherwise humanizing ethos of feminism and cultural studies, the self-driven rehearsals of one's own autobiography supposedly serve to validate the critic's arguments by dint of their elucidation of his or her subjectivity; at the same time, that critic entraps authorial intentionality, subjectivity, and agency within a written text that has itself become a person.[34] In the classroom, moreover, it all makes for a cacophony of subjectivities, which, unfortunately, do not tell us very much about right and wrong: a situation that may result in Hirsch's fearsomely "chaotic democracy of 'readings'" in which no one—even a teacher—could "claim that his 'reading' is more valid than that of any pupil" (*VI*, 4–5).[35] Meanwhile, outside the classroom, such critical postures and posturing render superfluous the underpinnings of our legal system. None of it means that the only possible validity is that of the receptive individual, whose personal validity has further mutated into a grand critical narrative of personal or group empowerment.

Whatever our reservations about Hirsch's validity in interpretation, the elusive meaning of texts and acts does not become any more valid by parceling it out to an endless variety of individual subjects. That practice does not solve the problem of intentionality, but merely substitutes one set of intentionalities and subjectivities for another or, more commonly, many others. However noble that democratizing effort, however fruitful the social dialogues that emerge from a decentered authorial subject, overindulgence in the personal is not immune from charges of critical narcissism.[36] Germane here is Bérubé's insistence on the separation between the "wholly personal" and the "wholly impersonal," lest "what may look like principled forbearance from one angle—*I will not commit the indignity of speaking for others*—may look like intellectual solipsism from another" (AS, 1068, 1065; his emphasis). But where Bérubé espouses a "laborious, hermeneutic, unstandardized process of reading," one might insist just as emphatically on a kindred process of *doing*. Problematic enough in the realm of literary texts, the overpersonalization of literary theory has effectively denied, in the realm of action, any logical relief to the discrepancies between meaning and doing, the very chasm that is regularly and artfully bridged by theater.

In his discussion of the "Banishment of the Author," Hirsch wrote, as if anticipating the work of Sean Burke, that "it is the job of the cultural historian to explain why this doctrine should have gained currency in recent times" (*VI*, 2). The answer seems to be "It's politics, stupid!" or, more elegantly for Buell, the "vexing problem of the relation or distinction between the personal and the sociopolitical" (IPE, 14). Whence my closing proposition—yes, political in and of itself—that intellectual politics, whether rightist or leftist, has fostered all three of the surrogacies above.

Nowhere do we see that more clearly than in the critical arenas in which authorial intention has never ceased to matter. Where would feminism be, for example, or cultural studies, if all narrative voices addressed their oppressors "unintentionally"? Surely no critic alive would dare to reject as irrelevant the intentions of an author who is writing as a woman, a person of color, or an inhabitant of a colonial or postcolonial culture. Without a minimal respect for biography and intentionality, we would never have experienced the huge paradigm shifts that helped to launch feminist approaches to literature or noncolonialist representations of race. There would be no legal storytelling movement, no politics of national literatures, no place for the personal at all. Thus, proponents of such agendas insist that those things are not only relevant but essential to literary analysis (even in the wake of a host of attacks on essentialism, such as Fuss's *Essentially Speaking*).[37] In the end, though, the contemporary reverence for subjectivity actually constitutes a thinly veiled effort to restore the intentional and biographical "fallacies" to literary criticism: in part, because intention and biography never *were* fallacies.

Agendas bespeak intentions that need to be explained and understood. It is illogical to accept some intentions, such as those associated with disenfranchised "others," and to deny others (and *other* others). Hegemonies are not malevolent because their members have (or had) intentions but because, in the past, present, and future, other people deem those intentions ignoble. Some intentions are not more equal than others; and if intentions are relevant for some, they are relevant for all. It is just as illogical to replace individual or collaborative authorial responsibility for texts and actions with collective sociocultural responsibility, or to replace the individual intentions related to causation with the politics of group reception. The current political fixation on art as a kind of group dynamic for social change—one that sometimes stifles individuality (the object of rectification) even within groups that share a political agenda[38]—has put the cart before the horse in a final irony: literary theorists themselves decide which voices it is acceptable to hear or restore.

Especially pertinent is Steiner's analysis of the "unholy alliance between the far left and far right" in the fight against pornography (*SP*, 61).[39] For

Steiner, the conservative attempts by the 1980s Meese Commission or by Jesse Helms to apply a special set of regulatory standards to art are just as problematic as MacKinnon's feminist argument that pornography causes violence against women (*SP*, 64–71). Like conservative fundamentalists, she contends, "Leftists are exerting a similar pressure to take art as real-world speech, to see it as dangerously efficacious, and to condemn the experts who argue for its virtuality" (*SP*, 60).[40] On the Left, proponents habitually cite Foucault in order to postulate that art-inspired violence is a fantasy perpetrated by police states that manufacture the threat of violence, the better to discipline and punish the arts.[41] On the Right, their apparent opponents believe that, since imaginary violence begets real violence, it is a good thing to lobby for censorship or V-Chips, the latter of which pre-empt the achievement of intentions only to watch, not to broadcast. Thus, the Left and Right unite, though for different reasons, around their shared conviction that certain types of art pose real dangers to the real lives of real citizens, manifesting a "naive nominalism" and an "illogical account of causality" (*SP*, 64) from which theater studies is not immune, as in Gould's intelligent urging that we avoid speaking of performativity solely in terms of effect.[42] Missing from the debate is this: If art is performative, it is not necessarily performative in a uniform way.

Unfashionable though a critical gesture like Steiner's might be in an age of both extreme political correctness and extreme conservatism, there has to be a better way of condemning violence than mutual accusations of extremism. If the Left fails to discuss morality in broad strokes (or applies leftist principles with rightist ardor), it abandons its critical province to the Right. If the Right uses broad strokes only, it abandons the specificity of individual consequences to the Left. I submit that the better way is to talk about the singularities of intention instead of, or at least along with, the plurality of reception. Short of an explicit reproblematization of the Intentional Fallacy, we are destined to an exercise in self-delusion.

Desperate times call for desperate measures; and we do no service to politics when we fail to deliberate deliberately about intentionality. Here, some will object anew that the mere shadow of that proposition is itself political, as in Read's warning that "theatre and its thought are possible only within a *polis*" (*TEL*, 3). I say that things need not be so dramatic. While Read is rightly fearful that "in the absence of an aesthetics and ethics . . . from within theatre, political demands are imposed from outside" (*TEL*, 1), it is also possible to shift our critical focus to the deliberate logic (or illogic) that undergirds political positions and political action.

During a 1959 interview, Sartre was once asked about the theatrical reception of his Marxism: "But haven't you had an opportunity since then to tell people what you really had intended?" "I did," he responded, "but I was wasting my breath. *Intentions don't count in the theater. What counts is what comes out.*"[43] What *counts* refers to what happens, what actors say and do as it is received and perceived by spectators. Brazen though it appears to say that towering figures like Stanislavski and Sartre are wrong, the central claim of this book has been that, while intention may not be the only thing that matters on stage, nothing counts in theater—or *as theater*—without it.

Part II / *The Theater and Its Trouble*

5 / The Theatrical Contract

> The question is, not whether the premises [of the theater] might
> not have been used for a legal purpose, but whether the contract
> between the parties, and their partnership, and their intentions,
> were not altogether to use them for an illegal purpose: and
> undoubtedly such was the fact.
> *Ewing V. Osbaldiston*, 1837

Is theater different from any other social contract? The enduring work of Erving Goffman, Victor Turner, and a variety of influential social anthropologists suggests that probably it is not. While Goffman
does not invoke the theatrical contract per se, he might as well have, given
his focus on its tacitly validated "official face" and its "interlocking obligations" (*FA*, 126, 346). The premise of this chapter is that theater has a legal
double called the theatrical contract: an implicit social contract between
those making it and those watching it, which is rarely recognized as such
and which has everything to do with intention.

Theorists have long pondered the role of intention in meaning, as when
Scott writes that "persons engaged in rhetorical communication recognize one another as intentional beings. If meanings are to be shared, intentions must to some degree be mutual."[1] Likewise, Knapp and Michaels
contend that meaning "is never anything more than a matter of intention"
(*AT2*, 5); while Hirsch emphasizes that "a word sequence means nothing
in particular until somebody either means something by it or understands
something from it" (*VI*, 4). But what about a *sequence of actions*? In human
communication—as in reading, for Iser or Jauss, and as in theater for Eco—
"theatrical messages are shaped also by the feedback produced from their
destination point" (ID, 110). Actors pretend, disseminate their pretense,
and, for the most part, based on multiple correct perceptions of that primary intent (including those of fellow theater-makers), audiences understand what is expected of them—and what they expect of themselves—at
the theater.[2] What has been obfuscated by decades of (mis)education in the
Intentional Fallacy are the complex interrelations between the following:
the ACTUAL INTENTIONS of a theater collective to represent something—
which intentions they DECLARE explicitly (or, more commonly, implic-

itly), regardless of whether the actants of that collective ACHIEVE or misa-
CHIEVE their ACTUAL INTENTIONS (again, happily or unhappily, faithfully
or unfaithfully). Their ACTUAL INTENTIONS hold, moreover, regardless of
the audience's correct or incorrect perception of those actants' ACTUAL and
ACHIEVED INTENTIONS (that is, the audience's PERCEIVED INTENTIONS of
what the actants mean to do and are doing). Thus, I endeavor to treat AC-
TUAL INTENTIONS first (to the extent that they can ever be identified sat-
isfactorily), before moving on to the audience's PERCEIVED INTENTIONS,
along with any subsequent changes in that nexus of intentions related to the
dynamics of feedback between actors and audiences.

From Aristotle's *Poetics* to Saint Augustine's *Confessions* to States's *Great
Reckonings,* it sounds like terribly old and, perhaps, literally tragic news to
say that actors represent and audiences look on, awaiting the pleasurably
painful (and painfully pleasurable) payoff of catharsis.[3] And yet, when all
the intentionalities coincide—not accidentally, but deliberately for the sake
of representation—we are in the presence of a theater in which intention
has always mattered and always will. Simply or, with my apologies, not so
simply put, the theatrical contract is this: *the reasonably successful achievement of an implicitly declared actual intention to represent, which is correctly perceived as such by an audience.*[4] To put it more polemically, everything else is
secondary or accidental, or it is coercion, voyeurism, or a value judgment.

To those who are already objecting that such a contractual definition of
theater is unhealthily juridical (*LT,* 119), coldly semiotic, or just plain old-
fashioned, I respond that they might be right, but not about this: to insist
on a bona fide theatrical contract does nothing to compromise the magic of
that art. It is merely an insistence that even theatrical magic is produced *by*
one or more persons *for* other persons, by one or more intending subjects
for other intending subjects. Furthermore, the acknowledgment of such a
contract allows us to speak in more systematic ways of the myriad events
that have come to inform the field of performance studies; and it enables
us, at long last, to rebut and reframe Austin's notorious exclusion of theater
from the category of performative utterances (*PP,* 228). However radical
the production, theater is a medium in which the implicit promise to represent might occasionally be broken by makers and watchers—but that promise is *to be respected by all parties.* By that phrase, I mean not a passive voice
but the absolute connoted by all the power of the Latin passive periphrastic
(by analogy to Cato's dictum, *Carthago delenda est* or "Carthage must be,
ought to be, is to be destroyed"): that is what theater *must be, ought to be,
should be, is to be.* Without such respect, it is impossible to understand, appreciate, and, yes, even to judge a theatrical event.

Consistent, then, with the initial taxonomies of this book, we analyze here the six discrete cases that make up the experience of theater, each defined in greater detail below. The first group includes the following:

CASE 1: ACTUAL INTENTIONS understood (or misunderstood) by AGENTS

CASE 2: ACHIEVED INTENTIONS understood or misunderstood (PERCEIVED or misPERCEIVED) by AGENTS

CASE 3: ACTUAL (and ACHIEVED) INTENTIONS DECLARED or UNDECLARED BY AGENTS (to AGENTS)—which, as we have previously noted, need never be declared by any agent at all.

The three remaining cases all concern the *reception of intention* or PERCEIVED INTENTION—perceived not by the agent but by others. I announce them provisionally only and with this caveat: Just because an agent intends to—and does—engage in a performance that enacts his or her ACTUAL INTENTIONS, that does not mean that anyone else need *receive* that performance (although an agreement to do just that is precisely what I mean by the theatrical contract). Thus, we consider the following:

CASE 4: ACTUAL INTENTIONS understood or misunderstood by AUDIENCES

CASE 5: ACHIEVED INTENTIONS understood or misunderstood by AUDIENCES

CASE 6: DECLARED INTENTIONS understood or misunderstood by AUDIENCES (a case that further muddies the critical waters by raising questions of sincerity or insincerity)[5]

Once we bear in mind the connections as well as the discrepancies between ACTUAL, ACHIEVED, DECLARED, and PERCEIVED intentions, we can finally take some of the mystery out of the unavoidable multiplicity of audience response.[6] We can also address a pesky issue that keeps popping up (not by happenstance) in the endless dialectic of communication. Without resorting to those good old Aristotelian beginnings, middles, and ends, we might even find that framing is just another way of talking about time: about the time and timing of intentions, the retrospective understanding of which must not come too late, as late as it did for the protagonists of Part I.[7]

I fully recognize that this taxonomy retains a seemingly older ontology that has fallen out of favor with most theorists of the theater: namely, the distinction between actor and audience, which can be traced nonetheless to the apocryphal origins of theater itself in the sixth century B.C., when

Thespis distinguished himself from his fellow worshippers of Dionysus by wearing the mask of a historical figure.[8] Good theater, they would argue, like good performance studies, depends on our intellectual embrace of the marginal, the messy, the slippery nature of any boundaries with which we might contain the theatrical experience.[9] But such slipperiness does not alter the basic principle that, regardless of how many of Bartsch's Roman actors are "in the audience," *some people are playing and others are not* (responsive though the former might be to the feedback of the latter).[10] As Goffman recalls, each player in social life has his or her "role": "We use the same word, 'role,' to cover both onstage and offstage activity and apparently find no difficulty in understanding whether a real role is in question or the mere stage representation of one" (*FA,* 128). Similarly, there is no difficulty in respecting the integrity of the roles of individual parties to any social contract, theatrical or otherwise.

CASE 1: ACTUAL INTENTIONS Understood (or Misunderstood) by AGENTS

Most of the time, people know what they are doing—at least in terms of their primary intentions—because they know what they are thinking, meaning, and intending when they are doing it. True, the entire profession of psychoanalysis exists to tell us differently: that people can go through their whole lives without self-reflexive investigations into just what they really intend (to say nothing of what they really mean). But it seems safe to say that people who are consciously doing things do not normally misunderstand what they think they are doing; if they do misunderstand—that is, if they are unable to access their own thoughts and intentions—we start to use terms like "psychosis," the better to designate thoughts that are so troubled we no longer like to think of them as thoughts at all, preferring such fantastical terms as "ideation." Theatrical agents and actants do not misunderstand their own ACTUAL INTENTIONS because, to put it squarely, they know and understand what they mean to do.[11]

It is also worth repeating that, barring certain pathologies or telepathies in others, an agent is chronologically the first to know what he or she intends to do. Until such time as he or she enacts, realizes, or achieves those ACTUAL INTENTIONS (successfully or "unsuccessfully"), those intentions are invisible to others—until such time (as we shall see in Case 6) that the agent decides to declare them, or otherwise display them, by means of language, gesture, or some other system of signs. We are all familiar with the numerous legal or extralegal defenses that are based on mental disease or defect, psychopathologies of denial, self-delusion, subconscious desires to fail, physical conditions like sleepwalking, or even the more commonplace situations of changing one's mind or forgetting, to which authors—and, to their great distress, actors—are not immune.[12] Those defenses are not interchangeable and they drive home the message that, notwithstanding Hirsch's contention that an author's forgetfulness is of no "theoretical interest whatever" (*VI*, 7), timing is of the essence even in an agent's understanding of his or her own ACTUAL INTENTIONS. Just as Coomaraswamy rightly advised against criticizing "an actual performance *ante factum*,"[13] one cannot claim amnesia *before the fact* and *prior to the act*. Meanwhile, in the legal arena, Leader-Elliot cites the well-worn defenses of drunkenness, drug-induced mania, or clinical insanity, which create an ad hoc "excuse for individuals who can satisfy the court that they suffered a mental impairment that diminished or destroyed their capacity for moral agency" (NI, 89). Underlying such legal strategies is an argument about an agent's capacity to form intent; and although such arguments are apparent in narrow legal definitions of *mens rea* or in the nullification of contracts whose signatories are not of the age to form legal intent, more germane to our study is the agent's ability (or inability) to distinguish between a moral and immoral course of aesthetic acts and action.

Why do ACTUAL INTENTIONS matter in the theater? For one thing, there is an entire collective on the line, an ensemble, a group of individuals who, both on and off stage, are all engaged in different yet related activities. Presumably, they have agreed to share an overarching ACTUAL INTENTION (or "covering intent") to make theater, which they implicitly DECLARE each time they show up for the work of play.[14] For another thing, while a host of legends (and the occasional reality) depict countless historical instances of actors' diminished capacities—the "crazy dancer" who went mad in ancient Greece while playing Ajax, the emotional breakdown of Stanislavski's Dasha, the impaired Nicol Williamson going off choreography and endangering Evan Handler, the enraged Bette Davis whacking Errol Flynn with undue force during the filming of *The Private Lives of Elizabeth and Essex*—theater itself is no accident.[15]

That is by no means to deny the importance of events that occur on and off stage accidentally, "accidentally on purpose," or downright deceptively: the comical *lapsus linguae,* the tragic slip of the hand (when the gun goes off "accidentally" as the suicidal man is cleaning it), or the fact that an agent can, on one hand, "produce *unintentionally* what usually is conceived to be *intentional*" and, on the other, "produce *intentionally* what is usually believed to be *unintentional*" (ID, 105; my emphasis).[16] Indeed, in a fascinating group of examples, Eco considers, from the standpoint of linguistic meaning, a phenomenon that we shall be considering from the standpoint of *action:* the *intentional* (and deceptive) production of the *appearance of the unintentional.* "What about a fictional character," he asks, "purposefully emitting French-like phonemes in order to mean 'I am French,' while he is perfectly all-American—maybe a CIA agent trying to get political information by talking with a French Communist?" (STP, 113).[17] And "what about an actor," he further asks, "who purposefully and caricaturally emits English phonemes with a French accent in order to tell his audience that he pretends (theatrically) to be a Frenchman who pretends (in theatrical reality) to be an American?" (ID, 105). Eco calls the deliberately produced appearance of an allegedly unintentional defect "double-pretense": a double-pretense that is redoubled in the theater.

Searle brings a welcome clarification to that state of affairs by creating a semiotic version of the safe house of theater: "In one sense of 'pretend,' to pretend to be or to do something that one is not doing is to engage in a form of deception, but in the second sense of 'pretend,' to pretend to do or be something is to engage in a performance which is *as if* one were doing or being the thing and is without any intent to deceive" (LSFD, 324–25; his emphasis).[18] Independent of whether the overarching intent to make theater has been compromised (by some*one* or some*thing*),[19] the ACTUAL INTENTIONS that go into making theatrical reality do not constitute a "false natural event, as when I purposely produce a false imprint in order to fool somebody. I can produce a false symptom by painting red spots on my face to pretend I have measles" (ID, 105). Painting spots on one's face is an off-stage trick, a deliberate deception, perhaps designed by its agent to elicit sympathy, alms, or relief for sufferers of Munchausen's syndrome. Theater is no such thing, notwithstanding centuries of antitheatrical polemic that equates it with lies. Nor, in most cases, does there intervene an unlucky accident, a "one-in-a-million piece of bad luck," an actant's change of mind, or a deliberate piece of malice that transforms a fake infirmity into a real one, all of which would present an improbably rare instance of the *converse of double-pretense.*[20]

As retrograde as this might sound, members of a theatrical collective intend to pretend and even to *entertain,* whether instructively, mindlessly, or even aggressively.[21] They present plays that are not "false natural events," not deceptions, not Baudrillardian simulations, not verisimilar vehicles for ill-gotten gains stolen out of the pockets of spectators. Theater is not highway robbery, no matter how ripped off one might feel at having paid $90 for a ticket to an abysmal Broadway show. It is representation, not misrepresentation.

Can someone *intend to appear to (pretend to) intend* to do something? Certainly Wilson thinks so, as does Kubiak when he understands the ever oxymoronic *verisimilitude* as theater's *"true perjury."*[22] But the feigned corporeal deception of painted measles, which succeeds as the simulation it *is*, or the linguistic errors that do *not* "succeed" as simulations because they are *not* simulations, are not bona fide theater in the most literal sense of the term: the intentional commitment to representation *in good faith*.

Therefore, despite the preoccupation of semioticians with whether one can intend to say the opposite (or a significant variant) of what one is saying,[23] it is both easier and harder to wonder, barring mental disease or defect: "Can one intend to *do* the opposite (or a significant variant) of what one is doing?" Theater traffics in that very question and mystifies the answers. Just as there is no murder by accident, just as one cannot mean what one does not mean, we may also say that one cannot intend to do what one does not intend—except in the theater, where actors regularly intend to, and do, represent the achievements and misachievements of the imaginary and historical subjects who take on fictive life as the intending subjects known as characters.

CASE 2: ACHIEVED INTENTIONS Understood or Misunderstood (PERCEIVED or MISPERCEIVED) by AGENTS

While intentions need not lead to actions, our focus remains on whether and how an agent follows through, as actant, on his or her ACTUAL INTENTIONS to do something, to enact ACTUAL INTENTIONS as ACHIEVED INTENTIONS. It makes a great deal of sense to say that agents are often the first to know that they have ACHIEVED their ACTUAL INTENTIONS, having intended the very achievements in question. Likewise, barring mental disease or defect, they do not normally *misunderstand* their own achievements, having intended them. But that is not always the case. The Olympic swimmer may well intend to win the gold medal; but she learns of her success only after she sees the posting of her official time and ranking (which she might even misperceive). Or, as we saw in the case of the unfortunate Henry D'Anoux, it is possible to misunderstand the consequences of one's own intended actions. Indeed, it is easy to misunderstand what one does not *primarily* intend: to misunderstand the infelicitous byproduct of a primary intent, a kind of collateral damage in agency or, if we prefer the happier flip side, a felicitous bonus.

Thus, Tallis fittingly cautions that actions "can never be totally transparent, even (or especially) to the actor" (*NS*, 234). What made Henry's death by dance so peculiarly infelicitous was the mortal combination of (ACTUAL) INTENTIONS that were both (partially) misACHIEVED and (initially) misPERCEIVED by the very person performing them: a misperception that was also (initially) shared by his audience. Such misperceptions are possible only when the (mis)achievements are as invisible or imperceptible as another's ACTUAL INTENTIONS, especially when an actant manages to achieve his or her ACTUAL (primary) INTENTIONS without a hitch.[24] That is a very different state of affairs from the unseen consequences of intentional actions: "By ingesting poison, I intend to die"; or, to take an example of affect, "By insulting you, I intend to wound you deeply": in the absence of tears and fallen faces, psychic wounds may also be invisible.[25]

It is also true that accidents need be neither as violent nor as theatrical as Henry D'Anoux's Dance of Death. It is not so hard to generate other scenarios, innocent and not so innocent, natural and not so natural, comic and tragic. Ask anyone who witnessed Janet Jackson's notorious "wardrobe malfunction." For Harris, it is the clumsy agent's slip of the hand as he knocks over the glass on the way to passing the roast beef (*LMRSL*, 91). For Austin, it is the not-so-amusing donkey-killer shooting the wrong beast (*PP*, 133n). For Sverdlik, it is the criminal agent who fails to murder because someone—or some*thing*—unforeseeable intervenes to stop it: the bird that intercepts a speeding bullet, the inanimate but deflective cigarette case (CML, 181–83).[26] Or, whether we characterize it as intentionless, agentless, or divine, perhaps it is the fury of the natural world that knocks a would-be killer off course (*NS*, 233) by means of a thunderbolt, an earthquake, or a tidal wave that prevents an agent's achievement of his or her ACTUAL INTENTIONS. The crucial point here is akin to our previous one that an accident is an event that occurs *on the way* from ACTUAL to ACHIEVED INTENTIONS: an ACTUAL INTENTION achieved successfully is an ACHIEVED INTENTION. An ACTUAL INTENTION that an actant *fails to achieve* is not an achievement.[27] Furthermore, barring such instances as a subconscious wish to fail or even changing one's mind (Case 1), in theater (as opposed to dramatic fiction), there ought to be no such thing as an intentional misachievement. That would be the theatrical equivalent of a fighter taking a dive.[28] Either that or, with connections to competency, taste, or *bienséance,* it would be the premise of Mel Brooks's *Springtime for Hitler* in *The Producers,* in which an actor is directed to "play it straight" so incompetently that his performance, having been conceived as a deliberate failure, becomes, unintentionally, an uproarious comic success.

Once again, questions of time and timing, being and becoming are paramount to any agent's post hoc determination of whether he or she has

ACHIEVED an ACTUAL INTENTION. On one hand, the ongoing chronology of life does not always offer the possibility of seeing Langer's achieved "acts in their entirety" (*FF*, 310). Some achievements simply take longer than others, like becoming a surgeon, a lawyer, or a Ph.D., to say nothing of becoming a *good* one. On the other hand, not everything we do constitutes an achievement at all, in that we may not even mean to be doing it (*MWM*, 231).[29] Needless to say, one cannot understand something as a completed, ACHIEVED action *before* that action has taken place—*ante factum* for Coomaraswamy ("Intentionality," 47)—although one indubitably can *imagine* it. We call that imagining ACTUAL INTENTION; in theater, we call it a rehearsal; and, in art, we call the virtuality that attends its fruition *suspense*.[30] One might even go so far as to say that, by its very nature, suspense exists when spectators, having correctly posited an agent's ACTUAL INTENTION(s), *perceive the* ACHIEVED INTENTION *before the* AGENT, who can also be in suspense but in different ways.

Agents constantly experience suspense while intentionally committing acts. But, beyond Austinian questions about perlocutionary effects such as "How will I feel when . . . ?"[31] if we keep the focus on the physical commission of acts rather than on the affect of their reception, we notice that agents can—and do—inquire self-reflexively about their intended achievements *prior to the enactment of those achievements*. Asks the athlete, "Will I make the jump?" or "Will I break my record?" Asks the pedestrian, "Will I get across the street before the light turns red?" Asks the teenager, "Will I wake up in time for school?" Asks the theater collective, "Will this play work?"—with the answer presumably foretold by their rehearsal(s). But when the would-be murderer asks, perhaps during a crisis of conscience, "Will I go through with this?"[32]—or when he or she asks even the apparently informational "What am I doing?"—such questions signal not only achievement in suspense but the actant's possible change of mind. A change of mind is a change of ACTUAL INTENTIONS, a change so noteworthy that, sometimes, it must be spoken out loud: not only as a declaration to others (the more usual Case 6) but as a declaration to oneself.

CASE 3: ACTUAL (and ACHIEVED) INTENTIONS DECLARED or UNDECLARED by AGENTS (to AGENTS)

On or off stage, the notion that people DECLARE their own ACTUAL and ACHIEVED INTENTIONS *to themselves* might appear odd; but it happens every day in such moments of self-coaching as "Come on, you can do it!" (SELF-DECLARATION of ACTUAL INTENTION) or "Good for you! You did it!" (SELF-DECLARATION of ACHIEVED INTENTION). But if agents need neither imply nor DECLARE their intentions to others, then they certainly need not do so to themselves—unless, of course, they do so as a matter of convention at the theater. For the cost of a ticket, as Gustave Cohen couches it charmingly, "[you] enter, with your gaze, into private rooms and into all the secrets of men who confide a thousand personal things to you that are none of your business; and you are not surprised to see people thinking out loud, which is a habit of lunatics."[33] We are not so far here from the issues of theater, madness, and intentionality that we explored in Case 1. That is to say that agents rarely misunderstand their own DECLARATIONS, the notable exceptions being all those true and apocryphal cases of demonic possession, hypnosis, or multiple personality disorder, in which a splintered psyche produces an almost unbelievable capacity to speak of content unknown— and in tongues indecipherable—to the declarant. Self-declaration of that order is a matter for physicians and psychiatrists; in Case 6 below, it will be a matter for observers; right now, theatrically, it is a matter for people who DECLARE their INTENTIONS (why, when, at all) not only while *talking to* themselves but while *acting for* themselves.

Beyond self-congratulation or self-recrimination, why would anyone self-declare an ACTUAL or an ACHIEVED INTENTION? The answer is relatively simple and relentlessly complex. Declarants tend to make such statements and counterstatements[34] to themselves, to others, or to both, when they are in doubt about whether an ACTUAL INTENTION is appropriate or ACHIEVABLE; when there is a discrepancy between ACTUAL and ACHIEVED INTENTIONS (accidents, contrary-to-fact conditions); or, in further communications, elaborations, explanations that arise from the feedback loop of PERCEIVED INTENTIONS (Cases 4–6), as when they fear that others will misunderstand either their ACTUAL INTENTIONS or their achievements of them. As previously noted, ACHIEVED INTENTIONS concern moments when the invisible becomes visible; and we *see them* especially when the usual becomes unusual, when the expected (by the actant) becomes the unexpected (for the actant).[35]

In that sense, DECLARATIONS of ACTUAL INTENTIONS also provide ways of talking about time. Agents issue such declarations ad hoc and in medias res, all without raising the specter of Cohen's lunatics. The self-coaching above may occur *prior to an act:* "Come on, you can do it!" or *during an act:* "You're almost there." Post hoc, however, self-coaching readily becomes either self-congratulation for an achievement—"I knew I could do it!"—or self-recrimination for failure or misachievement: "How could I have blown it so badly?" What is recrimination, after all, if not a post hoc reflection on

ACTUAL INTENTIONS misACHIEVED, which intentions have "expired," as it were? More important, regardless of their timing, self-DECLARATIONS do not refer at all times to all sorts of intentions, a point that seems obvious but is well worth articulating in the context of all the accidents of theater that we have been studying. Although ACTUAL INTENTIONS are subject to changes of mind, to accidents, or to other interventions that impede an agent's completion of his or her ACTUAL INTENTION to do something, one may make an ad hoc declaration about ACTUAL INTENTIONS only. It is at best confident, and at worst arrogant, to declare ad hoc an ACHIEVED INTENTION: "I will have executed my intention to do X" is, at most, a prediction of an achievement, not an achievement itself.[36] It is an ACTUAL INTENTION. Elsewhere, in the long-standing juridical and extrajuridical practices of allocution and confession, post hoc DECLARATIONS normally focus on the relationship between ACTUAL and ACHIEVED intentions, the latter of which make sense only in light of the former.[37]

In the theater, such DECLARATIONS are implicit on the part of actors (traditionally, the only officially "seen" members of the theater collective).[38] They look something like this: "I intend to impersonate the imaginary intending subject who is Hamlet" (ad hoc); "I am (executing my intention by) playing Hamlet" or, for the more committed of method actors, "I *am* Hamlet" (in medias res); and "I played Hamlet" (post hoc), after which the act of representation is over—unless one happens to be a devil of Bar-le-Duc or a literary critic determined to make it last a lifetime. In any event, once agents of theater implicitly (or explicitly) DECLARE their INTENTIONS to others, they invite interpretation in the endlessly interesting and occasionally dangerous world of reception.[39] They enter the realm of PERCEIVED INTENTIONS, to which we turn in our next three cases.

CASE 4: ACTUAL INTENTIONS Understood or Misunderstood, PERCEIVED or MisPERCEIVED by AUDIENCES

While agents and actants generally know their own ACTUAL INTENTIONS ad hoc, in medias res, and post hoc, audiences, listeners, spectators, observers, fellow actors, and other members of the theatrical collective can only *think* that they know the ACTUAL INTENTIONS of those around them. When such spectators are present—which they need not be—they make assumptions, read or misread signs, and engage in interpretations about the ACTUAL INTENTIONS of others, of which they may also be completely unaware, even when faced with an actant's explicitly DECLARED INTENTION(S) (Case 6). As Goffman asserts, they are usually right, such that all their split-second or long-pondered assessments promptly disappear into the "smooth flow of activity" (*FA,* 39).⁴⁰ They are usually right about theater as well because they rely, in large part correctly, on a theatrical collective's tacit but also conventional DECLARATION of a common ACTUAL INTENTION to represent, to put on a play. (Whether the collective succeeds or fails, jointly or severally, is a matter for Case 5; and whether their production is received according to their plan or to others' taste is still another matter.) But until someone violates that tacit promise of representation (as various individuals will do in our next chapter), audiences continue to be mostly right in their assumptions in two important respects:

On one hand, audiences tend to be right about their perceptions of the ACTUAL INTENTIONS they attribute to those performing a play, not only because of the collective's IMPLIED DECLARATION but because *actors,* on behalf of that collective, have ratified, through their own acts of representation, the theatrical contract. As Eco observes of the theatrical "double-pretense" with which "an actor hobbles along, pretending to be a lame person," the *"addressee understands that he is doing it voluntarily"*—as opposed to an extratheatrical, simulated limp, which "the addressee consciously receives . . . [as] unintentional" (ID, 106; my emphasis).⁴¹ In other words, an addressee's correctly PERCEIVED INTENTIONS refer to the actor's ACTUAL INTENTIONS: on stage, Eco's term *voluntary* means *intentional.*

On the other hand, theater audiences are usually right about their perceptions because they have asked and answered the right questions about the ACTUAL INTENTIONS of the actors before them (and, sometimes, of those behind the scenes). When a spectator asks (silently, we hope), "What is that actor doing?" more often than not the question means: "What does he or she intend to do?" or even "What is he or she going to do?" Unless we are in the presence of the beloved literary topos that shows such personages as Montesquieu's Rica wondering, in the *Lettres Persanes,* about the papal magic by which bread becomes wine, spectators ask such questions about the representation of theatrical acts in which they recognize the object of the imitation.⁴² Naturally, they also pose such questions of the *characters* the actors are portraying: "What is Othello going to do? Will he really strangle Desdemona?" But to pose such questions *of actors* is to wonder about others' motives and mental states as predictive of action. It is also to wonder about the virtuality, the potentiality, and the imminence (if not necessarily as fearful as it was in chapter 3) of the crucial if elusive moment when "I intend to" becomes "I am doing."⁴³ The answer to any such question is not anybody's guess and certainly not the guess of Cavell's yokel (*MWM,* 327–31).⁴⁴ Rather, it is any proverbially reasonable person's guess: an educated guess that is based, at least in part, on the intentions that the illusorily ideal spectator attributes to the actor as a party to the theatrical contract.

Once again, time is of the essence to the challenge of ACTUAL INTENTIONS PERCEIVED, so it is helpful to be explicit about the following: When actors are *about to act,* spectatorial understanding of their ACTUAL INTENTIONS involves interpreting, some would say *reading,* forward. When actors are *in the midst of acting,* their ACTUAL INTENTIONS are achievements-in-progress, coming into focus for spectators who interpret those acts both backward and forward, anticipating the moment when the Baudrillardian signs will eventually "incline to one side [or] the other" (*SW,* 178). Finally, when actors *have acted* or have completed a given act, spectators interpret backward (even if anticipating what is to come), engaging in Langer's retrospective (*FF,* 310) in order to determine whether the person who acted has also ACHIEVED his or her ACTUAL INTENTIONS.

CASE 5: ACHIEVED INTENTIONS Understood
or Misunderstood by AUDIENCES

This is an intriguing case because, in a way, it is not one: its meaning is dependent upon Case 4, and it is related to my objection in chapter 2 that, at the heart of the alleged Intentional Fallacy lies the misguided view that the only relevant disconnect in human action is that between an agent's ACHIEVED INTENTIONS and an audience's PERCEIVED INTENTIONS. What audiences, spectators, or onlookers PERCEIVE to be the ACHIEVED INTENTIONS of others is correct only when those audiences identify—not misidentify—acts in light of the ACTUAL INTENTIONS of the actant. For example, we cannot say that murder is not murder because we choose to see it that way; it is not murder because the actant does not intend it as such. Self-conscious or self-reflexive actants might well want to read post hoc the signs of their own ACHIEVED INTENTIONS, the better to gain insight into any subconscious (unACTUALized?) INTENTIONS that prompted their own successes and failures past. An individual like Henry D'Anoux might even share with an audience, at some stage, a misunderstanding about his own ACHIEVED INTENTIONS. But audiences have little choice in the matter: faced with something that may or not be an achievement at all, they cannot form opinions about an actant's ACHIEVED INTENTION(s) until such time as they have PERCEIVED that person's ACTUAL INTENTIONS—but with this significant exception. Sometimes, it is only during someone else's intended achievement-in-progress that they come to PERCEIVE the ACTUAL INTENTIONS of others in the first place—just as they did subconsciously, instinctually, invisibly in 1380, 1384, 1395, and 1504, when something exceptional compelled their attention as it now compels ours.

When confronted with the achievements and misachievements of others, when armed with the rarely spoken knowledge that an accident is something that occurs on the way from ACTUAL to ACHIEVED INTENTIONS, spectators ask and answer their questions to their own satisfaction (which is not the same thing as "correctly"). They make their determinations based on both the visible and the invisible: What have they seen—an interruption? an accident? a natural disaster? an Austinian shooting of the wrong donkey (*PP,* 133n)? a bird intercepting a bullet in flight (CML, 183)? a Macbeth who takes the dagger he sees before him and turns it on the actress playing Lady Macbeth to slay her? And what have they posited about the unseen intentions of the actant? criminal intent? change of mind? inattention?

It is a process that occurs post hoc each time observers wonder about whether something they have seen—something that someone else has done—was *supposed to happen.* This is the point at which we began our study: Does the achievement correspond to the actant's ACTUAL INTENTION? That inquiry occurs in medias res when observers engage in similar musings about what someone else is doing, is trying to do, or intends to do. And, perhaps most interesting of all, it occurs ad hoc when, in the veritable definition of suspense, spectators predict the achievements of a given actant, based on either their correct perception of that actant's ACTUAL INTENTIONS or on their prickly intuition that something else, unseen or unknown to the actant, is *about to happen:* the chandelier is about to fall to the ground; the psychic "just knows" that something awful is about to happen. In the extreme case of suspense, what is so thrilling and, sometimes, so terrifying for audiences is the possibility that they will perceive correctly—and *before the actant,* whose ACTUAL INTENTIONS they have posited correctly—what is *about to happen* in that oh-so-ephemeral moment during which ACTUAL INTENTIONS become ACHIEVED (or miSACHIEVED) INTENTIONS.

Suspense is an empathic fear of imminence *for someone else,* for the agent unaware of the acts and, oftentimes, of the misachievements to come, of the "unintended consequences" of his or her actions (ASCM, 173). For example, someone at the Blanchair wedding feast of 1504 notices, *before* Henry D'Anoux takes to the dance floor, that the knives seem improperly attached and thinks silently "This could be dangerous!" or even "This could be good!" Such a moment is, of course, a convention of a genre like the slasher film, as when the moviegoer sees something, knows something that the hapless protagonist does not: the murderer is lying in wait. But the situation need not be quite so dramatic: I see that you are gesticulating so animatedly that you are about to knock over your wine glass. The sports fan sees that the athlete will make the jump but also sees that his headgear will fall off and that he will both achieve the jump and injure himself. Nor are the types of suspense experienced by spectators all of a piece; as in the case studies of Part I, the spectators may fear imminence rightly, not so rightly, or not at all.

Henry D'Anoux's fellow dancers did not misperceive his ACTUAL INTENTIONS—nor did Henry himself who, having danced the *tordion, did not* misachieve that ACTUAL INTENTION. Everyone got that right; but, initially, they also got wrong that something had, at the same time, gone wrong accidentally (Appendix, Document 4.1). Mrs. Coton and her husband perceived all too clearly the evil intentions of a group of rapists in 1395; but in a narrative of hideous foreboding, the law officer Jehan Martin elected not to intervene to assist them (Appendix, Document 3.3). In 1384, Fremin Severin, from within and without a play, was himself a spectator of Perrin Le Roux's extratheatrical action, shouting out a warning based on his best guess about the latter's intentions. Perrin either did not hear the warning or did not hear it in time; perhaps he heard it and did not care; perhaps he disbelieved the dangers (Appendix, Document 2.1). And in 1380, if anyone witnessed the mortal wounding of Jehan Hemont by cannon fire, there was no time to intervene to stop something that the collective had never intended at all: it was already too late (Appendix, Document 1.1).

CASE 6: DECLARED INTENTIONS Understood
or Misunderstood by AUDIENCES

Whether implicit or explicit, oral or written, auditory or visual, DECLARED INTENTIONS must be heard, seen, understood, and, ultimately, counted or discounted by those to whom agents declare them. Recall the infamous cases in which they are not, as when radio listeners in 1938 panicked that the earth was under attack by Martians, having missed the declaration that a performance of the fictional drama *War of the Worlds* was about to take place. Declarants may announce their ACTUAL INTENTIONS (which, again, they need not do at all), just as they may announce their ACHIEVED INTENTIONS (even though it might be superfluous to do so). The declaration of an ACTUAL INTENTION to someone who believes otherwise is often called protesting, defending, even confessing; the declaration of an ACHIEVED INTENTION to someone who has not witnessed its enactment is called reporting (or, to someone who *has* seen it, confirming, even boasting); more recently, contemporary culture has even witnessed the disturbing birth of what we might call (once it is discovered post hoc), the retrospective, *pre-performative declaration*. Witness the ideological contortions of Brian Williams when justifying, on 18 April 2007, NBC's airing of portions of the edited videotapes in which Seung-Hui Cho, prior to the shootings at Virginia Tech, issued threats about his murderous rampage to come. As in our Case 3, agents tend to make such DECLARATIONS under contrary-to-fact conditions, but they can clearly do so in order to preserve the urgency of a real threat in a real time (now past). Nor are those the only conditions under which agents DECLARE their intentions.

As anyone who has ever read an authorial preface knows full well, a host of circumstances, accidents, emotions, and even legal imperatives surround the statements and misstatements of speakers, actants, and authors (broadly construed). Likewise, a listener, viewer, or reader also knows that, once someone DECLARES his or her ACTUAL or ACHIEVED INTENTIONS, that individual does so *to someone*,[45] broaching three crucial issues: timing (as in Case 3); medium of communication; and sincerity, the bedrock of law, literature, and much literary theory.

First, regarding timing, there are substantial differences among the following types of declaration: "You are misreading my (actual) intentions"; "You were not present at the enactment of my actual intentions"; "You have misconstrued my achievement"; or "I didn't do it/I am not doing what you think/I will not do anything," the last phrase meaning "There was/is/will be no enactment." Consider these examples: "I knew that I wouldn't be able to complete the Race for the Cure," says the breast cancer survivor, Ellen, "but I absolutely had to try: I meant only to do a mile or two." Here, she declares her ACTUAL INTENTION, the better to cast her "failure" to ACHIEVE it as a personal triumph. If she does so, moreover, in response to her sense that spectators deem her a failure, we might even begin to speak of an entity that is not the subject of this book but is quite intriguing: something that we might call ATTRIBUTED PERCEIVED INTENTION.[46] Or Bernard says: "I didn't mean to kill my wife; I was just cleaning my gun." Even if that is the truth, the gap is between intending to clean and the "unintended achievement" of a so-called murder by accident. Or, when eyed with suspicion, the Macy's shopper says: "No, no, I'm just getting a handkerchief from my coat pocket" (that is, "I'm not shoplifting a watch"). Or the Baudrillardian shopping-simulator (*SW*, 178) might say: "No, no, I am only playing at intending" (that is, "My achievement, apparently in progress, is part of an elaborate pretense which the law, by the way, will have a hard time punishing").

Second, in terms of medium, intending subjects make DECLARATIONS orally, in writing, even gesturally. When I point outside and cover my ears before getting up to close the door during your lecture, it is to signal my intent to help everyone with the noise level outside and not to imply: "You're so boring that I'm walking out!" The language and medium of such declarations is of no small consequence. On one hand, questions such as these arise: Are the declarations pronounced or mispronounced? If extant only in writing, are they transcribed accurately or inaccurately? Are they linguistically or grammatically correct or incorrect? (Imagine that Susan declares her intention in French to someone who does not speak French. Or that she logically declares it in French while in Paris, only to find that she is speaking to someone who does not understand French, who is deaf, and so on). On the other hand, individuals may interrupt—accidentally or on purpose—the oral or gestural declarations of others (and we shall see them do so at the theater in chapter 7); written documents are interrupted by authorial intervention, editorial cut-and-paste, ripping out of pages, post hoc establishment of their texts. By the same token, it is much easier (if not necessarily more successful, given the possibility of lies or insincerity) to cross-examine a declarant who is speaking in the presence of others than it is an extant fourteenth-century letter of remission—notwithstanding the reliance of our legal systems on the unwavering demand that declarations, testimony, and allocutions be truthful.

Third, in terms of sincerity, agents make declarations in order to clarify or obfuscate (their meanings), or to fulfill any number of rhetorical goals. That is true despite the handy dismissal of "declared intention" by proponents of the Intentional Fallacy: Stallman recalls that "irrelevant to the objective status of the work *as* art are criteria which dissolve the work back into the historical or psychological or creative process from which it came" ("Intentions," 399; his emphasis). One cannot dismiss quite so handily the scores of questions that individuals ask every day about what motivates the statements that they see, hear, or read. Who declares? under what circumstances? Are the declarations true or false? informed or misinformed? sincere or insincere? Witness Jehan Martin of our chapter 3; witness the long-standing debate about the reliability of literary narrators (the bread and butter of both Enlightenment studies and autobiography, with Jean-Jacques Rousseau as a favorite test case).[47] Are declarations given freely or coerced, as by an aggressive police interrogator, a prosecutor, or even a persistent romantic partner? Once again, the list of questions can be extended virtually ad infinitum; but in theater studies, we can sum it up this way: On stage, is the actor honestly, if implicitly, declaring his or her intention to represent? Or does that actor actually intend something altogether different?

We come full circle to the good faith of the theatrical contract, which is, in the end, an entity quite different from a horizon of expectation during reading.[48] Wimsatt and Beardsley once insisted that we separate "aesthetic achievement" from such "passwords of the intentional school" as sincerity, authenticity, and genuineness, themselves declaring of the perceived equivalency between them that "this is not so" (IF, 9). In theater, where parties commit to the reciprocal interaction of living beings in an ethical world, it *is* so. And it should be.

Based on the aesthetically elusive but morally imperative IMPLIED DECLARATION that imitation or make-believe is what happens at the theater, the theatrical contract begins with an implicit promise that a collective's primary intent is to represent.[49] Normally, collectives do not intend or promise to kill, to maim, to insult, or even to engage in innumerable anodyne activities such as eating, drinking, primping, and so on, even though certain "naturalistic" or avant-gardist tendencies have them doing just that. I submit that, if they do, they are not (primarily) engaged in theater. When a RATT actor beats a woman unconscious, when one actor in the Living Theatre's *Paradise Now* rapes another on stage,[50] those specific acts are not accidents and not representations. Those who perpetrated them must surely have intended battery or rape, even if they battered and raped without full cognizance of the legal definitions of those crimes, and even if their colleagues "consented." Likewise, representation in such cases is, at the very minimum, secondary, tertiary, and so on, even if the perpetrators subscribed to the fantasy that they intended their real violence as subservient to representation. A rape or a battery preempts representation; and the theatrical frame does not insulate actors from criminal liability (*FA,* 1).

Once someone with the standing to represent chooses, deliberately, to alter, abandon, or preempt representation, then we are no longer speaking of theater at all—unless we are prepared to accept such a morally bankrupt definition as Black's: "if murder can be experienced aesthetically, the murderer can in turn be regarded as a kind of artist—a performance artist or anti-artist whose specialty is not creation but destruction" (*AM,* 14).[51] In that respect, our earlier notion of the theatrical enthymeme as the unspoken premise of a theatrical contract proves most useful to renewed reflection upon the events that have long troubled theater's history. If any contract requires consideration, not coercion, then one may deduce that, in the Roman amphitheater, acting is but a means to another end: staying alive. RATT's allegedly "consensual assault" is oxymoronic to the point of defying the very definition of assault, to say nothing of that of theater. Similarly, just because spectators *want to* watch a car crash or a snuff film, that does not mean that anyone has produced one for them. Just because Black believes in "the beholder's subjective experience, *regardless of whether or not the object of this experience was intended as a work of art* or designed for the beholder's aesthetic enjoyment," that does not mean that that object *is* art, despite his statement that "*any* object or idea [his emphasis] may be experienced or interpreted by a beholder (or witness, in the case of someone who is present at an event or an act) as a work of art—again, according to whatever the beholder's definition of 'art' may be" (*AM,* 12; my emphasis).[52] And just because a group of dancers stood by and watched as a man was dying in 1504, that does not mean that Henry D'Anoux wanted or intended to die; nor was it art because they saw it or enjoyed it as such. Individuals who do not intend to make theater but who find themselves on display before others (who are booing or cheering them nonetheless) are not making theater. If anything, such "audience" responses begin to outline a theory not of aesthetics but of cruelty. Theater resides not just in the eye of the beholder but in the eye of the performer—and in the mutual consideration and ethically "interlocking obligations" between them (*FA,* 346).

What makes the consideration of "murders by accident" so difficult is that, in the theatrical world of impersonation, any shift from a primary collective intention (impersonation, pretense, representation) to a different primary intention—say, of one person in the collective to kill—precipitates not a change in frame but a change in both the theatrical contract and in that larger contract known as civilization. Theatrical norms are well and good, as are theatrical contracts; but, sometimes, contracts are meant to be broken—and in ways that finally illuminate what theater is not.

6 / In Flagrante Theatro

Every murder turns on a bright hot light, and a lot of
people have to walk out of the shadows.
MARK HELLINGER

      In approaching a variety of interlocking social obligations,
Goffman deploys a terminology of adherence and transgression that is as
germane to breaking the frame as it is to breaking the law. In addition to the
"unratified" participation of observers (*FA*, 130), he invokes *delicts:* "Should
one participant fail to maintain prescribed attention, other participants are
likely to become alive to this fact and perforce involved in considering *what
the delict means and what should be done about it*—and *this* involvement [his
emphasis] necessarily removes them from what they themselves should be
involved in. So one person's impropriety can create improprieties on the
part of others" (*FA*, 346; my emphasis).[1] As we shall see, one twist, one turn
in the path of agency, one fun-house mirror-image of Goffman's own image of the mirror and the lady (*FA*, 39), and we go through the looking glass
into a theatrical world that represents infinitely more than the sum of its
parts and its parties.

      Let us imagine, and call it SCENARIO 1, that a woman is dining at her
favorite sushi restaurant in New York. While she is enjoying her yellowtail,
a masked gunman enters the restaurant. He opens fire, bullets fly, and her
companion slumps over as bright red blood begins to trickle out of the left
side of his mouth. The woman applauds. As Eco noted of Goffman's curious
lady (ID, 105), this is irregular.

      SCENARIO 2: A woman is at a Broadway theater and, from her loge, she
sees a man—an actor who is disguised as a gunman—enter from stage left
into the sushi bar. From the loge, the set looks very much like a real restaurant because it has been designed by its makers to appear thus and, of
course, because the woman has been in a restaurant before and is capable of
recognizing the restaurant so represented.[2] The man appears to open fire,
gunshots ring out, and an actor seated center stage slumps over his spicy

tuna roll (or its plastic double) as what looks to be bright red blood begins to trickle out of the left side of his mouth. The woman calls the police. This is irregular.

In Scenarios 1 and 2, both the restaurant and the theater constitute frames in which certain types of activity normally take place, in which observers normally expect them to take place, and, most important, in which occupants of those spaces normally behave in accordance with their own culturally and historically contingent understanding(s) of those frames. It is "irregular" for the woman at the sushi restaurant to applaud a death that is neither framed as a representation nor intended as one by the shooter. Under the rule of law, murder is always "out of frame."[3] Likewise, it is "irregular" for the woman at the theater to seek legal or, for that matter, medical intervention for a death that has indeed been framed explicitly (by one or more intending subjects) as a representation. To decide between applauding or calling the police is to make at least two decisions: "This is reality" vs. "This is simulation"; and "I will respond in one or more ways appropriate to watching theater" vs. "I will respond in one or more ways appropriate to witnessing a crime." The first question is the subject of the present chapter, the second of chapter 7; but neither decision is possible without an understanding of intention.

By applauding a death at a restaurant or calling the police to the scene of a staged gunshot, our own curious lady, a direct descendant of Goffman's and Eco's, highlights the insufficiency of simply noticing that the "contextual frame" changes the meaning of "sushi-to-be-eaten" vs. "sushi-on-display-as-prop."[4] The restaurant above is still a restaurant and the theater is still a theater, regardless of whether the meal—or the show—goes on; so, unless we want to say otherwise, we have a problem. Of the gunman at the sushi restaurant, it seems inappropriate to theorize that an audience's gaze is already built into the "culinary frame" or that, short of blowing up the building, even an act of violence has caused a restaurant to cease to be one. It would be equally preposterous to postulate that, inside the restaurant, the people who are doing what they expected to be doing (and what others expected them to be doing)—*dining*—forfeit their status as "diners" the moment they put down their forks to assess the events taking place before them. And it would also be preposterous to state—once the ambulance or the police has come and gone (the former taking the body, the latter statements from witnesses)—that, just as suddenly, the restaurant has become a restaurant again. The persons inside the restaurant might well have become something more than diners during the hail of gunshots—namely, witnesses at the scene of a crime—but they have never ceased to be diners.

Regarding Scenario 2, if diners can truly become something more than diners, actors are always already "more than" who they are by dint of their impersonating others: but they can become still more than that.[5] On the sushi bar set, for instance, a hungry actor might easily become a diner of sorts if he or she takes a bite of the real (not plastic) sushi that serves as prop, a drinker of sorts when sipping the amber-colored water in the decanter (if not necessarily a drinker of scotch).[6] The question that has been before us all along concerns the quality of the acts that render a play more than a play (as in 1380 and 1384), a devil more than a character in Bar-le-Duc in 1485, a mimed dance more than a dance in 1504, and theater simultaneously more than theater and less than art. At this stage, the answer seems to be that, when a play becomes more than a play, it is not because a frame has become more than a frame. Nor is it necessarily because a frame has been broken: on a university campus, fraternity brothers engaging in acts of hazing might be respecting the secondary frame of their frat house, but not the primary university frame that subsumes that frame and outlaws the behavior. In this chapter, I argue, initially from the standpoint of the theater collective, that, with the exception of natural and other disasters (tidal waves, earthquakes, electrical blackouts), a play becomes more than a play *because of something that someone does accidentally or on purpose;* and, if that (here, largely illegal) thing is indeed done on purpose, we are talking not about broken frames but broken contracts. Given Eco's warning that, oftentimes, theorists "incorrectly put together natural and unintentional signs . . . [b]ut we should disambiguate [them]" (ID, 105), one can but agree that we should do so, too.

Let us further imagine, then, several variations on the theme of our first two scenarios:

VARIATION A: A woman is dining at her favorite sushi restaurant in San Francisco. While she is enjoying her yellowtail, the "big one" occurs—a massive earthquake that sends dishes, fishes, and furniture flying.[7] The woman applauds. This is irregular.

VARIATION B: A woman is seated in her loge at a theater near San Francisco's Union Square when she sees, entering from stage left, an actor disguised as a gunman. As he appears to open fire, the big one hits and, in the ensuing disarray, she calls the police. This may or may not be irregular.

VARIATION C: While at the theater, the woman is watching a scene that calls for an earthquake—perhaps a revival of the Crucifixion scene from a Passion play. At the very same moment of the simulated quake, a real earthquake occurs. She applauds. Or she calls the police. This may or may not be irregular.

One could multiply exponentially such variations and contingencies of space, time, place, age (of actants and observers), and mode of dissemination or observation. Our curious lady might have been present at the mortal fourteenth-century woundings of Jehan Hemont or Perrin Le Roux, where she applauded. Maybe she finds herself at a modern rehearsal in her capacity as an investor or an insurer. Or maybe she is still at the sushi restaurant but, before the gunman arrives, she is using one of the restaurant corridors as a catwalk to model her new designer dress for her friends. Or yet another lady uses the "restaurant" as "office" when she whips out her cell phone to call her broker because of something she has just seen on Headline News at the bar. Or yet another lady, a judge, has the "restaurant" *used for her* as "office" when her clerk pages her because she must sign a search warrant. Or yet another lady—the waitress who is serving the first lady—is the one who pulls out the gun and begins shooting.

It also bears mentioning that the countless acts of the natural world and of humankind that alter theatrical life need not be earth-shatteringly violent.

VARIATION D: Our exemplary lady is American, and she is attending not the Lillian Gish on Broadway but a Kabuki theater in Tokyo. She finds herself surrounded by Japanese spectators who are holding on their laps *obento* filled with delectable sushi and sashimi. At each pause in the soirée, they open the boxes and dine.

As a tourist unfamiliar with a frame capacious enough to encompass both "theater" and "restaurant" (albeit the latter only during intermission), the lady might find those activities irregular. Then again, as the performance reaches the fourth, then the fifth hour, she might be sufficiently hungry to consider it regular enough to buy a box of fish at theater prices. If, however, a gunman were to rush the stage and open fire (as he will, in truth and in fiction, in our next chapter), would it really matter to *any* attendee *which frame* (the theater or the restaurant) had been broken?

VARIATION E: Theater, murder, and dining are all taking place at a medieval tavern in which our gunman is now a swordsman. The lady either applauds or runs to fetch a *prevost fermier* (like Jehan Martin of chapter 3?). Which is irregular?

VARIATION F: A woman is attending a tournament in the fourteenth century. During a joust, she sees a man, who appears to be a knight, fall to the ground as blood trickles down his mouth. She applauds. This may or may not be irregular.

VARIATION G: A woman is attending a meeting of the Society for Creative Anachronism or a Saturday-night event at "Medieval Times" in the suburbs of Chicago. During a joust, she sees a man, who appears to be a knight, fall to the ground, and she sees what appears to be blood trickling down his mouth. She applauds. Or she calls a doctor. Or she calls the police. Any one of those choices may or may not be irregular.

If anything, the farcical medieval *Jeu de la Feuillée* suggests, for Variation E, that the medieval "dinner theater" was more commonplace than the schlock dinner theaters of the United States, or the new-wave dinner theaters that offer up participatory murder mystery events, especially when the latter go wrong.[8] For Variation F, as spectacular an event as jousting was in the Middle Ages, it would have been irregular *not to anticipate* the possibility of real violence, despite the pseudohistorical wisdom that it was rare for persons to die during such events.[9] And, for the efforts at spectacular historical realism of Variation G, which are reminiscent of those that killed Jehan Hemont and Perrin Le Roux, what, if anything, has changed except some vague notion that safety precautions have improved over time?

VARIATION H: A woman is eating in a restaurant in Bosnia . . . or Baghdad . . . or Los Angeles. She sees a group of men open fire on a man in the crowd, who falls bleeding to the ground. She tries to round up her friends so that they might come to watch the show.

VARIATION I: A woman is watching the NBC *Nightly News*. As part of a report on urban violence, a correspondent airs some footage from a surveillance camera installed in a Japanese restaurant. She sees a masked gunman enter a restaurant and open fire. After the bullets have flown, she sees a diner slumped over, with blood trickling out of his mouth. She wonders who is playing the dead man and where she can catch the whole thing. Or she calls the police.

VARIATION J: With special relevance to the man on the freeway (the subject of our concluding chapter), a woman is watching, let us say, *Dr. Phil*, when the network affiliate interrupts that program with breaking news. She watches as cameras follow a masked gunman into a restaurant; he opens fire and a man slumps over, blood trickling out of his mouth. Horrified, she wonders what to do.

In Variation H, it is irregular that observers of war would question the reality of casualties (unless, of course, they have taken in as fact, not fiction, a movie like *Wag the Dog*). In Variation I, it is just as irregular to perceive that televised reports of war have recorded actors who are in the appearance of danger, not soldiers who are in actual danger. To call the televised report a trumped-up montage[10] would be the equivalent of denying the realities of the deaths of all those who perish during wars, which is precisely the kind of thinking that leads to Holocaust revisionism. In a less sinister and more morally palatable scenario, it would also be irregular, in Variation I, if our new lady were to call the police to report the shooting at the Japanese restaurant. That would be irregular because what she is seeing is no longer "live."[11] Rather, it is a reconstruction of a real past that was happening then and airing "now" (because someone is airing it)—but not "happening now." It is a recorded past into which (unless she is a film editor changing its *presentation*) she can no longer intervene—at least, not in time to stop the shooting. Moreover, with the exception of movies like *Network,* it is also irregular to think that a television broadcast *calls for* some kind of *intervention* into the airing of the current events depicted (beyond their interpretation, which might even inspire some viewers to social action, as in the new trial for Randall Dale Adams that was largely instigated by Errol Morris's *Thin Blue Line* of 1988),[12] notwithstanding the complications wrought to those so-called norms by the tip-lines of *America's Most Wanted* or the voting-lines of *American Idol.* One might even argue that the success of reality television derives in large part from a refusal (by all parties) to bracket art from life.

Although a master narrator like Brian Williams, Charles Gibson, or Katie Couric stands in for whoever has restructured the random (or seemingly random) events of life into stories (which, in defiance of Dershowitz, suggest that life *is* a dramatic narrative),[13] the actual footage that the lady sees in Variation J is more complex still. In contrast to the more scripted, rehearsed "nightly news," breaking news shares much with theater in that it truly *is* "happening now," playing out in real time, brought to public view by a community of agents working together.[14] Furthermore, breaking news is itself "unexpected" by viewers in ways that theater is not, because theater is a *prearrangement about performance:* even if it breaks out spontaneously, a spur-of-the-moment decision is nonetheless a decision *ante factum.*

With regard to Variations H and I, for example, what is the effect if we learn that NBC has acquired (or purchased) the violent footage from a tourist who was present at the scene and who had filmed the crime at her risk and peril? What if it is from that same tourist who elected to film rather than to offer life-saving assistance? (Without sounding like Charles V or Charles VI, we can still acknowledge that, in subsequent civil actions, the video evidence might prove helpful to the complainants, descendants of those medieval *amis charnelz,* or "blood relations.") Or what if the videotape had been handed over by a reporter for the *National Enquirer,* who had first sold it to *Hard Copy* before NBC re-aired it? What if we learn that our curious lady turned on the news at 11:00 P.M. after having seen a trailer at 6:00 hinting that the entire drama would be re-aired at that time? What if, in the variations presented here, theater, murder, or dining are taking place during rehearsals? On off-Broadway instead of Broadway? In Chicago instead of Tokyo? Baghdad instead of Washington, D.C.? Are those events taking place on television or on the Internet? In the twenty-first century, the fourteenth, or the fourth? Fortunately, theatricality is not a matter of quantity but of quality and, more precisely, of the quality of intention.

In the scenarios to come, we follow our imaginary lady to the theater; since we are about to spend a great deal of time with her, let us call her "Emily." For the time being, we concentrate on what those before her mean and *intend to do*. We do so regardless of whether Emily understands their intentions and regardless of whether she acts on her perceptions and misperceptions (based on her own sense of law, ethics, morality, or lack thereof), transforming PERCEIVED INTENTION (as she will in chapter 7) into audience action or inaction.[15] What matters in this chapter are questions like these: What is happening (or has happened)? What is/was *supposed to be happening* at the theater? Who is causing it (or has caused it) to happen? What does (or did) the "doer" intend—consciously, subconsciously, even self-consciously? And, difficult though the task might be, to what extent is it important to identify those intentions correctly? Are spectators gazing at an evening of murder, an evening of theater, or both?[16]

While the presence of witnesses can make the difference between life and death, we turn to them only after having considered the related questions in chronological as well as moral order. To the extent that each new scenario poses a problem for reception at all, it is as a result of acts committed intentionally or unintentionally by actants: by all the people who create acts in the theater, such as playwrights, producers, directors, backers, crews, actors, and so on. Thus, Emily will perceive with variable speed "what is really going on": "from an individual's particular point of view, while one thing may momentarily appear to be what is really going on, in fact what is actually happening is plainly a joke, or a dream, or an accident, or a mistake, or a misunderstanding, or a deception, or a theatrical performance, and so forth" (*FA*, 10).

If my examples are about to become increasingly macabre and seemingly far-fetched, that is only in keeping with murder by accident, with Austin's own frequent propensity for violent examples, and also—not too heartlessly, I hope—with Sverdlik's decision to "stick to one type of harm—death—in order to simplify discussion" (CML, 183). I prefer to "simplify" the present discussion (whose function is nonetheless to complexify the nature of acts on stage) by focusing on perplexing theatrical delicts and misfires that are precipitated either by actors or by other members of the theatrical collective—all as a prelude of sorts to those precipitated by the audience (or nonaudience). Our dozen dramatic scenarios may well be the kind of peculiar exceptions that law students love to ponder and which confound how things usually are—and usually appear—to that proverbial "reasonable person." They may well stage violence, insofar as its demonstrable excesses provide an instructive counterpoint to what is not excessive. But, once again, the illegal illuminates the legal, the inartistic the artistic, the unreasonable the reasonable, as Emily will now discover when faced, like members of the theatrical collective and like us, with the need to make a decision about this: Is something happening *in flagrante delicto* or *in flagrante theatro* . . . or both . . . or neither?

Gone now is the restaurant as we accompany Emily to her loge at a play-in-progress at a Broadway theater, where she is about to witness a variety of strange events. Given their complexity, it will be helpful to become better acquainted with some of our other characters. On the critical stage with theatergoer Emily is one actor who is brandishing a firearm, whom we shall call "Bob," and another actor in the role of his victim (real, represented, simulated, or manqué), whom we shall call "George."[17] We recall, from Scenario 2, that Emily sees Bob, who is disguised as a gunman, make his entrance onto the restaurant set. Apparently in character, Bob opens fire, bullets seem to fly, and George, who is center stage and also in character, slumps over as what looks like bright red blood begins to trickle out of the left side of his mouth. What does Emily do?

SCENARIO 3A: Something has happened behind the scenes about which Emily knows nothing. Nor, for that matter, does George. Bob, who is playing the gunman, learned earlier that day that George (playing his victim) has been having an affair not with Bob's character's wife but with Bob's real, legally wedded wife, Lydia.[18] Before the performance, Bob switched the gun he had been issued by the props master with a real one, which he has really fired and which has discharged a real bullet. The blood is real, and the victim from the play—a character who is scripted to die, as performed by an actor representing death—is presently dying.

In contradistinction to the accidental deaths of Jehan Hemont and Perrin Le Roux, Scenario 3a depicts Bob's attempt to commit murder during a play, which he executes successfully. Bob knows full well, moreover, that impersonating a killer makes for a great cover to murder: theatrically, it will look all the more like the real thing because it *is* the real thing.[19] Scenario 3a is a case in which we need to know that a member of a theater collective has said to himself: "I am participating in the theater today because

I hope to kill someone." When Bob shoots George, he no longer intends to represent (which is how he began his performance), he is not representing, and he has substituted an intent to murder for an intent to imitate, even as he commits his murder during what, up to that moment, was—and may still be—art-in-progress. As for George, unlike the RATT actress who allegedly consented to be beaten (*SRT,* 21), he does not *want* to be shot; and unlike the man on the freeway (to whom we return in our Talk-Back), he by no means wants to die. Very much like, however, the ultimately unrescuable Henry D'Anoux (whose knife wound was too deep or whose medieval surgeon was too medically challenged), George will survive Bob's attempt to kill him if, and only if, someone else figures out in time "what is really going on" (*FA,* 10).

In Scenario 3a, the "frame" has not changed as a result of all the possible interruptions (accidental or deliberate, natural or unnatural), which are not part of the collective, collaborative intent—and attempt—to make theater. Nor has the definition of theater changed for anyone but Bob, who views it—and uses it—as a venue for murder, transforming art into the host form for a criminal act that is not representation, even as it takes place *during* one.[20] Life itself has changed and hangs in the balance; and George needs help from anyone willing and able to offer it, from on or off stage. Chances are that the actors or those behind the scenes will catch on first that it is the actor—not the character—who is in peril, given their familiarity with what was *supposed to happen,* having rehearsed it (although something of the sort is also possible for audiences familiar with the book, the story line, the previous performance, the history of theatrical mishaps, and the like). It would be irregular, for instance, that at such a moment (during which fellow actors become theatergoers of sorts), one of them in the same scene, rattled by the commotion, would merely turn to the prompter and say, "Line, please."[21] Instead, a regular response to the irregular here would be another actor rushing off stage to call 911, perhaps triggering a chain reaction of audience comprehension as spectators who suddenly "get it" whip out their previously turned off (we hope) cell phones and the proverbial doctor in the house hurries to the stage, jostling Emily, who finally gets it . . . upon which we may now ask: What about Emily? The critical curtain is about to fall on Scenario 3a. What does she do? Does she applaud? call the police? do nothing at all?

On one hand, if Emily applauds, she does so as Goffman's "onlooker," who "gives herself over" and "collaborates in the unreality onstage. [S]he sympathetically and vicariously participates in the unreal world generated by the dramatic interplay of the scripted characters." And if she applauds as onlooker, doubtless along with many others, she is morally unlucky, with George unluckier still, because she has failed to pick up on important cues to the theatergoer. It is a failure that renders her neither immoral nor unethical but—if only as temporarily, as a group of dancers once was in 1504—ignorant. On the other hand, if she calls the police, she does so as the "theatergoer" who has "untheatrical activity to sustain" as "the one who makes the reservations and pays for the tickets, comes late or on time, and is responsive to the curtain call after the performance" and who "takes the intermission break" (*FA,* 129–30).

And yet, there is another possibility. Perhaps Emily is a yokel and she calls the police not because she understands what is really going on but because, like Cavell's famous personage, she does *not* understand that theater is supposed to be an imitation of life, not life itself. Even then, her seemingly yokel-like intervention would prove warranted, "happy," morally lucky, and lifesaving: the *visual* equivalent of what Knapp and Michaels discussed in terms of the *sound* of speech acts: "If you really think that a noise you hear is someone shouting 'Fire!' you might call the fire department" ("Reply," 143). That is, "if one somehow does hear as a speech act what is really just noise, then one is nevertheless not simply pretending to hear words but genuinely hearing them, even if what was heard was not really uttered" (AT2, 19). Furthermore, what if there *were* someone else in the audience in a better position than Emily to understand that what only *seems* an act of real violence really *is* an act of violence?

While we have limited our spectators thus far to Emily and to the doctor in the house, we can now expand that focus to include at least one more individual. Imagine that, in a variation on Scenario 3a, we were to find, seated next to Emily, Bob's best friend, Dick. Dick has the perfect grasp of reality because he is Bob's accomplice; and Emily would have been a great deal more afraid had she known that a criminal was sitting next to her. Dick is the one who supplied the real gun. Obviously, Dick does not call the police; but he is concerned when he sees Emily whip out her cell phone. He should be—or, depending on the outcome of the events that he has plotted with Bob, maybe he should not be. Maybe Bob will misfire in such a way that his attempted murder also misfires as an "act that we purport to perform . . . [that does] not come off" (*PP,* 225).

SCENARIO 3B: Bob has still switched the gun that he has been issued by the props master with a real one. He still intends to kill George. And he still discharges a real weapon, which he believes to contain a real bullet. But then nothing happens. No sound. The gun does not go off; but George, in character, slumps over anyway as what looks like bright red blood begins to trickle out of the left side of his mouth. Does Emily applaud, call the police, or do something else?

At this point, whatever Emily does, the "accident" here, at least from Bob's perspective, is the continuation of theater. Certainly George is lucky in this scenario; and, difficult though it might be to accept that an immoral man is morally lucky, so too here is Bob. Bob meant to, intended to kill George, but he did not succeed. He appeared instead to succeed in what everyone else in the company—and the audience too—presumed to be his participation in the collective's intent to make theater.

In Scenario 3a, Bob has, in all likelihood, committed murder or, depending on how long it takes the ambulance to arrive, the nature of the wound, and so on, attempted murder. In Scenario 3b, he has attempted murder and failed. Scenario 3b is an accidental survival, a "nonmurder" by accident, a moment akin to that of Sverdlik's birds (CML, 183), when murder almost happens but does not. And one could envision any number of further variations along the lines of moral luck or Austinian donkeys (PP, 133n), dead or alive: Bob takes aim to shoot to kill, only to have a spotlight fall on his hand and stop him before he pulls the trigger. Bob has a muscle spasm as he fires his gun, which causes the real bullet to hit the wall. Perhaps he has no muscle spasm but is simply a lousy shot, and instead of hitting George, he hits a lamp, or another player, or, as we shall hypothesize later, a member of the audience. In any or all of those cases, Bob is still a would-be or virtual killer, if not yet an actual killer; and his indisputable intent to kill has increased the odds that he will not misfire the next time (if there *is* a next time).

Nor need we cast Dick or Bob as criminals in these scenarios to convey the value of intentionality at the theater:

SCENARIO 4: We find Emily still in her loge—Dick isn't there—still watching Bob play the shooter and George play the victim. This time, after the sound of gunshots, George slumps over because he is really dying. What no one knows is that George is already dying of a terminal illness and that he wishes to do any or all of the following: bring attention to the disease; avoid a slow, painful death; go out with a bang. It is George who has switched the props gun for a real one. Emily does what?

Unlike some of his celebrated predecessors who allegedly died on stage due to natural causes—Mr. Bond during Voltaire's *Zaïre,* Mr. Palmer during *The Stranger,* Molière during the *Malade Imaginaire*[22]—George *wants to* die; and, as a member of the theatrical collective, he has plotted his own death intentionally, without the full knowledge of that collective. George's death in Scenario 4 looks like an accident for Bob, who intended to—and did—fire a fake gun; while for George, it is suicide by theater, not suicide by accident.[23] For Bob, theater is—or was?—still theater, while George has broken the theatrical contract as someone with both the standing (however improperly he uses it) and the opportunity to alter the company's collective intent. If the actors stop the show in its tracks once they realize that George is dead,[24] the play is still a play, but that particular performance is *no longer* theater (which, as we shall see in chapter 7, may also be so compromised from outside the collective). Or perhaps George has had some assistance from someone else:

SCENARIO 5: With Emily in the theater audience, Bob appears to shoot George, who is dying of pancreatic cancer. This time, it is another cast member, George's friend Irma, who has switched the guns in order to euthanize him. Whether George asked for her assistance or whether Irma provided it on her own will doubtless come out during the murder trial to follow, as it foists anew into the headlines the larger cultural debate about assisted suicide. What does Emily do now? And what if Irma were *not* a friend or a cast member but a crew- or audience member?

While in Scenario 4, George has committed suicide, in Scenario 5, his death appears to be an accident to everyone but Irma, for whom it is no accident. In an act unexpected by actors and audience alike, Irma has used her standing to alter the collective's intent, such that her primary intention (shared or unshared with George) is no longer to make theater but to produce an assisted suicide. In both scenarios, however, actors have engaged in what we shall call, in our next chapter, *theater nullification,* prompting this variation of our own opening question: If murder by accident is just as impossible as theater by accident, then can two wrongs make a right?

SCENARIO 6: Emily is still at the Broadway theater, where the props master, Steve, always does a fabulous job. He seems uncannily able to find just the right item, whatever the needs of the play. This particular play calls for an antique pistol to inflict the mortal wound, and Steve has found just the right one at Lillie's Antiques on East 77th St. The antique dealer, however, failed to mention to Steve—perhaps because she did not know—that the piece (for which Steve shelled out $650 on a tightly budgeted production) was not purely ornamental. Like our earlier weapon imagined by Knapp and Michaels, it was loaded.[25] Steve had meant to check it, but forgot one day, having turned his attention to a loud argument between Bob and George about the latter's affair with Bob's wife, Lydia. (George has been restored to excellent health in this scenario.) Accidentally, Steve has given Bob a loaded gun that discharges a real bullet when Bob fires it. Emily calls the police.

Theater itself has misfired here because the collective intent to represent, to perform, to play roles on stage has been compromised by a show-stopping, potentially life-stopping accident: a bona fide accident decipherable only post hoc but to which Bob, George, and Steve catch on immediately. The play has *not* come off as the imitation of life intended and rehearsed by everyone involved (*PP*, 225). Meanwhile, the directors and producers, terrified for their legal liability, are extremely happy that Emily has called the police and further realize that calling an ambulance is still more pressing. On stage, the other actors have surrounded George, and Bob is calling his attorney. So, too, is the properties master Steve, who suspects that he will soon find himself the object of a civil lawsuit for negligence. So, too, for that matter, will similar thoughts cross the mind of Lillie, once she reads about the gunshot wound in the paper: as the antique dealer, she should perforce have exercised a higher standard of care. Steve's legal defense will remind us, moreover, of Tallis's earlier point about chance and agency (*NS*, 233). There can be no doubt that Steve intended to pick up some gun or other as the properties master (while Bob merely took what Steve gave him); but the choice of that particular gun out of the many that he might have purchased for the play was left to chance. Lillie will have a much harder time when trying to rationalize her negligence for having sold a loaded gun. As for the cuckolded Bob, he had truly wished that George were dead, and he is even a little bit cheered by the prospect of his colleague dying. But he would never have shot him.

What about Steve? Would he have picked up the gun and taken aim?

SCENARIO 7: Emily is still at the theater. Steve is still an excellent props master who has procured the perfect gun; but this time, there was no negligent antique dealer in the picture. Steve is good with guns: he and his wife both have carry permits for their pistols (as both gave state's testimony last year against a convicted felon who has threatened them both). Steve has still overheard a number of heated arguments between Bob and George about Bob's wife, Lydia. As a result, he has not only wondered about the potential affair between George and Lydia, but has even come to suspect George of interest in his own wife, Sue. As he was preparing the props for tonight's performance, Steve became so distracted by those musings that he picked up his own loaded gun instead of the unloaded props gun and gave it to Bob. George is still bleeding, Emily is still calling the police, the producer is still calling an ambulance, and now Steve is calling his attorney.

Did Steve commit a lapsus? Scenario 7 seems neither intentional nor accidental since Steve wasn't even aware of having wished George dead. In an affective misfire, a piece of psychically immoral luck, he had no intention—and could not have had one—to enact that of which he is not even conscious. By analogy to our earlier case of ACTUAL INTENTIONS misunderstood by agents themselves,[26] it is almost impossible to identify Steve's true intentions and, consequently, the very nature of a misfire, of which there are many kinds, among them the possibility that, following our loaded gun analogy of chapter 1, someone *other than an actor* (or other member of the collective) enters the theatrical line of fire. In other words, what if Bob's loaded weapon were to hit Emily?

From ancient Greece onward, when a performance of the *Eumenides* allegedly struck children dead and when Lucian's mad Ajax dealt a fellow actor a blow to the head,[27] theater history has been replete with such incidents, in the form of both physical harm and affective assaults of innumerable kinds. Of the former, Larwood reports that a highly visible off-stage duel erupted in 1702 during a performance of *The Scornful Lady,* during which one gentleman "plunged his sword twelve inches" into his opponent. He also cites another account of a "real tragedy in the pit of Drury Lane Theatre, where Mr. Scrope received a mortal wound from Sir T. Armstrong, and died presently, after being removed to a house opposite the theatre" (*TA,* 50–51). Of the latter, we find it harder to gauge the "emotional distress" (akin to that of legal proceedings), in that those making theater often seek to promulgate just such distress, be it on the road to catharsis or not. But there was nothing ambiguous about another actor's alleged castigation *from the stage* of an unidentified nonpaying theatergoer. With a "vigilant eye [that] was cocked on the pit-entrance," he "instantly" forgot King Richard's situation in favor of his own, states Larwood, "and pointing at the offender, he exclaimed, 'That man in the grey coat came in without paying!'" (*TA,* 32–33).[28] That last personage in particular, having trespassed upon theatrical proceedings, assists us in moving (at long last, sigh some), from actor to spectator, to the pleasures and pains of a final group of scenarios in which theater becomes hazardous to its audiences.

SCENARIO 8: Emily is still nicely dressed and nicely seated in her loge as a member of a large audience at a Broadway theater. She still sees Bob, disguised as a gunman, enter stage left onto the restaurant set. Apparently in character, Bob opens fire, and bullets fly as George, truly in character, slumps over. What looks like bright red blood begins to trickle out of the left side of his mouth. But this time, something else has happened as well—*to Emily.* As he had once done behind the scenes of Scenario 3a, Bob, in a jealous rage, has substituted a real firearm for the one issued by Steve, which he has really fired and which has discharged a real bullet as he attempts to murder George. The blood is real; but since Bob is not a good shot, the blood that is flowing is not George's but Emily's. Emily is in no condition to applaud, to call the police, or to take any other course of action. She must rely on another Emily to do it for her.

In Scenario 8, Bob has misfired, rendering George lucky, Bob morally unlucky, and Emily plain out of luck; and, in a way, that scenario might serve as a variation on many of our previous scenarios. In the extratheatrical Scenario 1, for example, a stray bullet might have hit Emily while she dined at her favorite sushi place. In Scenario 4, George's attempt at suicide could have been foiled by Bob's bad shot, which ricocheted to hit Emily; or, in Scenario 5, so too could Irma have missed her shot. Emily might also have found herself in the theatrical line of fire of Scenarios 6 or 7, where both shots were accidental, the former due to Lillie's and Steve's negligence, the latter from Steve's lapsus. Only in two scenarios is Emily perfectly safe. In Scenario 3a, which depicts a murder successfully achieved by a felonious Bob, she is unhurt because she is not the intended victim. And in Scenario 2— *ordinary theatrical verisimilitude successfully achieved*—Emily watches a play, along with everyone else, from the normally safe distance of her seat. Only Scenario 2 is true to the theatrical contract, true to what theater is. None of the other events belong at the theater or *to the theater* at all. Especially not this one, in which a member of the theatrical collective *intentionally* inflicts physical harm upon a person or persons in the audience:

SCENARIO 9A: Emily is still in her loge as a theatrical scene of a restaurant shooting unfolds. Apparently in character, Bob opens fire upon George who, in character all the while, slumps over as what looks like bright red blood begins to trickle out of the left side of his mouth. But, this time, it is no accident that Emily finds herself in the line of fire. It turns out that Bob hates Emily: she is the best friend of Bob's wife, Lydia; and Emily has been encouraging Lydia to divorce Bob. The gun is loaded because, as in Scenario 8 (or 3a), Bob has loaded it himself with a real bullet; and, ill advised though it is to commit murder in the full view of anyone who paid enough money for a decent seat, Bob takes aim directly at Emily and shoots. The gentleman on her left applauds; the one behind her calls the police.

SCENARIO 9B: Bob has still switched the props gun from Steve with a real one. He still intends to kill Emily; he still discharges a real weapon, which he believes to contain a real bullet. As usual, George bites down on his blood packet and slumps over. But then . . . nothing. Emily is fine; and Bob's attempted murder misfires as the theater that it always should have been. Emily is free to do what she pleases: to applaud, to call the police, to find the realism lacking, and so on.

Scenario 9a rings true to anyone familiar with the assassination of President Abraham Lincoln at the theater. In Scenario 9b, Bob shoots to kill and misses the mark: he "legitimately" attempts to murder Emily and fails, causing, at least for him, an unlucky legitimacy (or is it a lucky illegitimacy?) that may be due to multiple causes: the gun does not go off; he hits Dick instead; an Austinian donkey wanders into the path of the speeding bullet. Or, perhaps, in one more twist that we have yet to hypothesize:

SCENARIO 9C: Bob has either committed—or attempted to commit—an *acte gratuit*, having sought not to kill Emily in particular but, like some character out of Malraux's *La Condition humaine*, to experience what killing is like. In another example of the cohabitation of chance and agency (*NS*, 233), Emily is no pebble next to a Wordsworthian lyric in the sand, but she *is* the random victim of Bob's experiment.

Regardless of whether Emily survives any of those last three events, her family may already be preparing a lawsuit. For his own part, the house manager may already be rushing to Emily's side with a release of liability for her to sign, this latter possibility bringing us about as close as we can get to that ill-fated performance of 1380 that took the life of Jehan Hemont.[29] (An analogous comparison to the *Théophile* of 1384, which took the life of Perrin Le Roux, would require Emily to have wandered into a theatrical production which she had never contracted to spectate in the first place— and to have failed to heed a warning.)

SCENARIO 10: Emily is still at the theater, where a play is unfolding exactly as planned by the collective in a "regular" performance in which imitations and simulations all take place expectedly and effectively. There are no accidents, no murder plots, and no one in the collective dies. There are only great performances of things that seem real enough for the spectators to suspend, as usual, their mostly collective disbelief and to accept that George's character—not George himself—is bleeding and dying. But Emily is not the sharpest pencil in the box. In this scenario, she really *is* a Cavellian yokel who misperceives the IMPLIED DECLARED INTENTION of theater (as described in chapter 4). During the simulation of gunfire, she is so shocked by what she believes to be a real murder that she has a heart attack and dies on the spot.[30]

Emily's survivors will sue; the respondents will argue that so naive an attendee is not "any reasonable person"; and Emily will join the apocryphal ranks of such terrified spectators as those who died at the *Eumenides* or those who allegedly fled the performance of a prophet play in 1204.[31] But is Emily really as silly as all that?

Not if we take heed of the widespread "generic confusion" between real and represented violence that is the hallmark of such events as the notorious 1938 radio dramatization of the *War of the Worlds,* the 1976 exploitation film *Snuff,* or NBC's made-for-TV Stephen King flick, *Storm of the Century,* which the network promoted by issuing "storm warnings" on the same video crawler that is customarily reserved for urgent weather bulletins.[32] What happens, moreover, if even naivete is regular?

SCENARIO 11: Emily is at the theater with her five-year-old daughter, Eloise. When the little girl sees the gunman opening fire on the set of the sushi place, bullets flying, and bright red blood trickling out of the left side of the victim's mouth, she is frightened beyond all measure and she screams bloody murder, despite Mommy's assurance that "it's just make-believe." (Unfortunately, Emily has not read *Must We Mean What We Say?* so she is unaware of Cavell's statement that "if the child cannot be brought out of the play by working through the content of the play itself, [s]he should not have been subjected to it in the first place" [329].) Traumatized, Eloise will have nightmares for years and Emily will pay for a decade of therapy. In the meantime, Eloise refuses to enter a restaurant. It will take years before she ever tries sushi.

As was the case in chapters 1 and 2, the legal issues are numerous. Today, one need only recall the long list of official warnings issued to audiences of theater and film that concern both emotional harm—Is the material suitable for children?[33]—and physical harm: Have the epileptic patrons received due notice about the production's use of seizure-triggering strobe lights? Have those who are (or who are not) prone to cardiac arrhythmia been alerted to the use of (simulated) gunfire (with blanks)? All such warnings amply confirm that theater is not above the law; and those spectators who proceed despite such warnings have a tougher legal road ahead of them, be it in a modern civil tort case in which the complainant argues that a warning sign was improperly displayed, or a fourteenth-century plea for royal forgiveness such as that of Fremin Severin, who had served the wretched Perrin Le Roux with due legal notice. Thus, in Scenario 11, Emily could sue, outraged that no kind of parental warning had been issued; then again, if the play had been *Assassins,* she would probably be out of luck. The attorney for the respondent will brand her a negligent parent and agree with Cavell.

Finally, we may also conceive a scenario that is slightly more plausible than all of our recent deadly sightings and sitings of Emily, and one in which Bob is not as stupid as he is in Scenario 11. Here, under cover of theater, his is primarily a murderer, not an actor, who feigns *a murder by accident which is not one:*

SCENARIO 12: Bob's gun is still loaded, and he still intends to kill. But when the time comes for the shooting scene, he feigns a misfire into the audience when "what is really going on" is that he is aiming at, and firing directly upon, Emily. He can display his ersatz intention[34] in any number of ways: pretending to have a muscle spasm, orchestrating a falling spotlight, and so on. But Emily's wound is no pretense. She is presently suffering from a gunshot wound that looks like the result of an accident which was *not* an accident.

In this pretense of a misfire in which Bob does exactly what he intends, our imaginary character brings us full circle to Baudrillard's classic simulation scenario as well as to Eco's theory of pretense, as when the latter imagines this possibility: Emitter A arranges for Addressee B to attribute a specific intention to A which is not, in point of fact, A's actual intention (ID, 105–7). A theatrical incarnation of the famous paradox of the liar who says "I am lying," Scenario 12 also illustrates Eco's double-pretense or Gregory Bateson's argument that "individuals can *intentionally produce framing confusion* in those with whom they are dealing," here doubly invisible in the *appearance of a misfire*.[35] Nor is there any need to dream up a Scenario 13 because real life readily provides more than enough scenarios in many theatrical and extratheatrical venues.

At around midnight on 17 April 2006, three roommates experienced the ultimate simulation when, in my own community, four Santa Barbara City College students "staged a home invasion robbery in Goleta as a prank—complete with masks and a realistic-looking fake gun." As if emerging from the pages of Baudrillard, they launched their "little prank" because "it sounded like fun at the time."[36] They quickly learned that even a harmless weapon in a "fake hold up . . . won't succeed: the web of artificial signs will be inextricably mixed up with real elements" (*SW*, 178). Mixed up they were. The students faced criminal charges because "the mock invasion . . . was so real that one woman who was in another room frantically dialed 911 when she heard her roommate say: 'Oh, my God, he's got a gun!'" Meanwhile, instead of Baudrillard's police officer who "will really shoot on sight," there were sheriff's deputies who, having just responded to a prior home invasion in the area, took the matter all the more seriously by "speeding to the residence with flashing lights and sirens in response to what they thought was a home invasion robbery in progress." Of the simulated home invasion and alleged prank, one of the roommates later reported that "the electricity went out. Four men rushed in, shining a bright light in [her] face":

> "One with a mask had a gun and was pointing it at me and saying, like, 'Who else is in the house?' and swearing and telling me not to move," said

Ms. Hobson, who said later that she knew two of the men but could not see their faces in the dark.

"They were telling me not to move, and I was just so scared . . . The other girls could see through the mirror what was going on and called 911. He kept the gun on me. Our roommate, Ernie, this really big guy, heard something going on and came out. The guy said not to move and to sit on the couch. I was shaking really bad and starting crying, and that's when they stopped."

The intruders took off their masks, announced to the four women and one man that the invasion was a joke, then fled before sheriff's deputies arrived.

As we asked earlier of Baudrillard's own elision of intent from both his imaginary theft at the department store and his imaginary hostage crisis, shouldn't the intruders have *foreseen* the roommates' response? Shouldn't they have anticipated such consequences as these? "One woman sleeps with the lights on, and each carries the bat to answer the door. The slightest noise at night startles them."[37] The intruders thus faced charges of "conspiracy, false imprisonment, *brandishing an imitation firearm,* unlawful entry into a residence, and interfering with a residential electrical current" (my emphasis). They also received a stern lecture from the deputies, who explained that, had the gang of four "lifted the real-looking gun toward them, the officers would have been legally justified in opening fire, not knowing it was a fake weapon."

Pranks are played—and staged—for (or against) someone; and the whole point is presumably the victim's real, not fake, reaction to the deceptive appearance of a verisimilar reality for which he or she never contracted. There is nothing "theatrical" about that. If the primary role of theater were to test the limits of simulation, then it would be—indeed, we shall see that, when taken to extremes, *it has been*—the moral equivalent of the infamous Milgram experiments. In a chilling portrait of both intention and moral luck, Stanley Milgram sought, beginning in 1961, to get to the bottom of how, among many other things, obedience to authority had led to the Holocaust. He presented to a group of student-volunteers a fiction of learning and retribution that was no fiction at all to some of the participants. Those in the role of "teachers" thought that they were administering electric shocks to other student-volunteers when the latter failed to answer questions correctly on several simple learning tasks. The "learners," however, were played by actors, while the "teachers" truly believed that they were disciplining their charges with punishments ranging from 45 to 450 volts of electricity. Thankfully, there was no electrical current delivered—but the "teachers" *thought* that there was.

The teachers were morally "lucky" in that their ersatz victims did not experience physical harm, even as the "teachers" were haunted for decades to come by what they had learned about themselves from having done what they had not done.[38]

Baudrillard might well have urged would-be simulators, in his hostage and holdup scenarios, to "stay close to the 'truth,' so as to test the reaction of the apparatus to a perfect simulation" (*SW*, 178). But experimental theater does not mean Milgram experiment.

7 / Theater Nullification

> I have no right to jeopardise life, nor to take away the other's
> right to death—but to recognise that, in the absence of critical
> thought, dangers arise from unforeseen corners and jeopardise
> both life and theatre.
>
> ALAN READ, *Theatre and Everyday Life*

On 15 July 2005, in Santa Barbara, a performance in progress of *The Beard of Avon* was rudely interrupted when, reports Barney
Brantingham, "real life drama burst into the theater." A thirteen-year-old
boy evading the police "dashed into the darkened Garvin Theatre on Friday
night, no doubt shocked to find himself with an audience of hundreds," after which "flashlight-waving officers gave chase."[1] "It had a Keystone Kops
air to it," Brantingham continues, "so at first we thought it was part of the
zany play." Was it? Or was it for real? Was it a prank of the sort that has
long graced theater history, elaborately staged by one of the actors?[2] Would
everyone at the theater continue what they were doing (or not doing)? Or
would they do something else? Would they intercept one or both of the ongoing activities—*The Beard* and the police pursuit? What *is* the role of the
audience in the social contract that is theater? How do spectators think they
should respond to theatrical events, and why?[3]

While the presence of an audience is not a sine qua non of theater, once
spectators are indeed present, we are dealing with the integrity, even the
politics, of a theatrical contract that is all too vulnerable from the outset to
violations, breakages, or delicts (*FA,* 346)—not only from those who have
consented to the contract but from those who have not.[4] In this chapter, we
explore intentionality at the theater as related to individuals who disrupt
theater, who break its frame, who manage—accidentally or on purpose—to
cause it to misfire, compromising (temporarily or permanently) a collective's primary intention to put on a theatrical performance.

Goffman does not invoke the audience as a party to the theatrical contract per se, but he implies just such a contract when paraphrasing legal
"consideration" in this way: "The *central understanding* is that the audience has *neither the right nor the obligation* to participate directly in the dra-

matic action occurring on the stage, although it may express appreciation throughout in a manner that can be treated as not occurring by the beings which the stage performers present onstage" (*FA,* 125; my emphasis). Audiences implicitly ratify that understanding, moreover, in the spectatorial version of IMPLIED DECLARED INTENTION, if from nothing other than the purchase of a ticket (which has come increasingly to constitute a waiver of certain liabilities). At the theater, they implicitly declare their intentions to do—and not to do—what Goffman mentions. They commit to a certain *inaction,* to the *absence of certain activities:* to sit still and, as so many *poleis* and municipalities have put it from Plato onward, to "shut up."[5] By the same token, any spectator who objects to any or all of the provisions of the theatrical contract, any individual either unwilling or unable to keep the provisions (as in the case of the Tourette's sufferer) should probably not attend the theater. As if seated in the exit-row of a contemporary airplane, at a minimum, he or she should announce that unwillingness or inability to meet the usual requirements, which Goffman goes on to characterize thus: the audience "responds indirectly, glancingly, following alongside, as it were, *cheering on but not intercepting*" (*FA,* 127; my emphasis).

What happens, though, when Goffman's "cheering on" really *should be* interception, and interception cheering on? What if the theatrical misfire occurs not because of some natural disaster like an earthquake, not because of a technical manager's negligent failure to check the shaky spotlight that tumbles to the ground, and not even because of the alterations deliberately wrought to a company's theatrical intentions by our protagonists of chapter 6? What if the misfire, the breakage, or the interception comes *from the audience*? Can audience members reject the rules of the theatrical game in the same way that contemporary juries reject the rule of law by substituting their own take on what laws and contracts *should be*? Is there such a thing as *theater nullification*? This chapter is devoted to the affirmative answer to that question.

As we shall see, when individuals who have voluntarily committed to spectatorship both perceive irregularities (correctly or incorrectly) and *do something about them,* they create irregularities of their own: breakages that are accidental or deliberate, welcome or unwelcome, and necessary or unnecessary.[6] So, too, in ways that must be disambiguated, do those who have little or nothing to do with theater at all. In either case, it is well worth emphasizing that such things happen only in live media like theater, which hosts thoughts, words, and *acts* in progress. Censorship can stop the proverbial presses ad hoc, such that a novel is never published or an art exhibit never sees the light of day; or post hoc, authorities or publishers can pull a book off the shelves. One can also break the frame of a painting, during which the art "inside" might or might not be destroyed. And, as noted earlier, modern editors "interrupt," through textual editing, a manuscript that might already have been interrupted. But physical artifacts are not (or are no longer) acts in progress. Let us return, then, to our opening conundrum of *The Beard of Avon:*

Fleeing the police was still a crime, the Garvin was still the Garvin, and the play was still a play, especially since the actors did not stop the show (with promises of refunds or reticketing). Instead, the show went on, however awkwardly: "Actors kept reciting their lines, in subdued fashion. But police soon collared the teen." In fact, Irwin Appel, playing the lead, later explained that, while it was clear from upstage that something was going on, he could not tell what that was: "It's funny, I'm a strange person to talk to about this because I was on stage, as you mentioned, at the time, up on a balcony far upstage, playing my great death scene! I only know what people told me—I couldn't see anything or tell what was going on. But it was the most bizarre thing that has happened to me on stage."[7] Elsewhere on the scene, the police had an opportunity to stop the show and did not; and the lad himself had a choice between stopping and continuing—that is, as soon as he figured out that he was at the theater. So, too, did the spectators have a choice about revising their own observance of the contract by intercepting, not cheering (*FA,* 127). At the beginning of the soirée, they might well have "willingly sought out the circumstances in which [they] could be temporarily deceived or a least kept in the dark, in brief, transformed into collaborators in unreality" (*FA,* 136); but once the fog of mimetic blindness had lifted, were they to be crime-stoppers or play-stoppers—both or neither?[8]

In normal accordance with the "interlocking obligations" of social life (*FA,* 346), audience members should not stop theater in progress; but if they can, they should indeed, or might want to, stop assault or murder in progress because those things are illegal and wrong. In most jurisdictions, moreover, and despite avant-gardist pretensions to the contrary, actors cannot assault, rape, murder, inject heroin, distribute LSD, or commit other felonies or misdemeanors during theatrical productions that are subject to the laws of the land.[9] Therefore, in the face of intentional acts of violence that are illegal, unethical, or morally unwatchable, spectators are in a position to do considerably more than ponder, under the rubric of PERCEIVED IN-TENTION, what thoughts, feelings, and intentions the theatrical collective attributes to *them.* Regardless of the usual power of a theatrical contract to block both thespian violence and audience interception—to the point of immobilizing Pywell himself in the face of the RATT assault (*SRT,* 22), to the point that Cavell once mused that "the first task of the dramatist is to gather us and then to silence and immobilize us" (*MWM*, 326)—they must *do something about* them. To act or not to act? That is the question, as spectators proceed to exhibit behaviors that are appropriate or inappropriate.

Naturally, on the spectatorial side of the theatrical contract, individual audience members have interpretations and decisions of their own to make about characters, actors, and those behind the scenes. True, they ponder what characters on stage mean to do as fictive or historical intending subjects. And it seems fair to say that, unless the acting is truly awful or unless spectators are "in the business," those fictive aspects of character(s) tend to be their primary consideration; spectators' thoughts will wander to directors and producers if and when the play is working either so exceptionally well or so exceptionally poorly that the situation warrants the identification of either the proper recipients of praise or the scapegoats for all manner of outrage. But spectators also decipher—however subtly, subconsciously, ephemerally—what the various agents and actants involved in a theatrical performance intend to do (playwright[s], actors, producers, directors, and eventually, even other audience members who are responding). That is, spectators regularly ask themselves questions about ACTUAL and ACHIEVED INTENTIONS (to which I have previously alluded): "Is this supposed to be happening?" "Is what I'm looking at a representation?" "Although no one declared it explicitly, wasn't this *supposed to be* a representation and not an assault?" At the theater, all such questions come down to this: "Is this an actor who intends to represent?" (ACTUAL INTENTIONS). "Is this an intentional representation misachieved?" (ACHIEVED INTENTIONS dependent on ACTUAL INTENTIONS). As we have already seen, their PERCEIVED INTENTIONS depend on their individual abilities to distinguish between illusion and reality, pretense and so-called natural behavior, bad acting and good acting, and so on.

In all those respects, Goffman's "central understanding" usually stands until something (like an earthquake) or someone (like a murderer) demands that it be revised: that is, when something or someone makes known to audience members, explicitly or implicitly, that their generally appropriate conduct—which is based on their generally correct perception of a collective's ACTUAL INTENTIONS (PERCEIVED INTENTIONS)—is no longer appropriate, be it to art or to life. The reintroduction at this stage, from the standpoint of the audience, of spectators' own implied declarations about their PERCEIVED INTENTIONS permits the resolution of several tenacious problems. At the same time, it leads to a new challenge: the assessment of how one set of PERCEIVED INTENTIONS (such as the actors') is itself perceived by an audience; and how an audience's own IMPLIED DECLARED INTENTIONS are themselves perceived by a theater collective. Such perceptions sometimes lead to acts that are initially *unexpected* by all parties—and by that I mean acts that no one expected either from others or from themselves. That dialectic in action, which we first glimpsed in the case of Henry D'Anoux, demonstrates that audience perceptions and misperceptions have a cyclical life of their own. They lead to what individual spectators do (or fail to do) based on what they see (or do not see)—which, in turn, suggests an awareness of their own ACTUAL INTENTIONS and, eventually, their own ACHIEVED INTENTIONS (which they too may announce—ad hoc, in medias res, and post hoc[10]—as DECLARED INTENTIONS). Asks the spectator who is trying to determine what is unfolding: "Does this actor intend to affect the audience with real, make-believe, or simulated behavior?" But then, "I think that that actress is in danger: What will happen if I rush the stage to save (the actress playing) Desdemona?"[11] But it also introduces a final piece to the puzzle of theatrical intentions that we are about to see in action.

Spectators, we have seen, also make judgments, especially during the notoriously violent events that have preoccupied us throughout, about the intentions that a theater collective *has apparently attributed to them.* For example, a theatergoer wonders: "Did the director think that I would want to see that?" or "What does that director think of me (or of spectators in general) to attribute such desires to me?"[12] But beyond that lies another question about what we called those ATTRIBUTED PERCEIVED INTENTIONS: "What intentions and sensibilities do I now attribute to the director, given my perception of the intentions that that director attributes to me?" It is a question that spectators tend to pose in moments of outrage regarding contrary-to-fact conditions (or alleged such conditions): "Those are not my desires," "Those are not my sensibilities," "I did not/do not/would not/will not want to see that." And the outrage may itself be a response, at least in part, to such ATTRIBUTED PERCEIVED INTENTIONS.

Imagine now, for instance, that in Bar-le-Duc in 1485, a voyeur is spying on the man in his devil-suit raping his wife and does not come to her aid. Imagine that a dancer in 1504 mistakes the grimaces of the *Grand Turdion* for an actual epidemic of plague and that he sends for a surgeon—*before* Henry D'Anoux even needs one. Or imagine that such a spectator *does not* send for a surgeon once it is clear that Henry is dying. From the standpoint of the spectator, we ought to be able to exclude from aesthetic consideration those who attend a performance thinking, secretly (or openly), something like this: "I am attending the theater because I hope to see someone die in real time." On one hand, I have argued that the sociability of the theatrical contract is so ingrained in Western culture, its legal integrity so powerful that even when an intervention into theater is the deliberate act of a non–audience member, a host of mitigating factors crop up (from the peanut gallery?) to suggest that even what is deliberate is really accidental: that person *didn't mean to do it;* the interruption is explainable, excusable. On the other hand, and more provocatively, such considerations demand that we assess whether interruptions (and consequential interceptions) can be artistic or desirable.

Our own critical stage has been set by the events of the Garvin, which provides yet another example of Tallis's observations about chance and agency (*NS,* 234): the juvenile in question intended to evade police, but in all likelihood, his "choice" of that particular locale as an escape route was happenstance. Even so, in the eyes of others, that choice transformed him into an actant who, as possibly perceived *actor,* was/might have been playing the unpredictable and unpredicted dénouement of a very different drama: a police chase at the theater. On that summer evening, an alleged criminal also transformed, quite unintentionally, a play in progress into police work in progress. In so doing, he issued unintentionally something that often functions intentionally: a *demand.*[13] In this case, it is a demand that theatergoers suspend their suspended disbelief, that they believe not in unreality and verisimilitude but in an ongoing reality, which, in a true coincidence,[14] required them to do (in the presence of police work) exactly what they do at the theater: sit or stand back quietly and without interference while the legal agents/actors do their jobs.

So it was that a young alleged criminal, who was a member of neither the theatrical collective nor the audience, accidentally hijacked *The Beard of Avon,* interfering (at least temporarily) with the actors' intent to perform and the audience's intent to spectate. He broke their theatrical frame, and he compromised an entity to which, as had once been the case for Perrin Le Roux in 1384, *he was not even a party:* the theatrical contract. Given that the gaze of an audience has been an ontological—even philological—component of the earliest definitions of theater,[15] we probe here several concluding critical questions about audience intentionality in the production not just of meaning but of meaningful action. If theater can be stopped, then by whom? Is it possible to break or to nullify someone else's contract? Law courts do it all the time, of course, in a wide range of rulings, from annulling marriages to voiding agreements that are against public policy. But is such a thing possible at the theater?

The events of the Garvin further complicate matters in that, while police officers do indeed possess the authority and standing to vacate or displace artistic practice by stopping a show, on 15 June 2005 they were not even aware (at least initially) that that was what they were doing. Meanwhile, the juvenile had no standing to break such a contract, despite inciting a re-vision (or re-vision) of it for spectators who had two things to go on. On one hand, it was exigent that spectators discern correctly the meaning of an officer's cry of "Halt!"—*if* the officer said it and if, unlike Appel, they actually *heard* it. On the other hand, they relied on their "central under-standing" of their rights and "interlocking obligations" in such a way as to ascertain—much as the dancers present at Henry D'Anoux's deadly *tor-dion* of 1504 had once done in the twinkling of an eye—the ACTUAL and ACHIEVED INTENTIONS of all present. The events at *The Beard* happened in rapid fire and threatened no one's life—although they *could have,* had the police drawn their weapons—and, for all we know, the young offender's life might never have been the same again after a stay in Juvenile Hall. But what was *supposed to happen*? That is another way of asking: What did those in the theater collective intend to do or *intend to have happen*?—to the extent that one can intend or will, rather than hope or wish, that someone else will do, think, or feel something.

Thus, we consider six final cases, peering through a distorted glass darkly at what Goffman calls the "ordinary troubles" of frame analysis (*FA,* chap. 9), only to see that there is nothing so ordinary about them. From obstreperous Cavellian yokels and airborne tomatoes at La Scala; to invited interventions at *The Mystery of Edwin Drood, Shear Madness,* or the Living Theatre; to the deliberate intervention into art in progress by spectators and nonspectators: such "theater trouble" offers fascinating glimpses into an artistic agency that solicits further agency from any and all present. How, when, and why do audiences and extratheatrical beings come to act or not to act, with or without respect to a theatrical contract? On what basis do theater audiences deem that the unexpected if "ordinary troubles" of that art are sufficient to prompt their reassessment, renewal, or rejection of the theatrical contract?[16] How stable is that contract, anyway, if the occasional piece of drama demands that it be reratified minute by minute ... by min-ute?[17] The contractual answer tends to be as simple as the experiential an-swer is complex.

Just as it behooved us, in our Introduction, to distinguish among four fundamental ways of committing acts, similar distinctions are in order for an almost infinite number of ways of bearing witness to acts. Again, mak-ing no apologies for the appearance of legalese, I present here six final cases (some requiring more explanation than others) that are often mistakenly conflated in the secondary literature. When it comes to the creation of real, actionable behaviors during a theatrical representation, it is essential to determine whether someone (with or without the proper standing to affect the performance) has violated the representation scenario expected by the majority of parties (actors, producers, stagehands, and spectators alike). Each case facilitates a reconsideration of the terminology we use to speak of such acts as *intervention, interception, interruption, disruption, interference, intrusion,* and Goffman's signature *breakage,* all characterized philologically by both intentionality and degrees of violence.[18] Above all, the six cases together show that, due to the ever variable intentions of parties "within" and "without" a given spectacle, there is no such thing as an unbreakable, tamper-proof, or accident-proof theater.[19]

In our first two cases, we explore accidental vs. deliberate disruptions of theater by individuals who are members of neither the audience nor the theatrical collective and whose involvement in the activities of the stage is always "uninvited" by that collective (regardless of whether such intruders, or avant-gardists, invited *themselves*). Indeed, the concept of the *invitation* proves a particularly useful way of speaking about the *intent to have others do something.* Case 1, exemplified by *The Beard of Avon,* represents the ACCIDENTAL breakage of theater by a NONAUDIENCE member (or members); while Case 2 refers to a DELIBERATE breakage by such NONAUDIENCE members (of which history provides a long list of comic, tragic, and even terroristic instances).

Next, we review in Case 3 the mythic phenomenon of divine and not-so-divine interventions into theater by entities who seem to be neither AUDIENCE MEMBERS nor NONAUDIENCE member(s). Case 3 is not limited to the actors who have long been audience members themselves, from ancient Rome to Kabuki to the theater manager Tate Wilkinson's practice of retaliating against any actor who defied his advice by "mount[ing] some night into the gallery and hiss[ing] him most strenuously" (*TA,* 42).[20] Case 3 also includes "interventions" by such protagonists as God, the Devil, Death (as the dancers at Jedburgh Abbey met him in 1285), or Providence (à la Witmore or Hamilton).[21] Even as eternal players of life, such personages did not usually attend life's theaters, thereby raising cultural and historical questions as to what it truly means even to *be* a member of a theater audience.

Afterward, we address the complex disruptions that originate with actual members of a theater audience in the form of verbal and nonverbal interjections (laughter, applause, boos, and hisses) as well as physical ones (rushing the stage). Each case problematizes the extent to which such interventions are deliberate or accidental, appropriate or inappropriate, invited or uninvited, and welcome or unwelcome by those with the standing to invite or to welcome them in the first place. At the same time, each case also problematizes the extent to which those disruptions may (or may not) demand immediate action and reaction: Are the so-called disruptions not just aesthetically but legally, morally, or ethically necessary (or unnecessary)? In Case 4, we turn to the ACCIDENTAL breakage of theater by one or more AUDIENCE member(s), whether that breakage is verbal, nonverbal, or physical. Case 4 ultimately suggests some fruitful distinctions between *accidental* and *involuntary* breakage; and it may even prompt the curious phenomenon of the accident that leads to other accidents or, more intriguing still, *the accident that becomes deliberate* (or seems to) when an actant revises his or her intentions based on that accident. Case 5 treats a type of audience intervention or breakage that seems neither ACCIDENTAL nor DELIBERATE and which, depending on its timing, may be welcome or unwelcome, invited or uninvited: phenomena like laughter and tears.[22]

Last, we explore in Case 6, which is complicated enough to warrant subdivision, the bona fide (or bad faith) deliberate interventions into theater by a person or persons in the audience, including, conversely to Case 5, *the deliberate intervention that turns into an accident.* Case 6A is devoted to the DELIBERATE breakage of theater (by a member or members of the AUDIENCE), which is both welcome and INVITED, directly or indirectly.[23] This case reframes the very nature of the "interruption," which, once invited, welcome, and more or less controlled, is no longer an interruption at all and should rather be designated "participation." Indeed, the "invited interruption" is just as oxymoronic on its own terms—if not nearly as dangerous—as the murder by accident, the accidental theater, or the accidental contract. Case 6B, however, requires that we return one last time to the disturbing events of the RATT assault (*SRT,* chap. 1). It concerns AUDIENCE members who break the theatrical frame by getting into the act in ways that may be uninvited, unwelcome, and often out of control.

In all these cases, our task is to comprehend what everyone on both sides of a variety of ever shifting theatrical lines in the sand intends to do—or not to do. And when all is said and done, it is intention, that fallacy which is not one, that sheds the greatest light on the sociability, antisociability, and, sometimes, asociability of theater, life, and death.

Our imaginary cast of characters from Chapter 6 has left the stage; we no longer need Bob or George, and, with the exception of several cameos to come, we no longer need Emily. That is because premodern manuscripts, early modern theatrical anecdote books, modern newspapers, and postmodern philosophy are positively exploding with case studies that depict the kaleidoscopic nature of audiences' correctly or incorrectly PERCEIVED INTENTIONS and, more precisely, how they declare them implicitly (IMPLIED DECLARED INTENTIONS) by their actions and inaction.

CASE 1: ACCIDENTAL Breakage of Theater
by a NONAUDIENCE Member (or Members)

As confirmed by the events that led to Fremin Severin's letter of remission of 1384 and to *The Beard of Avon* of 2005, an individual who has nothing to do with an existing theatrical contract (between theatrical collectives and their audiences) can disrupt a play in progress which he or she has never committed to attend in the first place. No proverbially reasonable person could have expected the police chase at the Garvin as part of the price of admission; nor could any reasonable medieval participant in the rehearsal of the *Miracle of Théophile* have expected a bystander like Perrin Le Roux to be killed while walking (inattentively? recklessly?) near the special effects . . . unless, of course, that reasonable person had heard about the unfortunate demise of Jehan Hemont four years earlier in Paris. In 2005, the show went on; in 1384, the rehearsal presumably did not, as those present dropped theatrical measures for life-saving ones. But in such cases, someone from the so-called "outside," who is engaged in another activity, does not intend to break the theatrical frame or to break into theater at all: as opposed to the other alleged critical coincidences cited earlier,[24] it just turns out that way.

Audiences, moreover, are pleasantly or unpleasantly, legitimately or illegitimately surprised by such interventional accidents.[25] Although theater scholars rightly attend to audiences who expect to, who contract to, who intend to see a play—and not to those who merely happen by it—cases such as these demonstrate that audiences themselves must occasionally focus on the accident that intervenes. The nature and degree of welcome or unwelcome interruptions govern whether or not theater should stop. Imagine, for instance, that the policemen had opened fire and wounded the fleeing youth at *The Beard of Avon,* or that a stray bullet had wounded a spectator, but that the show went on when ethics and morality dictate that it should not.

CASE 2: DELIBERATE Breakage of Theater
by a NONAUDIENCE Member (or Members)

Individuals who are not members of a theater audience can and do interrupt that art in progress, whether amusingly and artistically, or shockingly and inartistically; and their extra-artistic interruptions provoke questions about the civil liberties of those doing the interrupting, as well as about the proper sphere of artistic control. Of the countless possibilities, I analyze here only a few; the rest is journalism, apocrypha, or the avant-garde.

Consider a French incident of 17 August 1539, which offers an intriguing counterpoint to *The Beard of Avon*. This time, a policeman allegedly burst onto the scene of the *Play of Saint Barbara*—with full knowledge afore-thought that it was a play that he was interrupting. He was attempting to arrest the thieving Montléon brothers who, in a nice piece of type-casting, were playing devils on stage. The officer in question was not making the-ater: he was making an arrest, and his disruption resulted in a hot pursuit.[26] Or consider that, sometime in the eighteenth century, the mad English ac-tress, Mrs. Montford, is said to have escaped from the sanatorium where she resided and stolen her way to the theater. She purportedly arrived there in time to upstage the actress playing Ophelia by beating her to the character's entrance in Act 4.5 and providing, along the way, a pertinent illustration of the mitigation of intention by madness (*TA*, 54–55).[27] And in 1880, reports Larwood, "a madman armed with a hatchet made his way on to the stage of the Teatro del Circo, at Madrid." He proceeded to kill an attendant, failed to respond to blank warning shots, and was ultimately killed himself when soldiers reloaded with real ammunition, after which "the audience returned to the places they had quitted in terror, and the performances were resumed at the point at which they had been interrupted by this little episode" (*TA*, 284). In contemporary life, one need look no further than such a terrifying incident as the Moscow theater hostage crisis of 23 October 2002, when a group of forty-two armed Chechen separatists seized control of a crowded theater during Act II of a sold-out performance of *Nord-Ost* at the House of Culture, demanding the withdrawal of Russian forces from Chechnya in exchange for over nine hundred hostages. On the third day of their siege, state troops gassed the theater, allegedly killing the vast majority of the ter-rorists along with, officially, 129 of the approximately 850 hostages, the lat-ter including members of both the theater collective and the audience.[28]

These examples represent more than an uninvited, unwelcome break-age that drains the magic circle of its magic and "wipes the make-believe away" (*FA*, 131). They illuminate both the limitations of Black's belief that one can "do murder beautifully" and the sinister theatricality of terrorism itself.[29] They also explain why, despite what would have been a lovely aes-thetic symmetry, I have not subdivided Case 2 into the invited vs. uninvited interruptions from "official" audience members, which we consider below in Cases 6a and 6b. For one thing, I contend that an "invited interruption" is not one; for another, even if extraspectatorial breakage is indeed "intended" *by the collective*—that is, even if the collective hopes for, wills, and does everything it can to bring about such breakage-which-is-not-one-because-invited from people who are *not* members of the audience (like inciting them to riot)—it is important to acknowledge the following: Whatever the nature of their commitment to making a spectacle of themselves and of others, those nonmembers do not themselves intend primarily to attend theater as audience members per se. And if they *do* intend to do so, if they have such a prior agenda, then they are not non–audience members but audience members. If they have no such intentions, then they cannot be considered good-faith parties to the theatrical contract.

CASE 3: (DELIBERATE) Breakage by a Spectator who is neither a Member nor a Nonmember of the AUDIENCE

Theater history is replete with mythic tales of divine intervention into theater by personages who are neither members nor "nonmembers" of the audience; helpful in that respect is Witmore's observation that "accidents constituted a recognizable subgroup of contingent events for which any foreseeable natural or human cause was lacking, but which were not miraculous either" (*CA*, 22). More familiar is the curious ontological status, invoked earlier, of actors in the audience; less familiar are our current protagonists: a literal deus ex machina, Death, and the Devil. In theory, and for the sake of symmetry, it might have been logical to divide Case 3 into accidental vs. deliberate interventions; but that would have been illogical in practice. The reality of this particular unreality (to all but true believers) is that the acts of God, Death, and the Devil are never accidental:[30] in accordance with a deistic world view, such personages are always watching, always players in terrestrial life.[31] In that sense, they also underscore the importance of an intentional universe in which men and women are merely players on a divine stage that is monitored by those ever beyond our imaginative reach, our legal system itself merely another endless rehearsal of how to get to the bottom of it all. It is a world of human interaction that religion explains by substituting, for randomness, a master plan, a divine causality, a deliberateness to everything that happens in this mortal coil.[32]

Among the more celebrated stories of the deliberate interception of theater by such actants (who are neither cross-examined about their motives nor needful of letters of remission) are these. Much as Death once appeared at Jedburgh Abbey in 1285, the Devil himself—that master of simulation—was a frequent and unwelcome (if intentional and artful) cast member or attendee of such plays as *Doctor Faustus,* allegedly appearing when summoned.[33] In 1547, a more agreeable interception was said to have been wrought by none other than God the Father, who purportedly took enough interest in a Valenciennes Passion play that He reprised, during the relevant scene, the miracle of the loaves and the fishes.[34] In contrast to Cases 5 and 6, the welcome vs. unwelcome nature of such interventions is character-driven for those who believe: diabolical and deathly interruptions are unwelcome, while divine interventions are most welcome (even if their ultimate and beneficent coherence to a divine plan escapes our grasp), nowhere more conspicuously than in this *pièce de résistance* from across the Channel in Beverley:

In or around the year 1220, during a graveyard performance of the *Resurrection of Our Lord,* a group of boys ascended the steps of the church, "intending, as I suppose, to see more easily." When church personnel gave chase, one of the boys mis-stepped and fell to the ground as he fled, where he lay "for some considerable time senseless and apparently dead" until God himself arranged to turn sorrow into joy and "lamentation into laughter." He did so in a theatrical feat of overrepresentation that began with the boy's "imitating Zaccheus who because he was of very small stature climbed a sycamore tree in order to see Jesus" and that culminated in an imitation so "distinctly like" the object of imitation that it *was* that thing: "[W]ishing to bear witness to the truth which was at the same time being shown in the representation of His Resurrection . . . [God] raised the apparently dead boy, so completely unharmed that no injury was to be seen anywhere on his body. And so it was brought about that those who, because of the crowds of people, could not be present at the representation outside the church, were able to see a miraculous token of the Resurrection inside the nave."[35] From the sublime to the silly, the nebulous status of the spectator-who-is-not-one is hardly limited to the divine or diabolical.

CASE 4: ACCIDENTAL Breakage of Theater
by an AUDIENCE Member (or Members)

On 5 February 1413, about halfway through a performance of the *Life of Saint Dorothy* (in Bautzen, Germany), several theatergoers, like our Zaccheus clone, also wanted a better view of the play; and, thanks to their "disobedience and imprudence," they "climbed onto the roof in front of the *Kaufhaus*" to get it. The result? A wall collapsed, "crushing many people of both sexes, so that 33 persons died that day and night."[36] Such breakage need not be violent, however; and virtually every theatergoer has a favorite Case 4, when there occurs, *in the audience,* an accident that is either excusable or inexcusable: something that the company has not intended, not invited, and does not welcome. Nor, for that matter, does the audience.

In my own case, it was a Broadway performance of *The Elephant Man* in the early 1980s, during which we were all suffering through the first act—not because there was anything wrong with the play or the performance, but because there was an ongoing auditory assault by a high-pitched ringing. Finally, the stage manager walked onto the stage, stopping the actors dead in their tracks, so that he could make an announcement to this effect: the technical team had conducted every conceivable test of their equipment and had come to the only possible conclusion. The sound could only have been emanating from a malfunctioning hearing aid issuing a dead battery signal and worn by someone in the audience. Suddenly, it all made sense. The man sitting directly in front of me (who had been complaining just as loudly throughout that he couldn't hear) turned off the device, the ringing stopped, he and his companion left the theater, and the play resumed.

Or consider the all-too-common instance of the massive coughing fit that spreads throughout the crowd or, for that matter, "the sympathetic laughter of one member of the audience [which] contagiously causes other members to take up the response" (*FA,* 131).[37] Following Austin's endeavor to distinguish between "by accident" and "by mistake" (*PP,* 133n), we are now in a position to notice the distinction, not only between *deliberate vs. accidental* and *voluntary vs. involuntary* behaviors, but also between *accidental vs. involuntary* behaviors. Sometimes events are under the frame- or contract-breaker's control: they are voluntary and intentional, and depending on a theater collective's invitation (or disinvitation), they are also *welcome* and, thus, *excusable* (in the sense that they do not require an excuse) or they are *unwelcome and inexcusable.* Sometimes such events are beyond the agent's control. For example, to the extent that one may call death a behavior,[38] they include involuntary acts like a heart attack, and they are always excusable as such. But sometimes, even involuntary behaviors are subject to degrees of control that render them *excusable vs. inexcusable.* In addition to the control that people regularly (try to) exercise (successfully or unsuccessfully) over coughing and laughing—instances that are so interesting that they form the basis for Case 5—consider this example: A boy is attending the theater when, to everyone's surprise including his own, he cries out "Motherfucker!" repeatedly as his as-yet-undiagnosed Tourette's Syndrome manifests itself for the first time. Given his unawareness of the disease, his interjections are both involuntary and excusable; but at his *next evening* at the theater, the excusability of his obscenities is open to question.[39]

A similar conclusion would obtain for the Parkinson's patient who, having refused to self-medicate before the show, is plagued by involuntary but controllable flailing gestures that disrupt the play for those around him: those behaviors are involuntary, but their (foreseeable) consequences are no longer accidental. Then again, the impaired spectator who attends the theater with full knowledge of the *possibility* or *probability*—not the certainty—of disruptive involuntary behaviors, and who commits the behaviors, does so not by accident, not by mistake, but not really deliberately, either. Consonant, in that respect, with various risk-seeking, death-defying, deliberate behaviors that are subject to "slips of the body,"[40] such instances of "living dangerously" at the theater have now prepared the critical terrain for one of the most curious cases of all: *the accident that becomes deliberate.*

We are all familiar with the domino effect or the chain reaction when, more dangerously than in fits of laughter or coughing, and less subject to self-control, one accident sets further accidents in motion: an actor trips and falls, causing others to trip and fall over the furniture that he has knocked over, and so on. But we might also envisage something like this: I am carelessly smoking a cigarette during the intermission of a particularly miserable play when I notice that my playbill has caught fire. I decide that this is a well-timed accident and that the theater *should* burn down (because the play was *that* bad?). (Had I been allowed to smoke *during the play,* my accidental and, eventually, *deliberate* disruption would have been all the more dramatic—and all the more difficult to justify during the ensuing criminal investigation.)

CASE 5: Breakage by an AUDIENCE Member (or Members)
that is neither DELIBERATE nor ACCIDENTAL

To what extent are laughter, tears, or yawns responses that individual spectators can control at all? Is the nonverbal, nonlinguistic phenomenon of laughter an act? a behavior? an involuntary response akin to its erstwhile opposite, crying? How do we determine whether its nature and degree are such that contagious laughter constitutes a breakage of theater and its contract at all?

Regardless of whether laughter and/or tears are *invited or uninvited* and *welcome or unwelcome* (as yawning is never welcome) by those with the standing to invite them, such meaningful reactions to theater may well be appropriate or inappropriate; but they also seem neither deliberate nor accidental. In that respect, the case of audience laughter reveals important distinctions between accidental and involuntary interventions, just as it grounds the whole nature of breakage in questions of appropriateness and timing. What is the audience *supposed to do*? Meaning: Do spectators deliver the very responses that members of the theater collective *intend to induce*?[41] Does the audience understand the nature of the collective's invitation—an invitation that is extended directly or indirectly, explicitly or implicitly, successfully or unsuccessfully, and always related to their communicative talents?

If Emily were back in our audience, and if she were to burst out laughing, she could do so in four different ways that will structure our final case. Let us disambiguate them here: (1) Emily is watching a piece of stage buffoonery and she laughs along with everyone else: her laughter is invited, welcome, and appropriate. (2) Emily is thinking of a joke that she just heard that day, which has nothing to do with the buffoonery on stage: her laughter is invited and welcome, but also inappropriate, even if its inappropriateness completely escapes detection. (3) Emily is thinking of that same joke and bursts out laughing during the death scene of a tragedy: her laughter is uninvited, unwelcome, inappropriate, and immediately perceptible. (4) Finally, as is not infrequently the case, a current event or something in the news all of a sudden, but completely contextually (and in ways unsought by the collective), renders funny a previously unfunny line of the script (or vice versa, as when the previously funny becomes unfunny): Emily laughs, alone or with others. If the former, Emily's laughter is uninvited but likely appropriate; if the latter, her failure (or refusal) to provide invited laughter may also be entirely appropriate.

Such invitations and disinvitations prompt further responses, along the lines of Goffman's contagious improprieties (*FA*, 346). But in addition to his insistence that Emily would be laughing in some instances as theatergoer, in others as onlooker, Goffman proposes a final example in which a character's laughter causes "onlookers to take up the *same* response." He concludes that "something deeply ungrammatical would have occurred" (*FA*, 131; his emphasis). Despite Dasenbrock's later assertion that "action does not have a syntax" (*TC*, 172), theater does indeed have a syntax.[42] And everything that we have seen thus far tells us that Goffman's grammar of response is also an ethics of response.

CASE 6A: DELIBERATE Breakage of Theater by a Member (or Members) of the AUDIENCE (INVITED)

When is an interruption not an interruption? Under what circumstances *should* spectators interrupt a play? And, if they should, is it an interruption at all? In theater, actors' deliberate solicitations of "breaks" from the audience are by no means rare: actors, for instance, routinely create prescribed spaces during which they invite (directly or indirectly) verbal, nonverbal, and even physical responses from spectators; and spectators respond appropriately or inappropriately to those invitations. Imagine now the distress of actors, spectators, and producers if no one at all laughed, even once, during a comedy.[43] From within theater, members of the collective already know (or think they know) the degree to which they welcome audience intervention; from outside the collective, audiences must figure out whether their "participation" or "interference" is aesthetically, legally, ethically, or morally welcome and/or necessary—or whether it is unwelcome and unnecessary on any or all counts. Invited breakage is no breakage at all but, rather, a *controlled illusion of breakage:* illusive, that is, with regard to its true status as "nonbreakage" committed by the audience and with regard to the alleged control by the members of the theatrical collective of events that may readily get out of hand.

In addition, then, to the converse of the accidental intervention of Case 4 that turns deliberate, this case raises the problem of the *deliberate intervention that turns accidental,* even to the point of not taking place. It might look like this: before a yokel can rise irate from his seat to rush the stage, he has a heart attack and dies. Of equal interest, and much less violent, are such examples as the actors in the 1980s production of *The Mystery of Edwin Drood* or the long-running *Shear Madness* who intentionally, "scriptedly," and directly invite participation, however stilted or limited that participation might be: Vote for the ending of the play! Vote for the song you'd like to hear! Tell us who the murderer is! In such plays, someone from outside the collective but inside the audience intervenes artfully into the play in ways that Goffman himself seems to deem impossible when specifying that "the onlooking aspect of the audience activity is not something that is a staged or simulated replica of a real thing, as is the action onstage" (*FA,* 130). During moments such as these, onlookers actually *do* perform that "simulated replica of a real thing":[44] in *Shear Madness,* they know very well that no one is dead, but accept the proposed role by playing along; in *Drood,* they may not even care about which song or which ending, or they may prefer a choice not on the menu but vote anyway for one of the options. To do any of those things—to act or not to act, to interrupt or to participate—they need to interpret the invitation correctly and judge it worthy of acceptance and also executable (the mute patron cannot cry out).

And yet, open invitations do not always produce the effect desired by the issuers. Even more intriguing is the possibility of a real break within the ersatz break, in which one or more spectators decline the invitations (or the alleged invitations, a concept to which we return shortly). What if the audiences of *Shear Madness* and *Drood* flatly refused to participate, period? What if they participated in ways that the players neither invited nor rehearsed? What if, in what would almost pass for heckling, someone boldly demanded an ending to *Drood* that the actors had not mentioned as a possibility? Or requested a song that the actors were not prepared to sing and would not sing, no matter how many requests they received to that effect, because it did not exist? If enough spectators were to behave in that manner, they could compromise the participatory "integrity" of the show, the enjoyment of it, and even the appearance of the enjoyment of it.[45] Sometimes the choices presented are not choices that we care to make, or choices at all. And, while they are a far cry from such hauntingly violent choices as those presented to prisoners about whether to be burned at the stake or hanged, shot or flayed alive,[46] it seems reasonable to assert (consistent with our earlier remarks about coercion) that theater must be a matter of choice.

CASE 6B: DELIBERATE Breakage of Theater by an AUDIENCE Member (or Members) (UNINVITED)

Even uninvited, the bona fide deliberate intervention into theater (as opposed to the bad-faith or criminal one) by a person or persons in the audience informs many a beloved theatrical anecdote. For example, in a wonderful mirror image of the celebrated Riga incident during which ignorant "heathen" fled the stage in 1204,[47] two separate chroniclers—Jehan Aubrion and Jacomin Husson—tendered the following account of a clerical performance in Metz on Sunday, 30 January 1502. It seems that the "little people" (*menuz peuple,* as opposed to those short in stature as from Beverley and Bautzen) were so frustrated by their inability to understand the Latin of the ecclesiastical thespians that they temporarily spoiled the show for the gentlemen attendees when they "rose up and revolted against the players, such that the gentlemen mentioned above were obliged to beat a hasty retreat. After that, the aforesaid little people overpowered the actors and stepped onto the stage, such that the actors barely had the time to get off before facing grave danger of a severe attack."[48] (Husson assures us that, the next day, the performance resumed in Latin, but only after the "doors were securely closed" so that the clergy and nobility alone could enter.)[49]

One need not "get medieval" about all this. In nineteenth-century Belgium, the performance of an opera allegedly erupted into a battle that turned into the Revolution.[50] Meanwhile, on a continent far, far away, a puppet performance of *Doctor Faustus* caused devilish trouble again, this time before the mountaineers of colonial Berryville, Virginia. Goffman reports, citing McPharlin, that a riot ensued when "a drunken member of the audience fired his rifle at one of the puppets playing the devil." This flesh-and-blood Cavellian yokel wounded not Emily but an assistant working behind the scenes: "When Mephistopheles appeared to bear Faustus off to the nether regions, a tall woodsman rose, unsteady with moonshine, cocked his rifle, yelled 'Git back, Devil, git back!' and took a shot at the puppet. This was worse than potato pitching. The bullet went through the backdrop and lodged in the shoulder of a Negro assistant who was hanging the puppets away. Alberto Lano was arrested by the city marshal for inciting the riot that ensued."[51] Meanwhile, the wounded body of the unlucky assistant, a descendant of sorts of Jehan Hemont of 1380, offers physical evidence of the momentous stakes of audience interventions that are uninvited and unwelcome.

What happens, moreover, when we find that even alleged mitigating factors are not so mitigating after all, perhaps on moral grounds? Imagine, for instance, a disturbingly informed intervention from a White Supremacist theatergoer, an unconscientious objector not to Othello's killing Desdemona but to his kissing her in an interracial cast? Goffman recalls what happened politically during a 1965 Living Theatre performance of *The Mysteries in Vienna*. As a response to the group's antiwar slogans, some thirty "tuxedo-wearing playgoers stormed the stage to prove, as one man put it, that 'this can be done by anyone.' Fist fights between the audience and the players broke out. There were screams and only after the curtain fell was order restored."[52] No matter how many real and hypothetical scenarios we adduce, they have this in common: all display a violation of the theatrical contract in which the audience does not watch the play in the spirit intended, meaning, *intended by those making theater.* All raise these final questions:

What if those very disruptions truly *are* intended, preplanned, even premeditated by either actors *or* spectators who mean all along to break the theatrical contract? What if the conventional invitation to welcome participation is really a disinvitation? Or what if the conventional disinvitation from unwelcome participation is really an invitation? What happens when the alleged invitation is not one? Whether the situation be medieval enough to necessitate mitigating explosive damages, stopping a rape or an assault, listening to—and hearing—a plea for help, or even stopping a death penalty in progress (which is, as a rule, illegal), sometimes it appears that participation itself is a fallacy which is not one.

To return one last time to that allegedly consensual RATT assault, a group of actors intentionally reversed the standard theatrical disinvitation *from* participation by issuing (through their commission of illegal acts) an implicit invitation, so they said, that audiences break the so-called fourth wall in favor of not breaking the law (as accomplices by accident at some point?). But we may or may not believe that was the true collective intention of RATT. I mean: What if the supposedly "welcome interventions" were really unwelcome by a troupe who, in reality, preferred criminal assault to aesthetic, metacritical representation? Under those circumstances, if the audience does *not* rush the stage, then are they breaking RATT's frame by refusing to break frame?

There is only one way to avoid a spiraling phenomenological reductio ad absurdum, which would be something on the order of the *disinvited nonbreak of the nonframe.*[53] Test though it might the limits of ethics, morality, and even law, theater cannot, should not violate basic social contracts. To investigate just how much horror an audience is willing to endure in passivity before intervening is indeed a theatrical version of the Milgram experiments.

In the final analysis, it is intention that permits the comparison of such an anodyne example as *Drood* with the violent activities of RATT or the Living Theatre. It is intention that makes possible the identification and the outright rejection of the theatrical invitation to violence, which may be aesthetically viable but which is morally repugnant. As in any form of communication, the artist issues an invitation of sorts to all those seeking the painful pleasures or the pleasurable pains of reception. In theater, it is a profoundly social invitation that is distinct from those issued in books, paintings, letters, or films. "Intervene inartistically as good Samaritans and bad theatergoers, or you're not human," says RATT, implicitly or indirectly inviting its audiences to stop an assault in progress that was their play in progress (*SRT,* 20–24). Fail to accept RATT's alleged call to Good Samaritanism and, artistic consequences notwithstanding, a life is at stake.[54] Fail to dialogue with *Drood* and, at worst, the play might flop. But nullify too much theater and social life itself is nullified.

Theatrical life is not—at least *not entirely*—a narrative of agency vs. victimhood, however recurrent that paradigm and however much social life itself does indeed feel that way because so often it *is* that way. Of doubled spectatorship in the law, Claudius Saturninus once wrote that "the person is looked at [*spectatur*] in two ways: the person who did the act and the person who suffered it."[55] Centuries later, Melia stated that, in reading, "the audience is, it seems to me, treated essentially as a passive victim of the potential inarticulateness of speakers" ("Response," 14). But even the much studied binary of agency vs. victimhood is insufficient when approaching theater and its troubled legal double, the contract.

In theater studies, the audience is no passive victim of the *potential misfires of actions*. If theater misfires, as it frequently does, it does so just as readily from action, inaction, and "mis-action" in the collective (decipherable only from the standpoint of intention) as from spectators' misperceptions and misattributions of the intentions of others: all different, all significant, and without all of which the sound and fury of theater signifies nothing. There can be no Intentional Fallacy in the theater.

Talk-Back / *Black Box and Idiot Box*

> From the point of view of action, one cannot compare
> a cinematic image which, poetic though it might be, is
> limited by the film, to a theatrical image which obeys
> all the exigencies of life.
>
> **ANTONIN ARTAUD,** *Theater and Its Double*

The incident was painful to watch. Traffic reports being what they are in Los Angeles, countless eyes and ears were attending to the news reporters' daily counsel about how best to navigate the complex system of freeways so that commuters could make their way home after a day's work. All of a sudden, the quotidian drama was replaced by a different one as local networks interrupted not just their news broadcasts but children's cartoon shows with the flavor-of-the-day called "breaking news." On that day in May 1998, as we first saw it in our Introduction, the breaking story of the man on the freeway promised a spectacle even more gripping than the infamous O. J. Simpson Bronco chase. Its protagonist lacked the name recognition of a Simpson: indeed, his name was never mentioned at all. He was, instead, a distraught Everyman who had parked in the left lane of the freeway and had draped over his truck a large banner bearing words that reflected a distinctly political agenda: "HMO's are in it for the money." He had not yet set his truck on fire. He had not yet flinched from remaining inside the automotive inferno. He had not yet raised a loaded rifle to his head and fired its lethal blast before everyone within eyeshot. But police officers had already blocked several lanes of traffic to monitor the situation. Miles away, exasperated motorists were probably already fuming, "there must have been an accident." The "accident" had not yet occurred.

All indications spoke to the seriousness of the man's threat to himself, his intention to air the final act of his life, and, for television network personnel (a "media collective" analogous to our theater collective), the interest to potential viewers. The unidentified man had timed his message about callous HMOs with rush hour, a moment when traffic helicopters were sure to be at hand: in fact, the words of his banner were legible only from the aerial shots. He might even have predicted that his threat would provoke conflict

within various news divisions as to what parts, if any, to air of his linguistic and bodily statements. But no one suggested that he committed suicide *because of* the politics of representation. Nor was there anything necessarily "political" about people watching the L.A. traffic report (beyond, perhaps, the debates about mass transit or about *everything* being political).

From the standpoint of the actant, there was nothing "accidental" about a man holding a gun, threatening to kill himself, and blowing his brains out. If anything, he appears to have issued implicitly an invitation not unlike the one issued explicitly by the convicted boy-murderer Kansas Charley in 1892 to his hanging, or by Gary Gilmore to his 1997 execution by a Utah firing squad. With literal gallows humor, Gilmore sent a postcard to a former cellmate which promised "Bang! Bang! / *A Real Live Shoot'em up!*" during which earplugs would be furnished.[1] Unless the man on the freeway had somehow changed his mind, unless a spasm caused him to pull the trigger,[2] he had intended to die and to perform a large-scale morality play that was, by our definition, not theater. It was not even theater by Wilshire's definition, which excludes the possibility of staging oneself dying because the theatrical performer "cannot as artist stand outside himself as dying character and aesthetically frame and bound himself" (*RPI*, 268).[3]

So it was that, when the man on the freeway set fire to his truck, the cameras never faltered. As Peter Jennings put it later that evening for ABC, "a lot of people, including a very large number of children, saw this poor man blow his brains out live."[4] News anchors returned immediately to their posts on screen, interrupting their prior interruptions and apologizing for having broadcast the very event that their camera crews had been following so rapaciously. "KTLA shares with its viewers their distress," said one local station manager.[5] Had the network also shared the pleasure of any viewer who had enjoyed the show? or, more disturbingly, any viewer who had anticipated it? In his self-reflexive, self-interested verdict of sorts, that station manager attempted to salvage and mitigate, on behalf of his media collective, the pleasure associated with the spectacular imminence of breaking news. He did so by broadcasting the station's noble intentions (and certainly not its negligence or incompetence). It all led to an oft-uttered contemporary entity that is surprisingly germane to the various nonaccidents that we have been studying: the apology which is not one.[6]

If the Middle Ages had letters of remission, the modern world has (non)apologies, issued profligately by a host of public figures (such as President William Jefferson Clinton on Monica Lewinsky, Trent Lott on Strom Thurmond, Don Imus on the Rutgers women's basketball team, or Jim Bakker, Jimmy Swaggart, and Ted Haggard on their respective "sins" of adultery and homosexuality). But the time may well have come to re-frame Artaud's call of "No More Masterpieces" (*TD*, 74–83) as "No more apologies"—at least, no more feigned ones, please. Apologies are usually welcomed by (or seem better than nothing to) the victims of accidents (and nonaccidents); and there are those who believe, with varying degrees of (religious) fervor, that apologies wipe the slate clean of evil intentions. But apologies do not alter post hoc what existed ad hoc: intentions.[7] Thus, the station manager of KTLA ruled the televised suicide an accident, an un-intended consequence, a collateral damage that was acceptable in light of the need to transmit newsworthy materials to viewers who are increasingly cast—and who increasingly cast themselves—as jurors of morality. For the most part, those jurors were not buying.

Ray Richmond of *Daily Variety* denounced the apologies as "a little bit disingenuous" and explained that "this is the money shot. This is what news directors long for."[8] ABC correspondent Brian Rooney firmly drove home a similar message when he emphasized that "we won't show what happened next, but several stations did show it live. The man put the gun to his head and viewers could clearly see his brains explode."[9] Others, like John Pal-minteri of my local Santa Barbara station, stressed the newsworthiness of the episode: "when two freeways are shut down in Los Angeles, it certainly becomes news there."[10] And yet, no one seriously believed that an impend-ing suicide had been aired for its newsworthiness to motorists. Had that been the intention of any one of a panoply of agents, the event could easily have been described as a "traffic situation" and paired with advice to take alternate routes. Just as plausibly, any shocked viewer might readily have cited what we have been calling ATTRIBUTED PERCEIVED INTENTIONS, angrily denouncing a given television station for having implied a public taste for blood lust: a perception that might or might not coincide with the actual desires and intentions of producers, directors, camera operators, or viewers (who were, likely, not of one mind on the subject).[11] Maybe there were members of the media collective who did not like the sight of blood at all, but only thought that the audience(s) would. Maybe others were right that bloodshed was exactly what some viewers hoped to see, regardless of whether disseminators or viewers admitted to those respective positions.

Oddly enough, the most persuasive justification for the noble intentions of the media was never made. Since, ad hoc, a happy dénouement was still possible, station managers might well have claimed that they had meant to air a drama of redemption: the uplifting and cathartic spectacle of cops successfully talking a man out of suicide, which is a staple of police dramas. No one said that, though. Instead, several news anchors invoked the cultural commonplace of their concern for children, defensively recalling that they had warned young viewers (with the presumed hope of illocutionary force)[12] to go fetch their parents so that the latter could determine whether the surprise dissemination was age-appropriate. The reason seems clear. Twist as they might in the ideological wind, station managers must surely have recognized a moment on that fateful day when a suicide was the odds-on favorite, especially after the man's initial but unsuccessful attempt to set himself on fire along with his truck. Likewise, with the possible exception of the confused children whose cartoons had been interrupted, any viewer (from within or without the collective that was doing the broadcasting) must also have recognized that that moment was at hand . . . all the more so given this comment from a reporter in a traffic helicopter: "Let's, uh, stay away from this picture now because, uh, at this time, this is not something we want to show on the air. . . . It's just getting worse and worse by the minute."[13] And it did get worse, such that he later exclaimed, during his play by play coverage, "Oh no!" It also got worse for the many parents who were interviewed later that day. Their outrage was as palpable as it was difficult to qualify: Were they scandalized because their children could not tell the difference between screen violence and real violence? or because they *could*?

This was not the first time—nor would it be the last—that a television network had essentially authorized the airing of a snuff film. Indeed, any media-literate American recalls (in addition to such indelible sights as the assassinations of John F. Kennedy, Robert Kennedy, and Martin Luther King before the eyes of a generation) a host of other incidents with which Aaron Brown contextualized the events of 6 May 1998 for ABC's *World News Tonight:* the murder of Lee Harvey Oswald on live television, or the "accidental" airing of the suicide of Budd Dwyer, a Pennsylvania state treasurer under criminal investigation.[14] With those, we may compare and contrast the following: videotapes of real police beatings (never intended by brutal officers to be seen by the public at all); the unspeakable snuff-in-progress murder of Daniel Pearl; Jim Wooten's report for ABC (7 May 2001) regarding genocide in the Congo, in which footage clearly showed two men opening fire upon a man whom they had just thrown from a bridge; the allegedly journalistic coverage of the 1999 murder trial of Charles Ng, which featured a videotape of a bound and "terrified young woman moments before her murder . . . [being] tormented by her captors as they threatened to rape and kill her"; the endlessly played 911 recording of the anguished Nicole Brown Simpson before her murder; the airing of audiotapes from Georgia's electric chair (released by all three major networks on 2 May 2001); an auditory snuff film about the murder of Eva Berwid, which was aired in 1981 by *60 Minutes;* or the moment when that same program upped the ante by airing, on 22 November 1998, the televised euthanasia of Thomas Youk by Dr. Jack Kevorkian in real time.[15] Youk was dying of Lou Gehrig's disease; and, via footage supplied by Kevorkian, he had memorialized his intention both to die at the age of fifty-two and, presumably, to have his death aired.[16]

The list is endless. But, as the preceding pages have shown, although fatal accidents occur every day, they do not normally occur before the eyes of audience members who have turned out expressly to watch something else. The difference between breaking news and snuff films (and snuff drama)—visual, auditory, or both—is *intention*. True, it is impossible to forget the honorable intentions that motivate breaking news in its most noble vein: at its most urgent, it may offer lifesaving advice about catastrophic events, such as the ones so readily associated these days with national security, as when the Twin Towers were destroyed. But the *60 Minutes* piece on Youk's euthanasia seems much less urgent to anyone other than the protagonists and those close to them. What then, was the excuse—or the explanation—for airing real death in real time? Even William F. Buckley and Alan Dershowitz managed to agree on the need to investigate the issue when debating the Youk exposé in the larger context of the question on the floor during their forum at Harvard University, "Censorship, Is it Ever Justified?" Of special interest is Buckley's characterization of the equation of breaking news to breaking death: he called it *theater.* "A venerable show has made itself an accomplice to a murderous farce," he objected, wondering whether we now needed "snuff films to certify to the bona fides of both parties."[17]

Buckley's is the wrong analogy. The very sociability of theater nurtures the opposite tendency. If spectators watch the real violence of a snuff film, what they are seeing is precisely *not theater.* Rather, it is war, it is journalism, it is Girardian "good violence," it is Reality TV, it is even rubbernecking on the highway; but it is not—and cannot be—theater. Without a conscious reckoning of intention, however, it *could have been theater,* which is why Buckley challenged Dershowitz with the further question of whether one could air a snuff film. Dershowitz said no, his initial response adhering to the letter of the law: "since murder was a felony, one couldn't produce a snuff film without committing the felony, so therefore he'd have to oppose it." But when Buckley riposted, "What if the snuff film were shot where it wasn't criminal to kill? There are no criminal codes in Antarctica," he reports with a certain pride that "Mr. Dershowitz backed off."[18] It is time for all of us to have that debate and to back off from any vestiges of the Intentional Fallacy.

Common sense, along with common-sense morality, demands that we reconsider one last time the categories of our Introduction, which we identified as follows:

1. Acts of real violence *committed accidentally* and *viewed—or experienced—deliberately*

2. Acts of real violence *committed accidentally* and *viewed or experienced accidentally*

3. Acts of real violence *committed deliberately* and *viewed or experienced accidentally*

4. Acts of real violence *committed deliberately* and *viewed or experienced deliberately*

Although, at first blush, the events of the L.A. freeway appear to correspond roughly to the third case, of acts of real violence *committed deliberately and viewed accidentally,* they are more complex still. Viewership itself was not accidental: rather, viewership of the man's threat and commission of suicide was accidental for some and deliberate for others. Subject to the vagaries of the timing of their understanding(s), which we studied earlier, one viewer might have channel-surfed and come upon the gunfire *accidentally;* another might have fathomed the predictable outcome of the breaking news and turned off the television; yet another, accepting the interruption, might have stuck with the new story for a variety of reasons. But one person's "accident" was another person's "on purpose"; one person's viewership, another's deliberate dissemination. A final refinement is thus in order and assists us in reintegrating theater into media studies at large:

CASE 1: There are acts of real violence *committed accidentally* and *aired deliberately* (or here we might further specify of the subject of that phrase: there are *primary acts*—as intended by those performing them and expected by those doing the filming—which are aired deliberately. Whether the "collateral media damage" of "unexpected" secondary acts is also deliberate is a matter for Cases 2 and 3. Case 1 may occur either in medias res (in real time) or post hoc, no longer live. On one hand, this case would include examples of the various violent events of chapter 6, which were witnessed by Emily in medias res: a spotlight falls or an earthquake occurs while a camera crew is at the theater that evening with a live feed of opening night; or a similar feed is ongoing at the grand opening of a sushi restaurant when a driver loses control of his vehicle and crashes through the storefront window. On the other hand, film of those events may be disseminated post hoc during the nightly news, in a video/DVD series such as *Faces of Death,* in television shows consecrated to *Pets Gone Bad, Stunts Gone Bad,* or in the more light-hearted fare of *America's Funniest Home Videos.*

CASE 2: There are acts of real violence *committed accidentally* and alleg-edly *aired accidentally* (in real time and usually live). Consider the on-air death of Owen Hart, who did not mean to die; the live crashes in medias res at NASCAR; the Olympic skier's mortal or near mortal jump; or even the nonviolent "wardrobe malfunction" of Janet Jackson. In each case, those disseminating the events readily claimed post hoc, in yet another spin on Tallis's point about chance and agency (*NS,* 233), that they had intended "only" to air a car race, a sport, a concert: they had *not* intended to air those specific secondary acts and consequences which, so goes the claim, were un-expected and unforeseeable. Regardless of whether we believe in the alleged "airing by accident," it tends to prompt, from those responsible for the dis-semination, embarrassment, excuses, and apologies. But unless we would now like to imagine a media-savvy somnambulist hooking up a camera, we normally conclude that such dissemination is never involuntary and never accidental. Even so, media-disseminated "airing by accident" is possible in ways that "theater by accident" or "murder by accident" are not. While we have seen in the preceding pages that theater and murder require the corre-sponding intentional state,[19] any given individual who takes charge of a live feed (on radio, television, or the Internet) can commit an error, can have a bona fide *accident.* In ways that are inconceivable for the actor who (short of delusions) forgets that he or she is acting, that individual who is feeding live truly *can* forget about being "on the air"; or someone else can misrepre-sent the termination of the feed, and so on,[20] all of which leads to Case 3.

CASE 3: There are acts of real violence *committed deliberately* and allegedly *aired live accidentally* (again, if we accept the latter premise at all). Analo-gous to such frequent contemporary instances as the "forgotten" hot mike or the live feed, this case corresponds to the airing as much of the assas-sination of President Kennedy as of the man on the freeway: in the first instance, disseminators and audiences were celebrating a motorcade, not anticipating the president's assassination (except for the one or more assas-sins who were); in the second case, disseminators had a harder time making the claim that the airing of a man's suicide was accidental. This case also corresponds to the alleged verbal violence of something like Kanye West's unscripted critique of George W. Bush in 2005 during a fundraiser for the victims of Hurricane Katrina (courtesy of NBC), the type of incident that has tended to proffer a fascinating solution of sorts to the *potential* for the embarrassment, excuses, and apologies of Case 2. Case 3 may culminate in the contemporary equivalent of the medieval fear of imminence: the *pre-emptive anticipation* of the *possibility of such accidents,* which is known as the time-delayed broadcast.[21]

CASE 4: There are acts of real violence *committed deliberately and aired live deliberately.* We recognize the extreme forms of this case on the computer screen, where individuals disseminate (and others watch) the sexual assaults against children in pornography or other snuff and snuff-like events. But we would also recognize it *if* all U.S. citizens were permitted by law to witness the death penalty in action: if, for example, KQED had won its 1991 lawsuit against the warden of San Quentin prison and aired the execution of Robert Alton Harris.[22] Indeed, one of the principal arguments against the death penalty is that such deliberate dissemination of a deliberately committed death viewed deliberately is important because it would acknowledge, once and for all, the *collective retributive intent* of societies that execute convicts in the name of the law. Most of the time, however, we witness examples in which the disseminators' presupposition (allegedly based on such factors as the law of the land, ethics, and even taste) is that the violence is not mortal enough to qualify as snuff: the spontaneous riot at the rugby stadium, the death-defying and deadly events of the circus, or the allegedly more anodyne dangers of *Survivor,* to say nothing of the psychic violence that is inflicted on a daily basis on the confessional stages of Oprah and Dr. Phil, the most obscene entry at the time of this writing being Fox's mercifully short-lived *Moment of Truth.*

With these cases in place, we are finally in a position to understand what happened with and to the man on the freeway. As if his death had been an instance of Case 3—that is, committed *deliberately* and aired *accidentally* (or even Case 2: committed *accidentally* and aired *accidentally*)—the various news teams and network executives who had broadcast the suicide proceeded to issue their plethora of apologies. Meanwhile, the public ruled with virtual unanimity that the hideous spectacle of breaking news had been a clear-cut example of Case 4: an act committed *deliberately* and aired *deliberately,* the televised equivalent of a snuff film. Whence the hue and righteous cry for those apologies: *viewers refused to equate accidental violence with accidental dissemination.* Instead, they characterized the news outlets as just what they were and just what they are: *media* that mediate our gaze, that serve as intermediaries. For those who had aired a suicide in real time, there had been no accident.

In that respect, Goldstein misses a crucial point when he finds that "most violent images and models produced for entertainment and recreation are not the real things; they carry clues to their false identity" (*WWW,* 2).

Like our medieval dramas of 1380 and 1384, like the posttheatrical rape of
Bar-le-Duc and the extratheatrical rape of Mrs. Coton, and like the Dance
of Death of Henry D'Anoux, the breaking news of 1998 also carried numerous clues to its *real identity* as both action and history. Critical conversa-
tions about the theater can no longer proceed as if no human agent ever
arranged for those clues to be seen in the first place or, more significantly, to
put them there. Granted, Goldstein's collection of essays is about audiences;
but when he finds himself drawn to violent events that are *"not intended*
[presumably by someone] *to entertain,"* it is crucial to recall that *events do
not have intentions.*[23] They do not emerge ex nihilo any more than do lyrics in
the sand. Nor does television have intentions, even though Eco himself prefers to speak of production, rather than intention, when ruminating about
how only one of many camera angles "emerges as the result" of a given
television report (*OW,* 107–10).[24] *People* have intentions—relentlessly elided
though their ever changing intentionalities might be. A television set may
well be an idiot box, but it is no equivalent of that crucial object recovered
after a plane goes down: the black box.

We may never fully understand the intentions of the man on the freeway
or of the men and women who filmed, aired, and watched him. But their
conduct involved intention and agency. To equate journalism with airing
all things at all times is to move even from our opening dichotomy of "entertaining news" vs. "newsy entertainment" to a distinctly unmedieval and
brave new world: a world dominated by, and dedicated to, something that
we might call the "transcription mode" as a pseudosolution to the fear of
imminence.

Capture and disseminate anything and everything! That seems to be the
new mantra not only for television and cinema, but for telejournalism as
well. Consider, for instance, Sasha Baron Cohen's efforts to capture rac-
ism and sexism in *Borat,* which prompted lawsuits alleging damages for the
unflattering(ly truthful) portrayal of some of the protagonists.[25] On television, moreover, the dissemination of "transcriptions" in real time is available in numerous arenas outside the nightly news programs that regularly
preserve the sights and sounds of murder:[26] Dr. Phil airs footage of real
child abuse, the better, presumably, to stop it. Chris Hansen catches—and,
we hope, *thwarts*—a predator for both *Dateline NBC* and society at large.
Prime Time Live airs one of the team's "What Would You Do?" segments,
which functions as a tougher version of the old *Candid Camera,* and an allegedly more anodyne one of the Milgram experiments: here, hidden cameras
reveal whether individuals will intervene in abuse, bullying, or cheating.
Proponents of the journalistic transcription mode intimate that anything

less is tantamount to censorship, as when another station manager, Jeff Wald, tendered no apology at all—is that better than a pseudoapology?—for his decision to air the gruesome media evidence from the Ng trial: "we warned our viewers before we showed [the tape], and we used a very short excerpt. . . . We're not in the censorship business. By showing what we did, we were indicating how horrific this case really is."[27]

Be all that as it may, the inanimate devices of a mediatized world have far surpassed Goffman's peephole at the work performance.[28] We now inhabit a culture in which transcription is all the rage, in which evidentiary compilation goes on, with or without our knowledge, collecting proof-in-the-making of any and all dangers and perceived dangers. Wiretapping (legal or illegal), along with its video descendants like the surveillance posts at commercial and domestic sites, legal "nannycams" or illegally and voyeuristically planted cameras and mikes seem to have replaced agency and intentionality altogether by monitoring everything within inanimate eyeshot. Thus, the technotranscriptions of surveillance cameras at the local Seven-Eleven or the ATM, the patriotic surveillance of telephone communications or book buying, and the black boxes—*which specific intending subjects arrange to place and to activate*—cannot, do not, and should not stand in for those intending subjects: intending human subjects who actively intervene in the world around us, the better, supposedly, to protect us, others, or ourselves *from* ourselves and from *what we do.* Those devices have no agency; rather, the people who install, monitor, and interpret them do—and their interpretations yield both truth and consequences. They create, moreover, the illusion of the peaceful passivity of things: of objects or filters that elide human agency but which, in reality, possess no agency and no intelligence, artificial or otherwise. The unbearable heaviness of things is now an ethereal fantasy of agentless transcription.

If Dershowitz contends that "life is not a dramatic narrative,"[29] then life is not a poem either, populated by objects that come alive because we breathe life into them. No matter how persistent the Pygmalion myth, no matter how prevalent today's predilection for robots and cyborgs over statues, Galatea will not walk, however tantalizingly beautiful Henri Michaux's poetry to that effect: "In my spare time, I've been teaching a statue how to walk. Given her exaggeratedly prolonged immobility, it is not easy. Not for her. Not for me. We are worlds apart. What matters is her first step. That first step is everything. I know it. I know it only too well. That's why I'm so worried."[30] A far greater source of worry is this: in transcription mode, the fear is real; the imminence may not be.

Like an airplane's black box, like all those commonplace customer service recordings that alert us that our telephone calls may be monitored (by whom?) for quality control, like automatic cameras at traffic intersections, recording devices are omnipresent and pointed (like a loaded gun?) at everything from the most banal to the most vile. Occasionally, and in apparent contradiction, we even encounter an almost human equivalent of the black box in accident-chasing amateur videographers who plant themselves at airports hoping to film a plane crash. But they are not agentless: they hope, rather, to turn the odds of Tallis's blend of chance and agency in their economic (or other) favor. Certainly, on 25 July 2000, some were able to do just that when the Concorde went down with a plane full of vacationing German tourists. The videographers were (morally un)lucky enough to catch the whole thing, which others went on to air and re-air ad infinitum—and which airing may well have helped with the aviational investigation. But even an airplane's black box has been programmed so that it erases its contents and starts over again with every new flight. So, too, should we start over, reboot, when reckoning with contemporary fears of the terrifying and even terroristic imminence in our world. None of that has anything to do with theater. Or does it?

Unless we wish to consider life itself as nothing more than an unfolding crime in progress, we do well to recall that theater issues an ethical call of its own for reflection upon the move from thought to action.

Maverick theater productions often take place in that special performance space called the black box, suitable for imagining almost any spatial configuration in which audiences interact with a theatrical piece of our world in ways more intimate than those of the *théâtre vitrine*. In theater, as in life, there is no transcription mode alive—because tape recorders and aeronautical black boxes are *not alive*—that can replace agency, no agentless transcription that can replace intentionality. This is no Hobson's choice between perpetual transcription and perpetual censorship, between seeing, hearing, showing, or disseminating *everything* vs. seeing, hearing, showing, or disseminating *nothing*. It is individual people, if they are able, who choose to act publicly or privately, and to disseminate their actions (or those of others) because they intend to do so. It is people who do those things. Not books. Not texts. Not plays. Not boxes. And at the time of their acts, authors, agents, and actants were alive, with intentions that motivated them to do what they did, despite our best efforts to murder them by accident.

In the end, the optimistically marvelous challenge of theater, life, and civilization is that intentions can change as a result of the responses from observers, readers, audiences, fellow citizens. If the author is not dead, neither is the agent. Indeed, as de Certeau teaches so elegantly, the dead are subject to resurrection by history, which "fashions out of language the forever-remnant trace of a beginning that is as impossible to recover as to forget" (*WH*, 47). Intention is the beginning, not the beginning of the end.

APPENDIX *Original Documents in French and Latin*

CHAPTER 1. Behind the Seen: All Hell Breaks Loose

DOCUMENT I.I

AN, JJ 116, no. 254, fols. 152v–53r. Cited by A. Thomas, "Le Théâtre à Paris et aux environs," *Romania* 21 (1892): 609–11.

Avril 1380. Lettres de rémission accordées par Charles V à Guillaume Langlois, cause involontaire d'un accident mortel survenu pendant une représentation de la Passion à Paris, le 27 mars 1380.

Charles, etc. Savoir faisons a touz presens et avenir a nous avoir esté exposé de la partie de Guillaume Langlois que comme, le mardi apres Pasques darr. passé, es jeux qui furent faiz et ordenez en l'onneur et remembrance de la Passion nostre Seigneur Jhesu Crit [*sic*] en nostre bonne ville de Paris par aucuns des bourgois et autres bonnes genz d'icelle, le dit exposant eust esté requis, prié et ordené de ceulx qui es diz jeux faisoient les personnages des figures des ennemis et deables de estre aux diz jeux pour getter des canons, quant temps seroit, afin que leurs personnages fussent mieulx faiz, si comme es diz jeux on a acoustumé a faire par chascun an a Paris, et lors avint que avec ledit exposant vint et s'embati illec amiablement Jehan Hemont, varlet d'estuves, pour lui cuidier aidier a jouer et faire getter des diz canons quant lieu et temps seroit, comme autreffoiz on a accoustumé a faire, et il soit ainsi que ilz ordenerent et mistrent a point iceulx canons pour getter et faire bruit sur l'appointement et arroy du cruxifiement que on a acoustumé a faire en iceulx jeux en remenbrance de la mort et passion de nostre seigneur Jhesu Crit [*sic*], et pour ce que illec ou lesdiz exposant et Jehan Hemon estoient fu mise une broche chaude et boutee en un canon estant ou dit lieu, la cheville d'icellui canon par force de feu s'en issy et sailli plus tost et autrement que cuidoient et pensoient yceulx exposant et Hemon par tele maniere que ledit Hemon d'icelle cheville fu feru et attaint d'aventure en l'une de ses jambes, et aussi fu ledit Guillaume par la force du feu qui en yssi embrasé et brulé parmi le visage et fu en grant doubte et en aventure d'estre mort ou affolé de touz poins; apres lesqueles choses ainsi avenues ledit Hemon, qui estoit bon et vray ami d'icellui exposant et qui ne vouloit que pour la bleceure qu'il avoit ainsi de la cheville dudit canon il fust aucunement dommagé ne poursuy pour luy ne a sa requeste pour lors ne ou temps avenir, ledit Jehan Hemon estant en bon et sain propos, de sa propre et bonne volenté, senz aucune induccion, quitta et clama quitte entierement, bonnement et absoluement pour lui et pour ses hoirs ou aians de lui cause ledit exposant dudit fait ainsi avenu et de tout ce qui pour raison d'icellui ou temps avenir s'en pourroit ensuir, en disant et confessant qu'ilz avoient esté et estoient bons amis ensemble, si comme plus a plain est contenu en certaines bonnes lettres de quittance passees par .ij. notaires le tiers jour de ce present moys d'avril et seellees du seel de nostre chastellet de Paris, et pour ce que depuis ledit fait, ainsi que le .xxvij. jour ou environ de ce present moys, ledit Jehan Hemon est alé de vie a trespassement, ledit exposant, nonobstans les choses et la quittance dessus dite sur ce faite, comme dit est, de doubte que il ne soit pour occasion de ce ores ou autreffoiz poursuiz, grevez ou travailliez en corps ou en biens, supplie par nous lui estre sur ce gracieusement et piteablement pourveu. Nous adecertes inclinans a sa supplicacion, considerans les choses dessus dites et attendu que les jeux qu'il faisoit estoient en significacion et exemple de bien et que ledit suppliant est de bonne vie, renommee et honneste conversacion, audit suppliant ou cas dessus dit ledit fait ainsi avenu avons remis, quittié et pardonné ... sauf le droit de partie, se aucun estoit, se aucun l'en vouloit poursuir civilement tant seulement. Si donnons en mandement au prevost de Paris. ...

Donné a Paris l'an de grace mil ccc et iiii^{xx} au mois d'avril et le XVIIe de nostre regne.

Es requestes de l'ostel.

N. GAIGNART. ROONY.

CHAPTER 2. The Final Run-Through

DOCUMENT 2.1

AN, JJ 125, no. 7, fols. 7v–8r. Cited by A. Thomas, "Le Théâtre à Paris," *Romania* 21 (1892): 611.

1384. Lettres de rémission accordées par Charles VI à Fremin Severin, cause in-volontaire d'un accident mortel survenu pendant une répétition de Théophile à Aunay-lès-Bondy, le 19 juin 1384.

Charles, etc. Savoir faisons a touz presens et avenir de la partie des amis char-nelz de Fremin Severin, demeurant a Aunay pres de Livry nous avoir esté signifié que comme les habitans de la dite ville d'Aunay et du pays d'environ eussent entrepris que le dimenche apres la nativité saint Jehan Baptiste ilz feroient uns jeux ou commemoracion du miracle qui a la requeste de la Virge Marie fust fait a Theophile, ou quel jeu avoir un personnage de un qui devoit getter d'un canon, et il soit avenu que le dimenche devant la dite feste saint Jehan derr. passé lesdiz habitans fussent en l'eglise de la dicte ville d'Aunay pour recorder leurs personnages, ledit Fremin qui devoit jouer du dit canon eust emplie de papier seulement la bouete du dit canon senz ce que fer ne boys y eust, et au temps qu'il devoit lachier ledit canon icellui Fremin eust dit aus gens qui la estoient "Traiez vous arriere; vous n'avez que faire de estre si prez pour touz perilz," néentmoins feu Perrin Le Roux se mist d'aventure au devant dudit canon quant vint a lachier et si que en lachant ledit canon le papier qui en la boite d'icellui canon estoit le frappa en l'eul, lequel feu Perrin Leroux est alé de vie a trespassement le vendredi apres ensuivant, pour laquelle chose nous ont supplié lesdiz amis que con-sidéré que ledit Fremin a tousjours esté de bonne fame et renommee . . . nous lui vueillons faire nostre grace, mesmement que ledit feu Perrin a dit qu'il estoit en coulpe dudit coup et non pas le dit Fremin. Nous, considerans les choses dessus dictes, audit Fremin Severin au cas dessus dit avons quitté et remis . . . le fait dessus dit . . . satisfaction faite a partie. Si donnons en mandement au prevost de Paris. . . .

Donné a Paris l'an de grace mil ccc iiii^{xx} et quatre, et de nostre regne le quart.

Es requestes de l'ostel.

J. CLERICI. T. D'ESTOU[TEVI]LE.

CHAPTER 3. Fear of Imminence and Virtual Ethics: Staging Rape in the Middle Ages

DOCUMENT 3.1

CPV, 3:114–15; Bruneau's emphasis. (Compare with *CVM,* 473.)

Ung enffans nés ayant la moitiet forme de diable. —Or avint que, en ce meisme tamps, fut juez ung jeux à Bar le Duc, auquelle estoient aulcuns hommes pourtant le parsonnaige de dyablez. Et, entre eulx, en y olt ung que en son habit voult avoir la compaignie de sa femme. Et elle le différoit, et demandoit qu'il volloit faire; et il luy respondit: "Je veult," dit il, "faire le dyable." Et, quoy que sa femme se sceût deffandre, force luy fut de obéyr. Cy avint qu'elle fut grosse et portait son tairme. Maix il avint qu'elle enfanta et délivra de ung corps qui estoit, dès le fault en aval, forme d'homme, et, dès le fault en amont, forme de dyable. De laquelle chose on en fut moult esbahis. Et ne l'oisairent baptiser jusques ad ce que l'on aroit estés à Romme pour sçavoir que l'on en feroit.

DOCUMENT 3.2
CMJH, 268–69, 346.

[1512]. Item, le xe. jour d'Octobre, ung dimanche fuit jué ung jeu sus Saint Illaire, de ii. gens estant en mariage. Après qu'ils eurent vesqus certain temps en mariage, heurent aiccord ensemble de vivre chaistement le demeurant de leur mariaige. Or avint que le marit volt avoir compagnie à sa femme, laquelle de son povoir y resistoit pour le voeu qu'ils avoient faict. Toutefois faullit qu'il fût. La femme courroucée dit que le diable y heust part, et que se elle concepvoit ung enffant que à diable fuit il et qu'elle ly donnoit; dont elle fuit mal avisée, car à celle heure elle conceut ung filz, de quoy elle en maldit l'heure plus de cent mil fois, car ce devint ung si bel enffant et si saige que point on en sceust trower; de quoy le père en avoit si grant joie que tout son reconffort estoit ondit enffant, et toutes fois que la mère le veoit, fondoit en larmes, de quoy le père s'en esmervilloit, et plusseurs fois ly en demandoit la cause, et aussy faisoit l'enffant, quant il commença à devenir grant, ce que jamaix ne leur voulut dire, tant que une fois que l'enffant, qui jay avoit environ xiii. ans d'aige, très instamment l'en prioit, laquelle ly dit qu'elle l'avoit donné à sa conception à diable et comment le diable l'infestoit et demandoit et ly disoit que dedans ces xv. ans il prenroit et emporteroit. Le pouvre enffant, bien estonné et esbahi, dit qu'il y porveroit et qu'il s'en iroit à Romme, se recommandant à la benoite Vierge Marie, laquelle moult humblement saluoit tous les jours. Or pour abrégier l'histoire, à bout des xv. ans, iii. diables le vinrent prenre: Sathan, Astarot et Leviatan et l'emportirent en enfer. Ce veant, la Vierge Marie priait Dieu Nostre Signour, son enffant, qu'il ly voulsist rendre cest enffant que les diables en avoient porté, qui estoit son bon ami. Nostre Signour permist et ly donnait congié de l'aller prendre tout dedans enffer, acompaignié de sainct Michiel, de sainct Gabriel et Raphael, qui fuit une chose bien belle à veoir, et de la joie que le père et la mère heurent de veoir leur enffant et d'estre quitte du diable, car il leur racontait tout ensy que la chose estoit avenue et des grants et horribles tor-ments d'enfer qu'il avoit veus; et fuit ledit jeux aussy bien jué qu'on en vit point de longtemps.

DOCUMENT 3.3
Lettre de rémission du 13 août 1395. AN, JJ 148, no. 144, fols. 74v–75r. (Reproduced in Cohen, "Le Théâtre à Paris et aux environs," in *EHTF,* 174–78.)

Charles, etc. Savoir faisons a tous presens et avenir nous avoir receüe l'umble supplicacion de Jehan Martin, prisonnier en nostre Chastellet de Paris, contenant que: comme le samedi, premier jour de may derr. passé, ledit suppliant feust venu de la ville de Courtery, où il demeure, en la ville de Chielle Sainte Baudour, dont il est prevost fermier pour les religieuses d'icellui liu, pour garder une feste qui, en remenbrance de la Passion Nostre Seigneur, y devoit l'endemain estre faicte, et, pour l'acompaignier, eust illec amenez Guillaume Guillier, Guillemin le Flament, Adenet de Lusigny, Pierre de Clercy et un chappellain de ladicte ville de Courtery, appellé Estienne; lequel suppliant, avec les dessus nommez, estant ledit samedi, environ soleil reconsant, a l'uis d'un des gens de ladicte ville de Chielle, nommé Jehan du Celier, feussent venuz pardevers lui Guillemin Coton et sa femme, lesquelx icellui suppliant ne congnoissoit alors, en lui disant teles paroles ou semblables en substance: "Sire, vous estes prevost de ceste ville, comme l'en nous a dit; moy et ma femme, qui yci est, avons trouvé compaignons en ceste ville qui nous veulent abussonner, et pour cause d'eulx l'en ne nous veult logier en ceste ville. Nous vous prions que vous nous faciez logier et baillier un lit pour nostre argent." Après laquelle complainte, icellui suppliant, acompaignié des dessus diz, qu'il avoit amenez, avec lui, comme dit est, mena lesdiz Guillemin Coton et sa femme en l'ostel d'un hostelier d'icelle ville, appellé Mahiet Thomas, pour les y faire logier. Ouquel hostel, tantost ou assez tost après que venus y furent, vindrent, pour cause d'icelle femme, pluseurs gens et compaignons d'icelle ville, jusques au nombre de douze ou environ, entre lesquelx estoient un prestre, qui a nom Guillaume, chappellain de Saint Andrieu dudit lieu, Jehan le Cave, Aubelet Caillet, les deulx filz Raoulet Robriquart et le filz Jehan Dairemes.

Et en icellui hostel soupperent ensemble touz les dessus diz suppliant, ceulx de sa compaignie, Guillemin Coton et sa femme et ceulx dudit lieu de Chielle, qui y estoient venus ou seurvenus, comme dit est. Auquel souper la dicte femme fu assise entre ledit suppliant et ledit chappellain de Saint-Andrieu, du bon gré d'icelle femme, sanz aucune contrainte. Duquel soupper chascun fut a un blanc d'escot et paia ladicte femme pour ledit suppliant. Et en souppant, ycellui chappellain de Saint Andrieu et lesdictes gens et compaignons dudit lieu de Chielle distrent a ladicte femme que ilz la congnoissoient bien et l'avoient vëue demourer avecques un prestre de la dicte ville, que l'en appelloit Thomas, duquel elle avoit esté chamberiere concubine. Laquelle respondit que il estoit vray, mais que elle n'y demouroit plus et est[oit] marié[e] audit Guillemin Coton et de ce en avoit bonnes lettres sur elle. Et adonc icellui suppliant lui dist qu'elle montrast ycelles letres et après qu'elle les eust monstrées et que les deux chappellains dessus diz les eurent leües, ilz distrent que elles ne valoient riens, riens. Et, après ce, ledit Jehanin le Cave dist audit suppliant a son oreille que s'il vouloit et pouoit tant faire que ladicte femme alast hors dudit hostel, eulx deux la congnoistroient charnelment. A quoy icellui suppliant respondi qu'il le vouloit bien, et, en oultre, ycellui suppliant, pour le desir qu'il avoit d'avoir compaignie charnelle a icelle femme, demanda audit Mahiet Thomas, hoste dudit hostel, un lit pour couchier celle nuit, lui et ladicte femme. Lequel respondi qu'ilz n'y coucheroient point. Et lors ycellui, a ce que icelle femme feust mise hors dudit hostel et qu'il peust avoir a faire a elle charnelment, defendi audit Mahiet qu'il ne la logast point, sur peine de soixante solz, disant que ledit Guillemin Coton estoit un ribaut rufien. Et après icellui suppliant avec les dessus nommez Pierre de Clercy, Guillaume Guillier, Guillemin le Flament et Estienne, chappellain dudit lieu de Courtery, se parti et s'en ala sur le pont de ladicte ville de Chielle, et oudit hostel laissa touz les autres dessus diz avecques ledit Jehanin de la Cave qui devoit prenre ladicte femme. Duquel pont ledit Pierre de Clercy et chappellain dudit Courtery, après ce que ilz y eurent un pou esté, se partirent et s'en alerent audit Courtery en leurs maisons, et lesdiz supplians et Guillemin le Flament avecques ledit Guillemin Guillier, qui estoit venuz a eulx sur ledit pont depuis que lesditz Clercy et chappellain s'en estoient partis et leur avoit dit que ledit Jehanin de la Cave et les autres compaignons qui estoient demourez oudit hostel dudit Mahiet emmenoient ladicte femme, s'en retournerent en ladicte ville de Chielle et alerent en l'ostel de Pierre le Maistre, tavernier en ycelle ville, ouquel hostel vint ledit Guillemin Coton par devers ledit suppliant et lui dist ces paroles ou semblables en substance: "Prevosts, ces compaignons ont emmené ma femme et encores le plus meschant d'eulx m'a donné une buffe, dont je suis plus courroucié que de tout le remenant. Je vous requiers raison et justice." Lequel suppliant lui demanda se il avoit point crié quant ledit cas fut fait et aussi ou estoient ceulx dont il se plaignoit. Et il respondi que il avoit bien crié, mais personne n'estoit venue a son aide et que ceulx qui lui avoient ce fait estoient alez aux champs et y avoient emmenée avec eulx sadicte femme. Et assez tost après, vint en icellui hostel l'un desdiz compaignons, appellé Aubelet, auquel ledit suppliant demanda ou estoit le flo desdiz autres compaignons, et il lui respondi que ilz estoient aux champs. Et aussi y vint ledit Jehanin de la Cave, qui parla audit Guillemin Coton a son oreille. Et puis lui et ledit Aubelet Cailliet se partirent d'icellui hostel et en enmenerent ledit Guillemin Coton. Et ledit suppliant, *en entencion d'avoir compaignie a ladicte femme* [*my emphasis*], acompaignié desdiz Guillemin Guillier et Guillemin le Flament, les suivit jusques aux champs, hors de ladicte ville, du costé de la porte de Paris, pour savoir s'il pourroit trouver ladicte femme, a ce qu'il peüst avoir a faire a elle comme les autres. Mais pour ce que ledit Guillaume Guillier, qui s'estoit parti desdiz suppliant et Guillemin le Flament et avencié devant pour savoir ou lesdiz compaignons et la femme estoient, retourna a iceulx suppliant et Flament, en leur disant qu'il avoit trouvé l'un desdiz compaignons tenant un grant plançon en sa main, lequel lui avoit demandé s'il les espioit et dit que, s'il ne s'en aloit, il seroit batu, iceulx suppliant, Flament et Guillier s'en retournerent en ladicte ville de Chielle, *ou il geurent celle nuit touz vestuz sur les eschaffaux qui avoient esté faiz pour ladicte feste* [*Cohen's emphasis*], sanz avoir compaignie a ladicte femme. Et l'endemain, qui fut jour de dimanche, oÿ ledit suppliant dire et aussi en commune renommée, en ladicte ville de Chielle, que ladicte femme avoit esté menée aux champs es prez de[s] religieuses d'icellui liu et illec congneüe charnelment de trois ou de quatre desdiz compaignons et entre les autres par ledit Guillaume, chappellain dudit saint Andrieu, et par les dessusdiz deux fils Robriquart et que, après ce, ladicte femme avoit esté rendue a son dit mary, qui l'avoit emmenée, et, nonobstant, la commune renommée dudit cas et que icellui suppliant veïst, en ladicte ville de Chielle, ledit jour de dimenche, ledit chappellain et l'un desdiz filz dudit Robriquart, il ne feist aucune diligence de les prenre ne son devoir es autres choses devantdictes, jasoit ce qu'il y feüst tenu comme prevost et justice d'icellui lieu. Pour cause desquelles choses dessusdictes ledit suppliant est detenu prisonnier en nostre Chastellet de Paris, en aventure de recevoir pour icelle[s] pugnicion corporelle, se par nous ne lui est sur ce estendue nostre grace, en nous humblement suppliant que, considéré que, en autres cas, il a esté et est homme de bonne vie et renommée, sanz avoir esté reprins ou convaincu d'aucun autre villain cas, et qu'il est chargié de femme et de cinq enfans, qui seroient en voye de mendier, il nous plaise nostre dicte grace lui estandre en ceste partie. Nous, eüe consideracion aux choses dessus dicte[s] et a la longue prison que ledit suppliant a pour ce soufferte et que partie ne poursuit plus a icelluy suppliant ou cas dessusdict, de nostre auctorité royal et grace especial avons mué le cas criminel dessusdit en civil et ledit crime remis, quitté et pardonné, remettons, quittons et pardonnons, avec toute peine, offense et amende corporelle et criminelle en quoy pour cause de ce, il puet ou pourroit estre dit encouru envers nous et justice et le restituons et remettons a sa bonne [fame] et renommée au païs et a ses biens non confisquez, satisfaction faicte a partie, se faicte n'est, et parmi ce aussi [qu'il] demourra encores prisonnier en nostredit Chastellet par un mois au pain et a l'eaue. Si donnons en mandement au prevost de Paris et a touz noz autres justiciers. . . .

Donné à Paris le xiiie jour d'aoust, l'an de grace mil CCC IIII^{xx} et quinze, et de nostre regne le quinziesme. Par le [roy], a la relacion du grant conseil ouquel vous, les evesques de Baieux et de Noyon et autres estiez. L. BLANCHET

DOCUMENT 3.4
DJ, 2:48.19.16.

Aut facta puniuntur, ut furta caedesque, aut dicta, ut convicia et infidae advocationes, aut scripta, ut falsa et famosi libelli, aut consilia, ut coniurationes et latronum conscientia quosque alios suadendo iuvisse sceleris est instar. Sed haec quattuor genera consideranda sunt septem modis: causa persona loco tempore qualitate quantitate eventu. Causa: ut in verberibus, quae impunita sunt a magistro allata vel parente, quoniam emendationis, non iniuriae gratia videntur adhiberi: puniuntur, cum quis per iram ab extraneo pulsatus est. Persona dupliciter spectatur, eius qui fecit et eius qui passus est. . . .

CHAPTER 4. Killing Himself by Accident: Of Broken Frames, Mimetic Blindness, and a Dance of Death

DOCUMENT 4.1
CPV, 34–36; Bruneau's emphasis.

Ung jonne homme bouchier tués par fortune en denceant. —Mais au lundemains, qui fut maicredi IXe jour du dit moix d'octobre, avint en ycelle saille une putte adventure et malvaise pour aulcuns; et fut le cas telz comme vous oyrés. Il est vray que, en celluy temps, y avoit en Mets ung robuste gallans, et encor jonne homme, bouchier, nommés Hanry d'Aulnoult, de la Viez Boucherie. Cellui Hanry, à celluy jour, ce tuait en la devent dicte saille par la plus estrainge fasson et maniers que jamaix fist homme. Il est vray que, le jour devant, il avoit servis a nopces, et puis, à celluy jour de lundemains, aincy comme il estoit homme joieulx et délibérés, après ce qu'il olt fait son devoir de servir le dînés, il c'en vint an la dicte saille pour dancer. Et, après plusieurs dance, l'on vint à dancer une dance qui ce dit *le grant turdion,* et ce meue celle dance de tel sorte que, après ce que l'on ait dancés tous ensemble,

tous les compaignons ce despairte à une pertie, et les fille à une aultre; puis
le premier qui maine la dance ce perte de sa plaisse et de son lieu, et permy
le paircque fait plusieurs tours et virailde, et puis, avec la fille, font plusieurs grimaiche; et la remaigne en son lieu. Et fait chacun einssy endroit
soy, quant son tour vient, tout le mieulx qu'il peult, soit de gambairde, de
soubresault ou aultrement; et font aincy les ung après les aultres jusques à
la fin. Or, quant ce vint au tour du dit Henry, il fist cenc mil grimache et
joieusetés. Entre lesquelles il avoit une coustume de faire ung tour, c'on dit
le cul tumerel, qui est essés fort à faire en la sorte qu'il le faisoit: car il saultel-
loit dessus ung piedz, et de l'une de ces mains il tenoit son aultre piedz, qui
estoit levés en hault, et l'aultre mains il la tenoit dessus son col et sa teste,
puis tout soudainement, sans laichier les mains, il boutoit la teste en terre et
faisoit le cul tumerel tout oultre en ce relevant, sans laichier les mains. Or
avint que, en faisant celluy tour, et qu'il remenoit la fille qu'il tenoit en son
lieu, come la dence le requier, il avoit dessus son cul deux lairge coustiaulx
de bouchier, nommés *rousse,* de quoy l'on acourche les beste; lesquelles, en
faisant cellui tours, par fortune saillirent dehors de la gaine, et, comme par
une malle adventure, et une chose que en mil fois ne advenroit, en cheant
qu'il firent, l'ung des dits coustiaulx ce dressait et thint le menche contre le
pavés, tellement que, en ce tournant cen dessus dessoubz, comme j'ai dit, la
pointe d'icellui coustiaulx entrait entre les chausse et le pourpoint, androy
du coustés, dessus la hainche, et luy antrait tout dedans le corps. Et, quant
il santit qu'il ce avoit blessé, non cuidant que ce fût ce que c'estoit, il remenait encor la dicte fille en son lieu; puis retournait en la plaice pour lever
ces coustiaulx. Mais, quant il n'en trouvait que l'ung, il fut bien esbays;
et alors, en ce relevent, il sentit le point. Et demenda confession: mais l'on
cuidoit qu'il ce juait ou truffait, jusques à tant que l'on le vît chaingier. Et,
dès incontinent, l'on le print par les bras, et fut menés chiez ung bouchiez
au Quairtal. Et fut confessés avent que on tirait le dit coustiaulx; lequelle
on olt en grant dificultés: car il estoit cy très dedens que à paine le veoit on;
et, avec ce, estoit fraippés en une os, tellement qu'il en estoit reboullés et
ploiez. Puis au bout de trois jours morut le dit Hanry. Dieu luy perdoint ces
faultes. Amen.

DOCUMENT 4.2
Philippe de Vigneulles, *Gedenkbuch,* ed. Michelant, 147–48.

En cest ainnée avint une aventure asses estrange d'ung homme qui par fortune se tuait, et ne vit-on, se croyiez, jamais homme mourir de mort pa-
reille, ne se tuer en la manière qu'il se tuait; pour ce la veulx-je mectre ycy.
Or avint que ung mecredy ix jour d'octobre, le lundemain des nopces Jehan

Blanchair, le filz Baudat Blanchair l'aman, que ung compaignon bouchier, lequel estoit mairié et demourait en viez Boucherie et se nommoit Hanry Dannoult, l'ung des forts hommes de Mets et l'ung des puissans, mais non pas hault de corps, ycellui Hanry Daulnoult dansoit en la newe saille, au lundemain des dites nopces et dansoit avec les aultres une danse c'on dit le grant turdion, car il estoit joieulx homme d'esperit, et ainsy qu'il voulloit remener sa baicelle, il fist le cul tumerel en se tenant aux mains, c'est assavoir qu'il tenoit l'une jambe devant l'aultre et en ploiant celle jambe et la tenant sans laichier faisoit le cul tumerel qui est aissez ung fort tour à faire, comme bien le savoit faire. Mais en ce faisant, il avoit deux coutiaulx de bouchier c'on dit roussé, en une gaigne sus son cul, qui saillirent hors de la gaigne et en cheant qu'ils firent, l'ung des dits coutiaulx se dressait et tint le manche contre le pavé, tellement que en faisant le cul tumerel, comme j'ay dit, luy entrait le dit coustiaulx tout dedans le corps, par entre le pourpoint et les chausses, par telle force et manière que à peine veoit-on le dit coustiaulx; et quand il sentit qu'il s'avoit fait mal, non cuidant que ce fut ce qu'estoit, il remenait la fille en son lieu avec les aultres et revint en la dite plaice pour serchier ses coustiaulx qu'il avoit sentus cheoir, et quant il n'en trouvait que l'ung il fut bien embais et en se redressant il sentist en prime le copt qu'il avoit et demandoit incontinent confession. Cy cuidoient tous qu'il se mocquait; mais on le vist tantost changier et le menait-on au quartaulx chiez ung aultre boucher et fut confessé avant c'on tirait le dit coustiaulx. Mais quant ce vint à le tirer, il y eust deux maistres bairbiers qui le tiroient avec des trecoizes et n'en savoient venir à bout de l'avoir; car à peine le veoit-on dehors du corps et estoit de ces lairges coustiaulx de quoy qu'ils escourchent les bestes, c'on appelle rousses. Et quant il fut dehors, il le trouvèrent tout ploié, car il estoit fraippé en la hanche en une os, et au bout de trois jours après le dit Hanry en mourut. Dieu ait son airme, car il estoit bon compaignon.

CHAPTER 7. Theater Nullification

DOCUMENT 7.1
LM, 1:444–45; Petit de Julleville's emphasis and ellipsis, also his footnotes.

Cependant, dès les premières années du XVIe siècle on essayait chez nous de remettre en honneur le théâtre des anciens; et ces premières tentatives étaient même fort mal accueillies du public. On en fit l'expérience à Metz dans des circonstances curieuses qu'a racontées le chroniqueur Aubrion:

Le diemenche penultieme jour de janvier (1502) fut commenciez ung jeuz après diney a la court l'Evescque, en la basse salle, nommey *Terance*. Et le jouoient plusieurs gens d'eglise et jonne clersons, tout en latin; et illec estoient... plusieurs... gens d'eglises et clercs et aultres menuz peuple; tellement que quant (*comme*) le diz menuz peuple qui n'estoit point clerc, ne povoit entendre ce que les personnaiges disoient, il se esmeut et se esleva par telle faiçon encontre lesdits joweuz qu'il convint que les sieurs dessus nommey trouvassent maniere de soy despartir tout doulcement de la place. Et ce fait ledit menuz peuple efforcet les dit personnaige et monta sur le hour tellement qu'il fuit tout bel audit personnaiges de decendre, car il furent en grant dangier d'estre très bien frontés. ... Le landemain après diney, que le dit peuple estoit chacun à sa besoigne, fuit juez le jeu en latin, comme dit est.[1]

_____

"Ils essevirent lour jeu," dit le chroniqueur Jacomin Husson,[2] mais seulement le lendemain, et quand ils eurent bien fermé "les huix, et n'y entroient que gens d'églize, seigneurs et clercs." C'est ainsi que le théâtre antique fit sa rentrée en terre gauloise, toutes portes closes et comme en cachette.

1. *Journal de Pierre* [sic] *Aubrion,* éditée par L. Larchey, p. 441.
2. *Mémoires de Jacomin Husson,* édit. Michelant, p. 214.

NOTES

Mise en Scène.

1. For the Intentional Fallacy, I will be focusing—mostly in the Introduction and Entr'Acte—on the classic essay, "The Intentional Fallacy" (hereafter IF), penned in 1946 by Wimsatt and Beardsley, as well as the numerous debates it has spawned, espe cially Knapp and Michaels, "Against Theory" (hereafter AT) and "Against Theory 2" (hereafter AT2), and many other works. For "performativity," I focus on Austin's two essays from *Philosophical Papers* (hereafter PP), "Pretending" and "Performative Utterances" (chaps. 10 and 11, respectively); and *How to Do Things with Words* (hereafter HDTW), essays 1 and 2. Especially germane are Witmore, *Culture of Accidents* (hereafter CA); and Hamilton, *Accident: A Philosophical and Literary History.* The latter work was released as my book was going to press, but I have alluded to it wherever possible.

2. *Medieval Civilization* (hereafter MC), trans. Barrow, 360–61.

3. See Turner, *From Ritual to Theatre* (hereafter FRT), especially 7–19, 61–88, 89–101, and "Acting in Everyday Life and Everyday Life in Acting," 102–23; de Certeau, *Practice of Everyday Life* (hereafter PEL); and Read, *Theatre and Everyday Life* (hereafter TEL). On theater's receptivity to social change, see Zumthor, *Essai de poétique médiévale,* 447; and Carlson, *Theatre Semiotics,* xviii.

4. For medieval theatricality in these arenas, see, e.g., Hardison, *Christian Rite and Christian Drama* (liturgy); Kipling, *Enter the King* (procession); Enders, *Rhetoric and the Origins of Medieval Drama* (hereafter ROMD) (courtroom and classroom); and Sponsler, *Drama and Resistance* (politics). For excellent introductions to the issue at large, see Clopper, *Drama, Play, and Game,* introd.; Axton, *European Drama of the Early Middle Ages,* chaps. 2 and 3; Zumthor, *Essai de poétique médiévale,* chap. 10; Olson, *Literature as Recreation;* along with the formative work of Schechner, especially *Between Theater and Anthropology* (hereafter BTA); Turner, *Dramas, Fields, and Metaphors;* and Ashley and Hüsken, eds., *Moving Subjects.*

5. *Mimesis,* 158. On theater as a widespread metaphor for human behavior, see

Wilshire, *Role Playing and Identity* (hereafter *RPI*), especially part 3. See also, on the "scene of the crime," Kottman, *Politics of the Scene,* 10.

6. Olson frames the problem nicely in "Plays as Play," 217.

7. Beyond McLuhan's influential *Gutenberg Galaxy,* Ong speaks of secondary literacy in, e.g., *Orality and Literacy.* It is a commonplace that rhetoric and literature were inseparable in early cultures; see Kennedy, *Classical Rhetoric* (hereafter *CR*), 5.

8. On the qualitative and quantitative differences between live theater and live television, see, e.g., Eco, *Open Work* (hereafter *OW*), 106; Weber, *Theatricality as Medium,* chaps. 2 and 3; and Auslander, *Liveness,* chap. 2 (to which I return in my concluding chapter).

9. Details follow in Part I, but I refer to Paris, Archives Nationales (hereafter AN), JJ 116, no. 254, fols. 152v–53r (Appendix, Document 1.1); AN, JJ 125, no. 7, fols. 7v–8r (Appendix, Document 2.1); and AN, JJ 148, no. 144, fols. 74v–75r (Appendix, Document 3.3). I thus revisit, from the standpoint of intention, several incidents to which I first alluded in *Death by Drama* (hereafter *DBD*), chaps. 4 (on two deaths by theatrical cannon-fire) and 7 (on various folkloric tales about diabolical intervention); in "Medieval Death"; and in "Spectacle of the Scaffolding." Petit de Julleville, e.g., found only a handful of earlier fragmentary records from 1290, 1333, 1351, and 1376 (catalogued chronologically in *Les Mystères,* hereafter *LM*). For an astute historical perspective, see Muir and Ruggiero, "Introduction: The Crime of History."

10. See, e.g., Isidore's treatment of armed combat, legal trials, sports, theater, gladiatorial battle, disputation, dice games, and so on, in *Isidori Hispalensis Episcopi Etymologiarum sive Originum Libri XX* (hereafter *Etymologiarum*), 2: book 18 (which I discuss at length in *ROMD,* 74–89).

11. For a helpful discussion of the philosophical distinctions between intentions, motives, and reasons, see, e.g., Anscombe, *Intentionality,* 13–20.

12. Rayner, *To Do, to Act, to Perform* (hereafter *DAP*), 3.

13. Eagleton, *Literary Theory* (hereafter *LT*), 119. Compare also with Brook's preference for a "healthy relation" between the real and the imaginary, in a 1972 interview cited by Croydon in *Lunatics, Lovers and Poets,* 278; discussed by Read, *TEL,* 14.

14. See, e.g., Geary, *Living with the Dead;* Ariès's classic, *Western Attitudes toward Death;* and Gertsman, "Pleyinge and Peynting."

15. Especially helpful in the historiography of political theater (a vast subject that lies beyond the scope of this book), are Cohen, *Drama of a Nation;* Kruger, *National Stage;* Fischer-Lichte, *Theatre, Sacrifice, Ritual,* chap. 1; Kershaw, *Politics of Performance* and "Curiosity or Contempt"; and, from a modern U.S. perspective, Cohen-Cruz, *Local Acts;* and Dolan, "Rehearsing Democracy."

16. Kubiak, *Stages of Terror,* 11.

17. Taylor Hackford, e.g., was reportedly outraged about the publicity ramifications of the liaison between Meg Ryan and Russell Crowe during the filming of *Proof of Life.*

18. I contest the "jadedness" of both cultures in *Medieval Theater of Cruelty* (hereafter *MTOC*), 20–24, 230–37.

19. For the *Eumenides* incident of ca. 460 B.C., see Nagler, *Source Book,* 5; and *DBD,* 74–75. On RATT, see Pywell, *Staging Real Things* (hereafter *SRT*), 21; and, e.g., Sell, *Avant-garde Performance and the Limits of Criticism* (hereafter *APLC*).

20. *Time on Fire,* 250–57. Compare also with the wrestler Owen Hart who, on 23 May 1999, plunged accidentally to his death during a spectacular aerial entrance into Kemper Arena. It was covered, e.g., on ABC's *World News Tonight* and NBC's *Nightly News* on 24 May 1999.

21. The notion that violence prompts the pleasurable accentuation of art rather than its ruinous compromise is, of course, the essence of sadomasochism, in the hands, e.g., of J. G. Ballard in *Crash.* See also Goffman on "orders of being" in *Frame Analysis* (hereafter *FA*), 62.

22. Robert Zemeckis could hardly have anticipated the popularity of the title of his *Back to the Future* (1985), which called up 23 million Google entries on 10 October 2006. See also Levinson, "New Historicism: Back to the Future."

23. Holsinger, in *Premodern Condition,* elucidates the importance of the Middle Ages to French theory in particular.

24. On this point, see Rayner, *DAP,* 13.

25. "Interpreting Drama" (hereafter ID), 103; my emphasis. An earlier, intriguingly different version of this essay appeared in 1977 as "Semiotics of Theatrical Performance" (hereafter STP).

26. On alterity, see especially Warning, "On the Alterity of Medieval Religious Drama" and *Ambivalences of Medieval Religious Drama;* and Jauss, "Alterity and Modernity of Medieval Literature" and *Question and Answer* (hereafter *QA*), 4. In my *MTOC,* I argue that a well-intentioned deference to alterity has masked contemporary complicity in the history of violence.

27. We return throughout to Goffman's ground-breaking *FA,* chap. 2; as well as to Eco, *Limits of Interpretation.* The similarities between medieval drama and modern telejournalism are the subject of my "Medieval Death."

28. Petit de Julleville cites this phrase about the *Play of Saint Catherine* in Montélimar on 15 May 1453: "*attento quod erit maximum exemplum honorque et utilitas et commodum ville,*" *LM,* 2:24. On the ritual continuity of heroism between Christian and pre-Christian societies, see the classic treatments by Auerbach, *Mimesis,* chap. 7; and Frye, *Anatomy of Criticism,* Third Essay.

29. Consider, e.g., the Texas celebration of "Jesus Day" on 10 June (as of 2000); or the controversy (2002) about the words "under God" in the Pledge of Allegiance.

30. For Horace on *dulce/utile,* see *Ars poetica,* 343. Konner and Shapiro made their remarks to media correspondent Terence Smith of the *Jim Lehrer News Hour* (13 January 1999).

31. Jane Pauley and Stone Phillips apologized on the air for that incident in March 1993.

32. Despite the endurance of the occasional "unimpeachable category" (like

Lamarque and Olsen's "'no truth' theory of literature" in *Truth, Fiction and Literature,* 1.13), most medievalists emphasize the dynamic historical interplay between historical "findings" and literary "inventions." See, e.g., White, *Metahistory,* 6–7; Davis, *Fiction in the Archives* (hereafter *FIA*), 4; Otter, *Inventiones,* 6; Mali, *Mythistory;* Le Goff, *History and Memory,* 101–3; Jauss, *QA,* 7; Riffaterre, *Fictional Truth;* Green, *Crisis of Truth;* Wilkinson, "Choice of Fictions"; and Davis, *Factual Fictions,* 9–10 (many of whom I discuss in *DBD,* prologue and introd.).

33. *Topica,* in *De inventione and Topica,* 7.33–34.

34. The signature work that unites the philosophy of the accident with both psychology and psychoanalysis is Hamilton's *Accident.*

35. Especially enlightening on the topic are such works as Austin's "Plea for Excuses," chap. 6 of *PP;* Cavell, *Must We Mean What We Say?* (hereafter *MWM*); Wilshire, *RPI;* Searle, *Intentionality;* Anscombe, *Intentionality;* Davidson, *Essays on Actions and Events;* Dennett, *Intentional Stance* (hereafter *IS*); Audi, *Action, Intention, and Reason* (hereafter *AIR*), chaps. 2–6; Shawcross, *Intentionality and the New Traditionalism;* Geach, "Kinds of Statement"; Williams, *Moral Luck;* Statman, ed., *Moral Luck;* Scheffler, ed., *Consequentialism and its Critics;* Witmore, *CA;* and, for a review of intention in rhetoric and philosophy, see Lyon, *Intentions.* As far as possible, I seek to avoid becoming embroiled in philosophical arguments about terminology (i.e., "intent" vs. "intentionality").

36. See the thoughtful analysis by Petrey, "French Studies/Cultural Studies."

37. Langer, *Feeling and Form* (hereafter *FF*), 57.

38. See, e.g., Goffman, *FA,* 125; and Kirby, *Formalist Theatre* (hereafter *FT*), x–xi; discussed below.

39. Tallis, *Not Saussure* (hereafter *NS*), 234. See also Harris, *Literary Meaning* (hereafter *LMRSL*), 94.

Introduction.

1. Full references for these events, and further justification of the analogy, appear in chapter 1 and our Talk-Back, respectively.

2. For medieval perspectives, see especially Minois, *History of Suicide;* and Murray, *Suicide in the Middle Ages.*

3. I return later to the critique of phenomenology and reception theory, the essence, e.g., of Lesser's objections to Black's *Aesthetics of Murder* (hereafter *AM*) in her *Pictures at an Execution* (hereafter *PE*), 5–17.

4. KTLA's Kelly Lang, 6 May 1998.

5. Schlegel describes historians thus in *Dialogue on Poetry and Literary Aphorisms* (1798), trans. Behler and Struc, aphorism 80. See Langer's discussion of this predicament, *FF,* chap. 17; and also Anscombe on "backward-looking motives" (*Intentionality,* 18–23). Langer's interest in the "dramatic mode" was positively clairvoyant for later developments in performance studies.

6. Giddens, "Action, Subjectivity, and the Constitution of Meaning" (hereafter ASCM), 173, also 165.

7. Although it is not my precise focus, we tend to see this debate in the context of censorship; see especially Steiner, *Scandal of Pleasure* (hereafter *SP*); Holquist, "Corrupt Originals"; and a debate between William F. Buckley Jr. and Alan Dershowitz, as detailed in Buckley, "Killer Doc." Closer to our case studies and still helpful is Hallays-Dabot, *Histoire de la censure théâtrale en France.*

8. Eagleton's emphasis on "actual," mine on the rest. In chapter 3, we return to Goffman's own legally charged terminology.

9. On this point (to which we return shortly), see especially Tallis, *NS,* 233; Witmore, *CA,* 10; and Huizinga, *Homo Ludens* (hereafter *HL*), chap. 4. Among Witmore's signal contributions is his explicit acknowledgment of theater as metaphor, through considerations of theology and rhetoricity—of what he calls the romance of Fortuna on one hand and the rhetorico-legal tradition on the other (*CA,* 7, 19).

10. The study of those narrative resonances is the primary contribution of Witmore and Hamilton: see especially *CA,* introd.; and *Accident,* introd. and chap. 1.

11. Hadrian: "qui hominem occidit, si non occidendi *animo* hoc admisit, absolvi posse, et qui hominem non occidit, sed vulneravit, ut occidat, pro homicida damnandum" (*Digest of Justinian* [hereafter *DJ*], 2: book 48, chap. 8, sec. 1, part 3; my emphasis). Alan Watson translates *animo* as "intention." All Latin citations of this text are drawn from *Digest of Justinian* (*Digesta*), ed. Mommsen; English translations are those of Watson. We return, especially in chapters 1 and 4, to the numerous ambiguities in the *Digest* on the matter of intention.

12. Here, Witmore cites Green, *Verdict according to Conscience,* 86-123.

13. See especially Davis's important discussion of the sixteenth-century jurist, Jehan Papon, *FIA,* 11-12. See also Witmore on *mens rea* in early English distinctions between manslaughter and murder, *CA,* 26. For ancient antecedents, see Evans, *Criminal Prosecution and Capital Punishment of Animals,* 9-10; for actual statistics, see, e.g., Given, *Society and Homicide;* and for the early modern period, see also, despite its minimalist bibliography, Wilson, *TT,* 10-11, which accords greater focus to economic context than I do here.

14. See Harris, *LMRSL,* 91; his emphasis. See Witmore's important historicization of the philology of accident, *CA,* 19-22, 29; and Hamilton, *Accident,* 17-19.

15. This is the stuff of philosopy. I reserve the related discussion of Freudian slips and psychopathology for chapters 5 and 6.

16. On this general point, see Harris, *LMRSL,* 91-96; and Tallis, *NS,* 233.

17. See especially Hirsch, *VI,* chap. 1. Useful in this respect is Alice Rayner's term *actant* (*DAP,* 2), to which we return shortly.

18. Graff, *Clueless in Academe,* especially introd.

19. Cavell is discussing here the specific possibility of medieval hagiographic inspiration (from Philomela) for *La Strada.* I will not be hypercorrecting earlier critics' use of the masculine pronoun.

20. Dasenbrock, *TC,* 172.

21. As recently as the Tony Awards of 2007, presenter Cynthia Nixon praised nominees for best director for their faithfulness to the original intentions of playwrights.

22. See especially Baudrillard, *Symbolic Exchange and Death;* and Butterfield, EVNA. Notable exceptions, to which we return throughout, include, in theater studies, Goffman, *FA;* Eco, STP; Kirby, *FT;* Rayner, *DAP;* Wilson, *TI,* introd.; Iser, "Representation"; and Ingarden's still illuminating "Functions of Language in the Theater" (hereafter FLT); in philosophy, the revelations of Witmore and Hamilton; and, in textual criticism, Melia, "Response"; Mailloux, *Interpretive Conventions;* Rabinowitz, *Before Reading;* Fish, "Interpreting the Variorum"; McGann, *Critique of Modern Textual Criticism;* Bowers, "Textual Criticism"; and Tanselle, *Textual Criticism.* We return to the critical history of the Intentional Fallacy at greater length in the Entr'Acte.

23. For exemplary work in law and literature, see Brooks and Gewirtz, eds., *Law's Stories* (hereafter LS); and Sarat and Kearns, eds., *Law in Everyday Life.*

24. See Barthes, "Death of the Author"; also Hirsch, *VI,* 1–6; and Burke, *Death and Return of the Author,* chap. 3.

25. We shall return, e.g., to Melia, "Response"; Mailloux, *Interpretive Conventions,* especially chap. 4; Rabinowitz, *Before Reading;* Fish, "Interpreting the Variorum"; McGann, *Critique of Modern Textual Criticism;* Bowers, "Textual Criticism"; and Tanselle, *Textual Criticism,* 26–71.

26. In the Entr'Acte, we return to that vast topic, as explored especially by Paul Ricoeur in *Interpretation Theory* (hereafter *IT*).

27. Key texts on that point include Marco de Marinis, *Semiotics of Performance,* especially 47–59; reprinted as "Performance Text," chap. 34 of *Performance Studies Reader* (hereafter *PSR*), ed. Bial. Even Hirsch termed the literary text an author's "actual performance . . . presented in his text" (*VI,* 11).

28. Natalie Zemon Davis revolutionized our understanding of the narrative conventions of letters of remission in *FIA* and *Return of Martin Guerre.*

29. On this point, see also Searle, *Intentionality,* 3 (discussed in chapter 1); and Robert Audi on "end-directed" vs. "simple" intentions, in *AIR,* chap. 2.

30. See, e.g., Stanislavski, *Actor Prepares* (hereafter *AP*), 176–78.

31. See Hamilton on the "intricacy of the interactions between accident as a quality and accident as an event" (*Accident,* 2, 17–19); and also Witmore, *CA,* 32–35.

32. We explore this point at greater length in Case 3 of chapter 7.

33. For a similar and eloquent point on textuality, see Ricoeur, *IT,* 30; also Hirsch, *VI,* 4.

34. I refer, e.g., to *L'Étranger* and *Les Caves du Vatican.* See also Dowling, "Intentionless Meaning"; Cavell on unconscious intent (*MWM,* 231); and Davidson, "Intending," 88.

35. Leader-Elliot, "Negotiating Intentions" (hereafter NI), 88.

36. As we shall see, especially in chapters 6 and 7, this is different, e.g., from affective impact prompting a fatal heart attack.

37. See Aristotle, *Poetics* 1452a; cited (Barnes trans.) by Witmore (*CA,* 40).

38. On that late arrival, see Case, *Performing Feminisms,* introd., 2; and Parker and Sedgwick, *Performativity and Performance,* introd., 2. Especially resonant for medieval performativity are, e.g., Geach on the "rediscovery" of the "sacramental forms of words" in such speech acts as promises, "Kinds of Statements," 223; and Gould's insightful "Unhappy Performative" (hereafter UP).

39. I.e., both are unmarried, the officiator has the proper credentials, and so forth. See *HDTW,* 14–16; and Searle on "direction of fit," *Intentionality,* 10–11.

40. Compare also with *HDTW,* 21–22; Cavell, *MWM,* 236; Searle, "Logical Status of Fictional Discourse" (hereafter LSFD), 324–25; and Walton, *Mimesis as Make-Believe* (hereafter *MM*), 81–89. For similar observations, see Goffman, *FA,* 10; and Issacharoff, *Discourse as Performance,* chap. 2.

41. On this point, discussed later, see Hirsch, *VI,* 4; and Ricoeur, *IT,* 30.

42. See also Dowling, "Intentionless Meaning."

43. Not helpful in clarifying such semantic confusion is Iser's title (to a textually oriented analysis): "Representation: A Performative Act."

44. See *FA,* chaps. 1 and 5; and Eco, ID.

45. See chapter 4; I discuss many such moments in *DBD,* chap. 3.

46. Isidore writes: "Theatrum autem ab spectaculo nominatum, apo tis theorias, quod in eo populus stans desuper atque spectans ludos contemplaretur," *Etymologiarum,* "De theatro," book 18, chap. 42. See also *ROMD,* 77–89; Olson, who treats Isidore briefly in his "Medieval Fortunes," 268, 270; and Henderson, *Medieval World of Isidore of Seville.* On etymology as medieval literary theory, see Bloch, *Etymologies and Genealogies.*

47. See especially Blau, *Audience;* and Bennett, *Theatre Audiences.*

48. Consider the moniker "closet drama," by which critics often translate audience displeasure with (or disregard of) a given play into *authorial intent not to stage it.*

49. We consider this type of event in Scenarios 9–10 of chapter 6.

50. For theater's "re-production" and unrepeatability, see Benjamin, *Illuminations,* 220; also discussed by Read, *TEL,* 15; and for Schechner's "restored behavior," see *BTA,* chap. 2. I make no excuses for my belief, substantiated throughout, that theater performed without an audience is still theater.

51. For an eerily compatible counterpart from conservative politics, see George Will's denunciation of the final murder in the 1976 exploitation film *Snuff,* which he finds equally despicable, "whether real or fake" (cited by Johnson and Schaefer, "Soft Core," 53). The machinations of fostering box-office success are clearly less important than determining whether a murder is real or fake.

52. "Simulacra and Simulations," in *Selected Writings* (hereafter *SW*), 178. In chapter 1, we consider his second example of the SWAT team at the more dangerous bank robbery (*SW,* 178).

53. Compare, e.g., with Kirby's so-called poles of acting vs. not acting, *FT,* chap. 1. On the postmodern rejection of the false binaries of reality vs. representation, true vs. false, or outside vs. inside, see also Read, *TEL,* 2; and Wilshire's critique of Goffman's binarism, *RPI,* 274–81.

54. In chapters 5 and 7, we consider the importance of time and timing.

55. LSFD, 325; my emphasis. See also Walton's discussion of this passage in *MM,* 81.

56. Compare also with our epigraph from Searle; and Knapp and Michaels's assertion that meanings and speech acts are always intentional (AT, 24).

57. In our Entr'Acte, we reconsider this problem in light of a slightly different argument, drawn from critical use of intentionless turns of phrase, that texts and objects do not have intentions: their agents do.

58. Again, the better to avoid frontloading theory, we return, in the Entr'Acte, to a brief discussion of the applied critical history of the Intentional Fallacy.

59. I discuss throughout the important exceptions cited in note 22; and, although it is not his principal focus, see Ridout, *Stage Fright,* especially chap. 4. Otherwise, even when Witmore (*CA,* chap. 4) and Hamilton (*Accident,* 81–91) discuss *Hamlet,* they emphasize the drama of the story's narrative arc over actual performance before spectators. Intention figures more prominently in work on rhetoric and theater semiotics: see, e.g., Burke, *Philosophy of Literary Form* (hereafter *POLF*), 103–32, 329–44; Pavis, *Problèmes de sémiologie théâtrale;* Pavis, *Voix et images de la scène;* Alter, *Sociosemiotic Theory of Theatre;* de Marinis, *Semiotics of Performance;* Carlson, *Theatre Semiotics;* Melrose, *Semiotics of the Dramatic Text;* and Issacharoff, *Discourse.*

60. See Witmore on Meyer's "Aristotle, Teleology, and Reduction," on Aristotle's *tuche* (luck or fortune) vs. *automaton* (chance), *CA,* 32–35.

61. Even Witmore's chap. 4, "*Hamlet* Interrupted," is about the dramatic theory (over the theatrical practice) of accidents.

62. On this point, the subject of much debate among philosophers, see, e.g., Anscombe, *Intentionality,* chap. 1; Davidson, "Intending," 83–88; Audi, *AIR,* chaps. 2, 3, and 6.

63. The discrete consideration of intention, action, and affect undergirds such approaches to speech acts as Austinian illocution and perlocution (*HDTW,* lecture 8); see also Gould, UP, 20. See also Audi for a consideration of intending to "bring about" certain states of affairs, *AIR,* 56–70. In chapter 7, we return to the extent to which one may intend *for others.*

64. See Zumthor on the "monumentalization" of language in *Essai de poétique médiévale,* 76–77. The nature of the theatrical archive is itself a hot topic in theater studies, in that audio- and videotapings can be multiplied ad infinitum. On the canonical duty of the orator to impel to action, especially in Cicero, see Kennedy, *CR,* 100.

65. Compare, e.g., with *DJ,* 2:48.19.16, to which I return in chapter 3 (Appendix, Document 3.4).

66. Eco, however, makes an argument (to which we return in chapter 4) that they *can be* things (ID, 102–3).

67. The master work on medieval animals on trial is Evans, *Criminal Prosecution,* which I treat at length in Enders, "Homicidal Pigs." On falling objects, see also *CA,* 6.

68. See Dershowitz, "Life Is Not a Dramatic Narrative." See also Huizinga on *judicium dei* (*HL,* 80–86). Witmore is citing Thomas Beard's *The theatre of gods judge-*

ments, a translation of Jean de Chassanion (*CA,* 7–8); see also his point that accidents "are a prime occasion for the recognition and expression of communal values which shape narrative representations of 'what happened'" (*CA,* 13).

69. See Suetonius, "Caligula," *Lives of the Caesars* (hereafter *LC*), 1: chap. 32; and on Nero's enjoyment of mortal accidents, "Nero," *LC,* 2:12.2; also cited and discussed by Bartsch, *Actors in the Audience* (hereafter *AA*), chap. 1; and by Shelton, *As the Romans Did,* 335n. See also Duncan, *Performance and Identity,* chaps. 5 and 6.

70. By analogy to snuff films (the notoriously elusive cinematic phenomenon in which a real death is ostensibly captured on film for pornographic purposes), I argued in "Medieval Snuff Drama" and in *DBD,* chap. 14, that there *is* or could be such a thing. For helpful approaches to the events that book-end the present inquiry, see Johnson and Schaefer, "Soft Core/Hard Gore," 46–47; and Schechner, *BTA,* chap. 7.

71. Buell, IPE, 9.

72. Sedgwick, *Epistemology of the Closet,* chap. 5.

73. See especially Eco on the feedback loop of theater, ID, 110. For classic work on readerly intent, see, e.g., Fish, *Is There a Text;* Holland, *Dynamics of Literary Response;* and, *5 Readers Reading;* Iser, *Act of Reading;* and Iser, *Implied Reader.* On the subject of time, still helpful is Ricoeur's exhaustive *Time and Narrative.*

74. It is not my purpose here to provide a comparative analysis of reading practices in classical antiquity and the Middle Ages (although the latter period proves especially rich for the interplay of oral tradition, textuality, and nascent practices of publication). For an excellent introduction to that vast and well-researched subject, see, e.g., Stock, *Implications of Literacy;* Saenger, "Silent Reading"; Treitler, "Oral, Written, and Literate Process"; Carruthers, *Book of Memory;* Huot, *From Song to Book;* Brantley, *Reading in the Wilderness;* and Brown, *Poets, Patrons, and Printers.*

75. For a disciplinary perspective on theater studies in higher education, see Jackson, *Professing Performance.*

76. See also Saenger, "Silent Reading"; Wimsatt and Beardsley, IF, 10–11, on language as both internal and public; and Eco on privacy before live telecasts, *OW,* 106. Web publishing of electronic editions represents, with emphasis on multimedia, some of the best critical efforts to recreate the polyvalent and even polyphonous nature of medieval manuscript culture.

77. On the importance of intentionality in the establishment of texts, see note 25.

78. Melia, "Response" (to Knapp and Michaels, AT2), 14; his emphasis.

79. For the debates in medieval studies, see Nichols, ed., *New Philology* (special issue of *Speculum*); Bloch and Nichols, eds., *Medievalism and the Modernist Temper;* Brownlee, Brownlee, and Nichols, eds., *New Medievalism;* and, more generally, Hunt, ed., *New Cultural History.* For *mouvance* and *variance,* see Zumthor, *Essai,* 65–72; Cerquiglini, *Éloge de la variante;* and, for oral tradition, Lord, *Singer of Tales;* and Foley, *Theory of Oral Composition,* which includes a superb bibliography.

80. I don't mean works of which only one copy is extant.

81. See also Anscombe, *Intentionality,* 7–9.

82. See Witmore on *Poetics* 1452a (*CA*, 40); and on the intersection of falling objects and divine justice (*CA*, 6).

83. I play, of course, on *This Sex Which Is Not One* (*Ce sexe qui n'en est pas un*). See especially Coomaraswamy, "Intention," discussed in chapter 1.

84. I adapt this terminology (to which we return in chapter 1 and throughout) from a variety of sources: especially Eco, ID, 101–10; Eco, "Overinterpreting Texts," 62–66; and Eco, *OW*, 106–15; Mailloux's superb analysis of "inferential intentions," *Interpretive Conventions*, 94–108; Anscombe on "executed intentions," *Intentionality*, 87–89; Stallman, "Intentions"; and Kirby, *FT*, chap. 4.

85. Here I allude especially to Turner, *FRT*, 61–88; see also Davidson, "Agency"; and Davidson, "Freedom to Act." On good faith, deception, and coercion, e.g., Audi, *AIR*, chap. 7; Ridout, *Stage Fright*, chap. 4; Searle, LSFD, 324–25; Walton, *MM*, 81; Eco, ID, 105 (all discussed in chapter 5); and the notorious Sokal hoax (see chapter 1).

86. See Ballard's *Crash*, as discussed by Butterfield in EVNA. In chapter 3, we consider a medieval version of that problem.

87. See the Mise en Scène for my caveats about political theater.

88. Of course, not everything that is experienced need be viewed (as we shall see in chapter 7 in the case of the blind theatergoer or the terrorist who releases anthrax in a crowded theater). But it is logical, in an inquiry into theater, to privilege acting, watching, and listening over acts of reading (Iserian or otherwise).

89. For a fascinating approach to "accidental reading," see Hamilton on Augustine, *Accident*, 30–41.

90. See especially Hamilton, *Accident*, 1; and Tallis on the random quality of some intentional acts, *NS*, 233; cited in chapter 4.

91. In our concluding Talk-Back, we shall see that that is not quite the case.

92. For an Aristotelian interpretation of the phenomenon, see Witmore, *CA*, 31.

93. For readability, these specific categories will appear in small capitals throughout. We explore and refine their relevance to theatrical action especially in chapters 5 and 6. Again, see Anscombe, *Intentionality*, 87–89.

94. Again, see Gould, UP.

95. See also Hamilton on Pascal, *Accident*, 107–10; and our chapter 3, for the literal embodiment of intentions.

96. We consider this type of example, the principal subject of Witmore's *CA* and Hamilton's *Accident*, in chapter 7, Case 3.

97. For confession as the "queen of proofs," see Peters, *Torture*, chap. 2. In chapter 5, we shall see that ACTUAL INTENTIONS also raise issues of self-knowledge, mental disease or defect, and timing.

98. Intending subjects need not follow through on their intentions, which is the topic of much debate in philosophy. Helpful introductions to the subject include Anscombe, *Intentionality*, 34–36; Audi, *AIR*, chap. 6; and Hirsch, *VI*, 11. One can also intend inaction or concealment (see chapter 6).

99. On this point, see Anscombe, *Intentionality*, 54–57.

100. For PERCEIVED INTENTION, which is sometimes called "inferential intention" (*TC*, 75), there seems no way to avoid the ellipsis of agency: perceived by whom? While it is technically part of the reception of ACTUAL and ACHIEVED INTENTIONS, I retain it here nonetheless, for its relevance to the consequences that befall actants.

101. In the Entr'Acte and chapter 7, we reconsider the specific intentions that the theatrical collective attributes to an audience—and vice versa.

102. The important philosophical work of Witmore and Hamilton in the history of accidents will prove crucial to this recuperation, as both return to the expansive inclusion, under the rubric of the largely Aristotelian "accident," of not just physical but mental events. See especially Hamilton, *Accident*, introd.; and Witmore, *CA*, chap. 1.

103. *Empty Space*, 17.

104. AN, JJ 125, no. 7, fols. 7v–8r (Appendix, Document 2.1).

105. Although this is not the subject of the present study, the performance setting of the letter of remission must join the ranks of protodramatic activities, as I describe them in *ROMD*, introd. and chap. 1. On the oral dimensions of the public performances of forgiveness, see Davis, *FIA*, chap. 1; Hanawalt, "Whose Story Was This?"; and Koziol, *Begging Pardon*, especially chap. 2 (in which he focuses nonetheless on the "iconic" over the theatrical); while even Stacey ignores the work of medieval theater scholars in her fascinating *Dark Speech*.

106. AN, JJ 148, no. 144, fol. 74v (Appendix, Document 3.3).

107. *La Chronique de Philippe de Vigneulles*, ed. Bruneau (hereafter *CPV*), 3:114–15; Appendix, Document 3.1.

108. *CPV*, 4:34–36; Appendix, Document 4.1.

109. That does not mean that I will avoid politics, which I address explicitly, especially in my Entr'Acte and Talk-Back.

110. Artaud's first chapter of *Theater and Its Double* is a meditation on the plague.

111. The term *collective* in no way excludes such phenomena as solo performance, a point presciently made, e.g., by Huizinga (*HL*, chap. 1), where he implies that the difference between childhood games and theatrical performance is one only of scale, degree, quantity of spectators, and so on. We consider legal standing in chapters 6 and 7.

112. See also Green's fascinating treatment of jury nullification in the thirteenth and fourteenth centuries in *Verdict according to Conscience*, chap. 2, especially 61–64. In chapter 7, we explore such nullification from the standpoint of the audience.

113. Indirectly relevant is the work especially of Jill Dolan's *Utopia in Performance*.

114. See, e.g., Futrell, *Blood in the Arena*; Kyle, *Spectacles of Death in Ancient Rome*; Plass, *Game of Death*; Cunningham, "Renaissance Execution and Marlovian Elocution"; Coleman, "Fatal Charades"; and Cohen on medieval scripting of death, *Crossroads of Justice*, 181–201.

115. Here I paraphrase, of course, Judith Butler's title, *Bodies That Matter*.

Chapter One.

1. AN, JJ 116, no. 254, fol. 152v; for the French document, see Appendix, Document 1.1 (a version of which also appears in *DBD*, 211–12). When citing it in this chapter, I refer parenthetically only to folio number. Our Cavell epigraph appears in *MWM*, 236–37; his emphasis.

2. As we shall see, the case of the unnamed man on the freeway is still more complex (Talk-Back). Compare also, e.g., with a medieval actor who supposedly *did* die for political reasons (*DBD*, chap. 13); and, for more on risk management see, e.g., from a legal perspective, Jackson, "How Decision Theory Illuminates Assignments of Moral Responsibility"; and from a medieval theatrical perspective, Evans, "When a Body Meets a Body."

3. Thomas, "Le Théâtre à Paris et aux environs," 609–11. A decontextualized excerpt from this document appears as no. E1a in Tydeman, ed. *Medieval European Stage* (hereafter *MES*), 285.

4. Compare, e.g., to Witmore's discussion of the narrative resonances of accident, *CA,* introd.

5. Vives, *Vives on Education (De tradendis disciplinis),* 177.

6. See especially Steiner, *SP,* chap. 2; see also discussion in Entr'Acte.

7. See Beale, "Sampler of Hell"; and Fletcher, "Tasteless as Hell." The signature work on medieval drama in America is Sponsler, *Ritual Imports.*

8. See Plato, *Laws,* ed. and trans. Bury, 700. For a historical overview, see Barish, *Antitheatrical Prejudice;* for specific medieval polemics, see *DBD,* chap. 8; and, for Enlightenment debates and beyond, see Marshall, *Surprising Effects of Sympathy* (hereafter *SES*).

9. See Witmore, *CA,* 5–7.

10. "Nihil interest, occidat quis an causam mortis praebeat," *DJ,* 2:48.8.15.

11. "Eventus spectetur, ut a clementissimo quoquo facta: quamquam lex non minus eum, qui occidendi hominis causa cum telo fuerit, quam eum qui occiderit puniat," *DJ,* 2:48.19.16.8. See also Marcian on the three categories of offense: by design, by impulse, or by accident (*aut proposito aut impetu aut casu*). Again, see Davis on a later period, *FIA,* 11–12.

12. "Nam si gladium strinxerit et in eo percusserit, indubitate occidendi *animo* id eum admisisse: sed si clavi percussit aut cuccuma in rixa, quamvis ferro percusserit, tamen non occidendi *animo.* [L]eniendam poenam eius, qui in rixa casu magis quam voluntate homicidium," *DJ,* 2:48.8.1.3; my emphasis. Watson weaves intentionality into his translations, e.g., when rendering *animo* as "intentionally" and *dolus* as "guilty intention" (*DJ,* 2:48.8.7; cited in chapter 2).

13. See the Introduction for the fourth category of our first taxonomy.

14. On Finley, see, e.g., Carr, "Unspeakable Practices"; as well as Dick's documentary on Flanagan, *Sick.*

15. We return in chapter 6 to suicide by theater; for theater-related suicide in the Middle Ages, see *DBD,* chap. 13.

16. On contemporary personages behind the scenes, who are (officially) both seen and unseen in different ways by audiences and actors, see Rayner, "Rude Mechanicals."

17. I discuss the special dangers of the staging—and filming—of the Crucifixion in *DBD*, chaps. 4 and 5; as well as in "Seeing Is Not Believing."

18. Again, on this point, see especially Witmore, *CA*, chap. 1; and Hamilton, *Accident*, chaps. 1 and 2.

19. Inherited by the Middle Ages via such widely disseminated texts as the *Rhetorica ad Herennium* (ed. Caplan; hereafter *RAH*), forensic stasis theory was a complex hierarchy of questions to be asked of any crime (*RAH*, 1.18–27); see chapters 2 and 3.

20. On believing, intending, and acting, see Searle, *Intentionality*, 3; on "true belief," see Knapp and Michaels, AT, 22–26; and Fish, "Consequences." Much ink has been spilled in philosophy about the interrelations of intention, motive, and belief: see, e.g., Anscombe, *Intentionality*, 15–26; Audi, *AIR*, chap. 8; Dennett, *IS*, chap. 2.

21. *Tropes, Parables, Performatives*, 139; cited and discussed by Gould, UP, 25.

22. On fol. 153r, we read that this was "fully recorded in our letter of remission delivered by two notaries on this third day of the present month of April and sealed with the seal of our Chastellet of Paris."

23. Here I paraphrase the famous dictum of McLuhan and Fiore in *Medium Is the Message*. The *didascalia* of extant plays, audience testimony, contracts, bills of sale, props lists, and so on amply indicate that medieval theatrical culture rose to the technical challenge of realism. Excellent work on medieval special effects includes Meredith and Tailby, eds., *Staging of Religious Drama*, and Gatton, "There Must Be Blood."

24. "Fu mise une broche chaude et boutee en un canon estant ou dit lieu," fol. 152v; my emphasis.

25. See also Witmore on accidents as (mis)adventures or contrivances associated with Fortuna (*CA*, 2–3).

26. See *PP*, 228; Austin's doctrine of "infelicities," *HDTW*, 14–24; and Gould's astute analysis of it in UP. The misfire is one of only three instances in which Goffman cites Austin (*FA*, 348).

27. Here, I draw on Burke, *POLF*, 155–58; I discuss this problem in *DBD*, chap. 4. The distinctions between *within* and *without, inside* and *outside,* are substantially blurred not only on the medieval stage but in such modern avant-gardist experiments as those of New York City's Squat. See, e.g., Schechner on Squat's performance of *Pig, Child, Fire!* (1977), complete with real cops and gunfire (*BTA*, 302–8).

28. Compare also with Searle, LSFD, 324–25; see our chapter 5.

29. See Blau's résumé (*Audience*, 165) of Scarry's thesis from *Body in Pain* (hereafter *BP*).

30. Eckstein, drawing on Elaine Scarry, Theodor Adorno, Hannah Arendt, and Michel Foucault, in *Language of Fiction in a World of Pain*, 181. See also Siebers, *Ethics of Criticism*, chap. 1.

31. This is the main premise of my *MTOC*, especially 38–48.

32. E.g., in the *Institutio oratoria* (hereafter *IO*), Quintilian advocated making au-

diences "feel as if they were actual eyewitnesses of the scene [*in rem praesentem*]" (ed. and trans. Butler, VI, 1.30–31); while medieval mystery plays addressed *témoins oculaires* (*MTOC*, 185–92). I also make those arguments in *ROMD*, chaps. 1 and 2.

33. I argue that point in chapter 7 and the Talk-Back.

34. Compare, e.g., the essays in Goldstein, ed., *Why We Watch* (hereafter *WWW*), with feminist legal theory like MacKinnon's on pornography.

35. See, e.g., *Lombard Laws,* ed. Drew, 60–73, 91–93; and Goebel, *Felony and Misdemeanor,* 98–117.

36. See Goffman's classic "Theatrical Frame" (*FA,* chap. 5). We return in chapters 2, 5, and 6 to issues of legal liability at the theater, including Goffman's own legalese (*FA,* 130, 346).

37. *Great Reckonings in Little Rooms* (hereafter *GR*), 34. On the "magic circle" of the medieval stage, see, e.g., Rey-Flaud's still helpful *Cercle magique;* Southern, *Medieval Theatre in the Round;* and Schmitt's reassessment, "Was There a Medieval Theatre in the Round?"

38. On the *théâtre vitrine,* see Rey-Flaud, *Pour une dramaturgie,* introd.; on the Thespian origins of drama, see such textbooks as Nicoll's *World Drama,* 6.

39. See, e.g., the invitation issued to the *populum circumstantem* of the Fleury Playbook *Herod* that they participate in adoring the Christ child (Bevington, ed., *Medieval Drama,* 58; also discussed by Tydeman, *Theatre in the Middle Ages* [hereafter *TMA*], 223). On actorly "invitations to breakage," see our chapter 7.

40. In *DBD,* chaps. 5, 8, and 11, I discuss such legislation (especially in Mons, 1501), along with its important rediscovery by Port, *Inventaire;* and Cohen, ed., *Le Livre de conduite* (hereafter *LCR*). I also reproduce that legislation in *DBD,* 213–14.

41. "Il était rare que ces assemblées si nombreuses ne donnassent pas lieu à quelque tumulte ou à quelque scène dramatique, on n'en revenait guère sans avoir été témoin ou acteur dans une bataille 'à sang et plaies,'" Arrêt de Parlement (Tournelle), 20 November and 23 March 1516; cited by Gosselin, *Recherches sur les origines,* 62. As we shall see in chapters 4 and 5, *unpremeditated* is not the same thing as *unintentional.*

42. See Ingarden, FLT; and the *Mystère de la Résurrection Angers (1456),* ed. Servet, vol. 1, Day 1, 218–25: "Je proteste publiquement / Pour tous joueurs generaument / De cest mistere, et pour chacun, / Que ou cas qu'il seroit par aucun / Contre la foy riens dit ou fait, / Il soit reputé pour non fait. / Car nous n'entendons dire ou faire / Riens qui soit a la foy contraire." Compare also with the Pseudo-Cicero's example of legal protection at the theater in *RAH,* 1.24.

43. For a review of this topos in the forensic rhetorical and medieval dramatic traditions, see *ROMD,* 89–110. See also Solterer, *Master and Minerva,* which demonstrates a medieval awareness of the problem long before the writings of Steiner in *SP* or Butler in *Excitable Speech.*

44. See, e.g., Eden on Plato's comparison of lawyers to actors (*Laws* 817b), *Poetic and Legal Fiction,* 29–30. The point of my *ROMD* was to demonstrate that medieval law and drama were of a piece in terms of verisimilitude, conflict, staging, costume, gesture, impersonation, and so forth.

45. AN, X1a, 4831, fol. 386, 4 March 1490, no. 25; cited by Delachenal, *Histoire des avocats,* 425–26; also *ROMD,* 153–55. This was no hard-and-fast rule, however: Krämer's *Malleus maleficarum* of 1486, for example, raises the threat of lawyerly guilt by association during the witch trials. See the English translation in Kors and Peters, *Witchcraft in Europe,* 159–61.

46. See Graver's agency-oriented "Actor's Bodies."

47. Although Cavell's work surprisingly appears nowhere in his bibliography, see also Walton, *MM,* 192–95.

48. On this topos of tort law, see Balkin, "Night in the Topics," 216.

49. Jackson, "How Decision Theory Illuminates," 29.

50. On 14 October 1984 the *New York Times* carried the Associated Press story, "Actor Wounds Himself on Set of TV Series."

51. See, e.g., Scenarios 6 and 7 in chapter 6.

52. See Austin, "Plea for Excuses" (*PP,* chap. 6); Baudrillard, *SW,* 178; and Cavell, *MWM,* 231–32, to which we return momentarily. Again, the better to introduce inductively the case studies that will prove the fallacy is not one, we return to the applied critical history of the Intentional Fallacy in the Entr'Acte. See also Kottman, following Primo Levi, on texts as loaded guns, *Politics of the Scene,* 14.

53. "Intention," 41–48; discussed in IF, 6.

54. Sverdlik is interested in the moral responsibility of the shooter in a variety of outcomes in "Crime and Moral Luck" (hereafter CML), 183.

55. They refer here to Gadamer, *Truth and Method,* 335. Compare also with Tallis on being "knocked off course" (*NS,* 233).

56. See also their discussion of Rousseau in AT2, 17.

57. See also on this point AT2, 19; and Knapp and Michaels, "Reply to Rorty," 142–44. Even Sofer's intriguing analysis of guns on stage is about "killing time," not *people* (*Stage Life,* chap. 5). In chapter 4, we return to the commonplace of shouting "Fire!" in a crowded theater.

58. Legal debates about "battered wife syndrome," for example, bridge the gulf between them; we return to them in chapter 3.

59. See Sokal's notorious exposé about his hoax in "A Physicist Experiments"; and the subsequent "Mystery Science Theater" and "Sokal Hoax: A Forum."

60. Sverdlik reprises Austin's donkey tale in human terms of moral luck in CML, 185–86. Compare, e.g., with George Carlin's quip that we commonly refer to the "near miss" of two airborne planes, something that is more rightly called a "near hit."

61. Likewise, we shall see that the suicidal man on the freeway might have been "hoping" that cameras would capture his suicide, but his answer must have been: "I am killing myself."

Chapter Two.

1. AN, JJ 125, no. 7, fols. 7v–8r; Appendix, Document 2.1. In the following discussion, this text is cited parenthetically by folio number. The text is also cited by Thomas, "Le Théâtre à Paris," 611; and discussed in *DBD,* 72–74. Petit de Julleville

picked up the trace of this incident in *LM*, 2:5–6. A decontextualized excerpt from this document appears as no. E1b in Tydeman, *MES*, 285.

2. On the ontological status of the rehearsal, see, e.g., Goffman, *FA*, 60–62, 126–27; Kirby, *FT*, x–xi; and Wilshire, *RPI*, 99. For liminality, see especially Turner's classic "Liminal to Liminoid," in *FRT*, 20–60; Flanigan, "Liminality, Carnival"; Ashley, *Victor Turner*; and States, *GR*, 197–206. The most famous performance site for religious dramas was the so-called liminal space of the *parvis*, or platform, set up right outside the expanding space of the church.

3. We return shortly to Goffman's work on "official" performances (*FA*, 126).

4. The historical insights of Koziol, *Begging Pardon and Favor*, and Pizarro, *Rhetoric of the Scene*, have yet to be incorporated into medieval theater criticism in any substantive way.

5. Although Kirby's work appeared almost twenty years after Goffman's *FA*, he stunningly never cites Goffman in *FT*.

6. We return in chapter 4 to the notion of mimetic blindness.

7. In addition to Ariès, *Western Attitudes toward Death*, see Black, *AM*, introd. and chap. 1.

8. "Car en terre commist l'outraige, / qui n'estoit q[u]'un pelerinaige / et une sente pour venir / au regne qui ne puet fenir"; Gréban, *Mystère de la Passion*, ed. Jodogne, 2709–2712.

9. In addition to the counterintuitive theoretical move of bringing liminality center stage, as it were, medieval theater itself played out (as for Turner) in what we call today liminal spaces. See especially McKenzie, *Perform or Else*, 49–53, reprinted as "The Liminal Norm," chap. 6 of *PSR*; also MacDonald, *Theater at the Margins*. On medieval theatrical space, see especially Symes, *Common Stage*, introd. and chap. 3; Carlson, *Places of Performance*, 14–23; Southern, *Medieval Theatre in the Round*; Konigson, *L'Espace théâtral médiéval*; and Hanawalt and Kobialka, eds., *Medieval Practices of Space*.

10. Compare, e.g., with Bloch on text as inquest, *Medieval French Literature and Law*, chap. 3.

11. Although the phrase is somewhat ambiguous—it implies that it is the *character* who is supposed to fire the cannon—there is no such militaristic character in the play. So it is probably safest to assume (positing the same kind of recovered intentionalities of textual editing discussed in my Introduction) that what the scribes *mean* is that *Perrin* was *also* supposed to be firing a cannon. See, e.g., Pauphilet's edition of Rutebeuf's *Miracle of Théophile*, 135–58, along with the English translation by Axton and Stevens.

12. See AN, X1a, 4831, fol. 386, 4 March 1490, no. 25; cited by Delachenal, *Histoire des avocats*, 425–26; discussed in my chapter 1; and, for a modern psychological take, see Rogoff, *Theatre Is Not Safe*. On reported speech in letters of remission, see Davis, *FIA*, chap. 1; and Hanawalt, "Whose Story."

13. Such events blatantly contradict Tydeman's optimistic affirmation that, on the medieval stage, "human lives plainly could not be put at risk," *TMA*, 176–77.

Thus, we see *cordons sanitaires* around theater (as in Mons in 1501): see Cohen, *LCR*, 591; also my *DBD*, 214.

14. In *DBD*, 73 (where my focus was not intentionality), I discuss briefly that irony relative to the plot of the play.

15. Oxymoronic though it might sound, any actor can attest to "unintended realism": the wind makes a bell toll at just the right moment; a bird flies into the hand of the Christ character as he preaches peace, and so on.

16. "In lege Cornelia *dolus* pro facto accipitur," *DJ*, 2:48.8.7; my emphasis.

17. I play here on the medieval French legal convention with which most official documents begin, in a tribute to the interplay of orality and literacy, *à tous ceux qui ces presentes lettres verront ou orront,* or "to all who see or hear the present letters," for which I've substituted "present warning."

18. See versions of this scriptural moment in, e.g, Gréban, *Mystère de la Passion,* 23531–23550; and Michel, *Mystère de la Passion,* ed. Jodogne, 25851–25879.

19. "Les coups de poing étaient plus rares que les coups de dague, d'espée et de bâtons, après lesquels il fallait bien venir s'expliquer devant la justice et lui raconter ces incidents imprévus, mais toujours assurés, du jeu d'un mystère," Gosselin on two edicts from Tournelle of 1516 in *Recherches,* 62; my emphasis. We have no record of who participated in the two productions of 1380 and 1384, and are thus in no position to make a guess about their surprise—and the accident's predictability—or the lack thereof.

20. The Mons edict regarding "nuls enffans qu'il n'ait x ans d'eaige, nulles anchiennes gens débilles, ne nulles femmes enchaintes" is cited by Cohen, *LCR*, 591; and in my *DBD*, 113, 270n.

21. Repeat visitors to RATT—that is, two-or-more-time viewers of twice-behaved behavior (*BTA*, chap. 2)—could no longer claim, e.g., that the violence was a surprise (*SRT*, 21).

22. As in most legal proceedings, the first subtype, the Absolute Issue, is not relevant here because no one contends that the act was right in and of itself (*RAH*, 1.24).

23. *RAH*, 1.25, 2.26.

24. On the fifteenth-century *procès de paradis,* see my *ROMD*, 169–204.

25. "[N]eque in hac lege culpa lata *pro dolo* accipitur. quare si quis alto se praecipitaverit et super alium venerit eumque occiderit, aut putator, ex arbore cum ramum deiceret, non praeclamaverit et praetereuntem occiderit, ad huius legis coercitionem non pertinet," *DJ*, 2:48.8.7; my emphasis. See also Witmore on falling objects (*CA*, 11).

26. The fascinating ramifications of this passage for spectatorship and feigning are lost in translation: "voluntatem in omnibus rebus *spectari* convenire; quae consulto facta non sint, ea *fraudi* esse non oportere," *RAH*, 2.25; my emphasis.

27. "Ea dividitur in inprudentiam, fortunam, necessitatem," *RAH*, 1.24. The Pseudo-Cicero repeats and expands that explanation in *RAH*, 2.23–24. Again, see Witmore, *CA*, 5–10.

28. For *purgatio* in various Latin translations of Aristotle's *Poetics*, see my *MTOC*, 1–2. See also the *DJ* on the cathartic *solacio* offered to communities when "notorious brigands" were hanged "on a gallows in the places which they used to haunt," *DJ*, 48.19.28.15; also discussed by Coleman, "Fatal Charades," 48–49.

29. "Deprecatio est cum et peccasse se et consulto fecisse confitetur, et tamen postulat ut sui misereantur"; repeated in almost identical language in *RAH*, 2.25–26. As is his habit, the Pseudo-Cicero subdivides the Plea for Mercy into subtypes (*RAH*, 2.25).

30. To those who might object here that rehearsal is an experiment with *performance*, not *intention*, I still reply that there is no theatrical performance *without intention* (with further clarifications to come in chapter 5).

31. Beyond the usual temporal purview of the forensic rhetorical genre—that is, the past-as opposed to the future-oriented deliberative genre—compare also with Augustine on the capacity of memory to negotiate simultaneously between past, present, and future. See *Confessions,* trans. Watts, book 11, chap. 11; and, for a summary of the temporal foci of forensic and deliberative rhetoric, see Kennedy, *CR*, 72–74.

32. "Life Is Not a Dramatic Narrative," 100–101; his ellipses. For a similar point, see *FA*, 149.

33. See also Sverdlik on foreseeable vs. unforeseeable consequences, CML, 181–86.

34. For Schlegel, *Dialogue on Poetry,* aphorism 80. Here I allude to Davidson, *Essays on Actions and Events,* especially "Intending."

35. In chapter 3, we reconsider Langer's work; and in chapter 5, we see that ACHIEVED INTENTIONS involve reading backward, while ACTUAL INTENTIONS involve reading both backward and forward.

36. For the law and literature movement, see Brooks and Gewirtz, eds., *LS;* and Sarat and Kearns, eds., *Law in Everyday Life.*.

37. See also Ridout, *Stage Fright,* 58–62.

38. On these apocryphal deaths, see my *DBD*, 52–54.

39. The accidental vs. deliberate nature of those interventions is the subject of chapter 7.

40. Compare, e.g., to *FA,* chaps. 3 and 5.

41. See especially Black on Thomas de Quincey in *AM,* chap. 1.

42. Compare, e.g., with the wisdom of Claudius Saturninus about legal doubling in *DJ*, 48.19.16; see also Appendix, Document 3.4.

43. For a superb introduction to that discipline, see Kirshenblatt-Gimblett, "Performance Studies," chap. 5 of *PSR*. Fake brawling is subject, of course, to Baudrillardian analysis as simulation. As of 2003, reality programming was a recognized category in the Emmy Awards.

44. There has been some fascinating work on the interplay of medieval theater and economics, including "corporate" sponsorship and even product placement. See

especially Ashley, "Sponsorship, Reflexivity, and Resistance"; and Sanok, "Performing Feminine Sanctity."

45. This use of *ad hoc* as "impromptu" is not the same thing as "before the fact."

46. See Suetonius, *LC*, "Nero," 12.2; discussed by Bartsch, *AA*, 6. See also Duncan, *Performance and Identity*, chap. 5; and Austin on the unhappy performative issued "under duress" (*PP*, 227). See also Ridout on theatrical coercion in the context of what he calls "corpsing" (*Stage Fright*, 130–46).

47. See *Etymologiarum*, 2: book 18, chap. 42; cited earlier.

48. See especially Marshall, *SES*, chap. 1.

49. In chapters 6 and 7, we explore who has the standing to intend in theater. Especially helpful, from another discipline, is Godlovitch, "Integrity of Musical Performance."

50. Temporally speaking, watching a rehearsal is not like watching a building go up. In the former, there is at least the possibility of seeing the whole thing, or Langer's act "in its entirety" (*FF*, 310). The latter would require time-lapse photography.

51. In addition to Le Goff, *MC*, 360–61, see also Huizinga, *HL*, chap. 1; and Axton, *European Drama*, chap. 2.

52. We consider such a case in chapter 6.

53. Theoretically, one could even rehearse a Baudrillardian simulation, which, I suppose, would be no simulation at all but a promise of a simulation to come.

54. That was allegedly the case when, in 1549, Philip II happened on a snuff drama (*DDD*, chap. 14). In chapter 5, we consider such cases as the infamous misunderstanding surrounding the radio dissemination of *The War of the Worlds*. See also Kirby on "accidental spectators," *FT*, xi. Difficult though it is, I am trying here to avoid the appearance—and the reality—of a tautology: Theater is representation. Representation is intentional. Ergo, "Not representation" = "Not theater."

55. In *DBD*, chap. 4, I discuss other cases of medieval pyrotechnics gone awry. See also Butterworth, *Theatre of Fire*, chap. 2.

56. See Searle, *Intentionality*; Wilson, *TI*; and Kirby, *FT*.

57. I consider such a case in Scenario 12 of chapter 6.

58. Here I allude to Rayner's work in *DAP*, especially chap. 1.

59. See Stanislavski's *Building a Character*. In chapter 5, I amplify this definition-in-progress as the dialectical relationship between the ACTUAL INTENTIONS of those making theater, which are ACHIEVED or misACHIEVED, and PERCEIVED or misPERCEIVED by spectators.

60. See *Chronique de Metz de Jacomin Husson* (hereafter *CMJH*), ed. Michelant, 285. For the complete citation, see *DBD*, 208–9. See also Goebel on the early Frankish regulation of theatrical space (*Felony and Misdemeanor*, 170–71).

61. See also Cavell on children at the theater, *MWM*, 329.

62. See *Poetics*, ed. Fyfe, 1449b.

63. We return briefly to the subject of terrorism in chapter 7.

Chapter Three.

1. On the erasure of rape from medieval theater history by Petit de Julleville (*LM*, 2:48) and others, see my "Spectacle of the Scaffolding;" thus, I use the term *rape* where many medieval sources would not. For an unusually compelling study of the legalities of bodily presence in art, see Hyde, *Bodies of Law,* introd.

2. For superb historical work on rape in medieval law and literature, see especially Hanawalt, "Whose Story"; Solga, "Rape's Metatheatrical Return"; Phillips, "Written on the Body"; Gravdal, *Ravishing Maidens;* Saunders, *Rape and Ravishment;* and Hyde, *Bodies,* 180–86.

3. On how "going through the motions" leads to the real thing in Pascal's famous bet, see *Pensées,* in *Oeuvres,* ed. Lafuma, p. 551, fragment 418, p. 233; and Dennett's assessment of what one might call a religious performative in *IS,* 114–15.

4. We return to this concept, which Austin would call "illocutionary" (*HDTW,* 109–11), in chapter 5.

5. *CPV,* ed. Bruneau, 3:114–15; Appendix, Document 3.1. All citations are from this edition, which reproduces "as is" Philippe's impressionistic "orthography" (as do I, also). We return shortly to this tale's similarities to various miracle plays.

6. *Parables for the Virtual,* 47 (his emphasis), where Massumi analyzes Ronald Reagan.

7. On the noble goals of medieval religious theater, see Petit de Julleville, *LM,* 2:24.

8. On this temporal issue in the enactment of intentions, see, e.g., Audi, *AIR,* 95–96.

9. See especially Walton, *MM,* 21–24.

10. Particularly insightful initiations to the rich subject of folk law include Green, *Crisis of Truth;* and Renteln and Dundes, ed., *Folk Law.*

11. For exceptional work in theater studies on this topic, see Olson, "Plays as Play"; Guynn, "Justice to Come"; and Read's more political *TEL.*

12. Plato, *Republic,* trans. Shorey, 606c–606d.

13. Quoted in Sainte-Beuve, *Tableau historique et critique,* 193. For examples of this legislation, see *DBD,* 77–78, 213, 221–22.

14. Feminist theologian Trible makes a similar point about a gruesome rape from Judges 19:1–30 in *Texts of Terror,* 65. On historiography as the resurrection of the dead, see especially de Certeau, *WH,* chap. 1; and Greenblatt, *Shakespearean Negotiations,* 1–4.

15. "Combat," 5 November 1953, cited in *Sartre on Theater,* ed. Contat and Rybalka, trans. Jellinek, 240; my emphasis.

16. Compare with Gould's treatment of the "illocutionary force of an utterance before the full battery of 'effects' has been discharged" (*UP,* 29); and also with Dershowitz, "Life Is Not a Dramatic Narrative."

17. See, e.g., Steiner on the "unholy alliance" between the Right and the Left (*SP,* 61); and Bérubé, "Against Subjectivity" (hereafter AS), 1065. On theater as "prospective," see our chapter 2.

18. Here I draw, of course, on Foucault's much studied theories from *Discipline and Punish* (hereafter *DP*); MacKinnon's signature *Toward a Feminist Theory of the State;* and Steiner, *SP*, 60, 44–51 (see our Entr'Acte). See also Wilshire, *RPI*, 250–52; and Hanawalt, "Whose Story," 137. Also relevant is a similar debate about the inflammatory airing even of still photographs: the tortures of Abu Ghraib; the airborne coffins of the military dead en route to their final resting places. In our concluding Talk-Back, we return to the phenomenon of the agentless recording device.

19. In *Sartre on Theater,* 73; see also States on Sartre, *GR*, 27–28.

20. Compare also with the version that appears in Jean François Huguenin's composite edition of several chronicles, the *Chroniques de la ville de Metz* (hereafter *CVM*), 473, in which the "body" is called a "child." See also Witmore, *CA*, 10, on embodiment; cited in our Introduction. Philippe's version of the story ends where we left it. Huguenin's version of the tale follows up with a new monstrous tale in which a mare allegedly gives birth to a son and a daughter (*CVM*, 473).

21. This notion has surfaced in recent scholarship on the interrelations of medieval theater and religion, especially Kobialka, *This Is My Body;* Beckwith, *Signifying God;* and Dominguez, "Le Corps dans les mystères."

22. This term is slightly ambiguous in that it could mean either "male" or "human."

23. For a fascinating if gruesome perspective on such monstrosity, see Favazza's medical assessment of bodily mutilation of the head in *Bodies under Siege,* chap. 5.

24. In a veritable explosion of work on monsters, see, e.g., Cohen, *Of Giants;* and Verner, *Epistemology of the Monstrous.*

25. On the historical role of the mother in making her imprint upon the child in her womb, see Pouchelle, *Body and Surgery in the Middle Ages;* and Paré's celebrated sixteenth-century work *On Monsters,* chaps. 1–4.

26. Berns, "Tales of Intention," 161.

27. See *Building a Character.* In chapter 4, we consider Goffman's "intention display" (*FA*, 235).

28. Passion plays were famous for their singing, chanting, dancing devils in numerous *diableries* (*DBD*, chap. 7).

29. "Riens n'y vault! Or est parfunie / ma sensuelle affection," *Le Viol de Dina,* in *Mystères de la procession de Lille,* ed. Knight, 1:151–52. Knight breaks the line (p. 298). Naturally, mimed displays of various length are possible independent of a script. For a list of known pantomimes of medieval France, see Petit de Julleville, *LM*, 2: chap. 15. For other problematic scenes of rape, see the anonymous *Mistere de la Sainte Hostie,* fol. 32r; and the sixteenth-century *Moralité nouvelle d'ung empereur qui tua son neveu qui avoit prins une fille a force,* in *Théâtre français avant la Renaissance,* ed. Fournier (hereafter *TFR*), 354–69. I discuss such texts in "Theater Makes History"; and "Spectacle of the Scaffolding."

30. There was evidence of such boasting in Chelles in 1395, where the gang-rape (to which we return shortly) was already *en commune renommée* the next day (AN JJ 148, no. 144, fol. 75r; Appendix, Document 3.3).

31. See, e.g., Jolibois, *La Diablerie de Chaumont.*

32. For a superb introduction to the "copycatting" that folklorists call "ostension," see Ellis, "Death by Folklore"; and Eco on theatrical ostension, ID, 103.

33. Consider, e.g., the case of the seventeenth-century actor, Mathew Coppinger, who played a judge on stage and a criminal highwayman once the show was over (see Larwood, *Theatrical Anecdotes* [hereafter *TA*], 215).

34. See Cannon, "Raptus in the Chaumpaigne Release"; and Cohen, *Of Giants,* 113–15.

35. The perfidious queen of the *Romance of Silence* (by Heldris de Cornuälle) does just that in a scene that attests to the legal dangers of pretense. See Thorpe's edition; or the translation by Roche-Mahdi, *Silence, a Thirteenth-Century Romance,* vv. 3711–4148.

36. See Woods, "Rape and the Pedagogical Rhetoric of Sexual Violence," especially 67–68; discussed in my *MTOC,* 129–36.

37. I discuss the suicide of Despair in *DBD,* chap. 13.

38. "Viollenentement et à force viollée et defflorée celle josne gairce ... et ... se desguisait et ... en tel habit, feindant d'aller laver en la riviere, passait par la porte du pont Thieffroy sans estre congneu et trouvait ainsy maniere d'eschaipper," *CVM,* 644.

39. Hagiography, e.g., is a rich source for such "good ostension"; consider the *imitatio Christi* of the *Life of Saint Faith,* when such a witness to martyrdom as Capraise proclaims his intent to follow in her footsteps. See *Lady as Saint,* ed. and trans. Cazelles, especially 588–99. For a superb initiation, see Elliott, *Proving Woman.*

40. *Moralité nouvelle d'ung empereur, TFR,* p. 361, col. 2 (Fournier's edition does not include verse numbers).

41. Stanislavski, *Creating a Role,* 224. Again, this theory of "no accidents," as related to their providential nature, is the subject of the work of Witmore and Hamilton.

42. I discuss the medieval resonance of Stanislavski's point to this effect (*AP,* 177) in *DBD,* chap. 3.

43. For a description of the *Miracle de l'enfant donné au Diable* and its manuscript sources, see Petit de Julleville, *LM,* 2:226–31; and Michelant's note in *CMJH,* 269n.

44. See the dénouement of Rutebeuf's *Théophile,* 155–58; and, for the importance of seals in the material culture of the medieval theater, see Symes, *Common Stage,* 246–58.

45. The term *perform/performance* derives from such a verb of legal completion: *parfournir.*

46. "Et, en disant ces mot[s], perdit la moitiet de luy, et ... ne jamaix ne polt plus pairfaitement perler," *CPV,* 4:136–37; also in *CMJH,* 270; and *CVM,* 680. I reproduce the first two versions in their entirety in *DBD,* 219, in the context of other "accidental" theatrical conjurings of the Devil (*DBD,* chap. 8). The definition of *parfaire* is consistent with that of *perform,* for which the *American Heritage Dictionary* lists first: "To begin and carry through to completion." See also Symes on the importance of such etymologies in medieval theater studies, in *Common Stage,* introd.

47. "Ung pouvre homme qui pourtoit vendre l'estrain parmy la cité, ne n'avoit aultre mestiés, par quoy l'on le appelloit comunement *Blan Trains*," *CPV*, 4:136; Bruneau's emphasis.

48. See Cohen, "Le Théâtre à Paris et aux environs," chap. 10 of *Etudes d'histoire du théâtre en France* (hereafter *EHTF*), 170. Thomas is also the archivist who discovered our two fatal performances of 1380 and 1384. We owe much to such archival quests for allusions to theater; but their erasure of rape is also a subject for history and historiography.

49. AN JJ 148, no. 144, fol. 74v; Appendix, Document 3.3; cited in this chapter parenthetically by folio number. To render more accessible this exceptional document and its often confusing events (which I discuss at length in "Spectacle of the Scaffolding," 171–75), I reproduce it in its entirety in the Appendix (Document 3.3), largely following the edition that appears in Cohen, *EHTF*, 174–78.

50. Claudius Saturninus, *DJ*, 2:48.19.16. I reproduce the full Latin text in the Appendix, Document 3.4.

51. Also cited in chapter 1. The *Digest* further details "seven aspects: the motive, the person, the place, the time, the quality, the quantity, and the outcome" (*DJ*, 2:48.19.16).

52. On this topic, see Leader-Elliott, NI; and Cane, "Mens Rea in Tort Law."

53. Fol. 75r. Martin was thus spared a "bodily penalty [*amende corporelle*]," spent four months in prison "on bread and water," and was directed to make financial restitution. This may be an indication that, having broken the law by taking Mr. Coton's "property," Martin paid in kind with property.

54. See *SW*, 178; discussed in our Introduction.

55. For the numerous holes in his story, see my "Spectacle of the Scaffolding," 171–76.

56. See Scheffler's introduction (1) to the wide-ranging essays in *Consequentialism and Its Critics*. "Outcome" is also crucial to MacKinnon in *Toward a Feminist Theory*, 183.

57. See *PP*, 133n; and Sverdlik, CML, 181–83; cited in our chapter 1.

58. See also Cavell, *MWM*, 231. We return, in our Talk-Back, to the ubiquitous contemporary apology.

59. Compare also with Hirsch, *VI*, 11; cited in our chapter 1.

60. In the late 1980s or early 1990s, I recall seeing harrowing news footage in which a Chicago Transit Authority worker did not intervene to stop the assault of a woman because he deemed it "only" a domestic dispute.

61. See my *ROMD*, chaps. 1 and 2. In that context, theatrical character comes together with rhetorical *hypokrisis* (delivery) and even religious casuistry as part of the eternally vexed debate (to which we return shortly) about sincerity vs. insincerity, authenticity vs. inauthenticity.

62. In *Intentionality*, Anscombe elucidates both popular and philosophical distinctions between motive, mental cause, and intention (18–24).

63. *DJ*, 2:48.19.16.2. Austin makes a similar distinction between justification and

excuse: "killing was done in battle (justification) or on the ground that it was only accidental if reckless (excuse)" (*PP*, 124–25). See also Girard on "good violence" in *Violence and the Sacred*, chap. 1.

64. In addition to the reported miscarriages at the *Eumenides* (Nagler, *Source Book*, 5), the RATT assault (*SRT*, chap. 1), and the deaths of Montfleury and Kean (cited in our chapter 2), see also an example of "snuff drama" in my *DBD*, chap. 14.

65. For a brief history of participatory murder mystery as dinner theater, see Wappler, "Guess Who's Coming to Dinner Theater?"

66. On Montfleury, see Ryan, *Dramatic Table Talk*, 1:143–44; his emphasis.

67. See Foucault, *DP*, part 3, chap. 2.

68. For examples of extant fifteenth-century legislation, see especially a ruling of 12 August 1486 in Angers; cited in my *DBD*, 213–16.

69. Articulated as early as Aristotle (*Poetics* 1448b), the safety of theatrical distance has been called into question by Pywell in *SRT;* Worthen, in *Modern Drama*, especially 138–39; Jauss, in *Aesthetic Experience and Literary Hermeneutics*, 268; and Rogoff, *Theatre Is Not Safe*. There is considerable doubt, moreover, as to whether the French ban on Passion plays of 1548 was even successful.

70. The curious instances in which they *do* intend primarily to commit crimes are the subject of our chapter 6.

71. *State v. Benjamin*, 345 S.C. 470, 549 S.E.2d 258 (2001). See also Jackson on the exculpatory functions of coercion in "How Decision Theory Illuminates," 27–29.

72. See *FIA*, 133. Davis reproduces the French original in *FIA*, 131–34.

73. *State v. Benjamin*, Cumulative Supplement FN 53; my emphasis.

Chapter Four.

1. Henry's story appears in Philippe de Vigneulles, *CPV*, 4:34–36; see Appendix, Document 4.1. Compare also with the account in *CVM*, 647, which I do not reproduce in the Appendix as it is virtually identical in content. Of the many variants of our protagonist's name, I use D'Anoux (with editor Bruneau). Philippe also relates this story, with some supplementary details, in his memoirs or *Gedenkbuch*, ed. Michelant, 147–48; Appendix, Document 4.2.

2. On the etymology of *turdion*, see Bruneau, ed., *CPV*, 4:35n. The *tordion* belongs to the larger class of popular dances called the *gaillarde* or galliard. See de Ménil, *Histoire de la danse*, 150–51; Bourcier, *Histoire de la danse en Occident*, 51–73; and Arbeau, *Orchésographie*, 47–53. In my translation, I preserve the dual meaning of *tour* as both "spin" and "trick."

3. On the *danse macabre*, see Bourcier, 59–61.

4. Compare also with *Gedenkbuch*, 148.

5. With such notable exceptions as Gertsman, the art of medieval dance has yet to reap the full benefits of performance studies. Once a holistic part of the ancient art of *mousike*, dance had long been partnered with mime, song, gesture, pedagogy, philosophy, sports, circus, and the law. For a masterful discussion of *mousike* in the

medieval world, see Holsinger, *Music, Body, and Desire;* and Isidore of Seville, *Etymologiarum,* 2: book 18. For the citation from Marcus Aurelius, see *Meditations,* 7.61.

6. *CPV,* 4:35–36. The term *reboulé* reflects the face-making, gaming, and even the sexuality that characterize the *drilling* of this dance insofar as it connotes grimaces, refusal, striking (as in skittles), and even circumcision. The depth of Henry's wound might have had something to with the fact that, while strong and powerful, Henry was "short in stature" (*Gedenkbuch,* 148).

7. See D'Ancona, *Origini del teatro,* 1:94–95; cited as no. G2 in *MES,* 430.

8. For superb commentary on the surprisingly neglected question of time on stage, see States, *GR,* 30–31; Rayner, *DAP,* 36–47; and Limon, "Play-within-the-Play"; as compared, e.g., with Ricoeur's narrativist approach to "Games with Time," *Time and Narrative,* 2: chap. 3.

9. On the commingling of such early performance genres, see especially Lucian, "Saltatio," ed. Harmon.

10. See especially Baxandall's influential discussion in *Patterns of Intention,* chap. 2.

11. See, e.g., Eco, ID, 109, on the theater semiotics of the Prague School, especially Bogatyrev's 1938 essay, "Semiotics in the Folk Theater."

12. On this vast subject, see, e.g., Stallybrass and White, *Politics and Poetics of Transgression.*

13. For "common consent" in the interpretation of pantomime, see Augustine, *De doctrina,* trans. Robertson, 61; and, more generally, *HDTW,* 14–24. See also the contemporary usage of that term in, e.g., the 1989 wilding attack on the Central Park jogger (Trisha Meili) or the notorious murder of Kitty Genovese in 1964.

14. We consider discrete cases of the dialectic between ACTUAL VS. ACHIEVED IN-TENTIONS, as DECLARED or UNDECLARED, PERCEIVED or MISPERCEIVED in chapters 5, 6, and 7.

15. However astute Iser's *Implied Reader* and *Fictive and the Imaginary,* e.g., they are works about textuality.

16. In much avant-garde theater, of course, the whole point is to call attention to and undercut blindness by replacing it with thespian self-consciousness. In "Performing Miracles," I argue that theater itself is the great "as if," not just in the large-scale metaphor of mimesis but in artistic practice.

17. See de Marinis, *Semiotics,* 6; and Pavis, *Problèmes de sémiologie,* introd.

18. See Heidegger, "Understanding the Appeal, and Guilt" in *Being and Time,* 325–35.

19. See, e.g., Sell, *APLC,* introd.; and Schechner, *BTA,* chap. 7.

20. See, e.g., Quintilian, *IO,* 5.14.24–26.

21. Expositors, narrators, and even preachers announce the intent of the players in the "Post-Reformation Banns," in the *Chester Mystery Cycle,* ed. Mills, 4–12; in Gréban's *Mystère de la Passion,* 19906–20103; and in the *Mystère de la Résurrection Angers (1456),* ed. Servet, vol. 1, Day 1, 218–25. (Many critics would argue that there is no such thing as an author's *porte-parole,* only fictional characters speaking.)

22. See especially Pavis, *Voix et images,* chap. 10; Alter, *Sociosemiotic Theory;* Mullaney, *Place of the Stage,* chap. 1; and Carlson, *Places of Performance.*

23. I play on *Blindness and Insight* by de Man, whose own intentions about concealing a Nazi past came under such close scrutiny.

24. See, e.g., *Arden Shakespeare,* Act 3.1.

25. For Hart, see the Mise en Scène, note 20; and on Young, see Zucco, "Boxing Match for Fun Turns Deadly."

26. On this point, see also Anscombe, *Intentionality,* 87; and Sverdlik, CML, 181; cited in our chapter 3.

27. *CPV,* 4:35–36. In the *Gedenkbuch,* Philippe already has Henry putting two and two together while dancing: he "felt the knives falling [*qu'il avoit sentus cheoir*]" (148). For another knife-wound that was "marvelously small," see Davis's discussion of the "strange passive homicide" of Toussaint Savary at the hands of his wife on 22 May 1540 when he "met her knife" while abusing her (*FIA,* 93–94, 135–37).

28. See, e.g., Dershowitz, "Life Is Not a Dramatic Narrative"; for a discussion of this passage from the *Ad Herennium* (IV, 53), see my *MTOC,* 30–32.

29. See also *NS,* 233; cited in our Introduction; and compare with Huizinga on the medieval confluence of play, law, and chance in *HL,* chap. 4.

30. In the Supreme Court case *Schenck v. United States* (1919), Justice Oliver Wendell Holmes penned the now famous opinion that "the most stringent protection of free speech would not protect a man in falsely shouting fire in a theatre and causing a panic." Compare also with the deaths in 1807 of twenty-three persons who were "trodden to death, owing to a false alarm of fire" during *Mother Goose* at Sadler's Wells (*TA,* 23).

31. "Saltatio," ed. Harmon, 36; see also Nagler's translation in *Source Book,* 28. For work on the visual logic, semantics, and verisimilitude of gesture, see Bremmer and Roodenburg, eds., *Cultural History of Gesture;* and Pavis on "theatrical gesture," *Voix et images,* chap. 7.

32. Compare also with *PP,* 228 (see our Introduction); the doctrine of "infelicities," *HDTW,* 14–24; and Ingarden, FLT.

33. On the theatricality of the medieval deathbed, see Paulson, "Death's Arrival and Everyman's Separation."

34. Peter Jennings, ABC's *World News Tonight,* 24 May 1999.

35. Boece, *Chronicles of Scotland,* 2:244; cited in Mill, ed. *Medieval Plays in Scotland,* 48; and as text no. D64 in *MES,* 268–69. For the iconographic and performative dimensions of the Dance of Death, see also Gertsman, "Pleyinge and Peyntinge." On interception, to which we return in chapter 7, see *FA,* 125–27; and Read, *TEL,* 125–28.

36. On this incident, see *Gesta Alberti Livoniensis Episcopi,* cited in translation by Tydeman in *TMA,* 223–24; and as no. C64 in *MES,* 180–81.

37. See *LM,* 2:12–13; and my *DBD,* chap. 4.

38. See especially Foucault, "Spectacle of the Scaffold," chap. 1:2 of *DP.*

39. See also Austin on "illocutionary suspense" and "perlocutionary delay," *HDTW,* 31; and Gould, UP, 21, 29.

40. In the *Gedenkbuch,* Henry was "making fun" or "kidding around" (*Cy cuidoient tous qu'il se mocquait*) (148); and in *CVM,* "people thought he was joking [*mais l'on cuidoit qu'il se juait en ce fait*]" (647). A similarly varied audience response obtained

in Lucian's story of the mad Ajax ("Saltatio," 82–83; my *DBD,* chap. 3); and also in the alleged snuff drama of 1549, which prompted "frenetic applause," "cries of indignation," and dispassionate approval from a visiting monarch. See Faber, *Histoire du théâtre en Belgique,* 14–15; cited in my *DBD,* 183, 243.

41. See also Ridout on laughter, *Stage Fright,* 129–46.

42. In chapter 7, we return to the problem of whether one can intend *for* or *on behalf of* other actants (or virtual actants).

43. For a comparatist approach to the much studied field of misogynistic literature, see, e.g., Blamires, *Woman Defamed;* and Fiero, Pfeffer, and Allain, eds., *Three Medieval Views.*

44. Compare with Goffman's own equation of acts to objects, both subject to the usual social definitions (*FA,* 39; cited in our chapter 1).

45. This is the larger subject of Sofer's fascinating *Stage Life of Props.*

46. See, e.g., on Nero, Bartsch, *AA,* chap. 1; and Kim, "Springtime for Kim Il-sung in Pyongyang."

47. Compare also with Tallis, *NS,* 233.

48. The invocation of primary, secondary, and even tertiary frames might sound complicated, but it need not be: a single-family dwelling is a frame in which kitchen and bedroom are frames within that frame; a university campus frames classrooms, sorority houses, and administrative offices; an arena frames football, patriotic displays, singing, cheerleading, even riots, and so on. See Goffman's "primary frameworks," *FA,* chap. 2.

49. In *L'Été meurtrier,* Japrisot depicts just that in the criminal premeditations of Elle which, despite their appearance of a *fait divers,* bespeak a psychotic rationale.

50. *Sartre on Theater,* 73; see also States, *GR,* 27–28.

51. See Isidore, *Etymologiarum,* "De theatro," book 18, chap. 42 (cited in our Introduction); and Huizinga on the *temenos* in *HL,* 77; also the blurring of *inside* vs. *outside,* discussed in chapter 1. In that sense, even those celebrated readerly "horizons of expectation," as derived, e.g., from the philosophy of Husserl by Jauss and Iser, must represent, at some level, an ever renewable dialectic between the responses of readers, viewers, and spectators to artistic efforts—intentional creative efforts, whether successful or unsuccessful—to shape those responses. See Jauss, *Towards an Aesthetics,* 22–32; and *QA,* 203–7 (in which he draws on Husserl, *Experience and Judgment*); and Iser, *Act of Reading,* 110–13.

Entr'Acte.

1. Again, I will not be hypercorrecting earlier critics' use of the masculine pronoun.

2. Without necessarily inscribing all positions within a male subjectivity, as Minow shows compellingly for legal rhetoric ("Stories in Law"), I believe nonetheless that it ought to be possible to assess literary theories based on their logic and rationality. By no means am I implying that logic does not serve political ends (to which I, too, marshal it, especially in our Talk-Back).

3. While somewhat outside the scope of this book, the poetics of sound (as disseminated live, in theater, over the radio, and even on the Internet) promises to be equally fruitful in our understanding of artistic agency. See, e.g., Auslander, *Liveness*, chap. 3.

4. Hirsch predicted that very thing in 1967 (*VI*, 3).

5. On the work of Sean Burke, Mailloux, Tanselle, Buell, and many others, see our Introduction.

6. His clever response? "They say it, but they do not mean it," Lipking, refuting Barthes ("Death of the Author," 148) in "Life, Death, and Other Theories," 184.

7. In addition to the authors cited in the Introduction, see Worthen, *Print and the Poetics of Modern Drama*, introd.; and Worthen, "Imprint of Performance." It is not my intention to rehearse the history of literary theory but rather to point out that many deconstructionists lost track of orality in a way that Derrida, for example, never did in such signature works as *Writing and Difference* and *Of Grammatology*.

8. See also Wellek and Warren, *Theory of Literature* (hereafter *TL*), chap. 7; along with Gang, "Intention." Ironically, the most celebrated studies of the Intentional Fallacy reflect the sometimes divergent intents of two or more coauthors. See also Anscombe, *Intentionality;* Patterson, "Intention"; Stallman, "Intentions, Problems of"; and the essays in Iseminger, ed., *Intention and Interpretation;* Diamond and Teichman, *Intention and Intentionality;* and Newton-De Molina, *On Literary Intention.*

9. Lang points out that the first edition of *TL* reads "any real critical importance." "Narcissus Jilted," 145. See also Beardsley and Wimsatt, IF, 11.

10. Coomaraswamy, "Intention," 48; my emphasis; also cited with some minor variations in Beardsley and Wimsatt, IF, 5–6.

11. On this point, see Ricoeur, *IT*, 30.

12. Or, following Witmore on coincidence (*CA*, 30); and Hamilton, at the very least, on what it is not *exclusively*. See Witmore, *CA,* introd., chaps. 1 and 5; Hamilton, *Accident,* introd. and chap. 1. Compare also with Gould's rereading of Austinian performative unhappiness in UP.

13. Stallman, "Intentions," 399; my emphasis. See also Hirsch on the distinctions between actual and achieved intentions, *VI*, 11; and contrast both with Searle's position on the necessary coincidence of a speech act with the expressed psychological state (*Intentionality*, 10–11; cited in our chapter 3).

14. See also *IT*, 19–22, on the ambiguity of *meinen* as both sense and reference; and Knapp and Michaels's work on Ricoeur in AT2, 6. Issacharoff also attempted such a distinction, though with nary a theatrical example, in *Discourse as Performance.*

15. Such gaps are possible, e.g., between what an aphasic says or writes and what he or she actually means (see also Knapp and Michaels, AT2, 19; and their "Reply," 142–44; cited in our chapter 1). In chapter 7, we consider the possible, related gap in action for sufferers of Tourette's syndrome.

16. In *ROMD*, 19–44, I discuss the philological consonance of advocacy/acting, which is relevant to the theatrical contract (chapter 5).

17. See, e.g., Poulet, "Une Critique d'identification"; and for a superb analysis of Nicholas of Cusa, see Colie, *Paradoxia Epidemica,* introd.

18. Again, see, Dowling, "Intentionless Meaning," discussed briefly in our Introduction.

19. Here Harris responds to Eco's 1992 essays (with Rorty, Culler, and Brooke-Rose) in Collini and others, *Interpretation and Overinterpretation.*

20. For a discussion of this passage, see also AT2, 7. Notwithstanding the vagaries of Hays's translation, compare also with Jauss's allusions to what texts are able to do (*QA,* 4). On the critique of the fascism or protofascism of Jauss and de Man, see Bérubé on the "reductive conflation of the scholar with the scholarship" (AS, 1066).

21. I am not disputing the fact that words on a page can move, teach, and impel to action long after the deaths of their respective authors: such a position would be as incompatible with rhetorical theory as it is to medieval studies or theater studies.

22. On the text as "friend," see Booth, *Company We Keep,* chap. 6; discussed by Buell, IPE, 13.

23. See Carruthers, *Book of Memory;* Huot, *From Song to Book;* Brantley, *Reading in the Wilderness;* and Brown, *Poets, Patrons, and Printers.*

24. For more on this enduring subject, see, e.g., Plato, *Phaedrus,* 276a; Stock, *Implications of Literacy,* chaps. 1 and 2; Chartier, *Order of Books,* chap. 1; and Chartier, *Forms and Meanings,* chap. 1.

25. "Depuis j'ay fort multiplié / Et ay mon texte publié"; "Noz chappitres tous bien escriptz, / Mon texte bien enluminé. . . . Arrière ce vieulx parchemin!" in *Farce Nouvelle de Digeste Vielle et Digeste Neufve,* ed. Cohen, vv. 103–23. One can only imagine their costumes, for which, unfortunately, no record survives nor any evidence of staging.

26. Compare, e.g., with Kirby's performance continuum, *FT,* chap. 1. In this play, the victor is another party, Custom, on "whom" the practices of customary law are based, and whose partner in the rhyme scheme is "costume" (*coutume/costume*).

27. See also Warning's pioneering *Rezeptionsästhetik;* along with Tompkins, ed., *Reader-Response Criticism;* and, from *PMLA,* "Four Views on the Place of the Personal in Scholarship" (Bérubé, Davidson, Molloy, and Palumbo-Liu).

28. Among the more obvious examples is Gallop's *Thinking through the Body.*

29. Davidson, "Critical Fictions," 1072.

30. For the non-Francophiles, I play here on Boileau's *Art poétique,* in which he declares that the seventeenth-century poet, Malherbe, rescued French literary history from its foolish medieval origins: *enfin Malherbe vint* (Chant 1, e.g., in the Collinet ed.).

31. Worthen makes a similar point about performance studies in "Drama, Performativity, and Performance," 1095.

32. The canonical example is Holland, *Five Readers Reading;* see also Burke's critique in *Death and Return,* 138–40.

33. On this point, see also Davidson, "Critical Fictions,"1069; and for its compatibility with medieval legal theories of confession, see Peters, *Torture,* chap. 2.

34. Another curious twist: sometimes, so-called sensitivity to humanization results in a desexualization that is the opposite of anthropomorphization, as when we refer to the agents formerly known as chairmen and chairwomen as pieces of furniture: the chair.

35. Compare also with Smith's "Egalitarian Fallacy," i.e., the "alleged belief/claim that all judgments are equally valid, all objects equally good, all practices equally justifiable" (*Contingencies of Value,* 152); see also Smith, *Belief and Resistance,* 77–78.

36. See, e.g., Molloy on the binary response to perceived critical narcissism, "Mock Heroics," 1074.

37. See our Introduction for the importance of intentionality in textual criticism. On feminist subjectivities and legal theory, see Minow, "Stories in Law"; and Farber and Sherry, "Legal Storytelling." See also Bérubé's refutation of the "genetic fallacy" in AS, 1066–67.

38. For political issues on collective intention and agency, see Dasenbrock, *TC,* chap. 7, especially 148–54.

39. Steiner's primary example is the unsuccessful 1990 prosecution of the Cincinnati Art Museum for having exhibited Robert Mapplethorpe's *Perfect Moment* (*SP,* 19–34). See also Bérubé on the similarly *unheimlich* couple of Mas'ud Zavarzadeh and Gertrude Himmelfarb (AS, 1065).

40. Under the rubric of "Topics of Film Genre," my colleague, Constance Penley, teaches the humor and liberation of pornography as the opposite of violence.

41. I refer, of course, to one of Foucault's primary theses of in *DP* (chap. 1.1); and Foucault, *Archaeology of Knowledge,* 40–49. Copeland illustrates the medieval resonance of the phenomenon in "Pardoner's Body."

42. See UP, 21; cited in our Introduction; and also Steiner, "Literalism of the Left: Fear of Fantasy," chap. 2 of *SP.*

43. Conversation with Françoise Giroud, Robert Kanters, François Erval, and Claude Lanzmann, published in *L'Express,* 17 September 1959; in *Sartre on Theater,* 68; his emphasis.

Chapter Five.

1. "Intentionality in the Rhetorical Process," 50. Compare also with Augustine on common consent in *De doctrina,* trans. Robertson, 61. Our epigraph appears in Mylne and Craig, *Reports of Cases Argued before the Chancery,* 85.

2. In chapter 6, we consider various noble, ignoble, and *deliberate* mutations of that primary intent.

3. In addition to Aristotle on catharsis in tragedy (*Poetics,* 1449b), see Augustine on passionately painful pleasures in *Confessions,* book 3, chap. 2.

4. As fictive and elusive an entity as "reasonableness" might be, we have little choice but to rely on it.

5. I draw my inspiration from Eco (ID, 106–10), who proposes eight scenarios for

the interrelations between an emitter's intentional vs. unintentional behaviors and "the intention that the addressee attributes (or does not attribute) to the emitter" (106), the latter of which I am calling PERCEIVED INTENTION.

6. Again, audience response, in the form of action or inaction, is the subject of chapter 7.

7. See *Poetics,* 1450b; and Ricoeur, *Time and Narrative,* especially "Historical Intentionality," 1: chap. 6, and "Games with Time," 2: chap. 3.

8. See Huizinga on the *temenos* (*HL,* 77). On Thespis as the father of drama, as well as audience vs. actors in the Dionysian liturgy—the stuff of such textbooks as Nicoll's *World Drama* (6)—Murphy provides a helpful summary in *Synoptic History,* 4–5; as does Miller in refuting the work of Else (*Aristotle's* Poetics, 172–78) in "Origins of Greek Drama," 131–33.

9. Along with McKenzie on the "liminal norm" (*Perform or Else,* 49–53), see Schneider, e.g., "Intermediality, Infelicity, and Scholarship on the Slip."

10. Witness, e.g., the medieval edicts regarding the physical containment of theater, as in Mons, cited in our chapters 1 and 2.

11. Again, for a psychoanalytical approach to the literary and philosophical theory of the accident, see Hamilton, *Accident,* especially 256–81.

12. Compare with Austin's own vocabulary of pathology in his doctrine of the "etiolations of language" (*HDTW,* 21–22); see also Baudrillard, *SW,* 167–68; and Boal's pathology of catharsis in *Theater of the Oppressed,* 28. For Hirsch, the forgetful author who "no longer understands his own text" is "like anyone else" (*VI,* 7); see also Eco's ingenious "An *Ars Oblivionalis*?" For the legalistic understanding of mental disease or defect, see, e.g., Leader-Elliott, NI, 89–94.

13. "Intention," 47; his emphasis; cited in our chapter 2.

14. On pretense as "covering" intentional activity, see Searle, LSFD, 324–35; and Wilson, *TI,* 11; discussed in our Introduction. What happens when they *do not* share that intent is the subject of Scenarios 3a, 3b, 4, and 5 of chapter 6.

15. See Lucian, "Saltatio," 83; and Stanislavski's tale of Dasha in *AP,* 151–52, both discussed in *DBD,* chap. 3. For the Williamson incident, see Handler, *Time on Fire,* 250–57; cited in our Mise en Scène.

16. Here Eco cites Freudian slips and the errors of foreign-language learners, the latter bespeaking both intentional features (the choice of English) and unintentional—even involuntary—ones (faulty pronunciation). See also *FA,* 186–92.

17. This passage did not survive the reincarnation of "Semiotics of Theatrical Performance" as "Interpreting Drama."

18. See also Walton's discussion of this passage in *MM,* 81; and, for medieval versions of the safe house of theater, see our chapter 2.

19. Actor-generated compromise is the subject of chapter 6; audience-generated compromise, of chapter 7.

20. Philippe de Vigneulles used the cited phrase to describe what happened to Henry D'Anoux, *CPV,* 4:35; Appendix, Document 4.1. We consider precisely these paradoxical situations in Scenario 12 of chapter 6.

21. On this spin on Horatian *dulce/utile,* see also *FT,* xi.

22. Kubiak, *Stages of Terror,* 28; his emphasis.

23. See, e.g., Knapp and Michaels on the example of "accidentally" saying "Turn left" when one means "Turn right," which can nonetheless be understood correctly as its opposite (AT2, 17); see also Cavell, *MWM,* 231; cited in our Introduction; and Dasenbrock, *TC,* 69–76.

24. Recall that even the surgeon could barely find the source of Henry's wound: above, *CPV,* 4:35; Appendix, Document 4.1; and *Gedenkbuch,* 148; Appendix, Document 4.2.

25. Compare, e.g., with Artaud's discussion of the unseen effects of the plague in *Theater and Its Double,* chap. 1; and Wilshire on broken hearts, *RPI,* 262; cited in our chapter 3.

26. Drawing on equivalence theory, Sverdlik finds that, in terms of "blameworthiness," "transferred intent," or "transferred malice," the shooter is equally culpable (CML, 183–86).

27. Compare also with Harris, *LMRSL,* 91; cited in our Introduction.

28. Given the burgeoning topic of the spectacle of sport in performance studies, such sports metaphors are hardly coincidental; see, e.g., Mazer, *Professional Wrestling.*

29. For the full passage, see the Introduction.

30. Compare also with Langer on "form in suspense" (*FF,* 310); cited in our chapter 2; Anscombe on the interrelations of intentionality and prediction, *Intentionality,* 1–7; and Dennett on "predictive strategies," *IS,* chap. 2.

31. On perlocution and affect, see *HDTW,* 108–20.

32. An excellent example of such a moment appears in [Jean Molinet], *Mystère de Judith et Holofernés,* ed. Graham Runnalls, where Judith delivers a soliloquy begging God's assistance in killing Holofernes. See Runnalls's translation, *Judith and Holofernes,* 2174–2230; and my discussion, *DBD,* chap. 14.

33. "[T]out n'est-il pas convention dans le théâtre? Vous vous rendez au spectacle et vous achetez au bureau le droit de pénétrer du regard tous les détours des appartements, tous les secrets des hommes qui vous confient mille choses personnelles où vous n'avez que faire; vous ne vous étonnez pas de voir des gens penser tout haut, ce qui est une habitude de maniaque" (*Histoire de la mise-en-scène,* 70).

34. See Burke on the "Status of Art," in *Counter-statement,* 63–91.

35. On the hypervisibility of the slip, see Cavell, *MWM,* 226–27; cited in our chapter 4.

36. Again, see Anscombe, *Intentionality,* 1–7.

37. For all these reasons, it did not seem fruitful to insist on subdividing, for the sake of symmetry, our cases in this way: ACTUAL INTENTIONS DECLARED or UNDECLARED to self; ACHIEVED INTENTIONS DECLARED or UNDECLARED to self; ACTUAL INTENTIONS DECLARED or UNDECLARED to others; ACHIEVED INTENTIONS DECLARED or UNDECLARED to others.

38. Here, I borrow Goffman's phrasing from *FA,* 39; cited in our chapter 4; see also Rayner on the theatrical unseen (stagehands and the like) in "Rude Mechanicals."

39. In chapter 7, we return to invited vs. uninvited audience feedback.

40. This passage is cited in chapter 4.

41. Simulation is always intentional, as Eco himself implies: "I simulate a limp *in order to make the addressee believe* that I am lame" (ID, 106; my emphasis).

42. See *Lettres persanes,* ed. Vernière, chaps. 24 and 26.

43. While Searle posits that there is no "I am intending," any parent asking a child, "What do you think you're doing?" would doubtless disagree (*Intentionality,* 3; cited in our chapter 1).

44. *Othello* has precipitated more than its fair share of comic and serious phenomenological crises. See Larwood, *TA,* 45–46, 107, 259.

45. Again, see Ricoeur, *IT,* 30; and Hirsch, *VI,* 4.

46. This would be Ellen's PERCEIVED INTENTION of the PERCEIVED INTENTIONS of others; we return, in chapter 7, to its theatrical equivalents.

47. See, e.g., Knapp and Michaels on de Man's "Purloined Ribbon" (AT, 21–24).

48. Here I allude, as earlier, to such work as Iser, *Act of Reading;* and Jauss, *Towards an Aesthetics.*

49. Spectators also make implicit declarations of their own, the subject of chapter 7.

50. On RATT, see *SRT,* chap. 1; on *Paradise Now,* see Martin, *Theater Is in the Streets,* chap. 2.

51. We explore the question of (legal) standing at the theater in chapter 7. Compare Black with Miller, *Tropes, Parables, Performatives,* 139; cited and discussed by Gould, UP, 25.

52. Compare also with Goldstein's introduction to *WWW,* in which he ponders "whether the allure [of violence] lies in the nature of the object or in the eye of the beholder" (4).

Chapter Six.

1. Compare also with Ridout on "corpsing," *Stage Fright,* chap. 4.

2. See, e.g., Aristotle on recognition of the object of imitation, *Poetics,* 1448b.

3. In our Talk-Back, we consider briefly the legal enactment of the death penalty in the United States, which is not out of frame but, for most, out of sight.

4. For the mirror-and-the-lady scenario, see *FA,* 39; and ID, 105; discussed in our chapter 4.

5. In addition to Graver, see, e.g., States on the curtain call, *GR,* 197–206.

6. Oddly, not even Sofer considers that possibility in his imaginative *Stage Life of Props.*

7. Compare, e.g., with the sudden collapse of a bridge during a Florentine festival of 1304: see D'Ancona, *Origini del teatro,* 1:94–95; cited in *MES,* 430, no. G2; or with Witmore's discussion of an accident in London in 1583 (*CA,* 93).

8. See Wappler, "Guess Who's Coming"; and Cowell, *At Play in the Tavern,* chap. 2.

9. For an elegant anthropological refutation of similar notions for still earlier periods, see Keeley, *War before Civilization.*

10. Compare, e.g., with Goffman's "riggings," dramatizations, and so on, cited in our chapter 2.

11. See, e.g., Eco, *OW,* chaps. 1, 3, and 4; and Auslander, *Liveness,* chaps. 1 and 4. A version of this scenario is the post hoc regret felt by many American viewers that they *could not intervene* to stop the atrocities depicted in the still photographs of the tortures of Abu Ghraib.

12. Adams had been wrongly convicted of murdering a police officer. See Lesser, *PE,* 84–92, 97–99, 173–75.

13. See his "Life Is Not a Dramatic Narrative," cited in our chapter 2.

14. As we shall see in chapter 7, a play can be interrupted by one person, by many people, by no person at all, by acts of God, and so on.

15. For a fascinating philosophical exploration of the problem—though one that shockingly neglects the work of Goffman and Baudrillard alike—see Walton, *MM,* chap. 7.

16. A comic strip from Berkeley Breathed's *Bloom County* illustrates that point very well when one character asks of the violence he is viewing on television, "Will somebody please tell me whether I should be enjoying this or not."

17. Our play could be, e.g., Sondheim's *Assassins.* The better to privilege agency and action over textuality, however, I have not named specific plays in our scenarios, which would also enmesh us in various Cavellian contortions of pointing (*MWM,* 328): "George playing Mussolini," and so on.

18. I could have switched the genders of our protagonists; but in the canonical examples of jealousy in crimes of passion, it is perhaps best to leave things as the highly imperfect stereotypes and conventions that they are rather than endorse new ones.

19. See, e.g., Lesser on the "blurry borderline between real murder and fictional murder" (*PE,* 1).

20. See chapter 3 on theatrical motive, means, and opportunity.

21. See also Goffman on the prompter, *FA,* 120.

22. I discuss both incidents (from *TA,* 198, 199) in *DBD,* 52–54; see also the death of Montfleury, discussed in our chapter 3.

23. I use those terms by analogy to "suicide by police" or "suicide by accident," the latter as in the death of Hexum ("Actor Wounds Himself"), both discussed in our chapter 1.

24. As previously, this is a matter of degree: the show is not liable to stop if one actor trips another, if wardrobe "malfunctions," if actors "break frame" by mingling with and engaging the spectators, and so on.

25. See AT2, 6; cited in our chapter 1.

26. See chapter 5, Case 1.

27. For the *Eumenides* incident of c. 460 B.C., see Nagler, *Source Book,* 5; and *DBD,* 74–75. See also Lucian, "Saltatio," 83.

28. The payoff: Thornton then "subjoined, with a burst of truly rational triumph, 'Richard is himself again'" (*TA,* 33).

29. Recall that Jehan Hemont signed a document in which he pronounced the innocence of his friend, Guillaume Langlois (fol. 153r; Appendix, Document 1.1).

30. Compare, e.g., to Baudrillard's holdup scenario (*SW,* 178), cited in our chapter 1.

31. On the Riga incident, cited earlier, see no. C64 in *MES,* 180–81.

32. The term *generic confusion* is from Johnson and Schaefer on snuff in "Soft Core/Hard Gore," 46–47. Compare also with Konner's equation of "entertaining news and newsy entertainment," cited in our Mise en Scène.

33. See the Mons legislation in Cohen, *LCR,* 591; cited in chapter 2.

34. Compare with Goffman's "intention display" (*FA,* 235), discussed in our chapter 4.

35. Bateson, "Theory of Play and Phantasy," as discussed by Goffman, *FA,* 7; my emphasis. Compare, e.g., with such staples as the *Jerry Springer Show,* in which participants seek to trick audiences that apparent misfires (in the form of real brawls) erupt spontaneously when, in reality, they are carefully orchestrated simulations.

36. Hobbs, "Terrifying Prank Not Funny to Authorities."

37. Compare with Baudrillard, *SW,* 178, discussed in our Introduction and chapter 1.

38. See Milgram, *Obedience to Authority;* and Blass, *Man Who Shocked the World,* chaps. 6 and 7.

Chapter Seven.

1. Brantingham, "Unusual Cop Chase."

2. We return later to the legend of the extra devil at *Doctor Faustus.*

3. Again, there is a vast critical literature on the audience; and I have earlier cited Bennett, Blau, Ridout, Bartsch, Eco, and Goffman himself. My focus remains, however, on the connection(s) of that response to issues of intentionality.

4. Technically, for Goffman, breakage is something that spectators do only in their capacity as "theatergoers," not "onlookers" (*FA,* 129–30).

5. On the imposition of silence in the medieval theater, see *DBD,* chap. 8. Compare with our earlier discussion in chapter 2 of Goffman on the display of a lack of affect (*FA,* 126).

6. On this point, see *FA,* 346; cited in our chapter 6. We have already seen that actors, e.g., have their own ways of doing something about them.

7. E-mail exchange with Irwin Appel, 13 May 2006.

8. In a movie like *The Accused,* cheering on but not intercepting is a crime; in the heinous murder of Sherrice Iverson in Las Vegas (25 May 1997), a University of California, Berkeley student, David Cash, was reviled for not intercepting, but his failure to act was not a crime in Nevada.

9. See, e.g., Schechner on Squat, *BTA,* 302–8; and Sell, *APLC,* chap. 2.

10. See chapter 5, especially Cases 3, 4, and 5.

11. In addition to Cavell (*MWM,* 328), see Walton on how and why we fear—not quite so vicariously as it seems—for fictional characters (*MM,* 241–59).

12. See especially Davidson on intention vs. desire, *Essays,* 96–101. For an interesting example of such perceptions and misperceptions in the Grand Guignol, see André de Lorde, *Théâtre de la mort,* 19; discussed in my *MTOC,* 232–33.

13. Here I mean that an individual, who is both conscious and aware of what it means to do so, explicitly *demands* something of others: not implicitly, as, e.g., the unconscious victim of an accident.

14. As opposed, here, to the false or misleading "coincidences" that we explored in the critical reception of the Intentional Fallacy (see the Entr'Acte).

15. See Isidore, *Etymologiarum,* "De theatro," book 18, chap. 42; cited earlier.

16. Chap. 1 of Kirby's *FT* is called "Acting and Not Acting."

17. For a philosophical approach to such temporality, see, e.g., Davidson, "Intending" (*Essays,* 88–89).

18. See, e.g., the twenty-seven definitions of *breakage* in the *American Heritage Unabridged Dictionary,* which emphasize the violence and intentionality inherent in "smashing, disrupting, hindering, impeding," as well as "confusion, disorder, interference, obstacles, hindrances, destruction, impropriety," and so on. Compare also with Godlovitch's claim that one of the "integrity conditions" of musical performance is the "continuity of Public Calm" ("Integrity of Musical Performance," 577). See also Wilshire's objection to Goffman's "binarism" in *RPI,* 274–81.

19. There is only an apparent contradiction here with my earlier remarks that theater does not stop being theater at such moments (chapters 4, 5, and 6): namely, the examples in this chapter elucidate the ontological compromise—and *sometimes* the cessation altogether—of theater from within and without the collective, all in ways that may or may not demand a principal concern with ontology.

20. That breakage then led to an intratheatrical breakage when, one night, Wilkinson's "remarkably audible" hiss backfired and, *from within the collective,* another actor cried, "Turn him out!" upon which "poor Wilkinson was unceremoniously handed down from his own gallery and ejected into the street" (*TA,* 42).

21. On Jedburgh Abbey, see *MES,* 268–69; cited in our chapter 4; on actors in the audience, see Bartsch, *AA;* and on divine intervention into medieval drama, see *DBD,* chaps. 4 and 12.

22. The better to avoid a *reductio ad absurdum,* I stop the chain reaction right here, even though Goffman does not. E.g., he identifies the ways in which an actor might pause to accommodate desirable audience laughter or, in response to undesirable laughter, might "move forward with his lines as fast as is practicable" (*FA,* 131). One might even include here the case of the actor who is entranced enough by the sympathetic laughter in the house either to crack up during the scene or even to *pretend* to crack up.

23. See also Walton, *MM,* chap. 6.

24. See Stallman, "Intentions," 399; cited in our Entr'Acte.

25. On the pleasant sort of upsurge of the real, see States, *GR,* 34.

26. On this incident, see Petit de Julleville, *LM,* 2:137–38; Gosselin, *Recherches,* 62–63; and my *DBD,* 93–95, 217–18.

27. See Leader-Elliott, NI, 88–89; cited in our chapter 5.

28. Statistics for these accounts vary. The number of terrorists is often estimated at 40–50; the number of hostages at 700–850. The military had arrived because some of the actors, who were *not* on stage at the time, had escaped so that they could intervene by calling the police. See, e.g., Dolnik and Pilch, "Moscow Theater Hostage Crisis."

29. See Black on "doing it beautifully," *AM,* 1–5; and Juergensmeyer on the "Theater of Terror," chap. 7 of *Terror in the Mind of God.*

30. The principal contribution of Witmore, however, and Hamilton, is to argue that the history of accidents allows for even the apparently oxymoronic "divine judgment through accident" (*CA,* 93).

31. See, e.g., the story of Blanctrain, *CPV,* 4:137; cited in our chapter 3.

32. Compare, e.g., with Dershowitz, "Life Is Not a Dramatic Narrative"; and Evans, *Criminal Prosecution,* 8–12.

33. On the appearance of the "extra devil" as early as 1594, see Cox, *Devil and the Sacred,* 125; and for a similar incident of 1824, see Ryan on an actor's prank to that effect, *Dramatic Table Talk,* 3:191; discussed in my *DBD,* chap. 7.

34. On this incident and its sources, see Enders, "Performing Miracles."

35. This text appears as no. C65 in *MES,* 181. The transformation of "lamentation into laughter" is a topos of such tales (see, e.g., my *DBD,* 106–7). See also Austin's discussion of distinct likeness (*PP,* 214).

36. See no. F33, in *MES,* 401.

37. See also Ridout, *Stage Fright,* 129–34.

38. On control as a criterion of art, whereby Wilshire rules out snuff, from the standpoint of the actor, see *RPI,* 249–72. Would he have ruled out the *Eumenides* of 460 B.C. from the standpoint of the audience? And what would he have said about laughter, over which agents can indeed assert a *degree* of control?

39. Compare with Cavell, *MWM,* 231–32; cited in our chapter 2.

40. For "slips of the body," see chapters 4 and 5. By no means am I implying that such persons should be barred from the theater; but their plight raises interesting questions of how individuals desire to and should participate in their communities, including the question of what makes up a community.

41. Here, it is important to include *all members of the collective:* even a set is designed (by someone) to induce response from audiences, as we see regularly when audiences applaud a theatrical set even before a play begins.

42. For the full passage from *TC,* 172, see our Introduction. See also Sheingorn's signature essay on theatrical iconography as a visual syntax of sorts in "Visual Language of Drama"; and Baxandall, *Patterns of Intention,* 41–42.

43. Kirby, e.g., treats such examples in *FT,* xiv–xv.

44. In *DBD,* chap. 3, I discuss a similar ancient Greek response by the spectators who politely applauded Lucian's mad Ajax ("Saltatio," 83).

45. Here, we could even imagine a truly clever director with a back-up plan in the form of an extra song or a character waiting in the wings on the off-chance that the audience would not play along.

46. I analyze several such medieval choices in my *DBD,* 188–89.

47. On the Riga incident, see no. C64 in *MES,* 180–81.

48. *Journal de Jehan Aubrion,* ed. Larchey, 441; cited by Petit de Julleville, *LM,* 1:445. See also Appendix, Document 7.1, which contains what is probably an erroneous reference to a Latin play *by Terence* and not called *Terance.* For a similar incident of 1508, see *LM,* 2:92–93.

49. *CMJH,* 214; also cited in *LM,* 1:445; see Appendix, Document 7.1.

50. For the eruption of the Belgian Revolution on 25 August 1830 after a performance of Auber's opera *La Muette de Portici,* see Gerhard, *Urbanization of Opera,* 127–33.

51. McPharlin, *Puppet Theatre in America,* 204; discussed in *FA,* 363. For his own part, McPharlin cites Hanck, "Frame Analysis of the Puppet Theater." Here, we also see anew the proffer of the mitigating circumstances of diminished capacity due to alcohol (NI, 88–89). Meanwhile, though we have lost all traces of the perhaps apocryphal mountaineer, there is nothing apocryphal about the celebrated family of puppeteers that began with grandfather Alberto Lano, who emigrated to the United States from Italy in 1825. See Fisler, "Phenomenology of Racialism," chap. 3.

52. *San Francisco Chronicle,* 8 December 1965; cited by Goffman (*FA,* 355) and reminiscent of the work of both Gosselin and Durkheim on spontaneous eruptions of violence during performance events. For Gosselin, see *Recherches,* 62–63; for Durkheim, see *Evolution of Educational Thought,* 142.

53. Compare to Goffman on the "dramatized, rigged match," and so on, *FA,* 127; cited in our chapter 2.

54. From a massive bibliography in comparative legal studies, see, e.g., Hayden, "Imposing Criminal and Civil Penalties for Failing to Help Another."

55. "Persona dupliciter spectatur, eius qui fecit et eius qui passus est," *DJ,* 48.19.16; see Appendix, Document 3.4.

Talk-Back.

1. See Brumberg, *Kansas Charley;* and Geraghty's review of it, 230. Lesser reproduces the Gilmore invite which, by analogy to wedding invitations, indicates that his mother, Bessie, was requesting the honor of the invitee's presence (*PE,* 118; her emphasis).

2. See Sverdlik, CML, 183; cited in our chapter 1.

3. For Konner's distinction between "entertaining news and newsy entertainment," see our Mise en Scène.

4. ABC's *World News Tonight,* 6 May 1998.

5. KTLA 5, *Today in LA,* 6 May 1998. Anchor Kelly Lang's apology on behalf of KTLA is cited in the Introduction.

6. See Searle, *Intentionality,* 10; discussed in our chapter 3, in the context of the nonapology there of Jehan Martin.

7. I do not wish to appear—or to be—uncharitable in neglecting the subject of forgiveness; but intention underlies both legal and theological approaches to re-

morse. And the intentions of those who forgive are different from those who *ask* forgiveness or who express their (real or feigned) remorse.

8. KEYT 3, *Key News,* 6 May 1998. The question of audience pleasure has been explored, e.g., by Black, *AM,* especially 5–17; and challenged by Lesser, *PE,* 9.

9. ABC's *World News Tonight,* 6 May 1998.

10. KEYT, *Key News,* 6 May 1998.

11. On this point, see both Goldstein, *WWW,* 1–2; and Eco, *OW,* 107–10.

12. On illocution, see, e.g., Austin, *HDTW,* lecture 8.

13. Footage from Skycam, KCAL 9; re-aired by KEYT 3 on *Key News,* 6 May 1998.

14. On Dwyer, see the virtually unmediated account of Kerekes and Slater, *Killing for Culture,* 200–202; and compare also with Scenario 4 of our chapter 6.

15. In *DBD,* 199–201, I discuss "Looking Out for Mrs. Berwid," produced by Norman Gorin, *60 Minutes,* 12 July 1981; on the Ng trial, see Robins, "When Is the News Just Too 'Horrific'?" 53–54.

16. The Michigan prosecutor David Gorcyga contended during various interviews that Dr. Kevorkian had acted with "premeditation and deliberation" and that the reality of Youk's consent was "not a viable defense in taking the life of another." Both ABC's *World News Tonight* and NBC's *Nightly News* aired excerpts from interviews with Gorcyga on 23 November 1998.

17. The first quotation is from "Killer Doc," 70, the second from "Dressed to Kill," 16.

18. "The question before the house was Censorship, Is It Ever Justified? He took the straight hard line (Never); I, an attenuated line (Sometimes)," Buckley, "Killer Doc," 70. On censorship, literature, and ethics, see Booth, *Company We Keep,* 26–28.

19. See especially Searle, *Intentionality,* 9–10; cited in our chapter 3.

20. Equally interesting, of course, and ever more in the news is the speaker or actant who, due to his or her knowledge deficit, proceeds *unaware* of the dissemination that is allegedly unintentional on the part of others.

21. Compare, e.g., to Auslander's discussion of the legal definition, as related to copyright law, of what it means to perform *live* (*Liveness,* chap. 4).

22. See Lesser on the 1991 case in which the public television station KQED sued Warden Daniel Vasquez for the right to televise the execution of Robert Alton Harris (*PE,* chap. 2).

23. Goldstein, *WWW,* 2; my emphasis. For the Aristotelian understanding of the accident, see Witmore, *CA,* chap. 1; and Hamilton, *Accident,* chap. 1.

24. See also Eco's "Overinterpreting Texts," 64–66. Compare to the "interruption that is not one," explored in Case 6a of our chapter 7. See also Auslander, *Liveness,* chap. 2.

25. Interestingly enough, the DVD extras contain at least one instance of Cohen's having (un)successfully captured the *absence of bigotry:* outside the "official" film, he includes the pointed real objection to his feigned anti-Semitism by a West Virginia animal control worker.

26. See Schechner, *BTA,* 301. In addition to the events especially of Cases 2 and 3, I discuss such incidents in *DBD,* 198–202.

27. Among those objecting were the girl's parents, who had seen the snuff tape for the first time while watching the news. Wald, cited by Robins, "When Is the News," 53–54.

28. On the peephole, see *FA,* 126–27; discussed in our chapter 2. That brave new world has a brave new literature devoted to it, to which I cannot do justice here. For that literature as related to theater studies, excellent places to start include Auslander, *Liveness,* chap. 2.

29. I refer again to his essay of that title in *LS.*

30. See, e.g., Haraway, *Simians, Cyborgs, and Women;* and Schneider, *Live Theory.* "A mes moments perdus, j'apprends à marcher à une statue. Etant donné son immobilité exagérément prolongée, ce n'est pas facile. Ni pour elle. Ni pour moi. Grande distance nous sépare . . . Ce qui importe, c'est que son premier pas soit bon. Tout pour elle est dans ce premier pas. Je le sais. Je ne le sais que trop. De là mon angoisse" ("La Statue et moi," in *Oeuvres complètes,* ed. Bellour, 948).

WORKS CITED

Primary Sources

Archives Nationales, Paris

JJ 116, no. 254, fols. 152v–53r.

JJ 125, no. 7, fol. 7r–v.

JJ 148, no. 144, fols. 74v–75r.

Aristotle. *The "Art" of Rhetoric*. Ed. and trans. John Henry Freese. Loeb Classical Library. 1926; rpt. Cambridge, Mass.: Harvard University Press, 1975.

———. *The Complete Works of Aristotle*. Ed. and trans. Jonathan Barnes. Princeton: Princeton University Press, 1984.

———. *Poetics*. Ed. and trans. W. Hamilton Fyfe. In *Aristotle, Longinus, Demetrius*. Loeb Classical Library. 1927; rpt. Cambridge, Mass.: Harvard University Press, 1946.

[Aubrion, Jehan.] *Journal de Jehan Aubrion, Bourgeois de Metz, avec sa continuation, par Pierre Aubrion, 1465–1512*. Ed. Lorédan Larchey. Metz: F. Blanc, 1857.

Augustine of Hippo. *Confessions*. Ed. and trans. William Watts. 2 vols. Loeb Classical Library. Cambridge, Mass.: Harvard University Press, 1950.

———. *On Christine Doctrine*. Trans. D. W. Robertson, Jr. 1958; rpt. Indianapolis: Bobbs Merrill, 1980.

Ballard, J. G. *Crash*. New York: Farrar, Straus, and Giroux, 1973.

Basin, Thomas. *Histoire des règnes de Charles VII et de Louis XI*. Ed. J. Quicherat. 4 vols. Paris: Renouard, 1859.

Bevington, David, ed. *The Medieval Drama*. Boston: Houghton-Mifflin, 1975.

Blamires, Alcuin, ed. *Woman Defamed and Woman Defended: An Anthology of Medieval Texts*. Oxford: Oxford University Press, 1992.

Boece, Hector. *The Chronicles of Scotland*. Trans. John Bellenden (1531). Ed. Edith C. Batho and H. Winifrid Husbands. 2 vols. Scottish Text Society, 3d ser., 10 and 15. Edinburgh: Blackwell, 1938–41.

Boileau, Nicolas. *Satires, Épîtres, Art poétique*. Ed. Jean-Pierre Collinet. Paris: Gallimard, 1985.

Camus, Albert. *L'Etranger, roman.* Paris: Gallimard, 1949.

Cazelles, Brigitte, ed. *The Lady as Saint: A Collection of French Hagiographic Romances of the Thirteenth Century.* Philadelphia: University of Pennsylvania Press, 1991.

Chassanion, Jean de. *The Theatre of Gods Judgements; or, a collection of histories out of sacred, ecclesiasticall, and prophane authors . . . Translated out of French and augmented by more than three hundred examples by Th. Beard.* London: Adam Islip, 1597.

Chaucer Life Records. Ed. Martin M. Crow and Clair C. Olson. Oxford: Clarendon Press, 1966.

The Chester Mystery Cycle. Ed. David Mills. East Lansing, Mich.: Colleagues Press, 1992.

The Chester Plays. Ed. Hermann Deimling. 2 vols. Early English Text Society. Vol. 1: 1892; rpt. Oxford: Oxford University Press, 1968. Vol. 2: 1916; rpt. Oxford: Oxford University Press, 1968.

La Chronique de Metz de Jacomin Husson, 1200–1525. Publié d'aprés le manuscrit autographe de Copenhague et celui de Paris. Ed. H. Michelant. Metz: Rousseau-Pallez, 1870.

Les Chroniques de la ville de Metz, recueillies, mises en ordre et publiées pour la première fois: Le Doyen de St. Thiébault, Jean Aubrion, Philippe de Vigneulles, Praillon. Annales Messines, etc., 900–1552. Ed. Jean François Huguenin. Metz: S. Lamort, 1838.

[Cicero]. *Ad C. Herennium.* Ed. and trans. Harry Caplan. Loeb Classical Library. 1954; rpt. Cambridge, Mass.: Harvard University Press, 1977.

Cicero. *De inventione and Topica.* Ed. and trans. H. M. Hubbell. Loeb Classical Library. 1949; rpt Cambridge, Mass.: Harvard University Press, 1968.

Cohen, Gustave, ed. *Le Livre de conduite du Régisseur et Le Compte des dépenses pour le Mystère de la Passion joué à Mons en 1501.* Paris: Champion, 1925.

———. *Recueil de farces françaises inédites du XVe siècle.* Cambridge, Mass.: Mediaeval Academy of America, 1949.

Cornuälle, Heldris de. *Le Roman de Silence.* Ed. L. Thorpe. Cambridge: W. Heffer, 1972.

———. *Le Roman de Silence.* Trans. Regina Psaki. New York: Garland, 1991.

———. *Silence, a Thirteenth-Century Romance.* Trans. Sarah Roche-Mahdi. East Lansing, Mich.: Colleagues Press, 1992.

Corpus iuris civilis. Vol. 1: *Institutiones,* ed. P. Krueger. *Digesta,* ed. T. Mommsen. Berlin, 1877.

Dick, Kirby. *Sick: The Life and Death of Bob Flanagan, Supermasochist.* Videotape. 1997.

The Digest of Justinian. Ed. Theodor Mommsen and Paul Krueger. Trans. Alan Watson. 2 vols. Philadelphia: University of Pennsylvania Press, 1985.

Drew, Katherine Fischer. *Law and Society in Early Medieval Europe: Studies in Legal History.* London: Variorum Reprints, 1988.

———. "Legal Materials as a Source for Early Medieval Social History." In *Medieval and Other Studies in Honor of Floyd Seyward Lear. Rice University Studies* 60, no. 4 (1974): 33–43.

——, trans. *The Laws of the Salian Franks.* Philadelphia: University of Pennsylvania Press, 1991.

——, trans. *The Lombard Laws.* Philadelphia: University of Pennsylvania Press, 1973.

Drew, Katherine Fischer, and Floyd Seyward Lear, eds. *Perspectives in Medieval History.* Chicago: University of Chicago Press, 1963.

Dumas, Alexandre. *Kean: Cinq actes.* Adaptation by Jean-Paul Sartre. Paris: Gallimard, 1954.

Farce Nouvelle de Digeste Vielle et Digeste Neufve où deux escoliers estudient, lesquelz ne peuvent trouver moyen d'avoir argent, si n'est par coustume et loix (à cinq personnages). In *Recueil de farces françaises inédites,* ed. Cohen, 333–40.

Fiero, Gloria K., Wendy Pfeffer, and Mathé Allain, eds. and trans. *Three Medieval Views of Women.* New Haven: Yale University Press, 1989.

Fournier, Édouard, ed. *Le Théâtre français avant la Renaissance.* 1872; rpt. New York: Burt Franklin, 1965.

Geoffrey of Vinsauf. *Poetria Nova.* In *The Poetria Nova and Its Sources in Early Rhetorical Doctrine.* Trans. Ernest Gallo. The Hague: Mouton, 1971.

Gide, André. *Les Caves du Vatican, Sotie.* Paris: Gallimard, 1922.

Gréban, Arnoul. *Le Mystère de la Passion.* Ed. Omer Jodogne. Brussels: Académie Royale, 1965.

Horace. *Satires, Epistles, and Ars poetica.* Trans. H. R. Fairclough. Loeb Classical Library. Cambridge, Mass.: Harvard University Press, 1926.

Isidore of Seville. *Isidori Hispalensis Episcopi Etymologiarum sive Originum Libri XX.* Ed. W. M. Lindsay. 2 vols. 1911; rpt. London: Oxford University Press, 1962.

Japrisot, Sébastien. *L'Été meurtrier.* Paris: Gallimard, 1981.

Jeux et sapience du Moyen Age. Ed. Albert Pauphilet. Librairie de la Pléiade. Paris: Gallimard, 1951.

Journal d'un bourgeois de Paris 1405–1449. Ed. A. Tuety. Paris, 1881. English translation: *A Parisian Journal, 1405–1449.* Trans. Janet Shirley. Oxford: Clarendon Press, 1960.

Judith and Holofernes: A Late Fifteenth-Century French Mystery Play. Trans. Graham A. Runnalls. Early European Drama Translation, 5. Fairview, N.C.: Pegasus Press, 2002.

Justinian. *Digest.* See *Digest of Justinian; Corpus iuris civilis.*

Kors, Alan C., and Edward Peters, eds. *Witchcraft in Europe 1100–1700: A Documentary History.* 1972; rpt. Philadelphia: University of Pennsylvania Press, 1986.

Krämer, Heinrich (Institoris) [and Jacob Sprenger] *Malleus malleficarum 1487.* Ed. Günter Jerouschek. Hildesheim and New York: G. Olms, 1992.

——. *Malleus malleficarum.* Trans. Montague Summers. 1928; rpt. London: Pushkin Press, 1951.

Lucian of Samosata. "Saltatio." Ed. and trans. A. M. Harmon. In *Works,* Vol. 5. Loeb Classical Library. 1936; rpt. Cambridge, Mass.: Harvard University Press, 1972.

Marcus Aurelius. *Meditations.* Trans. Martin Hammond. Penguin Classics. London: Penguin, 2006.

Marivaux. *Oeuvres de jeunesse.* Ed. Claude Rigault. Librairie de la Pléiade. Paris: Gallimard, 1972.

Meredith, Peter, and John E. Tailby, eds. *The Staging of Religious Drama in Europe in the Later Middle Ages: Texts and Documents in English Translation.* Early Drama, Art and Music, 4. Kalamazoo, Mich.: Medieval Institute Publications, 1983.

Michaux, Henri. *Oeuvres complètes.* Ed. Raymond Bellour. Librairie de la Pléiade. Paris: Gallimard, 2001.

Michel, Jean. *Le Mystère de la Passion (Angers 1486).* Ed. Omer Jodogne. Gembloux, Belgium: J. Duculot, 1959.

Le Mistere de la Sainte Hostie. Bibliothèque Nationale, Paris, MS Réserve, Yf 2915.

Le Mistére du Viel Testament. Ed. James de Rothschild. 6 vols. 1878; rpt. New York: Johnson Reprints, 1966.

[Molinet, Jean?]. *Le Mystère de Judith et Holofernés: Une édition critique de l'une des parties du "Mistere du Viel Testament."* Ed. Graham A. Runnalls. Geneva: Droz, 1995.

Montesquieu. *Lettres persanes.* Ed. Paul Vernière. Paris: Garnier, 1975.

Moralité nouvelle d'ung empereur qui tua son neveu qui avoit prins une fille a force. In *Théâtre français avant la Renaissance,* ed. Fournier, 354–69.

Mylne, J. W., and R. D. Craig. *Reports of Cases Argued and Determined in the High Court of Chancery during the Time of Lord Chancellor Cottenham.* 5 vols. Vol. 2. London: Saunders and Benning, 1838.

Le Mystère de la Résurrection Angers (1456). Ed. Pierre Servet. 2 vols. Geneva: Droz, 1993.

Les Mystères de la procession de Lille. Vol. 1: *Le Pentateuque.* Vol. 3: *De Salomon aux Maccabées* Ed. Alan E. Knight. Geneva: Droz, 2001, 2004.

Nagler, A. M. *A Source Book in Theatrical History.* 1952; rpt. New York: Dover, 1959.

Paré, Ambroise. *On Monsters and Marvels.* Trans. Janis L. Pallister. Chicago: University of Chicago Press, 1982.

Pascal, Blaise. *Oeuvres complètes.* Ed. Louis Lafuma. Paris: Seuil, 1963.

Plato. *Gorgias.* In *Lysis, Symposium, Gorgias.* Ed. and trans. W. R. M. Lamb. Loeb Classical Library. 1925; rpt. Cambridge, Mass.: Harvard University Press, 1975.

———. *Laws.* 2 vols. Ed. and trans. R. G. Bury. Loeb Classical Library. 1926; rpt. Cambridge, Mass.: Harvard University Press, 1942.

———. *Phaedrus.* Trans. R. Hackforth. 1952; rpt. Cambridge: Cambridge University Press, 1972.

———. *The Republic.* 2 vols. Ed. and trans. Paul Shorey. Loeb Classical Library. Cambridge, Mass.: Harvard University Press, 1935.

Port, Célestin. *Inventaire analytique des archives anciennes de la mairie d'Angers.* Paris: J. Dumoulin; Angers: Cosnier et Lachèse, 1861.

Quintilian. *Institutio oratoria.* Ed. and trans. H. E. Butler. 4 vols. Loeb Classical Library. 1920; rpt. Cambridge, Mass.: Harvard University Press, 1980.

Rutebeuf. *Le Miracle de Théophile*. Ed. Albert Pauphilet. In *Jeux et sapience*, 135–58. English translation in *Medieval French Plays*, 165–92. Trans. Richard Axton and John Stevens. Oxford: Basil Blackwell, 1971.

Shakespeare, William. *The Arden Shakespeare Complete Works*. Ed. Richard Proudfoot, Ann Thompson, and David Scott Kastan. Walton-on-Thames: Nelson, 1998.

Sondheim, Stephen, and John Weidman. *Assassins*. New York: Theatre Communication Group, 1991.

Suetonius. *The Lives of the Caesars*. 2 vols. In *Works*, ed. and trans. J. C. Rolfe. Loeb Classical Library. Cambridge, Mass.: Harvard University Press, 1914.

Tydeman, William, ed. *The Medieval European Stage, 500–1550*. Theatre in Europe: A Documentary History. Cambridge: Cambridge University Press, 2001.

de Vigneulles, Philippe. *La Chronique de Philippe de Vigneulles*. Ed. Charles Bruneau. 4 vols. Metz: Société d'Histoire d'Archéologie de la Lorraine, 1927–33.

———. *Gedenkbuch des Metzer Bürgers Philippe von Vigneulles aus den Jahren 1471–1522*. Ed. Heinrich Michelant. Stuttgart, 1852; rpt. Amsterdam: Rodopi, 1968.

Vives, Juan Luis. *Vives on Education (De Tradendis Disciplinis)*. Trans. Foster Watson. 1913; rpt. Totowa, N.J.: Rowman and Littlefield, 1971.

Secondary Sources

"Actor Wounds Himself on Set of TV Series." Around the Nation. From Associated Press. *New York Times*, 14 October 1984.

Alter, Jean. *A Sociosemiotic Theory of Theatre*. Philadelphia: University of Pennsylvania Press, 1990.

D'Ancona, Alessandro. *Origini del teatro italiano. Libri tre con due appendici sulla rappresentazione drammatica del contado toscano e sul teatro mantovano nel sec XVI*. 2 vols. 1891; rpt. Rome: Bardi, 1966.

Anscombe, G. E. M. *Intentionality*. 2d ed. 1957; rpt. Cambridge, Mass.: Harvard University Press, 2000.

Arbeau, Thoinot [Jean Tabourot]. *Orchésographie*. 1588; Geneva: Slatkine, 1970.

Ariès, Philippe. *Western Attitudes toward Death: From the Middle Ages to the Present*. Trans. Patricia M. Ranum. Baltimore: Johns Hopkins University Press, 1974.

Artaud, Antonin. *Le Théâtre et son double*. Vol. 4 of *Oeuvres complètes*. 2d ed. Paris: Gallimard, 1978. English translation: *The Theater and Its Double*. Trans. Mary Caroline Richards. New York: Grove Weidenfeld, 1958.

Ashley, Kathleen M. "Sponsorship, Reflexivity, and Resistance: Cultural Readings of the York Cycle Plays." In *Performance of Middle English Culture*, ed. Paxson, Clopper, and Tomasch, 9–24.

———, ed. *Victor Turner and the Construction of Cultural Criticism: Between Literature and Anthropology*. Bloomington: Indiana University Press, 1990.

Ashley, Kathleen M., and Wim Hüsken, eds. *Moving Subjects: Processional Performance in the Middle Ages and the Renaissance*. Amsterdam: Rodopi, 2001.

Audi, Robert. *Action, Intention, and Reason*. Ithaca: Cornell University Press, 1993.

Auerbach, Erich. *Mimesis: The Representation of Reality in Western Literature.* Trans. Willard R. Trask. 1953; rpt. Princeton: Princeton University Press, 1974.

August, Roland. *Cruelty and Civilization: The Roman Games.* New York: Routledge, 1994.

Auslander, Philip. *Liveness: Performance in a Mediatized Culture.* London: Routledge, 1999.

Austin, J. L. *How to Do Things with Words.* Ed. J. O. Urmson and Marina Sbisà. 2d ed. Cambridge, Mass.: Harvard University Press, 1978.

———. *Philosophical Papers.* Ed. J. O. Urmson and G. J. Warnock. 2d ed. Oxford: Clarendon Press, 1970.

Axton, Richard. *European Drama of the Early Middle Ages.* London: Hutchinson, 1974.

Balkin, J. M. "A Night in the Topics: The Reason of Legal Rhetoric and the Rhetoric of Legal Reason." In *Law's Stories,* ed. Brooks and Gewirtz, 211–24.

Barish, Jonas. *The Anti-Theatrical Prejudice.* Berkeley: University of California Press, 1981.

Barthes, Roland. "The Death of the Author." In *Image—Music—Text,* trans. Stephen Heath, 142–48. New York: Hill and Wang, 1977.

Bartsch, Shadi. *Actors in the Audience: Theatricality and Doublespeak from Nero to Hadrian.* Revealing Antiquity, 6. Cambridge, Mass.: Harvard University Press, 1994.

Bateson, Gregory. "A Theory of Play and Phantasy." *Psychiatric Research Reports* (American Psychiatric Association) 2 (1955): 39–51. Reprinted in *Steps to an Ecology of Mind: Collected Essays in Anthropology, Psychiatry, Evolution, and Epistemology,* 177–93. New York: Ballantine, 1972. Also in *Performance Studies Reader,* ed. Bial, chap. 18.

Baudrillard, Jean. *Selected Writings.* Ed. and trans. Mark Poster. Stanford, Calif.: Stanford University Press, 1988.

———. *Symbolic Exchange and Death.* Trans. Iain Hamilton Grant. London: Sage, 1993.

Baxandall, Michael. *Patterns of Intention: On the Historical Explanation of Pictures.* New Haven: Yale University Press, 1985.

Beale, Lewis. "A Sampler of Hell, as One Church Pictures It, Anyhow." *New York Times,* 10 November 2002, sec. 2, p. 27.

Beardsley, Monroe C. and W. K. Wimsatt, Jr. "The Intentional Fallacy." *Sewanee Review* 54 (1946). Reprinted in Wimsatt, *The Verbal Icon: Studies in the Meaning of Poetry,* 3–18. Lexington: University of Kentucky Press, 1954.

Beckwith, Sarah. *Signifying God: Social Relations and Symbolic Action in York's Play of Corpus Christi.* Chicago: University of Chicago Press, 2001.

Benjamin, Walter. *Illuminations.* Ed. Hannah Arendt, trans. Harry Zohn. New York: Schocken Books, 1969.

Bennett, Susan. *Theatre Audiences: A Theory of Production and Reception.* 2d ed. London: Routledge, 1997.

Berns, Sandra. "Tales of Intention: Storytelling and the Rhetoricity of Judgment." In *Intention in Law and Philosophy,* ed. Naffine, Owens, and Williams, 161–86.

Bérubé, Michael. "Against Subjectivity." In "Four Views on the Place of the Personal in Scholarship." *PMLA* 111 (1996): 1063–68.

Bial, Henry, ed. *The Performance Studies Reader.* 2d ed. London: Routledge, 2007.

Birringer, Johannes. *Theatre, Theory, Postmodernism.* Bloomington: Indiana University Press, 1991.

Black, Joel. *The Aesthetics of Murder: A Study in Romantic Literature and Contemporary Culture.* Baltimore: Johns Hopkins University Press, 1991.

Blass, Thomas. *The Man Who Shocked the World: The Life and Legacy of Stanley Milgram.* New York: Basic Books, 2004.

Blau, Herbert. *The Audience.* Baltimore: Johns Hopkins University Press, 1990.

Bloch, R. Howard. *Etymologies and Genealogies: A Literary Anthropology of the French Middle Ages.* 1983; rpt. Chicago: University of Chicago Press, 1986.

———. *Medieval French Literature and Law.* Berkeley: University of California Press, 1977.

Boal, Augusto. *Theater of the Oppressed.* Trans. Charles A. McBride and Maria-Odilia Leal McBride. New York: Urizen, 1979.

Bogatyrev, Petr. "Semiotics in the Folk Theater." In *Semiotics of Art: Prague School Contributions,* ed. Ladislav Matejka and Irwin R. Titunik, 33–50. Cambridge, Mass.: MIT Press, 1976.

Booth, Wayne. *The Company We Keep: An Ethics of Fiction.* Berkeley: University of California Press, 1988.

Bourcier, Paul. *Histoire de la danse en Occident.* Paris: Seuil, 1978.

Bowers, Fredson. "Textual Criticism." In *The Aims and Methods of Scholarship in Modern Languages and Literatures,* ed. James Thorpe, 29–54. 2d ed. New York: MLA, 1970.

Brantingham, Barney. "Unusual Cop Chase Twist in SBCC Play." *Santa Barbara News Press,* 20 July 2005, A2.

Brantley, Jessica. *Reading in the Wilderness: Private Devotion and Public Performance in Late Medieval England.* Chicago: University of Chicago Press, 2007.

Brecht, Bertolt. *Brecht on Theatre: The Development of an Aesthetic.* Ed. and trans. John Willett. New York: Hill and Wang, 1964.

Bremmer, Jan, and Herman Roodenburg, eds. *Cultural History of Gesture: From Antiquity to the Present Day.* Cambridge: Polity Press, 1991.

Briscoe, Marianne G., and John C. Coldewey, eds. *Contexts for Early English Drama.* Bloomington: Indiana University Press, 1989.

Brook, Peter. *The Empty Space.* Harmondsworth, Middlesex, England: Penguin, 1972.

Brooks, Peter, and Paul Gewirtz, eds. *Law's Stories: Narrative and Rhetoric in the Law.* New Haven: Yale University Press, 1996.

Brown, Cynthia J. *Poets, Patrons, and Printers: Crisis of Authority in Late Medieval France.* Ithaca: Cornell University Press, 1995.

Brownlee, Marina S., Kevin Brownlee, and Stephen G. Nichols. *The New Medievalism*. Baltimore: Johns Hopkins University Press, 1991.

Brumberg, Joan Jacobs. *Kansas Charley: The Story of a Nineteenth-Century Boy Murderer*. New York: Viking, 2003.

Buckley, William F. "Dressed to Kill." *National Review*, 21 December 1998, 16.

——. "Killer Doc." *National Review*, 21 December 1998, 70.

Buell, Lawrence. "In Pursuit of Ethics." Introduction to special issue, *Ethics and Literary Study*. *PMLA* 114 (1999): 7–19.

Burke, Kenneth. *Counter-Statement*. 1931; rpt. Berkeley: University of California Press, 1968.

——. *The Philosophy of Literary Form: Studies in Symbolic Action*. 3d ed. 1941; rpt. Berkeley: University of California Press, 1973.

Burke, Sean. *The Death and Return of the Author: Criticism and Subjectivity in Barthes, Foucault, and Derrida*. Edinburgh: Edinburgh University Press, 1992.

Butler, Judith. *Bodies That Matter: On the Discursive Limits of "Sex."* New York: Routledge, 1993.

——. *Excitable Speech: A Politics of the Performative*. New York: Routledge, 1997.

——. *Gender Trouble: Feminism and the Subversion of Identity*. London: Routledge, 1990.

Butterfield, Bradley. "Ethical Value and Negative Aesthetics: Reconsidering the Baudrillard-Ballard Connection." *PMLA* 114 (1999): 64–77.

Butterworth, Philip. *Theatre of Fire: Special Effects in Early English and Scottish Theatre*. London: Society for Theatre Research, 1998.

Cane, Peter. "Mens Rea in Tort Law." In *Intention in Law and Philosophy*, ed. Naffine, Owens, and Williams, 129–59.

Cannon, Christopher. "Raptus in the Chaumpaigne Release and a Newly Discovered Document concerning the Life of Geoffrey Chaucer." *Speculum* 68 (1993): 74–94.

Carlson, Marvin. *Places of Performance: The Semiotics of Theatre Architecture*. Ithaca: Cornell University Press, 1989.

——. *Theatre Semiotics: Signs of Life*. Bloomington: Indiana University Press, 1990.

Carr, C. "Unspeakable Practices, Unnatural Acts: The Taboo Art of Karen Finley." In *Acting Out*, ed. Hart and Phelan, 141–52.

Carruthers, Mary. *The Book of Memory*. Cambridge: Cambridge University Press, 1990.

Case, Sue-Ellen. "Introduction." In *Performing Feminisms*, 1–13.

——, ed. *Performing Feminisms: Feminist Critical Theory and Theatre*. Baltimore: Johns Hopkins University Press, 1990.

Cavell, Stanley. *Must We Mean What We Say? A Book of Essays*. New York: Scribner's, 1969.

Cerquiglini, Bernard. *Éloge de la variante: Histoire critique de la philologie*. Paris: Seuil, 1989.

de Certeau, Michel. *The Practice of Everyday Life*. Trans. Steven Rendall. Berkeley: University of California Press, 1988.

——. *The Writing of History.* Trans. Tom Conley. New York: Columbia University Press, 1988.

Chambers, E. K. *The Mediaeval Stage.* 2 vols. Oxford: Oxford University Press, 1903.

Chartier, Roger. *Forms and Meanings: Texts, Performances, and Audiences from Codex to Computer.* Philadelphia: University of Pennsylvania Press, 1995.

——. *The Order of Books: Readers, Authors, and Libraries in Europe between the Fourteenth and Eighteenth Centuries.* Trans. Lydia G. Cochrane. Stanford, Calif.: Stanford University Press, 1994.

Clopper, Lawrence M. *Drama, Play, and Game: English Festive Culture in the Medieval and Early Modern Period.* Chicago: University of Chicago Press, 2001.

Cohen, Esther. *The Crossroads of Justice.* Leiden: E. J. Brill, 1993.

Cohen, Gustave. *Études d'histoire du théâtre en France au Moyen-âge et à la Renaissance.* 7th ed. Paris: Gallimard, 1956.

——. *Histoire de la mise en scène dans le théâtre religieux français du moyen-âge.* 2d ed. Paris: Champion, 1951.

Cohen, Jeffrey Jerome. *Of Giants: Sex, Monsters, and the Middle Ages.* Medieval Cultures, 17. Minneapolis: University of Minnesota Press, 1999.

Cohen-Cruz, Jan. *Local Acts: Community-Based Performance in the United States.* New Brunswick, N.J.: Rutgers University Press, 2005.

Coleman, Kathleen. "Fatal Charades: Roman Executions Staged as Mythological Enactments." *Journal of Roman Studies* 80 (1990): 44–73.

Colie, Rosalie. *Paradoxia Epidemica: The Renaissance Tradition of Paradox.* Princeton: Princeton University Press, 1966.

Collini, Stefan, with Umberto Eco, Richard Rorty, Jonathan Culler, and Christine Brooke-Rose. *Interpretation and Overinterpretation.* Cambridge: Cambridge University Press, 1992.

Coomaraswamy, Ananda K. "Intention." *American Bookman* 1 (1944): 41–48.

Copeland, Rita. "The Pardoner's Body and the Disciplining of Rhetoric." In *Framing Medieval Bodies,* ed. Miri Rubin and Sarah Kay, 138–59. Manchester: Manchester University Press, 1994.

Cowell, Andrew. *At Play in the Tavern: Signs, Coins, and Bodies in the Middle Ages.* Stylus: Studies in Medieval Culture. Ann Arbor: University of Michigan Press, 1999.

Cox, John D., and David Scott Kastan, eds. *A New History of Early English Drama.* New York: Columbia University Press, 1997.

Croydon, Margaret. *Lunatics, Lovers, and Poets: The Contemporary Experimental Theatre.* New York: McGraw Hill, 1974.

Cunningham, Karen. "Renaissance Execution and Marlovian Elocution: The Drama of Death." *PMLA* 105 (1990): 209–22.

Dasenbrock, Reed Way. *Truth and Consequences: Intentions, Conventions, and the New Thematics.* University Park: Pennsylvania State University Press, 2001.

Davidson, Cathy N. "Critical Fictions." In "Four Views on the Place of the Personal in Scholarship." *PMLA* 111 (1996): 1069–72.

Davidson, Donald. "Agency (1971)." In *Essays on Actions and Events*, 43–61.

———. *Essays on Actions and Events*. Oxford: Oxford University Press, 1980.

———. "Freedom to Act (1973)." In *Essays on Actions and Events*, 63–81.

———. "Intending (1978)." In *Essays on Actions and Events*, 83–102.

Davis, Lennard J. *Factual Fictions: The Origins of the English Novel*. 2d. ed. Philadelphia: University of Pennsylvania Press, 1996.

Davis, Natalie Zemon. *Fiction in the Archives: Pardon Tales and Their Tellers in Sixteenth-Century France*. Stanford, Calif.: Stanford University Press, 1987.

———. *The Return of Martin Guerre*. Cambridge, Mass.: Harvard University Press, 1983.

Davis, Tracy C., and Thomas Postlewait, eds. *Theatricality*. Cambridge: Cambridge University Press, 2003.

Delachenal, Roland. *Histoire des avocats au Parlement de Paris (1300–1600)*. Paris: Plon, 1885.

de Man, Paul. *Blindness and Insight: Essays in the Rhetoric of Contemporary Criticism*. Introduction by Wlad Godzich. 2d ed. Theory and History of Literature, 7. Minneapolis: University of Minnesota Press, 1983.

———. "The Purloined Ribbon." *Glyph* 1 (1977): 28–49.

Dennett, Daniel C. *The Intentional Stance*. Cambridge, Mass.: MIT Press, 1987.

Derrida, Jacques. *Of Grammatology*. Trans. Gayatri Chakravorty Spivak. Baltimore: Johns Hopkins University Press, 1976.

———. *Writing and Difference*. Trans. Alan Bass. Chicago: University of Chicago Press, 1978.

Dershowitz, Alan M. "Life Is Not a Dramatic Narrative." In *Law's Stories*, ed. Brooks and Gewirtz, 99–105.

Diamond, Cora, and Jenny Teichman, eds. *Intention and Intentionality: Essays in Honour of G. E. M. Anscombe*. Ithaca: Cornell University Press, 1979.

Dolan, Jill. "Rehearsing Democracy: Advocacy, Public Intellectuals, and Civic Engagement in Theatre and Performance Studies." *Theatre Topics* 11, no. 1 (2001): 1–17.

———. *Utopia in Performance: Finding Hope at the Theater*. Ann Arbor: University of Michigan Press, 2005.

Dolnik, Adam, and Richard Pilch. "The Moscow Theater Hostage Crisis: The Perpetrators, Their Tactics, and the Russian Response." *International Negotiation* 8, no. 3 (2003): 577–611.

Dominguez, Véronique. "Le Corps dans les mystères de la Passion français du XVe siècle: discours théologiques et esthétique théâtrale." Doctoral diss., Université de Paris IV Sorbonne, 1999.

Dowling, William C. "Intentionless Meaning." In *Against Theory*, ed. Mitchell, 89–94.

Duncan, Anne. *Performance and Identity in the Classical World*. Cambridge: Cambridge University Press, 2006.

Durkheim, Emile. *L'Évolution pédagogique en France: des origines à la Renaissance*. Paris: Félix Alcan, 1938. English translation: *The Evolution of Educational Thought*. Trans. Peter Collins. London: Routledge and Kegan Paul, 1977.

Eagleton, Terry. *Literary Theory: An Introduction*. Minneapolis: University of Minnesota Press, 1983.

Eckstein, Barbara J. *The Language of Fiction in a World of Pain: Reading Politics as Paradox*. Philadelphia: University of Pennsylvania Press, 1990.

Eco, Umberto. "An Ars Oblivionalis? Forget It!" *PMLA* 103 (1988): 254–61.

———. "Interpreting Drama." In *The Limits of Interpretation*, 101–10. Reprint of "Semiotics of Theatrical Performance" (1977).

———. *The Limits of Interpretation*. Bloomington: Indiana University Press, 1990.

———. *The Open Work*. Trans. Anna Cancogni. Cambridge, Mass.: Harvard University Press, 1989.

———. "Overinterpreting Texts." In *Interpretation and Overinterpretation*, ed. Collini, 45–66.

———. "Semiotics of Theatrical Performance." *Drama Review* 21 (1977): 107–17.

Eden, Kathy. *Poetic and Legal Fiction in the Aristotelian Tradition*. Princeton: Princeton University Press, 1986.

Elliott, Dyan. *Proving Woman: Female Spirituality and Inquisitional Culture in the Later Middle Ages*. Princeton: Princeton University Press, 2004.

Ellis, William. "Death by Folklore: Ostension, Contemporary Legend, and Murder." *Western Folklore* 48 (1989): 201–20.

Else, Gerald F. *Aristotle's Poetics: The Argument*. Cambridge, Mass.: Harvard University Press, 1957.

Enders, Jody. *Death by Drama and Other Medieval Urban Legends*. Chicago: University of Chicago Press, 2002.

———. "Homicidal Pigs and the Antisemitic Imagination." *Exemplaria* 4, no. 1 (2002): 201–38.

———. "Medieval Snuff Drama." *Exemplaria* 10, no. 1 (1998): 171–206.

———. *The Medieval Theater of Cruelty: Rhetoric, Memory, Violence*. Ithaca: Cornell University Press, 1998.

———. "Performing Miracles: The Mysterious Mimesis of Valenciennes (1547)." In *Theatricality*, ed. Davis and Postlewait, 40–64.

———. *Rhetoric and the Origins of Medieval Drama*. Rhetoric and Society, 1. Ithaca: Cornell University Press, 1992.

———. "Seeing Is Not Believing." In *The Passion of the Christ*, 187–93. Ed. Tim Beal and Tod Linafelt. Chicago: University of Chicago Press, 2005.

———. "The Spectacle of the Scaffolding: Rape and the Violent Foundations of Medieval Theatre Studies." *Theatre Journal* 56 (2004): 163–81.

———. "Theater Makes History: Ritual Murder by Proxy in the *Mistere de la Sainte Hostie*." *Speculum* 79 (2004): 991–1016.

Evans, E. P. *The Criminal Prosecution and Capital Punishment of Animals: The Lost History of Europe's Animal Trials*. 1906; rpt. London: Faber and Faber, 1988.

Evans, Ruth. "When a Body Meets a Body: Fergus and Mary in the York Cycle." *New Medieval Literatures* 1 (1997): 193–212.

Faber, Frédéric. *Histoire du théâtre en Belgique depuis son origine jusqu'à nos jours:*

d'après les documents inédits reposant aux Archives Générales du Royaume. 5 vols. Vol. 1. Brussels: Olivier; Paris: Tresse, 1878.

Farber, Daniel A., and Suzanna Sherry. "Legal Storytelling and Constitutional Law: The Medium and the Message." In *Law's Stories,* ed. Brooks and Gewirtz, 37–53.

Favazza, Armando R. *Bodies under Siege: Self-Mutilation and Body Modification in Culture and Psychiatry.* 2d ed. Baltimore: Johns Hopkins University Press, 1996.

Fischer-Lichte, Erika. *Theatre, Sacrifice, Ritual: Exploring Forms of Political Theatre.* New York: Routledge, 2005.

Fish, Stanley. "Consequences." In *Against Theory,* ed. Mitchell, 106–31.

———. "Interpreting the Variorum." *Critical Inquiry* 3, no. 1 (1976): 191–96.

———. *Is There a Text in This Class?: The Authority of Interpretive Communities.* Cambridge, Mass.: Harvard University Press, 1980.

Fisler, Benjamin Daniel. "The Phenomenology of Racialism: Blackface Puppetry in American Theatre, 1872–1939." Ph.D. diss., University of Maryland, 2005.

Flanigan, C. Clifford. "Liminality, Carnival, and Social Structure: The Case of Late Medieval Biblical Drama." In *Victor Turner and the Construction of Cultural Criticism,* ed. Ashley, 42–63.

Fletcher, John. "Tasteless as Hell: Community Performance, Distinction, and Countertaste in Hell House." *Theatre Survey* 48, no. 2 (2007): 313–30.

Foley, John Miles. *The Theory of Oral Composition: History and Methodology.* Bloomington: Indiana University Press, 1989.

Foucault, Michel. *The Archaeology of Knowledge.* Trans. A. M. Sheridan Smith. New York: Pantheon, 1972.

———. *Discipline and Punish: The Birth of the Prison.* Trans. Alan Sheridan. New York: Pantheon, 1977.

Frye, Northrop. *Anatomy of Criticism.* 1957; rpt. Princeton: Princeton University Press, 1973.

Fuss, Diana. *Essentially Speaking: Feminism, Nature, and Difference.* London: Routledge, 1989.

Futrell, Alison. *Blood in the Arena: The Spectacle of Roman Power.* Austin: University of Texas Press, 1997.

Gadamer, Hans-Georg. *Truth and Method.* 2d rev. ed. Trans. Joel Weinsheimer and Donald G. Marshall. New York: Crossroad, 1989.

Gallop, Jane. *Thinking through the Body.* New York: Columbia University Press, 1988.

Gang, T. M. "Intention." *Essays in Criticism* 7 (1957): 175–86.

Gatton, John Spalding. " 'There Must Be Blood': Mutilation and Martyrdom on the Medieval Stage." In *Violence in Drama,* ed. Redmond, 79–92.

Geach, Peter. "Kinds of Statement." In *Intention and Intentionality,* ed. Diamond and Teichman, 221–35.

Geary, Patrick J. *Living with the Dead in the Middle Ages.* Ithaca: Cornell University Press, 1995.

Geraghty, Thomas F. "Review: Trying to Understand America's Death Penalty System and Why We Still Have It." *Journal of Criminal Law and Criminology* 94, no. 1 (2003): 209–38.

Gerhard, Anselm. *The Urbanization of Opera: Music Theater in Paris in the Nineteenth Century*. Trans. Mary Whitall. Chicago: University of Chicago Press, 1998.

Gertsman, Elina. "Pleyinge and Peyntinge: Performing the Dance of Death." *Studies in Iconography* 27 (2006): 1–43.

Giddens, Anthony. "Action, Subjectivity, and the Constitution of Meaning." In *The Aims of Representation: Subject/Text/History,* ed. Murray Krieger, 159–74. 1987; rpt. Stanford, Calif.: Stanford University Press, 1993.

Girard, René. *Violence and the Sacred*. Trans. Patrick Gregory. Baltimore: Johns Hopkins University Press, 1977.

Given, James Buchanan. *Society and Homicide in Thirteenth-Century England*. Stanford, Calif.: Stanford University Press, 1977.

Godlovitch, Stan. "The Integrity of Musical Performance." *Journal of Aesthetics and Art Criticism* 51, no. 4 (1993): 573–87.

Goebel, Julius, Jr. *Felony and Misdemeanor: A Study in the History of Criminal Law*. Philadelphia: University of Pennsylvania Press, 1976.

Goffman, Erving. *Frame Analysis: An Essay on the Organization of Experience*. Cambridge, Mass.: Harvard University Press, 1974.

Goldstein, Jeffrey H. "Introduction." In *Why We Watch*, 1–6.

——, ed. *Why We Watch: The Attractions of Violent Entertainment*. New York: Oxford University Press, 1998.

Gosselin, E. *Recherches sur les origines et l'histoire du théâtre à Rouen avant Pierre Corneille*. Rouen, 1868.

Gould, Timothy. "The Unhappy Performative." In *Performativity and Performance,* ed. Parker and Sedgwick, 19–44.

Graff, Gerald. *Clueless in Academe: How Schooling Obscures the Life of the Mind*. New Haven: Yale University Press, 2003.

Gravdal, Kathryn. *Ravishing Maidens: Writing Rape in Medieval French Literature and Law*. Philadelphia: University of Pennsylvania Press, 1991.

Graver, David. "The Actor's Bodies." *Text and Performance Quarterly* 17 (1997): 221–35.

Green, Richard Firth. *A Crisis of Truth: Literature and Law in Ricardian England*. Philadelphia: University of Pennsylvania Press, 1999.

Green, Thomas Andrew. *Verdict according to Conscience: Perspectives on the English Criminal Trial Jury, 1200–1800*. Chicago: University of Chicago Press, 1985.

Greenblatt, Stephen. *Shakespearean Negotiations: The Circulation of Social Energy in Renaissance England*. Berkeley: University of California Press, 1988.

Guynn, Noah D. "A Justice to Come: The Role of Ethics in *La Farce de Maistre Pierre Pathelin.*" *Theatre Survey* 47, no. 1 (2006): 13–31.

Hallays-Dabot, Victor. *Histoire de la censure théâtrale en France*. 1862; rpt. Geneva: Slatkine, 1970.

Hamilton, Ross. *Accident: A Philosophical and Literary History*. Chicago: University of Chicago Press, 2007.

stifyameveanginkyarnbynav

Hanawalt, Barbara. "Whose Story Was This? Rape Narratives in Medieval English Courts." In *Of Good and Ill Repute: Gender and Social Control in Medieval England,* 124–41. New York: Oxford University Press, 1998.

Hanawalt, Barbara, and Michal Kobialka, eds. *The Medieval Practices of Space.* Minneapolis: University of Minnesota Press, 1999.

Hanck, Gerold. "A Frame Analysis of the Puppet Theater." Unpublished paper, University of Pennsylvania.

Handler, Evan. *Time on Fire: My Comedy of Terrors.* New York: Henry Holt, 1997.

Haraway, Donna J. *Simians, Cyborgs, and Women: The Reinvention of Nature.* New York: Routledge, 1991.

Hardison, O. B., Jr. *Christian Rite and Christian Drama in the Middle Ages: Essays in the Origin and Early History of Modern Drama.* Baltimore: Johns Hopkins University Press, 1965.

Harris, Wendell V. *Literary Meaning: Reclaiming the Study of Literature.* New York: New York University Press, 1996.

Hayden, Angela. "Imposing Criminal and Civil Penalties for Failing to Help Another: Are 'Good Samaritan Laws' Good Ideas?" *New England International and Comparative Law Annual* 6 (2000): 6. Available online: http://www.nesl.edu/intljournal/vol6/hayden.pdf (accessed 24 April 2007).

Heidegger, Martin. *Being and Time.* Trans. John Macquarrie and Edward Robinson. New York: Harper and Row, 1962.

Henderson, John. *The Medieval World of Isidore of Seville: Truth from Words.* Cambridge: Cambridge University Press, 2007.

Himmelfarb, Gertrude. *The De-moralization of Society: From Victorian Virtues to Modern Values.* New York: Alfred A. Knopf, 1995.

Hirsch, E. D. "Against Theory?" In *Against Theory,* ed. Mitchell, 48–52.

———. *Validity in Interpretation.* New Haven: Yale University Press, 1967.

Hobbs, Dawn. "Terrifying Prank Not Funny to Authorities." *Santa Barbara News-Press,* 27 April 2006, 1, 13.

Holland, Norman N. *The Dynamics of Literary Response.* New York: Columbia University Press, 1968.

———. *Five Readers Reading.* New Haven: Yale University Press, 1975.

Holquist, Michael. "Corrupt Originals: The Paradox of Censorship." Introduction to special issue, *Literature and Censorship. PMLA* 109 (1994): 14–25.

Holsinger, Bruce Wood. *Music, Body, and Desire in Medieval Culture: Hildegard of Bingen to Chaucer.* Stanford, Calif.: Stanford University Press, 2001.

———. *The Premodern Condition: Medievalism and the Making of Theory.* Chicago: University of Chicago Press, 2005.

Huizinga, Johan. *Homo Ludens: A Study of the Play Element in Culture.* 1950; rpt. Boston: Beacon Press, 1972.

Hunt, Lynn, ed. *The New Cultural History.* Berkeley: University of California Press, 1989.

Huot, Sylvia. *From Song to Book: The Poetics of Writing in Old French Lyric and Lyrical Narrative Poetry.* Ithaca: Cornell University Press, 1987.

Hüsken, Wim. "Politics and Drama: The City of Bruges as Organizer of Drama Festivals." In *The Stage as Mirror,* ed. Knight, 165–87.

Husserl, Edmund. *Experience and Judgment: Investigations in a Genealogy of Logic.* Trans. J. Churchill and K. Ameriks. Evanston, Ill.: Northwestern University Press, 1973.

Hyde, Alan. *Bodies of Law.* Princeton: Princeton University Press, 1997.

Ingarden, Roman. "The Functions of Language in the Theater." In *The Literary Work of Art,* appendix, 377–96.

———. *The Literary Work of Art: An Investigation on the Borderlines of Ontology, Logic, and Theory of Literature.* With an Appendix on the Functions of Language in the Theater. Trans. George G. Grabowicz. Evanston, Ill.: Northwestern University Press, 1973.

In the Theatre of Consciousness. Special issue, *Journal of Consciousness Studies* 4, no. 4 (1997).

Irigaray, Luce. *Ce sexe qui n'en est pas un.* Paris: Éditions de Minuit, 1977. English translation: *This Sex Which Is Not One.* Trans. Catherine Porter with Carolyn Burke. Ithaca: Cornell University Press, 1985.

Iseminger, Gary. "An Intentional Demonstration?" In *Intention and Interpretation,* ed. Iseminger, 76–96.

———, ed. *Intention and Interpretation.* Philadelphia: Temple University Press, 1992.

Iser, Wolfgang. *The Act of Reading: A Theory of Aesthetic Response.* Baltimore: Johns Hopkins University Press, 1978.

———. *The Fictive and the Imaginary: Charting Literary Anthropology.* Baltimore: Johns Hopkins University Press, 1993.

———. *The Implied Reader: Patterns of Communication in Prose Fiction from Bunyan to Beckett.* Baltimore: Johns Hopkins University Press, 1974.

———. "Representation: A Performative Act." In *Aims of Representation,* ed. Krieger, 217–32.

Issacharoff, Michael. *Discourse as Performance.* Stanford, Calif.: Stanford University Press, 1989.

Jackson, Frank. "How Decision Theory Illuminates Assignments of Moral Responsibility." In *Intention in Law and Philosophy,* ed. Naffine, Owens, and Williams, 19–36.

Jackson, Shannon. *Professing Performance: Theatre in the Academy from Philology to Performativity.* Cambridge: Cambridge University Press, 2004.

Jauss, Hans Robert. *Aesthetic Experience and Literary Hermeneutics.* Trans. Michael Shaw. Minneapolis: University of Minnesota Press, 1982.

———. "The Alterity and Modernity of Medieval Literature." *New Literary History* 10 (1979): 181–227.

——. *Question and Answer: Forms of Dialogic Understanding.* Trans. Michael Hays. Theory and History of Literature, 68. Minneapolis: University of Minnesota Press, 1989.

——. *Towards an Aesthetics of Reception.* Trans. Timothy Bahti. Theory and History of Literature, 2. Minneapolis: University of Minnesota Press, 1982.

Johnson, Eithne, and Eric Schaefer. "Soft Core/Hard Gore: Snuff as a Crisis in Meaning." *Journal of Film and Video* 45 (1993): 40–59.

Jolibois, Émile. *La Diablerie de Chaumont.* Chaumont, 1838.

Juergensmeyer, Mark. *Terror in the Mind of God: The Global Rise of Religious Violence.* Berkeley: University of California Press, 2000.

Juhl, P. D. *Interpretation: An Essay in the Philosophy of Literary Criticism.* Princeton: Princeton University Press, 1980.

Keeley, Lawrence H. *War before Civilization.* New York: Oxford University Press, 1996.

Kennedy, George A. *Classical Rhetoric and Its Christian and Secular Tradition from Ancient to Modern Times.* Chapel Hill: University of North Carolina Press, 1980.

Kerekes, David, and David Slater. *Killing for Culture: An Illustrated History of Death Film from* Mondo *to* Snuff. London: Creation Books, 1995.

Kershaw, Baz. "Curiosity or Contempt: On Spectacle, the Human, and Activism." *Theatre Journal* 55, no. 4 (2003): 591–611.

——. *The Politics of Performance: Radical Theatre as Cultural Intervention.* New York: Routledge, 1992.

Kim, Suk-Young. "Springtime for Kim Il-Sung in Pyongyang: City on Stage, City as Stage." *TDR: The Drama Review* 51, no. 2 (2007): 24–40.

Kipling, Gordon. *Enter the King: Theatre, Liturgy, and Ritual in the Medieval Civic Triumph.* Oxford: Clarendon Press, 1998.

——. "Theatre as Subject and Object in Fouquet's 'Martyrdom of St. Apollonia.'" *Medieval English Theatre* 19 (1997): 26–80.

Kirby, Michael. *A Formalist Theatre.* Philadelphia: University of Pennsylvania Press, 1992.

Kirshenblatt-Gimblett, Barbara. "Performance Studies." In *Performance Studies Reader,* ed. Bial, 43–55.

Knapp, Steven, and Walter Benn Michaels. "Against Theory." In *Against Theory,* ed. Mitchell, 11–30. Originally published in *Critical Inquiry* 8, no. 4 (Summer, 1982): 723–42.

——. "Against Theory 2: Sentence, Meaning, Hermeneutics." *Colloquy* (Center for Hermeneutical Studies in Hellenistic and Modern Culture) 52 (1986): 1–11.

——. "The Impossibility of Intentionless Meaning." In *Intention and Interpretation,* ed. Iseminger, 51–64.

——. "A Reply to Rorty: What Is Pragmatism." In *Against Theory,* ed. Mitchell, 13–46.

Knight, Alan E., ed. *The Stage as Mirror: Civic Theatre in Late Medieval Europe.* Woodbridge, Suffolk, England: D. S. Brewer, 1997.

Kobialka, Michal. *This Is My Body: Representational Practices in the Early Middle Ages.* Ann Arbor: University of Michigan Press, 1999.

Konigson, Élie. *L'Espace théâtral médiéval.* Paris: CNRS, 1975.

Kottman, Paul A. *A Politics of the Scene.* Stanford, Calif.: Stanford University Press, 2008.

Koziol, Geoffrey. *Begging Pardon and Favor.* Ithaca: Cornell University Press, 1992.

Krieger, Murray, ed. *The Aims of Representation: Subject/Text/History.* 1987; rpt. Stanford, Calif.: Stanford University Press, 1993.

Kruger, Loren. *The National Stage: Theatre and Cultural Legitimation in England, France, and America.* Chicago: University of Chicago Press, 1992.

Kubiak, Anthony. *Stages of Terror: Terrorism, Ideology, and Coercion as Theatre History.* Bloomington: Indiana University Press, 1991.

Kyle, Donald G. *Spectacles of Death in Ancient Rome.* New York: Routledge, 1998.

Lamarque, Peter, and Stein Haugom Olsen. *Truth, Fiction, and Literature: A Philosophical Perspective.* Clarendon Library of Logic and Philosophy. Oxford: Clarendon Press, 1994.

Lang, Cecil Y. "Narcissus Jilted: Byron, Don Juan, and the Biographical Imperative." In *Historical Studies and Literary Criticism,* ed. McGann, 143–79.

Langer, Susanne K. *Feeling and Form: A Theory of Art Developed from Philosophy in a New Key.* New York: Charles Scribner's Sons, 1953.

Larwood, Jacob. [H. D. J. van Schevichaven]. *Theatrical Anecdotes or Fun and Curiosities of the Play, the Playhouse, and the Players.* London: Chatto and Windus, 1882.

Leader-Elliott, Ian D. "Negotiating Intentions in Trials of Guilt and Punishment." In *Intention in Law and Philosophy,* ed. Naffine, Owens, and Williams, 73–105.

Le Goff, Jacques. *History and Memory.* Trans. Steven Rendall and Elizabeth Claman. New York: Columbia University Press, 1992.

——. *Medieval Civilization, 400–1500.* Trans. Julia Barrow. 1988; rpt. Oxford: Blackwell, 1995.

Lesser, Wendy. *Pictures at an Execution: An Inquiry into the Subject of Murder.* Cambridge, Mass.: Harvard University Press, 1993.

Levinson, Marjorie. "The New Historicism: Back to the Future." In *Rethinking Historicism,* ed. Levinson, Butler, McGann, and Hamilton, 18–63.

Levinson, Marjorie, Marilyn Butler, Jerome McGann, and Paul Hamilton, eds. *Rethinking Historicism: Critical Readings in Romantic History.* Oxford: Basil Blackwell, 1989.

Limon, Jerzy. "The Play-within-the-Play: A Theoretical Perspective." In *Enjoying the Spectacle: Word, Image, Gesture,* ed. Jerzy Sobieraj and Dariusz Pestka, 17–32. Torun: Wydawnictwo Naukowe Uniwersytetu Mikolaja Kopernika, 2006.

Lipking, Lawrence. "Life, Death, and Other Theories." In *Historical Studies and Literary Criticism,* ed. McGann, 180–98.

"Looking Out for Mrs. Berwid." Produced by Norman Gorin. *60 Minutes* 13, no. 43, 12 July 1981.

Lord, Albert. *The Singer of Tales.* Harvard Studies in Comparative Literature, 24. Cambridge, Mass.: Harvard University Press, 1960.

de Lorde, André. *Théâtre de la mort. Les Charcuteurs.—Le Vaisseau de la Mort.— L'Homme mystérieux.* Paris: Eugène Figuière, 1928.

Lyon, Arabella. *Intentions: Negotiated, Contested, and Ignored.* University Park: Pennsylvania State University Press, 1998.

MacDonald, Erik. *Theater at the Margins: Text and Post-Structured Stage.* Ann Arbor: University of Michigan Press, 1993.

MacKinnon, Catherine A. *Toward a Feminist Theory of the State.* Cambridge, Mass.: Harvard University Press, 1989.

Mailloux, Steven. *Interpretive Conventions: The Reader in the Study of American Fiction.* Ithaca: Cornell University Press, 1982.

Mali, Joseph. *Mythistory: The Making of a Modern Historiography.* Chicago: University of Chicago Press, 2003.

de Marinis, Marco. *The Semiotics of Performance.* Trans. Áine O'Healy. Bloomington: University of Indiana Press, 1993. Reprinted as "The Performance Text," in *Performance Studies Reader,* ed. Bial, 280–99.

Marshall, David. *The Surprising Effects of Sympathy: Marivaux, Diderot, Rousseau, and Mary Shelley.* Chicago: University of Chicago Press, 1988.

Martin, Bradford. *The Theater Is in the Street: Politics and Public Performance in Sixties America.* Amherst: University of Massachusetts Press, 2004.

Massumi, Brian. *Parables for the Virtual: Movement, Affect, Sensation.* Durham, N.C.: Duke University Press, 2002.

Mazer, Sharon. *Professional Wrestling: Sport and Spectacle.* Jackson: University Press of Mississippi, 1998.

McConahay, John. "Pornography: The Symbolic Politics of Fantasy." *Law and Contemporary Problems* 51 (1988): 31–69.

McGann, Jerome J. *Critique of Modern Textual Criticism.* Charlottesville: University Press of Virginia, 1992.

———, ed. *Historical Studies and Literary Criticism.* Madison: University of Wisconsin Press, 1985.

McKenzie, Jon. *Perform or Else.* London: Routledge, 2001. Reprinted as "The Liminal Norm," in *Performance Studies Reader,* ed. Bial, 26–31.

McLuhan, Marshall, and Quentin Fiore. *The Medium Is the Message.* New York: Random House, 1967.

McPharlin, Paul. *The Puppet Theatre in America.* New York: Harper and Brothers, 1949.

Melia, Daniel F. "Response." *Colloquy* (Center for Hermeneutical Studies in Hellenistic and Modern Culture) 52 (1986): 12–16.

Melrose, Susan. *A Semiotics of the Dramatic Text.* New York: St. Martin's Press, 1994.

de Ménil, Félicien. *Histoire de la danse à travers les âges.* 1905; rpt. Geneva: Slatkine, 1980.

Meyer, Susan Suavé. "Aristotle, Teleology, and Reduction." *Philosophical Review* 101, no. 4 (1992): 791–825.

Milgram, Stanley. *Obedience to Authority: An Experimental View.* New York: Harper Collins, 1975.

Mill, Anna Jean, ed. *Medieval Plays in Scotland.* St. Andrews University Publications, 24. Edinburgh: St. Andrews University, 1927.

Miller, J. Hillis. *Tropes, Parables, Performatives: Essays on Twentieth-Century Literature.* Durham, N.C.: Duke University Press, 1991.

Miller, N. P. "The Origins of Greek Drama: A Summary of the Evidence and a Comparison with Early English Drama." *Greece and Rome,* 2d ser., 8, no. 2 (1961): 126–37.

Minois, Georges. *History of Suicide: Voluntary Death in Western Culture.* Trans. Lydia G. Cochrane. 1995; rpt. Baltimore: Johns Hopkins University Press, 1999.

Minow, Martha. "Stories in Law." In *Law's Stories,* ed. Brooks and Gewirtz, 24–36.

Molloy, Sylvia. "Mock Heroics and Personal Markings." In "Four Views on the Place of the Personal in Scholarship." *PMLA* 111 (1996): 1072–75.

Muir, Edward, ed., and Guido Ruggiero. *History from Crime.* Trans. Corrada Biazo Curry, Margaret M. Galluci, and Mary M. Galluci. Baltimore: Johns Hopkins University Press, 1994.

———. "Introduction: The Crime of History." In *History from Crime,* vii–xviii.

Mullaney, Steven. *The Place of the Stage: License, Play, and Power in Renaissance England.* Chicago: University of Chicago Press, 1988.

Murphy, James J. *Rhetoric in the Middle Ages: A History of Rhetorical Theory from Saint Augustine to the Renaissance.* 1974; rpt. Berkeley: University of California Press, 1981.

———. *A Synoptic History of Classical Rhetoric.* New York: Random House, 1972.

Murray, Alexander. *Suicide in the Middle Ages.* Vol. 1, *The Violent against Themselves.* Oxford: Oxford University Press, 1998. Vol. 2, *The Curse on Self-Murder.* Oxford: Oxford University Press, 2000.

"Mystery Science Theater." *Lingua Franca* (July–August 1996): 54–57.

Naffine, Ngaire, Rosemary Owens, and John Williams, eds. *Intention in Law and Philosophy.* Burlington, Vermont: Ashgate, 2001.

Newton-De Molina, David. *On Literary Intention.* Edinburgh: Edinburgh University Press, 1976.

Nichols, Stephen G. "Modernism and the Politics of Medieval Studies." In *Medievalism and the Modernist Temper,* ed. Bloch and Nichols, 25–56.

———, ed. *The New Philology.* Special issue, *Speculum* 65 (1990).

Nicoll, Allardyce. *World Drama from Aeschylus to Anouilh.* 1949; 2d. ed., New York: Harper & Row, 1976.

Olson, Glending. *Literature as Recreation in the Later Middle Ages.* Ithaca: Cornell University Press, 1982.

———. "The Medieval Fortunes of 'Theatrica.'" *Traditio* 4 (1986): 265–86.

———. "Plays as Play: A Medieval Ethical Theory of Performance and the Intellectual Context of the *Tretise of Miraclis Pleyinge.*" *Viator* 26 (1995): 195–221.

Ong, Walter J. *Orality and Literacy.* New York: Methuen, 1982.

Otter, Monika. *Inventiones: Fiction and Referentiality in Twelfth-Century English Historical Writing.* Chapel Hill: University of North Carolina Press, 1996.

Parker, Andrew, and Eve Kosofsky Sedgwick. "Introduction." In *Performativity and Performance,* ed. Parker and Sedgwick, 1–18.

———, eds. *Performativity and Performance.* New York: Routledge, 1995.

Parker, Hershel. *Flawed Texts and Verbal Icons: Literary Authority in American Fiction.* Evanston, Ill.: Northwestern University Press, 1984.

Patterson, Annabel M. "Intention." In *Critical Terms for Literary Study,* ed. Lentricchia and McLaughlin, 135–46.

Paulson, Julie. "Death's Arrival and Everyman's Separation." *Theatre Survey* 48, no. 1 (2007): 121–41.

Pavis, Patrice. *Problèmes de sémiologie théâtrale.* Quebec: Presses de l'Université de Québec, 1976.

———. *Voix et images de la scène: Pour une sémiologie de la réception.* Lille: Presses Universitaires de Lille, 1985.

Peters, Edward. *Torture.* 1985; expanded ed., Philadelphia: University of Pennsylvania Press, 1996.

Petit de Julleville, L. *Les Mystères.* Vols. 1 and 2 of *Histoire du théâtre en France.* 1880; rpt. Geneva: Slatkine, 1968.

Petrey, Sandy. "French Studies/Cultural Studies: Reciprocal Invigoration or Mutual Destruction." *French Review* 68 (1995): 381–92.

Phillips, Kim M. "Written on the Body: Reading Rape from the Twelfth to Fifteenth Centuries." In *Medieval Women and the Law,* ed. Noël James Menuge, 125–44. Woodbridge, Suffolk, England: Boydell, 2000.

Pizarro, Joaquín Martínez. *A Rhetoric of the Scene: Dramatic Narrative in the Early Middle Ages.* Toronto: University of Toronto Press, 1989.

Plass, Paul. *The Game of Death in Ancient Rome: Arena Spirit and Political Suicide.* Madison: University of Wisconsin Press, 1995.

Postlewait, Thomas. "Writing History Today." *Theatre Survey* 41 (2000): 83–106.

Postlewait, Thomas, and Bruce A. McConachie, eds. *Interpreting the Theatrical Past: Essays in the Historiography of Performance.* Iowa City: University of Iowa Press, 1989.

Pouchelle, Marie-Christine. *Corps et chirurgie à l'apogée du Moyen-Age.* Paris: Flammarion, 1983. English translation: *The Body and Surgery in the Middle Ages.* Trans. Rosemary Morris. New Brunswick, N.J.: Rutgers University Press, 1990.

Poulet, Georges. "Une Critique d'identification." In *Les Chemins actuels de la critique,* 9–23. Paris: 10/18, 1968.

Pywell, Geoff. *Staging Real Things: The Performance of Ordinary Events.* Lewisburg, Pa.: Bucknell University Press, 1994.

Rabinowitz, Peter J. *Before Reading: Narrative Conventions and the Politics of Interpretation.* Ithaca: Cornell University Press, 1987.

Rayner, Alice. "Rude Mechanicals and the Specters of Marx." *Theatre Journal* 54 (2002): 535–54.

——. *To Do, to Act, to Perform: Drama and the Phenomenology of Action.* Ann Arbor: University of Michigan Press, 1994.

Read, Alan. *Theatre and Everyday Life: An Ethics of Performance.* London: Routledge, 1993.

Redmond, James, ed. *Violence in Drama.* Themes in Drama, 13. Cambridge: Cambridge University Press, 1991.

Renteln, Alison Dundes, and Alan Dundes, eds. *Folk Law: Essays in the Theory and Practice of Lex Non Scripta.* 2 vols. New York: Garland, 1994.

Rey-Flaud, Henri. *Le Cercle magique: essai sur le théâtre en rond à la fin du moyen âge.* Paris: Gallimard, 1973.

——. *Pour une dramaturgie du moyen-âge.* Paris: Presses Universitaires de France, 1980.

Ricoeur, Paul. *Interpretation Theory: Discourse and the Surplus of Meaning.* Fort Worth: Texas Christian University Press, 1976.

——. *Time and Narrative.* Trans. Kathleen McLaughlin and David Pellauer. 3 vols. Chicago: University of Chicago Press, 1984.

Ridout, Nicholas. *Stage Fright, Animals, and Other Theatrical Problems.* Cambridge: Cambridge University Press, 2006.

Riffaterre, Michael. *Fictional Truth.* Baltimore: Johns Hopkins University Press, 1990.

Robins, J. Max. "When Is the News Just Too 'Horrific'?" Robins Report. *TV Guide,* 21–27 November 1999, 53.

Rogoff, Gordon. *Theatre Is Not Safe: Theatre Criticism, 1962–1986.* Evanston, Ill.: Northwestern University Press, 1987.

[Ryan, Richard]. *Dramatic Table Talk; or Scenes, Situations and Adventures, Serious and Comic, in Theatrical History and Biography.* 3 vols. London: J. Knight and H. Lacey, 1825.

Saenger, Paul. "Silent Reading: Its Impact on Late Medieval Script and Society." *Viator* 13 (1982): 367–414.

Sainte-Beuve, Charles Augustin. *Tableau historique et critique de la poésie française et du théâtre français au seizième siècle.* Rev. ed. Paris: Charpentier, 1869.

Sanok, Catherine. "Performing Feminine Sanctity in Late Medieval England: Parish Guilds, Saints' Plays, and the Second Nun's Tale." *Journal of Medieval and Early Modern Studies* 32, no. 2 (2002): 269–303. 5

Sarat, Austin, and Thomas R. Kearns, ed. *Law in Everyday Life.* Ann Arbor: University of Michigan Press, 1993.

Sartre, Jean-Paul. *Sartre on Theater.* Documents assembled, edited, introduced, and annotated by Michel Contat and Michel Rybalka. Trans. Frank Jellinek. New York: Pantheon, 1976.

Saunders, Corinne. *Rape and Ravishment in the Literature of Medieval England.* Cambridge: D. S. Brewer, 2001.

Scarry, Elaine. *The Body in Pain: The Making and Unmaking of the World.* 1985; rpt. New York: Oxford University Press, 1987.

Schechner, Richard. *Between Theater and Anthropology.* Philadelphia: University of Pennsylvania Press, 1985.

Scheffler, Samuel, ed. *Consequentialism and Its Critics.* Oxford: Oxford University Press, 1988.

Schlegel, Friedrich. *Dialogue on Poetry and Literary Aphorisms.* Trans. Ernst Behler and Roman Struc. University Park: Pennsylvania State University Press, 1968.

Schmitt, Natalie Crohn. "Was There a Medieval Theatre in the Round? A Re-examination of the Evidence." In *Medieval Drama: Essays Critical and Contextual,* ed. Jerome Taylor and Alan Nelson, 292–315. Chicago: University of Chicago Press, 1972.

Schneider, Joseph. *Donna Haraway: Live Theory.* New York: Continuum, 2005.

Schneider, Rebecca. "Intermediality, Infelicity, and Scholarship on the Slip." *Theatre Survey* 47, no. 2 (2006): 253–60.

Scott, Robert L. "Intentionality in the Rhetorical Process." In *Rhetoric in Transition: Studies in the Nature and Uses of Rhetoric,* ed. Eugene E. White, 39–60. University Park: Pennsylvania State University Press, 1980.

Searle, John. *Intentionality: An Essay in the Philosophy of Mind.* Cambridge: Cambridge University Press, 1983.

———. "The Logical Status of Fictional Discourse." *New Literary History* 6 (1975): 319–32.

Sedgwick, Eve Kosofsky. *Epistemology of the Closet.* Berkeley: University of California Press, 1990.

Sell, Mike. *Avant-garde Performance and the Limits of Criticism: Approaching the Living Theatre, Happenings/Fluxus, and the Black Arts Movement.* Ann Arbor: University of Michigan Press, 2005.

Shawcross, John T. *Intentionality and the New Traditionalism: Some Liminal Means to Literary Revisionism.* University Park: Pennsylvania State University Press, 1991.

Sheingorn, Pamela. "The Visual Language of Drama: Principles of Composition." In *Contexts for Early English Drama,* ed. Briscoe and Coldewey, 173–91.

Shelton, Jo-Ann. *As the Romans Did: A Sourcebook in Roman Social History.* New York: Oxford University Press, 1988.

Siebers, Tobin. *The Ethics of Criticism.* Ithaca: Cornell University Press, 1988.

Smith, Barbara Herrnstein. *Belief and Resistance: Dynamics of Contemporary Intellectual Controversy.* Cambridge, Mass.: Harvard University Press, 1997.

———. *Contingencies of Value: Alternative Perspectives for Critical Theory.* Cambridge, Mass.: Harvard University Press, 1988.

Sokal, Alan D. "A Physicist Experiments with Cultural Studies." *Lingua Franca* (May–June 1996): 62–64.

"The Sokal Hoax: A Forum." *Lingua Franca* (July–August 1996): 58–64.

Solga, Kim. "Rape's Metatheatrical Return: Rehearsing Sexual Violence among the Early Moderns." *Theatre Journal* 58 (2006): 53–72.

Solterer, Helen. *The Master and Minerva: Disputing Women in Old French Literature.* Berkeley: University of California Press, 1995.

Southern, Richard. *The Medieval Theatre in the Round*. London: Faber and Faber, 1957.

Sponsler, Claire. *Drama and Resistance: Bodies, Goods, and Theatricality in Late Medieval England*. Medieval Cultures, 10. Minneapolis: University of Minnesota Press, 1997.

———. *Ritual Imports: Performing Medieval Drama in America*. Ithaca: Cornell University Press, 2004.

Stacey, Robin Chapman. *Dark Speech: The Performance of Law in Early Ireland*. Philadelphia: University of Pennsylvania Press, 2007.

Stallman, Robert W. "Intentions, Problems of." In *Princeton Encyclopedia of Poetry and Poetics* (enlarged ed.), ed. Alex Preminger, 398–400. Princeton: Princeton University Press, 1974.

Stallybrass, Peter, and Allon White. *The Politics and Poetics of Transgression*. Ithaca: Cornell University Press, 1986.

Stanislavski, Constantin. *An Actor Prepares*. Trans. Elizabeth Reynolds Hapgood. New York: Theatre Arts, 1936.

———. *Building a Character*. Trans. Elizabeth Reynolds Hapgood. New York: Theatre Arts, 1949.

———. *Creating a Role*. Trans. Elizabeth Reynolds Hapgood. 1961; rpt. New York: Routledge, Theatre Arts, 1988.

States, Bert O. *Great Reckonings in Little Rooms: On the Phenomenology of Theatre*. Berkeley: University of California Press, 1985.

———. *The Pleasure of the Play*. Ithaca: Cornell University Press, 1994.

Statman, Daniel, ed. *Moral Luck*. Albany: State University of New York Press, 1993.

Steiner, Wendy. *The Scandal of Pleasure: Art in an Age of Fundamentalism*. Chicago: University of Chicago Press, 1995.

Stock, Brian. *Implications of Literacy: Written Language and Models of Interpretation in the Eleventh and Twelfth Centuries*. Princeton: Princeton University Press, 1983.

Sverdlik, Steven. "Crime and Moral Luck." In *Moral Luck*, ed. Statman, 181–94.

Tallis, Raymond. *Not Saussure: A Critique of Post-Saussurean Literary Theory*. Basingstoke, England: Macmillan, 1988.

Tanselle, G. Thomas. *Textual Criticism and Scholarly Editing*. Charlottesville: Bibliographical Society of the University Press of Virginia, 2003.

Thomas, A. "Le Théâtre à Paris et aux environs." *Romania* 21 (1892): 606–12.

Tompkins, Jane P., ed. *Reader-Response Criticism: From Formalism to Post-Structuralism*. Baltimore: Johns Hopkins University Press, 1980.

Treitler, Leo. "Oral, Written, and Literate Process in the Transmission of Medieval Music." *Speculum* 56 (1981): 471–91.

Trible, Phyllis. *Texts of Terror: Literary-Feminist Readings of Biblical Narratives*. Philadelphia: Fortress Press, 1984.

Turner, Victor W. *Dramas, Fields, and Metaphors: Symbolic Action in Human Society*. Ithaca: Cornell University Press, 1974.

———. *From Ritual to Theatre: The Human Seriousness of Play*. 1982; rpt. New York: PAJ, 1992.

Tydeman, William. *The Theatre in the Middle Ages: Western European Stage Conditions, c. 800–1576.* Cambridge: Cambridge University Press, 1978.

Verner, Lisa. *The Epistemology of the Monstrous.* Medieval History and Culture. New York: Routledge, 2005.

Vitz, Evelyn Birge. "Rereading Rape in Medieval Literature: Literary, Historical, and Theoretical Reflections." *Romanic Review* 88 (1997): 1–26.

Walton, Kendall L. *Mimesis as Make-Believe.* Cambridge, Mass.: Harvard University Press, 1990.

Wappler, Margaret. "Guess Who's Coming to Dinner Theater?" *Los Angeles Times,* 10 March 2007, E28–31.

Warning, Rainer. *The Ambivalences of Medieval Religious Drama.* Trans. Steven Rendall. 1974; rpt. Stanford, Calif.: Stanford University Press, 2001.

———. "On the Alterity of Medieval Religious Drama." *New Literary History* 10 (1979): 265–92.

———. *Rezeptionsasthetik: Theorie und Praxis.* Munich: W. Fink, 1975.

Weber, Samuel. *Theatricality as Medium.* New York: Fordham University Press, 2004.

Wellek, René, and Austin Warren. *Theory of Literature.* 3d ed. New York: Harcourt Brace and World, 1970.

White, Hayden. *Metahistory.* Baltimore: Johns Hopkins University Press, 1981.

Wilkinson, James. "A Choice of Fictions: Historians, Memory, and Evidence." *PMLA* 111 (1996): 80–92.

Will, George. "Naive Hopes and Real Decadence." *Washington Post,* 28 March 1976, C7.

Williams, Bernard. *Moral Luck: Philosophical Papers, 1973–1980.* Cambridge: Cambridge University Press, 1981.

Wilshire, Bruce. *Role Playing and Identity: The Limits of Theatre as Metaphor.* 1982; rpt. Bloomington: Indiana University Press, 1991.

Wilson, Luke. *Theaters of Intention: Drama and the Law in Early Modern England.* Stanford, Calif.: Stanford University Press, 2000.

Witmore, Michael. *Culture of Accidents: Unexpected Knowledges in Early Modern England.* Stanford, Calif.: Stanford University Press, 2001.

Woods, Marjorie Curry. "Rape and the Pedagogical Rhetoric of Sexual Violence." In *Criticism and Dissent,* ed. Copeland, 56–86.

Worthen, W. B. "Drama, Performativity, and Performance." *PMLA* 113 (1998): 1093–1107.

———. "The Imprint of Performance." In *Theorizing Practice: Redefining Theatre History,* 213–34. New York: Palgrave-Macmillan, 2007.

———. *Modern Drama and the Rhetoric of Theater.* Berkeley: University of California Press, 1992.

———. *Print and the Poetics of Modern Drama.* Cambridge: Cambridge University Press, 2006.

Yates, Frances. *The Art of Memory.* Chicago: University of Chicago Press, 1966.

Young, Karl. *The Drama of the Medieval Church.* 2 vols. Oxford: Clarendon Press, 1933.

Zucco, Tom. "Boxing Match for Fun Turns Deadly." *St. Petersburg Times Online,* 18 June 2003. http://www.sptimes.com/2003/06/18/State/Boxing_match_for_fun_.shtml Accessed 21 August 2008.

Zumthor, Paul. *Essai de poétique médiévale.* Paris: Seuil, 1972.

critical self, as replacement for author, 115–20

Crowe, Russell, 210n17

"dance of death" (Henry D'Anoux, Metz, 9 October 1504), 89–91, 95–102

D'Anoux, Henry, 23, 89–91, 95–103, 137

Dasenbrock, Reed Way, 5, 15, 178

Davidson, Donald, 116

Davis, Natalie Zemon, 4, 85, 214n28

Death, intervention into theater, 174–75

death penalty, 181,192

de Certeau, Michel, 115, 196

declared intentions, 19–21, 23, 29, 86–87, 92–94, 102, 112, 125, 133, 158, 164, 167, 172; understood or misunderstood by audiences (case 6), 137–40. *See also* implied declared intentions

deconstructionism, 110, 236n7

delicts, 143, 150

Dershowitz, Alan, 14, 56, 189, 194

Devil, intervention into theater, 174–75

devil, of Bar-le-Duc, 67–72

diableries, 73, 229n28

didascalia, 72, 221n23

Digest of Justinian, 4, 31–32, 54, 77, 81–82, 204, 226n28

disinvitation, 176, 178, 181–82. *See also* invitation

disinvited nonbreak of nonframe, 182

divine intervention into theater, 174–75

double-pretense, 128, 134, 160

Eagleton, Terry, xvii, 4, 24, 33, 66, 124

Eckstein, Barbara J., 36

Eco, Umberto, xviii–xix, 99, 104–05, 114, 123, 127–28, 134, 143, 145, 160, 193, 238n5

electronic publishing, 217n76

emotions, 9, 13, 43, 69, 127, 138, 156, 159

enthymeme, 94–95, 140

essentialism, 118

ethics, theatrical, 65–87

ethics, xvii, 38, 63, 65, 68–70, 72–73, 78, 82, 85, 95, 101, 113, 119, 149, 172, 178, 182, 192

ethics of agency, 14–15

evil, problem of, in theater, 55, 67–87, 187

Exculpation, in forensic rhetoric, 54

expectations, of audience, violation of, 1–3, 134, 163, 170, 181–82

falsely shouting fire in a theater, 97, 234n30

Farce de Digeste Viel et Digeste Neuve, 115

fear of imminence, 23, 69–87, 136–37, 192–93

Fish, Stanley, 6

follow-through, on intentions, 218n98

forensic rhetoric, 52–55, 226n31

forgetting, 127, 191

forgiveness, 7, 30, 33, 46, 51, 54–55, 66, 78–80, 83, 113, 159, 246n7

form in suspense, 57, 70, 131

fourth wall, of theater, 39, 182

frame analysis, 22, 24, 38, 91. 93. 169. *See also* Goffman, Erving

frames, multiple, 98, 235n48; primary, 66, 145, 190–91

framing, 24–25, 91, 93–94, 104–7. *See also* breaking frame

French, as academic discipline, xxii

future action, rehearsal and, 55–56

gang-rape (Chelles, 1395), 77–81, 229n30

Geary, Patrick, xvii

generic confusion, between real and represented violence, 158–59, 243n32

Gibson, Mel, 209n2

Giddens, Anthony, 3, 87, 114, 136

Gilmore, Gary, 186

God, 14, 76, 94, 96, 170, 211n29; intervention into theater, 174–75. *See also* acts of God

Goffman, Erving, xx–xxi, 10, 13, 22–24,